THE GUINNESS
MOTORCYCLE SPORT
FACT BOOK

THE GUINNESS MOTORCYCLE SPORT FACT BOOK

Ian Morrison

GUINNESS PUBLISHING

Editor: Charles Richards
Text design and layout: Steve Leaning
Cover design: Ad Vantage

Published in Great Britain by Guinness Publishing
Ltd, 33 London Road, Enfield, Middlesex.

Typeset in Baskerville/Helvetica by Ace Filmsetting
Ltd, Frome, Somerset

Printed and bound in Great Britain by The Bath
Press, Bath

'Guinness' is a registered trademark of Guinness
Publishing Ltd

British Library Cataloguing in Publication Data
Morrison, Ian
   Motorcycle racing fact book. – (Fact book).
   1. Racing motorcycles. Racing
   796.75

ISBN 0-85112-953-6

Front cover, top *Isle of Man Senior TT, May 1914*
(Hulton Picture Company)
Middle *Wayne Gardner, Portuguese Grand Prix,
1987* (Action-Plus)
Bottom *British sidecar pair Simon Webster and
Gavin Simmons at the West German Grand Prix in
1990* (Allsport)

CONTENTS

AUTHOR'S NOTE

The title 'Motorcycle Sport' brings many different branches of motorcycling under one umbrella and very few have been ignored in compiling this book. Speedway, however, is one area that is omitted, because I feel it is a sport that would not have justice done to it if included in a book of this nature. The sport has such a long history that it could justifiably be the subject of a book in its own right.

Leaving aside what has *not* been included in this book, a large part of text has been dedicated to the World Road Race Championships. Despite the fact that the 500cc class is fast losing its appeal – because of the high cost of entering these finely tuned machines – it has, over the years, provided race fans with some outstanding personalities and duels. The Agostini–Hailwood clashes of the sixties were legendary, as were those between Barry Sheene and Kenny Roberts a decade later.

The 750cc Superbikes are now gaining in popularity and may soon be the Road Race Championships' premier category; their presence will no doubt continue to enhance the fascination that these championships have held over the years.

But motorcycle sport does not begin and end with the Road Race Championships, and the likes of moto-cross, trials, enduro, racing in the United States and, of course, the Isle of Man's great races, the Tourist Trophy and Manx Grands Prix, all gain their rightful place in this comprehensive coverage of motorcycle sport.

Ian Morrison
January 1991

ACKNOWLEDGEMENTS

The author would like to thank the following for their assistance with the compilation of this book:
His wife Ann for yet more hours of typing and checking of manuscript; Manchester Reference Library for their continued support; Anne-Marie Gerber of the Fédération Internationale Motocycliste (FIM); Angie Myers of the American Motorcyclist Association (AMA); Mary Kerr of the Auto-Cycle Union (ACU); Peter Neal, Isle of Man co-ordinator and commentator; R J Hewitt of the Motor Cycle Union of Ireland; Jock Wilson, team manager of the England Enduro team; Mary Twelvetree and Brian Woolett of EMAP Publishing; Gary van Voortis of the Daytona International Speedway; Jim McColm, secretary of the Edinburgh and District Motor Club Limited; and finally, the man who invented the fax machine – it doesn't half make life a lot easier!

Black & white illustrations courtesy of EMAP Archives, apart from the following:

Hulton: pp 41, 119, 125, 129, 133, 165, 177, 179, 187.
Allsport: pp 90, 171.
Gamma: p 157

Colour illustrations courtesy of Allsport and Gamma except the following:

Hulton: pp 2 (top), 5, 6 (top).
Daily Telegraph: pp 6 (Sheene), 15 Bottom)

ABBREVIATIONS

Arg	Argentina	Fin	Finland	SRho	Southern Rhodesia
Aus	Australia	Fra	France	SAf	South Africa
Aut	Austria	FRG	Federal Republic of Germany (West Germany)	Spa	Spain
Bel	Belgium			Swe	Sweden
Bra	Brazil	Hol	Netherlands	Swi	Switzerland
Can	Canada	Hun	Hungary	UK	Great Britain & Northern Ireland
Chi	Chile	Ire	Republic of Ireland	Uru	Uruguay
Col	Colombia	Ita	Italy	USA	United States of America
Cze	Czechoslovakia	Jap	Japan	USSR	Soviet Union
Den	Denmark	Lie	Liechtenstein	Ven	Venezuela
GDR	German Democratic Republic (East Germany)	NZ	New Zealand		
		Por	Portugal		

A HISTORY OF MOTORCYCLE SPORT

When the German Gottlieb Daimler manufactured and patented the first motorcycle in 1885, little did he know that a hundred years later man would be travelling at speeds in excess of 170 miles per hour as motorcycle racing became one of the world's most exciting and popular spectator sports.

Daimler's single-cylinder four-stroke machine was capable of producing 700 revolutions per minute and was first ridden by his son Paul, who drove the bike the six-mile round trip from his home town of Cannstatt to Untertürkkeim and back on 10 November 1885.

A century later the powerful Grand Prix bikes were capable of producing well in excess of 20 000rpm, but Daimler had none of the modern-day sophistications. His machine consisted of internal flywheels, a fan cooling system and a mechanically-operated exhaust valve with an automatic inlet valve. It was to serve as a useful part of the experiments which led to him developing the first four-wheeled petrol-driven car the following year.

Inevitably the petrol-driven motorcycle was also developed and in 1894 Alois Wolfmüller, together with Heinrich and Wilhelm Hildebrand, started production of the world's first commercial machine, the 2.5hp Motorrad, at their Munich factory. In the two years from November 1894 they produced a thousand of these 760cc water-cooled machines; while in August 1896, the New Beeston Cycle Company of Coventry started producing the Beeston Tricycle, the first commercial motorcycle in Britain.

Motorcar racing was already popular in Europe by then, but on 20 September 1896 motorcyclists engaged in their first organised race from Paris to Nantes and back. The 152km/94.45 mile race was won by M. Chevalier who beat seven other riders on his Michelin-Dion and covered the distance in 4hr 10min 37sec at an average speed of 22.61mph/36.39kph.

On 29 November the following year, Mr Charles Jarrott of the Motor-Car Club organised the first race for two-wheeled motorcycles at Sheen House, Richmond, and he himself won the 1 mile/1.6km race on a Fournier in a time of 2min 8sec.

By the turn of the century, motorcycling had become popular in both Britain and the rest of Europe. The first national organisation, the Motor Cycle Union of Ireland, was formed in 1901, shortly before the formation of the Motor Cycling Club in London on 19 November that year.

As racing became increasingly popular there was the need to set up a governing body and in Britain the Auto-Cycle Club was formed in 1903 – it changed its name to its present style of Auto-Cycle Union (ACU) in 1907.

Two pioneers of motorcycle sport at the turn of the century – the Collier brothers, Harry and Charlie, seen here at the Olympia Race Track in 1904

City-to-city races were very popular on the Continent as cars and motorcycles raced together along the open roads of France, Belgium and Spain. But after a large number of fatalities involving spectators during the 1903 Paris–Madrid race, which was abandoned before the contestants crossed the French border, this kind of racing was outlawed.

The following year, the Auto-Cycle Club de France organised the first official international race on closed roads. It became known as the International Cup and was a chance for rider and manufacturer to show off their skills and talents. However, the British were outclassed by their European counterparts. In addition, they had to endure a great deal of hostility from the French and there were more than a few allegations of cheating made by the British riders.

The event was appallingly organised and it was after this farce that a meeting of those associations involved in the first International Cup was called. In Paris on 21–22 December 1904 a governing body, to be known as the *Fédération Internationale des Club Motorcyclistes* (FICM) – later the *Fédération Internationale*

Motorcycliste (FIM) – was formed. It remains the sport's world governing body.

After the débâcle in France, the British were determined to set about improving standards, but found little co-operation from the powers-that-be in Westminster, who refused to close public roads for the purpose of testing and racing machines. This was a setback to the British manufacturers' hopes of establishing themselves as market leaders in the motorcycle industry.

However, the Isle of Man authorities stepped in and made available the island's roads for the purpose of running elimination races for the International Cup; and on 28 May 1907, less than a year after the demise of the International Cup in July 1906, the first Tourist Trophy (TT) races were held on the island and soon established themselves as the most important in the world, a status they carried for many years.

Also in 1907 the famous banked closed circuit at Brooklands was opened and it soon became established both as a home of motorcar and motorcycle racing and as a testing ground for manufacturers.

It remained a popular venue until the outbreak of the Second World War.

There was very little racing in France after the end of the International Cup; in the years between 1907 and the end of the First World War, motorcycle racing supremacy switched from France to Britain.

It was not until after the war that the Isle of Man TT races faced any serious rivals. A French Grand Prix had been run in 1913, but the 1914 race was cancelled because of the war. However, it resumed in 1920 and was joined a year later by races in Hungary and Holland. Motorcycle racing was truly expanding as an international sport, albeit predominantly in Europe at that time.

The British were still dominant, because many clubs had sprung up all around the country and riders had the chance to take part in some form of racing most weekends. No other nation had developed so much. But the so-called 'Roaring Twenties' soon altered that, as motorcycle sport took off across Europe.

Grand Prix racing, and indeed the Isle of Man's most important races, were divided into three classes: 250cc, 350cc and 500cc. The latter was originally the most popular, just as it has been in recent times. But the sport was not quite so well organised. Races were frequently more than 300 miles long and the three classes often competed together. It was confusing for the spectators.

As the Second World War approached, the FICM had started reducing race distances and holding separate races for the individual classes. In 1938 they made the first move towards an eventual world championship when they launched the European Championship. But it ran for only two

Brooklands, England's first purpose-built race track and the home of British motor sport in the 1920s

years before the war intervened.

Motorcycle racing resumed in 1946. At their Spring Congress in Luxembourg, in April 1949, the FICM approved the change of name to the FIM and within a couple of months they launched their inaugural World Championships for five categories: 125cc, 250cc, 350cc, 500cc and sidecars, which had first been introduced into the TT programme in 1923.

Since then, other categories have been granted 'world championship' status. The 50cc class was introduced in 1962 and was replaced in 1984 by the slightly larger 80cc class, which in turn ceased at the end of 1989. A 750cc class was held briefly from 1977–9, and since 1977 there has been a Formula One

Right *One of the riders in the 1903 Paris–Madrid race, abandoned because of the high number of fatalities.*
Below *Motorcycle racing was very popular in the 1920s and 1930s, as this crowd at Crystal Palace for the 1928 Essex Cup race shows*

World Championship which was formed after the FIM took world championship status away from the Isle of Man TT races.

Motorcycle sport, however, covers far more than the closed-circuit road races of the Grands Prix and the classic road racing

on the Isle of Man. There is long-distance racing, which formed the basis of the sport in the early days, and such races as the Bol d'Or and Le Mans 24-Hour race are classics amongst endurance races. An endurance championship, previously known as the FIM Coupe

Club racing is the arena from which most budding stars emerge, whether it be as a road race champion or scrambler. Here at the Southend club's Whit Monday Scramble in 1965, two of Britain's finest moto-cross exponents can be seen: Jeff Smith (50) and Vic Eastwood (48)

nents and have themselves established a degree of supremacy.

But motorcycling as a sport does not end there. There is also drag racing and sprinting, which is popular on both sides of the Atlantic, and in America dirt-track racing has a large following.

All branches of motorcycling are reliant upon sponsorship, which is very much a part of modern-day sport in general. Motorcycling is perhaps luckier than many other sports because riders at the grass-roots level generally receive some sort of assistance from a local motorcycle dealer. But at the highest level, big-name sponsors are needed to pay the sort of money required to attract the best riders. Fortunately, because of its standing as a great spectator and television sport, there has been no shortage of such sponsors in the world of motorcycling, particularly in Grand Prix and Superbike racing.

Sadly, though, the cost of Grand Prix racing has soared in recent years and the sport's premier event, the 500cc World Championship, is losing much of its appeal because of the restricted number of riders who can attract the sort of sponsorship money required to compete. Consequently, fields in the 500cc road race championship rounds are dwindling all the time, and its status as road racing's number one event may soon be threatened.

Each form of motorcycle sport requires a different technique and each has its own specially designed machine. But all have one thing in common: the rider must have courage and a sound command of his machine. And there is no finer sight than a leading exponent, whether he be a road racer, moto-cross specialist or trials expert, in full flow.

d'Endurance, has existed since the 1970s but in 1980 it was granted world championship status and became known as the World Endurance Championship.

Speedway, whilst not covered in this book, is another form of motorcycle sport. Dirt-track racing was seen in the United States in 1902 and the first speedway race in anything like its present form was at the West Maitland Agricultural Show in New South Wales, Australia, on 22 December 1923. It made its way to England in 1927 and was first demonstrated at Camberley in Surrey. The first race meeting was at Droylesden, Manchester, on 25 June 1927. The first on a cinder track was at High Beech, Essex, on 19 February 1928. Grass tracking, a form of speedway but on grass, was also popularised in the 1920s.

One of the oldest forms of motorcycle sport is trials riding, in which man tests his machine against rivals for reliability and other performances, like manoeuvrability, over tough and demanding courses. They are not races as such, but are a test of the rider's skill and the

machine's capability. Points are gained and lost according to the skill of the rider, who must display control over his machine. The most famous of all trials is the Scottish Six Day Trial, inaugurated in 1909. The first International Six Day Trial was in 1913, but this became known as the International Six Day Enduro in 1984 when Enduro riding, a form of trials but without observed points, became increasingly popular. The inaugural World Trials Championship took place in 1975.

Moto-cross, also known as scrambling, is another form of motorcycle sport which has many enthusiasts in Britain and on the Continent. Held over pre-planned undulating dirt circuits, it developed from trials riding in the 1920s and the first meeting over a pre-determined course was at Camberley in 1924.

Predominantly a British sport for the first twenty years, it became international in 1947 with the introduction of the Moto-Cross des Nations, an international team event. While the Europeans dominated for many years, the Americans have since become moto-cross expo-

DEVELOPMENT OF THE RACING MACHINE

The earliest motorcycles were little more than conventional cycles fitted with an engine. But as the sport of racing became increasingly popular, manufacturers, notably on the Continent, began to design bikes specifically for racing.

However, the British manufacturers were against such a move because they were of the opinion that the purpose of racing was to produce better touring machines. Consequently they refused to build machines solely for the purpose of racing. While their decision was commendable, it did have adverse results on the track as the overseas bikes were dominant in the early International Cup races, which stipulated only that bikes should weigh no more than 50 kilograms unladen.

With the opening of Brooklands in 1907, the British manufacturers had the opportunity to develop better and faster bikes and in 1908 Charlie Collier built a 1000cc machine on which he established the world 1-hour record at the Surrey track, covering 70 miles/112.65km in 60 minutes. The record stood until 1920.

British machines dominated the early Isle of Man TT races but in 1911 they received a jolt when the Americans 'invaded' the island and took the first three places in the Senior TT with their famous Indian marque, a 1.5hp single-cylinder machine weighing just 98lb/44.45kg. However, the Ameri-

can clean sweep of the world's premier race was just the spur the British manufacturers needed. AJS, Brough Superior, Rudge, Velocette and Norton all set about re-designing their machines; and they soon regained their dominance.

Early racing machines were little more than 'souped-up' versions of commercial machines and races were categorised according to engine capacity. However, as the sport became more competitive, and manufacturers sought to make machines faster all the time, the first major development was the

introduction of the multi-cylinder engine – previously, all had been single cylinders. Multi-cylinder engines were an unknown quantity and because of their unproven record the governing bodies allowed manufacturers to produce engines with a larger total capacity than the single-cylinder engines. But as the design of the multi-cylinder machines improved and they became more powerful, their permitted cubic capacity advantage was gradually reduced, and by the time the First World War intervened, fixed-capacity classes had been created irre-

Oliver Godfrey astride the American-made Indian on which he won the Senior TT at the Isle of Man in 1911, the first time a foreign machine had won the race. As can be seen, it was little more than a pedal cycle fitted with an engine

Sidecars are now sleek one-piece units, but their design was considerably different back in 1923

spective of whether the machine was two-stroke, four-stroke, single or multi-cylinder.

The design of the racing bike changed very little during the 1920s, but speeds were increasing all the time thanks to the improvement in quality of the engines, as engineers started to fully understand the principles of the four-stroke engine and were able to apply those principles. An improvement in tyre manufacture also meant faster speeds, but equally it meant that machines were better to handle, and consequently there was an improvement in safety standards.

Manufacturers were given a boost in the 1930s when the FICM authorised the use of superchargers and streamlining. However, the British manufacturers were again reluctant to change, and remained loyal to the unsupercharged single-cylinder machines. Inevitably they got left behind as the Italians and Germans produced superb machines, notably at the Gilera, Moto Guzzi and BMW factories. And it was Guzzi who first confirmed the arrival of the new Italian machines when Stan Woods rode the innovative 120°

V-twin, with rear springing, to victory in the 1935 Senior TT.

It was the first win by a foreign bike since the American Indians' victory in 1911, and a double blow to British pride followed in 1939 when Germany's Georg Meier won the Senior TT on a BMW. It was the first time the most prestigious race in the world had been won by an overseas rider on a Continental machine. Meier's powerful twin was to lose its supremacy later in the year, though, when Dorini Serafini won the Ulster Grand Prix on a supercharged, water-cooled, four-cylinder Gilera at an average speed of 97.85mph/ 157.44kph, to make it the fastest road race in the world. AJS and Velocette had led the way for the British factories who were trying to re-establish themselves; both had produced four-cylinder supercharged machines and, during the same race, Walter Rusk established a lap record at a staggering 100.03mph/ 160.95kph on his AJS.

The Germans and Italians both saw motorcycle racing as a political platform for supremacy, just as they had done in car racing, and both nations set aside plenty of money for the

development of bikes solely for racing purposes. But whilst the overseas machines were far more advanced technically than the British machines, and capable of much greater speeds, they still lacked the reliability of the British bikes.

BMW's triumph at the Senior TT had seemed to bode ill for the British machines. But they were saved by the war years; when racing returned in 1946, the governing body banned the use of superchargers, and the fortunes of the British manufacturers took an upward turn at a time when it was feared they were going to lose what little credibility they still had. However, while the ban on superchargers gave renewed hope to the single-cylinder British machines, the reprieve was only short-lived and by the mid-fifties, the British manufacturers once more posed little threat to the Italians and Germans.

Norton stuck with their reliable single-cylinder engine in the early post-war years, but they mounted it in a new frame with revolutionary rear springing. The Norton 'Featherbed' was a magnificent bike to handle and was excellent at cornering, which made up for its lack of acceleration on the straight.

But, as so often happens, the innovators ultimately suffered from their own skills. Before long, the overseas manufacturers had copied the Norton style of frame, and the Germans and Italians reigned supreme once more. It was Guzzi who were one of the first to produce an engine that needed less power for the performance required of it. Consequently they took full advantage of streamlining and produced a very lightweight machine, with a small front. In terms of aerodynamics it was magnificently designed.

Their 350cc model which won the 1954 Junior TT was probably one of the most scientifically designed racing bikes in the world, and it made full use of the low centre of gravity. That same year Guzzi also launched their amazing eight-cylinder 500cc machine.

Another of the outstanding streamlined bikes of the 1950s was the NSU, and for many years it was the only unsupercharged petrol engine capable of producing 125 brake horsepower (bhp). By then the British manufacturers, AJS, Velocette and Norton, had withdrawn factory support from racing.

By the mid-fifties, streamlining was a major feature of most, if not all, racing bikes as manufacturers extended the small front fairing to a large enclosure covering all parts of the bike in front of the rider. It had its desired effect as speeds rose to beyond 150mph/ 241.35kph, but to curb this trend the FIM outlawed full streamlining at the end of the 1957 season.

While the Italians were producing superb racing machines they were paying the price for concentrating on the racing side, and their successes at Grand Prix level did little to enhance sales of road bikes, just as the British manufacturers had predicted at the turn of the century. All but MV Augusta withdrew from Grand Prix racing at the end of 1957. Not surprisingly, MV dominated the World Championship over the next couple of years – until the arrival of Honda.

The Japanese manufacturer was keen to engage on a sales drive and, despite the domestic Italian market not having benefited from the nation's Grand Prix successes, Honda still entered the world of Grand Prix racing, at the 1959 Isle of Man TT races. By the early sixties, they were the biggest name in road racing – their gamble, and investment, certainly paid off.

They were experts in designing engines with very small cylinders but plenty of them, a feature which proved exceptionally successful on their smaller machines. They produced a four-cylinder 250cc

machine capable of 16 000rpm, and a five-cylinder 125cc model which touched 20 000rpm. These kinds of figures had previously only been associated with the larger bikes. Honda's design was to set the trend for the years to come and the days of the pioneer, the single-cylinder machine, were numbered.

Since Honda's innovative moves in the late fifties, the world of motorcycle racing has been dominated by the Japanese as Suzuki and Yamaha became equal masters at producing small-engined machines.

In the 500cc class, MV Agusta managed to hold off the Japanese challenge because they redesigned their original four-cylinder model and built a lighter three-cylinder machine. In time, however, the Japanese took charge of the 500cc event too, and since the mid-1970s the water-cooled, four-cylinder two-strokes of Honda, Yamaha and Suzuki have been dominant.

Whilst engineers were still looking to produce more powerful engines all the time, the designers were looking at ways of improving the frames and it soon became apparent that a successful machine was one that could corner well in addition to having power. Consequently, a great deal of attention was paid to the positioning of the centre of gravity; the lower it became, the greater the cornering speed.

Telescopic and hydraulic suspension systems have helped to improve the racing bike's performance and handling. The moving away from drum to disc brakes was another major feature in its development, as was the introduction of the high-grip tyres. But no matter what has been done over the years to make the racing machine faster, safer and better to handle, it all comes down to the rider, in whose hands the success or failure of a bike remains.

This 1956 Mondial highlights the use of full streamlining, which the FIM outlawed the following year

THE WORLD ROAD RACE CHAMPIONSHIPS

THE POINTS SYSTEM

Between 1949 and 1976, a rider's points total was not ultimately accumulated over every race, only a certain number of races. As a general rule, the number of races which could be counted towards the final total was derived from the number of championship rounds, divided by two, plus one. So if there were a total of 8 races, then 5 would count towards the championship. (If there were 9 then it would still be 5, fractions were ignored.)

The figures in brackets, in the final points tables listed, indicate the number of points a rider/manufacturer actually obtained, while the other figures are those which counted towards the championship. Since 1977, all races have counted.

Only a manufacturer's best position in a race counts towards the manufacturers' title.

THE CHAMPIONSHIP POINTS SYSTEM

The points scoring in individual races has also changed as follows:

1949		1969–87		1988–90	
1st . . . 10 pts		1st . . . 15 pts		1st . . . 20 pts	
2nd . . . 8 pts		2nd . . . 12 pts		2nd . . . 17 pts	
3rd . . . 7 pts		3rd . . . 10 pts		3rd . . . 15 pts	
4th . . . 6 pts		4th . . . 8 pts		4th . . . 13 pts	
5th . . . 5 pts		5th . . . 6 pts		5th . . . 11 pts	
		6th . . . 5 pts		6th . . . 10 pts	
Plus one point for the rider		7th . . . 4 pts		7th . . . 9 pts	
recording the fastest lap,		8th . . . 3 pts		8th . . . 8 pts	
provided he finished the race		9th . . . 2 pts		9th . . . 7 pts	
		10th . . . 1 pt		10th . . . 6 pts	
1950–68	1st . . . 8 pts			11th . . . 5 pts	
	2nd . . . 6 pts			12th . . . 4 pts	
	3rd . . . 4 pts			13th . . . 3 pts	
	4th . . . 3 pts			14th . . . 2 pts	
	5th . . . 2 pts			15th . . . 1 pt	
	6th . . . 1 pt				

1949

BRITISH GRAND PRIX (TOURIST TROPHY)

Isle of Man, 13–15 June
500cc
1 Harold Daniell (UK), Norton, 86.93mph/139.90kph
2 Johnny Lockett (UK), Norton
3 Ernie Lyons (UK), Velocette
Fastest lap: Bob Foster (UK), Guzzi, 89.75mph/144.44kph

Other winners:
350cc: Freddie Frith (UK), Velocette, 83.15mph/133.82kph
250cc: Manliff Barrington (Ire), Guzzi, 77.96mph/125.46kph

SWISS GRAND PRIX

Berne, 2–3 July
500cc
1 Leslie Graham (UK), AJS. 88.06mph/141.72kph
2 Arciso Artesiani (Ita), Gilera
3 Harold Daniell (UK), Norton

Fastest lap: Ted Frend (UK), AJS, 90.00mph/144.84kph
Other winners:
350cc: Freddie Frith (UK), Velocette, 84.89mph/
136.62kph
250cc: Bruno Ruffo (Ita), Guzzi, 81.21mph/130.69kph
125cc: Nello Pagani (Ita), Mondial, 71.37mph/114.86kph
Sidecar: Eric Oliver/Denis Jenkinson (UK), Norton,
73.48mph/118.25kph

DUTCH TT

Assen, 9 July
500cc
1 Nello Pagani (Ita), Gilera, 91.52mph/147.29kph
2 Leslie Graham (UK), AJS
3 Arciso Artesiani (Ita), Gilera
Fastest lap: Pagani, 93.68mph/150.76kph
Other winners:
350cc: Freddie Frith (UK), Velocette, 85.68mph/
137.89kph
125cc: Nello Pagani (Ita), Mondial, 68.84mph/110.79kph

BELGIAN GRAND PRIX

Spa-Francorchamps, 17 July
500cc
1 Bill Doran (UK), AJS, 95.25mph/153.29kph
2 Arciso Artesiani (Ita), Gilera
3 Nello Pagani (Ita), Guzzi
Fastest lap: Artesiani, 96.28mph/154.95kph
Other winners:
350cc: Freddie Frith (UK), Velocette, 89.58mph/
144.17kph
Sidecar: Eric Oliver/Denis Jenkinson (UK), Norton,
75.33mph/121.23kph

ULSTER GRAND PRIX

Clady Circuit, Belfast, 21 August
500cc
1 Leslie Graham (UK), AJS, 96.49mph/155.29kph
2 Artie Bell (UK), Norton
3 Nello Pagani (Ita), Gilera
Fastest lap: Graham, 98.08mph/157.84kph
Other winners:
350cc: Freddie Frith (UK), Velocette, 89.12mph/
143.42kph
250cc: Maurice Cann (UK), Guzzi, 80.08mph/128.88kph

ITALIAN GRAND PRIX
(GRAND PRIX DES NATIONS)

Monza, 4 September
500cc
1 Nello Pagani (Ita), Gilera, 97.90mph/157.55kph
2 Arciso Artesiani (Ita), Gilera
3 Bill Doran (UK), AJS
Fastest lap: Pagani, 101.10mph/162.70kph
Other winners:
250cc: Dario Ambrosini (Ita), Benelli, 89.40mph/
143.88kph
125cc: Gianni Leoni (Ita), Mondial, 77.80mph/125.21kph
Sidecar: Ercole Frigerio/Edoardo Ricotti (Ita), Gilera,
80.80mph/130.03kph

The first world 500cc champion, Leslie Graham

LEADING CHAMPIONSHIP POSITIONS

500cc
Riders
1 Leslie Graham (UK) 30(31)pts
2 Nello Pagani (Ita) 28(40)pts
3 Arciso Artesiani (Ita) 25(32)pts
4 Bill Doran (UK) 23pts
5 Artie Bell (UK) 20pts
6 Harold Daniell (UK) 17pts
Manufacturers
1 AJS 32(48)pts
2 Gilera 31(46)pts
3 Norton 25(37)pts

350cc
1 Freddie Frith (UK) 33(54)pts
2 Reg Armstrong (Ire) 18pts
3 Bob Foster (UK) 16pts
Manufacturers' title: Velocette

250cc
1 Bruno Ruffo (Ita) 24pts
2 Dario Ambrosini (Ita) 19pts
3 Ron Mead (UK) 13pts
Manufacturers' title: Guzzi

125cc
1 Nello Pagani (Ita) 27pts
2 Renato Magi (Ita) 14pts
3 Umberto Masetti (Ita) 13pts
Manufacturers' title: Mondial

Sidecar
1 Eric Oliver (UK) 27pts
2 Ercole Frigerio (Ita) 18pts
3 Frans Vanderschrick (Bel) 16pts
Manufacturers' title: Norton

1950

BRITISH GRAND PRIX (TOURIST TROPHY)

Isle of Man, 5–9 June
500cc
1 Geoff Duke (UK), Norton, 92.27mph/148.49kph
2 Artie Bell (UK), Norton
3 Johnny Lockett (UK), Norton
Fastest lap: Duke, 93.33mph/150.20kph
Other winners:
350cc: Artie Bell (UK), Norton, 86.33mph/138.93kph
250cc: Dario Ambrosini (Ita), Benelli, 78.08mph/
125.66kph

BELGIAN GRAND PRIX

Spa-Francorchamps, 2 July
500cc
1 Umberto Masetti (Ita), Gilera, 101.09mph/162.69kph
2 Nello Pagani (Ita), Gilera
3 Ted Frend (UK), AJS
Fastest lap: Geoff Duke (UK), Norton, 103.84mph/
167.11kph
Other winners:
350cc: Bob Foster (UK), Velocette, 97.26mph/156.52kph
Sidecar: Eric Oliver (UK)/Lorenzo Dobelli (Ita), Norton,
82.50mph/132.77kph

DUTCH TT

Assen, 8 July
500cc
1 Umberto Masetti (Ita), Gilera, 91.70mph/147.58kph
2 Nello Pagani (Ita), Gilera
3 Harry Hinton (Aus), Norton
Fastest lap: Carlos Bandirola (Ita), Gilera, 95.42mph/
153.56kph
Other winners:
350cc: Bob Foster (UK), Velocette, 88.41mph/142.28kph
125cc: Bruno Ruffo (Ita), Mondial, 75.06mph/120.80kph

SWISS GRAND PRIX

Geneva, 22–23 July
500cc
1 Leslie Graham (UK), AJS, 78.46mph/126.27kph
2 Umberto Masetti (Ita), Gilera
3 Carlos Bandirola (Ita), Gilera
Fastest lap: Bandirola, 82.80mph/133.25kph
Other winners:
350cc: Leslie Graham (UK), AJS, 78.26mph/125.95kph
250cc: Dario Ambrosini (Ita), Benelli, 75.96mph/
122.25kph
Sidecar: Eric Oliver (UK)/Lorenzo Dobelli (Ita), Norton,
71.71mph/115.41kph

ULSTER GRAND PRIX

Clady Circuit, Belfast, 18 August
500cc
1 Geoff Duke (UK), Norton, 99.56mph/160.23kph
2 Leslie Graham (UK), AJS
3 Johnny Lockett (UK), Norton
Fastest lap: Duke, 101.77mph/163.78kph
Other winners:
350cc: Bob Foster (UK), Velocette, 91.38mph/147.06kph
250cc: Maurice Cann (UK), Guzzi, 82.73mph/133.14kph
125cc: Carlo Ubbiali (Ita), Mondial, 77.46mph/124.66kph

ITALIAN GRAND PRIX
(GRAND PRIX DES NATIONS)

Monza, 10 September
500cc
1 Geoff Duke (UK), Norton, 102.34mph/164.70kph
2 Umberto Masetti (Ita), Gilera
3 Arciso Artesiani (Ita), MV Agusta
Fastest lap: Masetti, 105.44mph/169.69kph
Other winners:
350cc: Geoff Duke (UK), Norton, 95.02mph/152.92kph
250cc: Dario Ambrosini (Ita), Benelli, 90.45mph/
145.57kph
125cc: Gianni Leoni (Ita), Mondial, 82.11mph/132.14kph
Sidecar: Eric Oliver (UK)/Lorenzo Dobelli (Ita), Norton,
85.91mph/138.26kph

LEADING CHAMPIONSHIP POSITIONS

500cc
Riders
1 Umberto Masetti (Ita) 28(29)pts
2 Geoff Duke (UK) 27pts
3 Leslie Graham (UK) 17pts
4 Nello Pagani (Ita) 12pts
5 Carlos Bandirola (Ita) 12pts
6 Johnny Lockett (UK) 9pts
Manufacturers
1 Norton 28(32)pts
2 Gilera 28(29)pts
3 AJS 21pts

350cc
1 Bob Foster (UK) 30pts
2 Geoff Duke (UK 24(28)pts
3 Leslie Graham (UK) 17pts
Manufacturers' title: Velocette

250cc
1 Dario Ambrosini (Ita) 24pts
2 Maurice Cann (UK) 14pts
3 Fergus Anderson (UK) 6pts
 Bruno Ruffo (Ita) 6pts
Manufacturers' title: Benelli

125cc
1 Bruno Ruffo (Ita) 17pts
2 Gianni Leoni (Ita) 14pts
3 Carlo Ubbiali (Ita) 14pts
Manufacturers' title: Mondial

Sidecar
1 Eric Oliver (UK) 24pts
2 Ercole Frigerio (Ita) 18pts
3 Hans Haldemann (Swi) 8pts
Manufacturers' title: Norton

1951

SPANISH GRAND PRIX

Montjuich, Barcelona, 7–8 April
500cc
1 Umberto Masetti (Ita), Gilera, 58.30mph/93.82kph
2 Tommy Wood (UK), Norton
3 Arciso Artesiani (Ita), MV Agusta
Fastest lap: Enrico Lorenzetti (Ita), Guzzi, 59.90mph/
96.40kph
Other winners:
350cc: Tommy Wood (UK), Guzzi, 58.39mph/93.97kph
125cc: Guido Leoni (Ita), Mondial, 53.50mph/86.10kph
Sidecar: Eric Oliver (UK)/Lorenzo Dobelli (Ita), Norton,
50.02mph/80.50kph

SWISS GRAND PRIX

Berne, 26–27 May
500cc
1 Fergus Anderson (UK), Guzzi, 80.01mph/128.76kph
2 Reg Armstrong (Ire), AJS
3 Enrico Lorenzetti (Ita), Guzzi
Fastest lap: Geoff Duke (UK), Norton, 89.40mph/
143.88kph
Other winners:
350cc: Leslie Graham (UK), Velocette, 80.04mph/
128.81kph
250cc: Dario Ambrosini (Ita), Benelli, 74.50mph/
119.90kph
Sidecar: Ercole Frigerio/Edoardo Ricotti (Ita), Gilera,
70.60mph/113.62kph

BRITISH GRAND PRIX (TOURIST TROPHY)

Isle of Man, 4–9 June
500cc
1 Geoff Duke (UK), Norton, 93.83mph/151.00kph
2 Bill Doran (UK), AJS
3 Cromie McCandless (UK), Norton
Fastest lap: Duke, 95.22mph/153.24kph
Other winners:
350cc: Geoff Duke (UK), Norton, 89.90mph/144.68kph

250cc: Tommy Wood (UK), Guzzi, 81.39mph/130.98kph
125cc: Cromie McCandless (UK), Mondial, 74.85mph/
120.46kph

BELGIAN GRAND PRIX

Spa-Francorchamps, 1 July
500cc
1 Geoff Duke (UK), Norton, 106.66mph/171.65kph
2 Alfredo Milani (Ita), Gilera
3 S Geminiani (Ita), Guzzi
Fastest lap: Duke, 107.80mph/173.49kph
Other winners:
350cc: Geoff Duke (UK), Norton, 100.52mph/161.77kph
Sidecar: Eric Oliver (UK)/Lorenzo Dobelli (Ita), Norton,
86.83mph/139.74kph

DUTCH TT

Assen, 7 July
500cc
1 Geoff Duke (UK), Norton, 95.55mph/153.77kph
2 Alfredo Milani (Ita), Gilera
3 Enrico Lorenzetti (Ita), Guzzi
Fastest lap: Umberto Masetti (Ita), Gilera, 97.28mph/
156.56kph
Other winners:
350cc: Bill Doran (UK), AJS, 88.60mph/142.59kph
125cc: Gianni Leoni (Ita), Mondial, 76.57mph/123.23kph

FRENCH GRAND PRIX

Albi, 14 July
500cc
1 Alfredo Milani (Ita), Gilera, 99.22mph/159.68kph
2 Bill Doran (UK), AJS
3 Nello Pagani (Ita), Gilera
Fastest lap: Milani, 100.68mph/162.03kph
Other winners:
350cc: Geoff Duke (UK), Norton, 87.97mph/141.57kph
250cc: Bruno Ruffo (Ita), Guzzi, 83.21mph/133.91kph
Sidecar: Eric Oliver (UK)/Lorenzo Dobelli (Ita), Norton,
82.45mph/132.69kph

ULSTER GRAND PRIX

Clady Circuit, Belfast, 18 August
500cc
1 Geoff Duke (UK), Norton, 95.18mph/153.18kph
2 Ken Kavanagh (Aus), Norton
3 Umberto Masetti (Ita), Gilera
Fastest lap: Alfredo Milani (Ita), Gilera, 97.27mph/
156.54kph
Other winners:
350cc: Geoff Duke (UK), Norton, 96.85mph/155.86kph
250cc: Bruno Ruffo (Ita), Guzzi, 86.93mph/139.90kph
125cc: Cromie McCandless (UK), Mondial, 73.15mph/
117.72kph
*Race did not count towards the World Championship
because of insufficient entries*

ITALIAN GRAND PRIX (GRAND PRIX DES NATIONS)

Monza, 9 September
500cc
1 Alfredo Milani (Ita), Gilera, 105.20mph/169.30kph
2 Umberto Masetti (Ita), Gilera
3 Nello Pagani (Ita), Gilera
Fastest lap: Milani, 107.18mph/172.49kph
Other winners:
350cc: Geoff Duke (UK), Norton, 85.13mph/137.00kph
250cc: Enrico Lorenzetti (Ita), Guzzi, 89.23mph/
143.60kph
125cc: Carlo Ubbiali (Ita), Mondial, 84.51mph/136.01kph
Sidecar: Albino Milani/Giuseppe Pizzocri (Ita), Gilera,
89.38mph/143.84kph

LEADING CHAMPIONSHIP POSITIONS

500cc
Riders
1 Geoff Duke (UK) 35(37)pts
2 Alfredo Milani (Ita) 31pts
3 Umberto Masetti (Ita) 21pts
4 Bill Doran (UK) 14pts
5 Nello Pagani (Ita) 10pts
6 Reg Armstrong (Ire) 9pts
Manufacturers
1 Norton 38(44)pts
2 Gilera 36(40)pts
3 AJS 22(23)pts

350cc
1 Geoff Duke (UK) 40pts
2 Bill Doran (UK) 19pts
3 Johnny Lockett (UK) 19pts
Manufacturers' title: Norton

250cc
1 Bruno Ruffo (Ita) 26pts
2 Tommy Wood (UK) 21pts
3 Dario Ambrosini (Ita) 14pts
Manufacturers' title: Guzzi

125cc
1 Carlo Ubbiali (Ita) 20pts
2 Gianni Leoni (Ita) 12pts
3 Cromie McCandless (UK) 11pts
Manufacturers' title: Mondial

Sidecar
1 Eric Oliver (UK) 30(32)pts
2 Ercole Frigerio (Ita) 26pts
3 Albino Milani (Ita) 19pts
Manufacturers' title: Norton

1952

SWISS GRAND PRIX

Berne, 17–18 May
500cc
1 Jack Brett (UK), AJS, 93.71mph/150.81kph
2 Bill Doran (UK), AJS
3 Carlos Bandirola (Ita), MV Agusta
Fastest lap: Brett, 96.70mph/155.62kph
Other winners:
350cc: Geoff Duke (UK), Norton, 91.54mph/147.32kph
250cc: Fergus Anderson (UK), Guzzi, 85.09mph/
136.94kph
Sidecar: Albino Milani/Giuseppe Pizzocri (Ita), Gilera,
79.07mph/127.25kph

BRITISH GRAND PRIX (TOURIST TROPHY)

Isle of Man, 9–13 June
500cc
1 Reg Armstrong (Ire), Norton, 92.97mph/149.62kph
2 Leslie Graham (UK), MV Agusta
3 Ray Amm (SRho), Norton
Fastest lap: Geoff Duke (UK), Norton, 94.88mph/
152.69kph

Other winners:
350cc: Geoff Duke (UK), Norton, 90.29mph/145.31kph
250cc: Fergus Anderson (UK), Guzzi, 83.82mph/
134.90kph
125cc: Cecil Sandford (UK), MV Agusta, 75.54mph/
121.57kph

DUTCH TT

Assen, 28 June
500cc
1 Umberto Masetti (Ita), Gilera, 97.19mph/156.41kph
2 Geoff Duke (UK), Norton
3 Ken Kavanagh (Aus), Norton
Fastest lap: Masetti, 102.92mph/165.63kph
Other winners:
350cc: Geoff Duke (UK), Norton, 92.96mph/149.60kph
250cc: Enrico Lorenzetti (Ita), Guzzi, 84.98mph/
136.76kph
125cc: Cecil Sandford (UK), MV Agusta, 78.80mph/
126.82kph

BELGIAN GRAND PRIX

Spa-Francorchamps, 6 July
500cc
1 Umberto Masetti (Ita), Gilera, 101.13mph/162.75kph
2 Geoff Duke (UK), Norton

3 Ray Amm (SRho), Norton
Fastest lap: Masetti, 109.34mph/175.97kph
Other winners:
350cc: Geoff Duke (UK), Norton, 101.71mph/163.69kph
Sidecar: Eric Oliver/Eric Bliss (UK), Norton, 89.77mph/
144.47kph

WEST GERMAN GRAND PRIX

Solitude Circuit, Stuttgart, 20 July
500cc
1 Reg Armstrong (Ire), Norton, 83.12mph/133.77kph
2 Ken Kavanagh (Aus), Norton
3 Sid Lawton (UK), Norton
Fastest lap: Leslie Graham (UK), MV Agusta, 84.86mph/
136.57kph
Other winners:
350cc: Reg Armstrong (Ire), Norton, 81.07mph/
130.47kph
250cc: Rudi Felgenheier (FRG), DKW, 77.91mph/
125.38kph
125cc: Werner Haas (FRG), NSU, 73.11mph/117.66kph
Sidecar: Cyril Smith/Bob Clements (UK), Norton,
72.10mph/116.03kph

ULSTER GRAND PRIX

Clady Circuit, Belfast, 14–16 August
500cc
1 Cromie McCandless (UK), Gilera, 99.79mph/160.60kph
2 Rod Coleman (NZ), AJS
3 Bill Lomas (UK), MV Agusta
Fastest lap: Leslie Graham (UK), MV Agusta, 105.94mph/
170.49kph
Other winners:
350cc: Ken Kavanagh (Aus), Norton, 94.88mph/
152.69kph

250cc: Maurice Cann (UK), Guzzi, 86.22mph/138.76kph
125cc: Cecil Sandford (UK), MV Agusta, 77.47mph/
124.68kph

ITALIAN GRAND PRIX
(GRAND PRIX DES NATIONS)

Monza, 14 September
500cc
1 Leslie Graham (UK), MV Agusta, 106.29mph/171.06kph
2 Umberto Masetti (Ita), Gilera
3 Nello Pagani (Ita), Gilera
Fastest lap: Graham, 108.09mph/173.95kph
Other winners:
350cc: Ray Amm (SRho), Norton, 97.59mph/157.06kph
250cc: Enrico Lorenzetti (Ita), Guzzi, 93.67mph/
150.75kph
125cc: Emilio Mendogni (Ita), Morini, 84.39mph/
135.81kph
Sidecar: Ernesto Merlo/Edoardo Magri (Ita), Gilera,
91.80mph/147.74kph

SPANISH GRAND PRIX

Montjuich, Barcelona, 5 October
500cc
1 Leslie Graham (UK), MV Agusta, 59.54mph/95.82kph
2 Umberto Masetti (Ita), Gilera
3 Ken Kavanagh (Aus), Norton
Fastest lap: Masetti, 61.21mph/98.51kph
Other winners:
125cc: Emilio Mendogni (Ita), Morini, 58.29mph/93.81kph
Sidecar: Eric Oliver (UK)/Lorenzo Dobelli (Ita), Norton,
53.85mph/86.66kph

LEADING CHAMPIONSHIP POSITIONS

500cc
Riders
1 Umberto Masetti (Ita) 28pts
2 Leslie Graham (UK) 25pts
3 Reg Armstrong (Ire) 22pts
4 Rod Coleman (NZ) 15pts
5 Jack Brett (UK) 14pts
6 Ken Kavanagh (Aus) 14pts
Manufacturers
1 Gilera 36(39)pts
2 Norton 32(35)pts
3 MV Agusta 30(33)pts

350cc
1 Geoff Duke (UK) 32pts
2 Reg Armstrong (Ire) 24(31)pts
3 Ray Amm (SRho) 21pts
Manufacturers' title: Norton

250cc
1 Enrico Lorenzetti (Ita) 28(30)pts
2 Fergus Anderson (UK) 24pts
3 Leslie Graham (UK) 11pts
Manufacturers' title: Guzzi

125cc
1 Cecil Sandford (UK) 28(32)pts
2 Carlo Ubbiali (Ita) 24pts
3 Emilio Mendogni (Ita) 16pts
Manufacturers' title: MV Agusta

Sidecar
1 Cyril Smith (UK) 24(28)pts
2 Albino Milani (Ita) 18pts
3 Jacques Drion (Fra) 17(18)pts
Manufacturers' title: Norton

1953

BRITISH GRAND PRIX (TOURIST TROPHY)

Isle of Man, 8–12 June
500cc
1 Ray Amm (SRho), Norton, 93.85mph/151.04kph
2 Jack Brett (UK), Norton

3 Reg Armstrong (Ire), Gilera
Fastest lap: Amm, 97.41mph/156.77kph
Other winners:
350cc: Ray Amm (SRho), Norton, 90.52mph/145.68kph
250cc: Fergus Anderson (UK), Guzzi, 84.73mph/
136.36kph
125cc: Leslie Graham (UK), MV Agusta, 77.79mph/
125.19kph

DUTCH TT

Assen, 27 June
500cc
1 Geoff Duke (UK), Gilera, 99.92mph/160.81kph
2 Reg Armstrong (Ire), Gilera
3 Ken Kavanagh (Aus), Norton
Fastest lap: Ray Amm (SRho), Norton, 100.91mph/
162.40kph
Other winners:
350cc: Enrico Lorenzetti (Ita), Guzzi, 93.44mph/
150.38kph
250cc: Werner Haas (FRG), NSU, 91.23mph/146.82kph
125cc: Werner Haas (FRG), NSU, 78.85mph/126.90kph

BELGIAN GRAND PRIX

Spa-Francorchamps, 5 July
500cc
1 Alfredo Milani (Ita), Gilera, 109.94mph/176.93kph
2 Ray Amm (SRho), Norton
3 Reg Armstrong (Ire), Gilera
Fastest lap: Geoff Duke (UK), Gilera, 112.33mph/
180.78kph
Other winners:
350cc: Fergus Anderson (UK), Guzzi, 103.32mph/
166.28kph
Sidecar: Eric Oliver/Stanley Dibben (UK), Norton,
90.55mph/145.73kph

WEST GERMAN GRAND PRIX

Schötten, 19 July
250cc: Werner Haas (FRG), NSU, 74.70mph/120.22kph
125cc: Carlo Ubbiali (Ita), MV Agusta, 69.24mph/
111.43kph

FRENCH GRAND PRIX

Rouen, 2 August
500cc
1 Geoff Duke (UK), Gilera, 80.73mph/129.92kph
2 Reg Armstrong (Ire), Gilera
3 Alfredo Milani (Ita), Gilera
Fastest lap: Armstrong, 82.44mph/132.67mph
Other winners:
350cc: Fergus Anderson (UK), Guzzi, 77.65mph/
124.97kph
Sidecar: Eric Oliver/Stanley Dibben (UK), Norton,
71.96mph/115.81kph

ULSTER GRAND PRIX

Dundrod Circuit, Belfast, 13–15 August
500cc
1 Ken Kavanagh (Aus), Norton, 89.81mph/144.54kph
2 Geoff Duke (UK), Gilera
3 Jack Brett (UK), Norton
Fastest lap: Duke, 91.74mph/147.64kph

Other winners:
350cc: Ken Mudford (NZ), Norton, 84.01mph/135.20kph
250cc: Reg Armstrong (Ire), NSU, 81.76mph/131.58kph
125cc: Werner Haas (FRG), NSU, 74.87mph/120.49kph
Sidecar: Cyril Smith/Bob Clements (UK), Norton,
77.79mph/125.19kph

SWISS GRAND PRIX

Berne, 22–23 August
500cc
1 Geoff Duke (UK), Gilera, 98.13mph/157.92kph
2 Alfredo Milani (Ita), Gilera
3 Reg Armstrong (Ire), Gilera
Fastest lap: Rod Coleman (NZ), AJS, 100.96mph/
162.48kph
Other winners:
350cc: Fergus Anderson (UK), Guzzi, 90.77mph/
146.08kph
250cc: Reg Armstrong (Ire), NSU, 88.31mph/142.12kph
Sidecar: Eric Oliver/Stanley Dibben (UK), Norton,
82.43mph/132.66kph

ITALIAN GRAND PRIX
(GRAND PRIX DES NATIONS)

Monza, 6 September
500cc
1 Geoff Duke (UK), Gilera, 106.84mph/171.94kph
2 Dickie Dale (UK), Gilera
3 Libero Liberati (Ita), Gilera
Fastest lap: Dale, 108.01mph/173.83kph
Other winners:
350cc: Enrico Lorenzetti (Ita), Guzzi, 99.55mph/
160.21kph
250cc: Enrico Lorenzetti (Ita), Guzzi, 98.53mph/
158.57kph
125cc: Werner Haas (FRG), NSU, 86.98mph/139.98kph
Sidecar: Eric Oliver/Stanley Dibben (UK), Norton,
88.79mph/142.89kph

SPANISH GRAND PRIX

Montjuich, Barcelona, 4 October
500cc
1 Fergus Anderson (UK), Guzzi, 59.99mph/96.54kph
2 Carlos Bandirola (Ita), MV Agusta
3 Dickie Dale (UK), Gilera
Fastest lap: Anderson, 63.35mph/101.95kph
Other winners:
250cc: Enrico Lorenzetti (Ita), Guzzi, 57.87mph/93.13kph
125cc: Angelo Copeta (Ita), MV Agusta, 58.10mph/
93.50kph

LEADING CHAMPIONSHIP POSITIONS

500cc
Riders
1 Geoff Duke (UK) 38pts
2 Reg Armstrong (Ire) 24(30)pts
3 Alfredo Milani (Ita) 18pts
4 Ken Kavanagh (Aus) 18pts
5 Ray Amm (SRho) 14pts
6 Jack Brett (UK) 13pts
Manufacturers
1 Gilera 40(54)pts
2 Norton 29(30)pts
3 AJS 10pts

350cc
1 Fergus Anderson (UK) 30(34)pts
2 Enrico Lorenzetti (Ita) 26pts
3 Ray Amm (SRho) 18pts
Manufacturers' title: Guzzi

250cc
1 Werner Haas (FRG) 28(35)pts
2 Reg Armstrong (Ire) 23pts
3 Fergus Anderson (UK) 22(26)pts
Manufacturers' title: NSU

125cc
1 Werner Haas (FRG) 30(36)pts
2 Cecil Sandford (UK) 20pts
3 Carlo Ubbiali (Ita) 18pts
Manufacturers' title: MV Agusta

Sidecar
1 Eric Oliver (UK) 32pts
2 Cyril Smith (UK) 26(30)pts
3 Hans Haldemann (Swi) 12pts
Manufacturers' title: Norton

1954

FRENCH GRAND PRIX

Reims, 30 May
500cc
1 Pierre Monneret (Fra), Gilera, 108.54mph/174.68kph
2 Alfredo Milani (Ita), Gilera
3 Jacques Collot (Fra), Norton
Fastest lap: Monneret, 114.67mph/184.54kph
Other winners:
350cc: Pierre Monneret (Fra), AJS, 95.57mph/153.81kph
250cc: Werner Haas (FRG), NSU, 101.03mph/162.59kph

BRITISH GRAND PRIX (TOURIST TROPHY)

Isle of Man, 14–18 June
500cc
1 Ray Amm (SRho), Norton, 88.12mph/141.82kph
2 Geoff Duke (UK), Gilera
3 Jack Brett (UK), Norton
Fastest lap: Amm, 89.82mph/144.55kph
Other winners:
350cc: Rod Coleman (NZ), AJS, 91.51mph/147.27kph
250cc: Werner Haas (FRG), NSU, 90.88mph/146.26kph
125cc: Rupert Hollaus (Aut), NSU, 69.57mph/111.96kph
Sidecar: Eric Oliver/Les Nutt (UK), Norton, 68.87mph/
110.84kph

ULSTER GRAND PRIX

Dundrod Circuit, Belfast, 24–26 June
500cc
1 Ray Amm (SRho), Norton, 83.87mph/134.98kph
2 Rod Coleman (NZ), AJS
3 Gordon Laing (Aus), Norton
Fastest lap: Amm, 85.02mph/136.83kph
*Race did not count towards the championship – it was
shortened due to adverse weather*
Other winners:
350cc: Ray Amm (SRho), Norton, 83.47mph/132.33kph
250cc: Werner Haas (FRG), NSU, 77.62mph/124.92kph
125cc: Rupert Hollaus (Aut), NSU, 77.01mph/123.94kph

Sidecar: Eric Oliver/Les Nutt (UK), Norton, 76.49mph/
123.10kph

BELGIAN GRAND PRIX

Spa-Francorchamps, 4 July
500cc
1 Geoff Duke (UK), Gilera, 109.51mph/176.24kph
2 Ken Kavanagh (Aus), Guzzi
3 Léon Martin (Bel), Gilera
Fastest lap: Duke, 111.90mph/180.09kph
Other winners:
350cc: Ken Kavanagh (Aus), Guzzi, 101.65mph/
163.59kph
Sidecar: Eric Oliver/Les Nutt (UK), Norton, 94.21mph/
151.62kph

DUTCH TT

Assen, 10 July
500cc
1 Geoff Duke (UK), Gilera, 104.24mph/167.76kph
2 Fergus Anderson (UK), Guzzi
3 Carlos Bandirola (Ita), MV Agusta
Fastest lap: Duke, 105.42mph/169.66kph
Other winners:
350cc: Fergus Anderson (UK), Guzzi, 97.65mph/
157.15kph
250cc: Werner Haas (FRG) NSU, 95.40mph/153.53kph
125cc: Rupert Hollaus (Aut), NSU, 85.32mph/137.31kph

WEST GERMAN GRAND PRIX

Solitude Circuit, Stuttgart, 25 July
500cc
1 Geoff Duke (UK), Gilera, 89.49mph/144.02kph
2 Ray Amm (SRho), Norton
3 Reg Armstrong (Ire), Gilera
Fastest lap: Duke, 91.60mph/147.42kph
Other winners:
350cc: Ray Amm (SRho), Norton, 83.59mph/134.53kph
250cc: Werner Haas (FRG), NSU, 84.58mph/136.12kph
125cc: Rupert Hollaus (Aut), NSU, 78.87mph/126.93kph
Sidecar: Wilhelm Noll/Fritz Cron (FRG), BMW, 76.26mph/
122.73kph

THE WORLD ROAD RACE CHAMPIONSHIPS 1954

SWISS GRAND PRIX

Berne, 21–22 August
500cc
1 Geoff Duke (UK), Gilera, 93.68mph/150.76kph
2 Ray Amm (SRho), Norton
3 Reg Armstrong (Ire), Gilera
Fastest lap: Duke, 96.82mph/155.82kph
Other winners:
350cc: Fergus Anderson (UK), Guzzi, 87.85mph/
141.38kph
250cc: Rupert Hollaus (Aut), NSU, 78.82mph/126.85kph
Sidecar: Wilhelm Noll/Fritz Cron (FRG), BMW, 80.79mph/
130.02kph

ITALIAN GRAND PRIX (GRAND PRIX DES NATIONS)

Monza, 12 September
500cc:
1 Geoff Duke (UK), Gilera, 111.46mph/179.38kph
2 Umberto Masetti (Ita), Gilera
3 Carlos Bandirola (Ita), MV Agusta

Fastest lap: Duke, 113.04mph/181.92kph
Other winners:
350cc: Fergus Anderson (UK), Guzzi, 101.64mph/
163.57kph
250cc: Arthur Wheeler (UK), Guzzi, 92.32mph/148.57kph
125cc: Guido Sala (Ita), MV Agusta, 90.97mph/146.40kph
Sidecar: Wilhelm Noll/Fritz Cron (FRG), BMW, 93.13mph/
149.88kph

SPANISH GRAND PRIX

Montjuich, Barcelona, 3 October
500cc:
1 Dickie Dale (UK), MV Agusta, 66.91mph/107.68kph
2 Ken Kavanagh (Aus), Guzzi
3 Nello Pagani (Ita), MV Agusta
Fastest lap: Kavanagh, 69.33mph/111.58kph
Other winners:
350cc: Fergus Anderson (UK), Guzzi, 65.89mph/
106.04kph
125cc: Tarquinio Provini (Ita), Mondial, 64.53mph/
103.85kph

LEADING CHAMPIONSHIP POSITIONS

Riders		
500cc	**350cc** 1 Fergus Anderson (UK) 32(38)pts	**125cc** 1 Rupert Hollaus (Aut) 32pts
1 Geoff Duke (UK) 40(46)pts	2 Ray Amm (SRho) 22pts	2 Carlo Ubbiali (Ita) 18pts
2 Ray Amm (SRho) 20pts	3 Rod Coleman (NZ) 20pts	3 Herman-Peter Müller (FRG) 15pts
3 Ken Kavanagh (UK), 16pts		
4 Dickie Dale (UK) 13pts	**250cc**	**Sidecar**
5 Reg Armstrong (Ire) 13pts	1 Werner Haas (FRG) 32(40)pts	1 Wilhelm Noll (FRG) 30(38)pts
6 Pierre Monneret (Fra) 8pts	2 Rupert Hollaus (Aut) 26(30)pts	2 Eric Oliver (UK) 26pts
	3 Herman-Peter Müller (FRG) 17(19)pts	3 Cyril Smith (UK) 22(26)pts

There was no official manufacturers' championship in 1954

1955

SPANISH GRAND PRIX

Montjuich, Barcelona, 1 May
500cc
1 Reg Armstrong (Ire), Gilera, 67.77mph/109.07kph
2 Carlos Bandirola (Ita), MV Agusta
3 Umberto Masetti (Ita), MV Agusta
Fastest lap: Ken Kavanagh (Aus), Guzzi, 69.09mph/
111.19kph
Other winners:
125cc: Luigi Taveri (Swi), MV Agusta, 64.63mph/
104.01kph
Sidecar: Willy Faust/Karl Remmert (FRG), BMW,
61.46mph/98.91kph

FRENCH GRAND PRIX

Reims, 15 May
500cc
1 Geoff Duke (UK), Gilera, 111.97mph/180.20kph

2 Libero Liberati (Ita), Gilera
3 Reg Armstrong (Ire), Gilera
Fastest lap: Duke, 116.73mph/187.86kph
Other winners:
350cc: Duilio Agostini (Ita), Guzzi, 97.33mph/156.64kph
125cc: Carlo Ubbiali (Ita), MV Agusta, 91.66mph/
147.51kph

BRITISH GRAND PRIX (TOURIST TROPHY)

Isle of Man, 6–10 June
500cc
1 Geoff Duke (UK), Gilera, 97.93mph/157.60kph
2 Reg Armstrong (Ire), Gilera
3 Ken Kavanagh (Aus), Guzzi
Fastest lap: Duke, 99.97mph/160.89kph
Other winners:
350cc: Bill Lomas (UK), Guzzi, 92.33mph/148.59kph
250cc: Bill Lomas (UK), MV Agusta, 71.37mph/
114.86kph
125cc: Carlo Ubbiali (Ita), MV Agusta, 69.67mph/
112.12kph
Sidecar: Walter Schneider/Hans Straus (FRG), BMW,
70.01mph/112.67kph

WEST GERMAN GRAND PRIX

Nürburgring, 26 June
500cc
1 Geoff Duke (UK), Gilera, 81.34mph/130.91kph
2 Walter Zeller (FRG), BMW
3 Carlos Bandirola (Ita), MV Agusta
Fastest lap: Duke, 81.79mph/131.63kph
Other winners:
350cc: Bill Lomas (UK), Guzzi, 79.43mph/127.83kph
250cc: Herman-Peter Müller (FRG), NSU, 77.48mph/
124.69kph
125cc: Carlo Ubbiali (Ita), MV Agusta, 68.61mph/
110.42kph
Sidecar: Willy Faust/Karl Remmert (FRG), BMW,
72.53mph/116.73kph

BELGIAN GRAND PRIX

Spa-Francorchamps, 3 July
500cc
1 Giuseppe Colnago (Ita), Gilera, 111.17mph/178.91kph
2 Pierre Monneret (Fra), Gilera
3 Léon Martin (Bel), Gilera
Fastest lap: Geoff Duke (UK), Gilera, 114.44mph/
184.17kph
Other winners:
350cc: Bill Lomas (UK), Guzzi, 105.62mph/169.98kph
Sidecar: Wilhelm Noll/Fritz Cron (FRG), BMW, 96.04mph/
154.56kph

DUTCH TT

Assen, 16 July
500cc
1 Geoff Duke (UK), Gilera, 79.85mph/128.51kph
2 Reg Armstrong (Ire), Gilera
3 Umberto Masetti (Ita), MV Agusta
Fastest lap: Duke and Armstrong, 81.40mph/131.00kph

Other winners:
350cc: Ken Kavanagh (Aus), Guzzi, 78.01mph/
125.54kph
250cc: Luigi Taveri (Swi), MV Agusta, 75.81mph/
122.00kph
125cc: Carlo Ubbiali (Ita), MV Agusta, 70.16mph/
112.91kph
Sidecar: Willy Faust/Karl Remmert (FRG), BMW,
72.09mph/116.02kph

ULSTER GRAND PRIX

Dundrod Circuit, Belfast, 11–13 August
500cc
1 Bill Lomas (UK), Guzzi, 92.30mph/148.54kph
2 John Hartle (UK), Norton
3 Dickie Dale (UK), Guzzi
Fastest lap: Lomas, 94.34mph/151.83kph
Other winners:
350cc: Bill Lomas (UK), Guzzi, 89.31mph/143.73kph
250cc: John Surtees (UK), NSU, 87.63mph/141.03kph

ITALIAN GRAND PRIX
(GRAND PRIX DES NATIONS)

Monza, 4 September
500cc
1 Umberto Masetti (Ita), MV Agusta, 110.16mph/
177.29kph
2 Reg Armstrong (Ire), Gilera
3 Geoff Duke (UK), Gilera
Fastest lap: Duke, 112.66mph/181.31kph
Other winners:
350cc: Dickie Dale (UK), Guzzi, 104.50mph/168.18kph
250cc: Carlo Ubbiali (Ita), MV Agusta, 102.21mph/
164.49kph
125cc: Carlo Ubbiali (Ita), MV Agusta, 93.91mph/
151.13kph
Sidecar: Wilhelm Noll/Fritz Cron (FRG), BMW, 93.24mph/
150.06kph

LEADING CHAMPIONSHIP POSITIONS

500cc
Riders
1 Geoff Duke (UK) 36pts
2 Reg Amstrong (Ire) 30pts
3 Umberto Masetti (Ita) 19pts
4 Giuseppe Colnago (Ita) 13pts
5 Carlos Bandirola (Ita) 10pts
6 Bill Lomas (UK) 8pts
Manufacturers
1 Gilera 40(54)pts
2 MV Agusta 25pts
3 Guzzi 15pts

350cc
1 Bill Lomas (UK) 30(36)pts
2 Dickie Dale (UK) 18pts
3 August Hobl (FRG) 17pts
Manufacturers' title: Guzzi

250cc
1 Herman-Peter Müller (FRG) 16(20)pts
2 Bill Lomas (UK) 13pts
3 Cecil Sandford (UK) 12(14)pts
Manufacturers' title: MV Agusta

125cc
1 Carlo Ubbiali (Ita) 32(44)pts
2 Luigi Taveri (Swi) 26pts
3 Remo Venturi (Ita) 16pts
Manufacturers' title: MV Agusta

Sidecar
1 Willy Faust (FRG) 30pts
2 Wilhelm Noll (FRG) 28pts
3 Walter Schneider (FRG) 22pts
Manufacturers' title: BMW

1956

BRITISH GRAND PRIX (TOURIST TROPHY)

Isle of Man, 4–8 June
500cc
1 John Surtees (UK), MV Agusta, 96.57mph/155.41kph
2 John Hartle (UK), Norton
3 Jack Brett (UK), Norton
Fastest lap: Surtees, 97.79mph/157.38kph
Other winners:
350cc: Ken Kavanagh (Aus), Guzzi, 89.29mph/143.70kph
250cc: Carlo Ubbiali (Ita), MV Agusta, 67.05mph/107.90kph
125cc: Carlo Ubbiali (Ita), MV Agusta, 69.13mph/111.25kph
Sidecar: Fritz Hillebrand/Manfred Grünwald (FRG), BMW, 70.03mph/112.70kph

DUTCH TT

Assen, 30 June
500cc
1 John Surtees (UK), MV Agusta, 82.46mph/132.70kph
2 Walter Zeller (FRG), BMW
3 Eddie Grant (SAf), Norton
Fastest lap: Surtees, 83.93mph/135.07kph
Other winners:
350cc: Bill Lomas (UK), Guzzi, 80.48mph/129.52kph
250cc: Carlo Ubbiali (Ita), MV Agusta, 78.20mph/125.85kph
125cc: Carlo Ubbiali (Ita), MV Agusta, 74.89mph/120.52kph
Sidecar: Fritz Hillebrand/Manfred Grünwald (FRG), BMW, 73.37mph/118.08kph

BELGIAN GRAND PRIX

Spa-Francorchamps, 8 July
500cc
1 John Surtees (UK), MV Agusta, 114.38mph/184.08kph
2 Walter Zeller (FRG), BMW
3 Pierre Monneret (Fra), Gilera
Fastest lap: Geoff Duke (UK), Gilera, 117.42mph/188.97kph
Other winners:
350cc: John Surtees (UK), MV Agusta, 109.65mph/176.46 kph
250cc: Carlo Ubbiali (Ita), MV Agusta, 104.82mph/168.70kph
125cc: Carlo Ubbiali (Ita), MV Agusta, 99.92mph/160.81kph

Sidecar: Wilhelm Noll/Fritz Cron (FRG), BMW, 97.27mph/156.54kph

WEST GERMAN GRAND PRIX

Solitude Circuit, Stuttgart, 22 July
500cc
1 Reg Armstrong (Ire), Gilera, 92.40mph/148.70kph
2 Umberto Masetti (Ita), MV Agusta
3 Pierre Monneret (Fra), Gilera
Fastest lap: Bill Lomas (UK), Guzzi, 95.38mph/153.5kph
Other winners:
350cc: Bill Lomas (UK), Guzzi, 90.84mph/146.19kph
250cc: Carlo Ubbiali (Ita), MV Agusta, 87.87mph/141.41kph
125cc: Romolo Ferri (Ita), Gilera, 84.99mph/136.78kph
Sidecar: Wilhelm Noll/Fritz Cron (FRG), BMW, 84.98mph/136.76kph

ULSTER GRAND PRIX

Dundrod Circuit, Belfast, 9–11 August
500cc
1 John Hartle (UK), Norton, 85.66mph/137.86kph
2 Bob Brown (Aus), Matchless
3 Peter Murphy (NZ), Matchless
Fastest lap: Geoff Duke (UK), Gilera, 94.47mph/152.03kph
Other winners:
350cc: Bill Lomas (UK), Guzzi, 90.26mph/145.26kph
250cc: Luigi Taveri (Swi), MV Agusta, 86.26mph/138.82kph
125cc: Carlo Ubbiali (Ita), MV Agusta, 81.00mph/130.36kph
Sidecar: Wilhelm Noll/Fritz Cron (FRG), BMW, 78.89mph/126.96kph

ITALIAN GRAND PRIX (GRAND PRIX DES NATIONS)

Monza, 9 September
500cc
1 Geoff Duke (UK), Gilera, 113.67mph/182.93kph
2 Libero Liberati (Ita), Gilera
3 Pierre Monneret (Fra), Gilera
Fastest lap: Duke and Liberati, 116.51mph/187.50kph
Other winners:
350cc: Libero Liberati (Ita), Gilera, 110.85mph/178.40kph
250cc: Carlo Ubbiali (Ita), MV Agusta, 103.78mph/167.02kph
125cc: Carlo Ubbiali (Ita), MV Agusta, 99.87mph/160.73kph
Sidecar: Albino Milani/Rossano Milani (Ita), Gilera, 98.13mph/157.92kph

LEADING CHAMPIONSHIP POSITIONS

500cc
Riders
1 John Surtees (UK) 24pts
2 Walter Zeller (FRG) 16pts
3 John Hartle (UK) 14pts
4 Pierre Monneret (Fra) 12pts
5 Reg Armstrong (Ire) 11pts
6 Umberto Masetti (Ita) 9pts
Manufacturers
1 MV Agusta 30(32)pts
2 Gilera 20pts
3 Norton 20(21)pts

350cc
1 Bill Lomas (UK) 24pts
2 August Hobl (FRG) 17pts
3 Dickie Dale (UK) 17pts
Manufacturers' title: Guzzi

250cc
1 Carlo Ubbiali (Ita) 32(40)pts
2 Luigi Taveri (Swi) 26(29)pts
3 Enrico Lorenzetti (Ita) 10pts
Manufacturers' title: MV Agusta

125cc
1 Carlo Ubbiali (Ita) 32pts
2 Romolo Ferri (Ita) 14pts
3 Tarquinio Provini (Ita) 12pts
Manufacturers' title: MV Agusta

Sidecar
1 Wilhelm Noll (FRG) 30pts
2 Fritz Hillebrand (FRG) 26pts
3 Pip Harris (UK) 24pts
Manufacturers' title: BMW

1957

WEST GERMAN GRAND PRIX

Hockenheim, 19 May
500cc
1 Libero Liberati (Ita), Gilera, 124.27mph/199.99kph
2 Bob McIntyre (UK), Gilera
3 Walter Zeller (FRG), BMW
Fastest lap: McIntyre, 129.56mph/208.51kph
Other winners:
350cc: Libero Liberati (Ita), Gilera, 106.81mph/171.89kph
250cc: Carlo Ubbiali (Ita), MV Agusta, 109.86mph/
176.80kph
125cc: Carlo Ubbiali (Ita), MV Agusta, 99.29mph/
159.79kph
Sidecar: Fritz Hillebrand/Manfred Grünwald (FRG), BMW,
101.09mph/162.69kph

BRITISH GRAND PRIX (TOURIST TROPHY)

Isle of Man, 3–7 June
500cc
1 Bob McIntyre (UK), Gilera, 98.99mph/159.31kph
2 John Surtees (UK), MV Agusta
3 Bob Brown (Aus), Gilera
Fastest lap: McIntyre, 102.12mph/164.35kph
Other winners:
350cc: Bob McIntyre (UK), Gilera, 94.99mph/152.87kph
250cc: Cecil Sandford (UK), Mondial, 75.80mph/
121.99kph
125cc: Tarquinio Provini (Ita), Mondial, 73.69mph/
118.59kph
Sidecar: Fritz Hillebrand/Manfred Grünwald (FRG), BMW,
71.89mph/115.70kph

DUTCH TT

Assen, 29 June
500cc
1 John Surtees (UK), MV Agusta, 82.56mph/132.87kph
2 Libero Liberati (Ita), Gilera
3 Walter Zeller (FRG), BMW
Fastest lap: Bob McIntyre (UK), Gilera, 85.53mph/
137.65kph
Other winners:
350cc: Keith Campbell (Aus), Guzzi, 82.28mph/
132.42kph
250cc: Tarquinio Provini (Ita), Mondial, 79.50mph/
127.94kph
125cc: Tarquinio Provini (Ita), Mondial, 76.68mph/
123.40kph

Sidecar: Fritz Hillebrand/Manfred Grünwald (FRG), BMW,
72.95mph/117.40kph

BELGIAN GRAND PRIX

Spa-Francorchamps, 7 July
500cc
1 Libero Liberati (Ita), Gilera, 114.93mph/184.96kph
2 Jack Brett (UK), Norton
3 Keith Bryen (Aus), Norton
Fastest lap: Keith Campbell (Aus), Guzzi, 118.56mph/
190.80kph
Other winners:
350cc: Keith Campbell (Aus), Guzzi, 114.28mph/
183.92kph
250cc: John Hartle (UK), MV Agusta, 106.51mph/
171.41kph
125cc: Tarquinio Provini (Ita), Mondial, 102.16mph/
164.41kph
Sidecar: Walter Schneider/Hans Straus (FRG), BMW,
98.96mph/159.26kph

ULSTER GRAND PRIX

Dundrod Circuit, Belfast, 8–10 August
500cc
1 Libero Liberati (Ita), Gilera, 91.56mph/147.35kph
2 Bob McIntyre (UK), Gilera
3 Geoff Duke (UK), Gilera
Fastest lap: John Surtees (UK), MV Agusta, 95.69mph/
154.00kph
Other winners:
350cc: Keith Campbell (Aus), Guzzi, 85.28mph/
137.24kph
250cc: Cecil Sandford (UK), Mondial, 83.30mph/
134.06kph
125cc: Luigi Taveri (Swi), MV Agusta, 78.45mph/
126.25kph

ITALIAN GRAND PRIX
(GRAND PRIX DES NATIONS)

Monza, 1 September
500cc
1 Libero Liberati (Ita), Gilera, 115.75mph/186.28kph
2 Geoff Duke (UK), Gilera
3 Alfredo Milani (Ita), Gilera
Fastest lap: Liberati, 118.11mph/190.08kph
Other winners:
350cc: Bob McIntyre (UK), Gilera, 111.89mph/180.07kph
250cc: Tarquinio Provini (Ita), Mondial, 109.44mph/
176.13kph
125cc: Carlo Ubbiali (Ita), MV Agusta, 99.20mph/
159.65kph
Sidecar: Albino Milani/Rossano Milani (Ita), Gilera,
99.08mph/159.45kph

LEADING CHAMPIONSHIP POSITIONS

500cc
Riders
1 Libero Liberati (Ita) 32(38)pts
2 Bob McIntyre (UK) 20pts
3 John Surtees (UK) 17pts
4 Geoff Duke (UK) 10pts

5 Jack Brett (UK) 9pts
6 Walter Zeller (FRG) 8pts
Manufacturers
1 Gilera 32(46)pts
2 MV Agusta 19(20)pts
3 Norton 13pts

350cc
1 Keith Campbell (Aus) 24(30)pts
2 Libero Liberati (Ita) 18(26)pts
3 Bob McIntyre (UK) 16(22)pts
Manufacturers' title: Gilera

250cc
1 Cecil Sandford (UK) 26(33)pts
2 Tarquinio Provini (Ita) 16pts
3 Sammy Miller (UK) 14pts
Manufacturers' title: Mondial

125cc
1 Tarquinio Provini (Ita) 24(36)pts
2 Luigi Taveri (Swi) 22(28)pts
3 Carlo Ubbiali (Ita) 16(22)pts
Manufacturers' title: Mondial

Sidecar
1 Fritz Hillebrand (FRG) 24(28)pts
2 Walter Schneider (FRG) 14(20)pts
3 Florian Camathias (Swi) 14(17)pts
Manufacturers' title: BMW

1958

BRITISH GRAND PRIX (TOURIST TROPHY)

Isle of Man, 2–6 June
500cc
1 John Surtees (UK), MV Agusta, 98.63mph/158.73kph
2 Bob Anderson (UK), Norton
3 Bob Brown (Aus), Norton
Fastest lap: Surtees, 100.58mph/161.87kph
Other winners:
350cc: John Surtees (UK), MV Agusta, 93.97mph/
151.23kph
250cc: Tarquinio Provini (Ita), MV Agusta, 76.89mph/
123.74kph
125cc: Carlo Ubbiali (Ita), MV Agusta, 72.86mph/
117.26kph
Sidecar: Walter Schneider/Hans Straus (FRG), BMW,
73.01mph./117.50kph

DUTCH TT

Assen, 28 June
500cc
1 John Surtees (UK), MV Agusta, 83.86mph/134.96kph
2 John Hartle (UK), MV Agusta
3 Derek Minter (UK), Norton
Fastest lap: Surtees, 85.36mph/137.37kph
Other winners:
350cc: John Surtees (UK), MV Agusta, 81.42mph/
131.03kph
250cc: Tarquinio Provini (Ita), MV Agusta, 77.90mph/
125.37kph
125cc: Carlo Ubbiali (Ita), MV Agusta, 77.53mph/
124.77kph
Sidecar: Florian Camathias (Swi)/Hilmar Cecco (FRG),
BMW, 74.31mph/119.59kph

BELGIAN GRAND PRIX

Spa-Francorchamps, 6 July
500cc
1 John Surtees (UK), MV Agusta, 115.32mph/185.59kph
2 Keith Campbell (Aus), Norton
3 John Hartle (UK), MV Agusta
Fastest lap: Surtees, 120.25mph/193.52kph
Other winners:
350cc: John Surtees (UK), MV Agusta, 110.48mph/
177.80kph
125cc: Alberto Gandossi (Ita), Ducati, 98.09mph/
157.86kph
Sidecar: Walter Schneider/Hans Straus (FRG), BMW,
103.05mph/165.84kph

WEST GERMAN GRAND PRIX

Nürburgring, 20 July
500cc
1 John Surtees (UK), MV Agusta, 69.96mph/112.59kph
2 John Hartle (UK), MV Agusta
3 Gary Hocking (SRho), Norton
Fastest lap: Surtees, 75.12mph/120.89kph
Other winners:
350cc: John Surtees (UK), MV Agusta, 80.47mph/
129.50kph
250cc: Tarquinio Provini (Ita), MV Agusta, 73.94mph/
118.99kph
125cc: Carlo Ubbiali (Ita), MV Agusta, 75.62mph/
121.70kph
Sidecar: Walter Schneider/Hans Straus (FRG), BMW,
70.09mph/112.80kph

SWEDISH TT

Hedemora, 26–27 July
500cc
1 Geoff Duke (UK), Norton, 102.76mph/165.38kph
2 Dickie Dale, UK), BMW
3 Terry Shepherd (UK), Norton
Fastest lap: Duke, 104.91mph/168.84kph
Other winners:
350cc: Geoff Duke (UK), Norton, 96.99mph/156.09kph
250cc: Horst Fügner (GDR), MZ, 94.20mph/151.60kph
125cc: Alberto Gandossi (Ita), Ducati, 91.28mph/
146.90kph

ULSTER GRAND PRIX

Dundrod Circuit, Belfast, 7–9 August
500cc
1 John Surtees (UK), MV Agusta, 86.73mph/139.58kph
2 Bob McIntyre (UK), Norton
3 John Hartle (UK), MV Agusta
Fastest lap: Surtees, 89.53mph/144.08kph
Other winners:
350cc: John Surtees (UK), MV Agusta, 80.46mph/
129.49kph
250cc: Tarquinio Provini (Ita), MV Agusta, 77.41mph/
124.58kph
125cc: Carlo Ubbiali (Ita), MV Agusta, 77.04mph/
123.98kph

ITALIAN GRAND PRIX
(GRAND PRIX DES NATIONS)

Monza, 14 September
500cc
1 John Surtees (UK), MV Agusta, 114.51mph/184.29kph
2 Remo Venturi (Ita), MV Agusta

3 Umberto Masetti (Ita), MV Agusta
Fastest lap: Surtees, 115.98mph/186.65kph
Other winners:
350cc: John Surtees (UK), MV Agusta, 107.65mph/
173.25kph

250cc: Emilio Mendogni (Ita), Morini, 104.52mph/
168.21kph
125cc: Bruno Spaggiari (Ita), Ducati, 96.81mph/
155.80kph

LEADING CHAMPIONSHIP POSITIONS

500cc
Riders
1 John Surtees (UK) 32(48)pts
2 John Hartle (UK) 20pts
3 Geoff Duke (UK) 13pts
4 Dickie Dale (UK) 13(16)pts
5 Derek Minter (UK) 10pts
6 Gary Hocking (SRho) 8pts
Manufacturers
1 MV Agusta 32(48)pts
2 Norton 26(35)pts
3 BMW 15(19)pts

350cc
1 John Surtees (UK) 32(48)pts
2 John Hartle (UK) 24(30)pts
3 Geoff Duke (UK) 17pts
Manufacturers' title: MV Agusta

250cc
1 Tarquinio Provini (Ita) 32pts
2 Horst Fügner (GDR) 16pts
3 Carlo Ubbiali (Ita) 16pts
Manufacturers' title: MV Agusta

125cc
1 Carlo Ubbiali (Ita) 32(38)pts
2 Alberto Gandossi (Ita) 25(28)pts
3 Luigi Taveri (Swi) 20(21)pts
Manufacturers' title: MV Agusta

Sidecar
1 Walter Schneider (FRG) 24(30)pts
2 Florian Camathias (Swi) 20(26)pts
3 Helmut Fath (FRG) 8pts
Manufacturers' title: BMW

1959

FRENCH GRAND PRIX

Clermont-Ferrand, 15–17 May
500cc
1 John Surtees (UK) MV Agusta, 74.80mph/120.38kph
2 Remo Venturi (Ita), MV Agusta
3 Gary Hocking (SRho), Norton
Fastest lap: Surtees, 75.64mph/121.73kph
Other winners:
350cc: John Surtees (UK), MV Agusta, 73.36mph/
118.04kph
Sidecar: Fritz Scheidegger (Swi)/Hans Burkardt (FRG),
BMW, 64.41mph/103.66kph

BRITISH GRAND PRIX (TOURIST TROPHY)

Isle of Man, 1–6 June
500cc
1 John Surtees (UK), MV Agusta, 87.94mph/141.53kph
2 Alastair King (UK), Norton
3 Bob Brown (Aus), Norton
Fastest lap: Surtees, 101.18mph/162.83kph
Other winners:
350cc: John Surtees (UK), MV Agusta, 95.38mph/
153.50kph
250cc: Tarquinio Provini (Ita), MV Agusta, 77.77mph/
125.16kph
125cc: Tarquinio Provini (Ita), MV Agusta, 74.06mph/
119.19kph
Sidecar: Walter Schneider/Hans Straus (FRG), BMW,
72.69mph/116.98kph

WEST GERMAN GRAND PRIX

Hockenheim, 14 June
500cc
1 John Surtees (UK), MV Agusta, 123.45mph/198.67kph
2 Remo Venturi (Ita), MV Agusta
3 Bob Brown (Aus), Norton
Fastest lap: Surtees, 125.23mph/201.54kph
Other winners:
350cc: John Surtees (UK), MV Agusta, 110.31mph/
177.53kph
250cc: Carlo Ubbiali (Ita), MV Agusta, 109.64mph/
176.45kph
125cc: Carlo Ubbiali (Ita), MV Agusta, 97.74mph/157.30kph
Sidecar: Florian Camathias (Swi)/Hilmar Cecco (FRG),
BMW, 104.96mph/168.92kph

DUTCH TT

Assen, 27 June
500cc
1 John Surtees (UK), MV Agusta, 84.86mph/136.57kph
2 Bob Brown (Aus), Norton
3 Remo Venturi (Ita), MV Agusta
Fastest lap: Surtees, 86.91mph/139.87kph
Other winners:
250cc: Tarquinio Provini (Ita), MV Agusta, 81.67mph/
131.44kph
125cc: Carlo Ubbiali (Ita), MV Agusta, 76.72mph/
123.47kph
Sidecar: Florian Camathias (Swi)/Hilmar Cecco (FRG),
BMW, 74.56mph/119.99kph

BELGIAN GRAND PRIX

Spa-Francorchamps, 5 July
500cc
1 John Surtees (UK), MV Agusta, 119.28mph/191.96kph
2 Gary Hocking (SRho), Norton
3 Geoff Duke (UK), Norton
Fastest lap: Surtees, 120.48mph/193.89kph
Other winners:
125cc: Carlo Ubbiali (Ita), MV Agusta, 98.75mph/
158.92kph
Sidecar: Walter Schneider/Hans Straus (FRG), BMW,
99.78mph/160.58kph

SWEDISH TT

Kristianstadt, 25–26 July
350cc: John Surtees (UK), MV Agusta, 92.58mph/148.99kph
250cc: Gary Hocking (SRho), MZ, 87.05mph/140.09kph
125cc: Tarquinio Provini (Ita), MV Agusta, 82.53mph/132.82kph

ULSTER GRAND PRIX

Dundrod Circuit, Belfast, 8 August
500cc
1 John Surtees (UK), MV Agusta, 95.28mph/153.34kph
2 Bob McIntyre (UK), Norton
3 Geoff Duke (UK), Norton
Fastest lap: Surtees, 96.73mph/155.67kph
Other winners:
350cc: John Surtees (UK), MV Agusta, 91.32mph/145.97kph

250cc: Gary Hocking (SRho), MZ, 89.26mph/143.65kph
125cc: Mike Hailwood (UK), Ducati, 81.92mph/131.84kph

ITALIAN GRAND PRIX (GRAND PRIX DES NATIONS)

Monza, 6 September
500cc
1 John Surtees (UK), MV Agusta, 115.22mph/185.44kph
2 Remo Venturi (Ita), MV Agusta
3 Geoff Duke (UK), Norton
Fastest lap: Surtees, 119.20mph/191.83kph
Other winners:
350cc: John Surtees (UK), MV Agusta, 107.14mph/172.43kph
250cc: Carlo Ubbiali (Ita), MV Agusta, 107.52mph/173.04kph
125cc: Ernst Degner (GDR), MZ, 96.14mph/154.72kph

LEADING CHAMPIONSHIP POSITIONS

500cc
Riders
1 John Surtees (UK) 32(56)pts
2 Remo Venturi (Ita) 22(24)pts
3 Bob Brown (Aus) 17(22)pts
4 Geoff Duke (UK) 12pts
5 Gary Hocking (SRho) 10pts
6 Bob McIntyre (UK) 8pts
Manufacturers
1 MV Agusta 32(56)pts
2 Norton 24(36)pts
3 BMW 7pts

350cc
1 John Surtees (UK) 32(48)pts
2 John Hartle (UK) 16pts
3 Bob Brown (Aus) 14pts
Manufacturers' title: MV Agusta

250cc
1 Carlo Ubbiali (Ita) 28(34)pts
2 Gary Hocking (SRho) 16pts
 Tarquinio Provini (Ita) 16pts
Manufacturers' title: MV Agusta

125cc
1 Carlo Ubbiali (Ita) 30(38)pts
2 Tarquinio Provini (Ita) 28(30)pts
3 Mike Hailwood (UK) 20(23)pts
Manufacturers' title: MV Agusta

Sidecar
1 Walter Schneider (FRG) 22(28)pts
2 Florian Camathias (Swi) 22pts
3 Fritz Scheidegger (Swi) 16(18)pts
Manufacturers' title: BMW

1960

FRENCH GRAND PRIX

Clermont-Ferrand, 20–22 May
500cc
1 John Surtees (UK), MV Agusta, 75.52ph/121.54kph
2 Remo Venturi (Ita), MV Agusta
3 Bob Brown (Aus), Norton
Fastest lap: Surtees, 76.73mph/123.48kph
Other winners:
350cc: Gary Hocking (SRho), MV Agusta, 70.68mph/113.75kph
Sidecar: Helmut Fath/Alfred Wohlgemuth (FRG), BMW, 66.51mph/107.04kph

BRITISH GRAND PRIX (TOURIST TROPHY)

Isle of Man, 13–17 June
500cc
1 John Surtees (UK), MV Agusta, 102.44mph/164.86kph
2 John Hartle (UK), MV Agusta

3 Mike Hailwood (UK), Norton
Fastest lap: Surtees, 104.08mph/167.50kph
Other winners:
350cc: John Hartle (UK), MV Agusta, 96.70mph/155.62kph
250cc: Gary Hocking (SRho), MV Agusta, 93.64mph/150.70kph
125cc: Carlo Ubbiali (Ita), MV Agusta, 85.60mph/137.76kph
Sidecar: Helmut Fath/Alfred Wohlgemuth (FRG), BMW, 84.10mph/135.35kph

DUTCH TT

Assen, 25 June
500cc
1 Remo Venturi (Ita), MV Agusta, 83.67mph/134.65kph
2 Bob Brown (Aus), Norton
3 Emilio Mendogni (Ita), MV Agusta
Fastest lap: Venturi, 86.43mph/139.10kph
Other winners:
350cc: John Surtees (UK), MV Agusta, 83.59mph/134.53kph
250cc: Carlo Ubbiali (Ita), MV Agusta, 82.90mph/133.41kph

125cc: Carlo Ubbiali (Ita), MV Agusta, 76.30mph/
122.79kph
Sidecar: Pip Harris/Ray Campbell (UK), BMW, 75.26mph/
121.12kph

BELGIAN GRAND PRIX

Spa-Francorchamps, 3 July
500cc
1 John Surtees (UK), MV Agusta, 120.53mph/193.98kph
2 Remo Venturi (Ita), MV Agusta
3 Bob Brown (Aus), Norton
Fastest lap: Surtees, 122.67mph/197.42kph
Other winners:
250cc: Carlo Ubbiali (Ita), MV Agusta, 113.53mph/
182.71kph
125cc: Ernst Degner (GDR), MZ, 100.12mph/161.13kph
Sidecar: Helmut Fath/Alfred Wohlgemuth (FRG), BMW,
100.24mph/161.32kph

WEST GERMAN GRAND PRIX

Solitude Circuit, Stuttgart, July 23–24
500cc
1 John Surtees (UK), MV Agusta, 92.77mph/149.30kph
2 Remo Venturi (Ita), MV Agusta
3 Emilio Mendogni (Ita), MV Agusta
Fastest lap: Surtees, 94.21mph/151.62kph
Other winners:
250cc: Gary Hocking (SRho), MV Agusta, 90.54mph/
145.71kph
Sidecar: Helmut Fath/Alfred Wohlgemuth (FRG), BMW,
80.29mph/129.21kph

ULSTER GRAND PRIX

Dundrod Circuit, Belfast, August 6
500cc
1 John Hartle (UK), Norton, 93.37mph/150.26kph
2 John Surtees (UK), MV Agusta
3 Alan Shepherd (UK), Matchless
Fastest lap: Surtees, 99.32mph/159.84kph
Other winners:
350cc: John Surtees (UK), MV Agusta, 93.39mph/
150.30kph
250cc: Carlo Ubbiali (Ita), MV Agusta, 90.83mph/
146.18kph
125cc: Carlo Ubbiali (Ita), MV Agusta, 83.38mph/
150.28kph

ITALIAN GRAND PRIX
(GRAND PRIX DES NATIONS)

Monza, 11 September
500cc
1 John Surtees (UK), MV Agusta, 115.02mph/185.11kph
2 Emilio Mendogni (Ita), MV Agusta
3 Mike Hailwood (UK), Norton
Fastest lap: Surtees, 118.33mph/190.43kph
Other winners:
350cc: Gary Hocking (SRho), MV Agusta, 109.73mph/
176.59kph
250cc: Carlo Ubbiali (Ita), MV Agusta, 109.05mph/
175.50kph
125cc: Carlo Ubbiali (Ita), MV Agusta, 97.76mph/
157.33kph

LEADING CHAMPIONSHIP POSITIONS

500cc
Riders
1 John Surtees (UK) 32(46)pts
2 Remo Venturi (Ita) 26pts
3 John Hartle (UK) 16pts
4 Bob Brown (Aus) 15pts
  Emilio Mendogni (Ita) 15pts
6 Mike Hailwood (UK) 13pts
Manufacturers
1 MV Agusta 32(54)pts
2 Norton 22(33)pts
3 Matchless 4pts

350cc
1 John Surtees (UK) 22(26)pts
2 Gary Hocking (SRho) 22pts
3 John Hartle (UK) 18pts
Manufacturers' title: MV Agusta

250cc
1 Carlo Ubbiali (Ita) 32(44)pts
2 Gary Hocking (SRho) 28pts
3 Luigi Taveri (Swi) 11pts
Manufacturers' title: MV Agusta

125cc
1 Carlo Ubbiali (Ita) 24(36)pts
2 Gary Hocking (SRho) 18(22)pts
3 Ernst Degner (GDR) 16(18)pts
Manufacturers' title: MV Agusta

Sidecar
1 Helmut Fath (FRG) 24(36)pts
2 Fritz Scheidegger (Swi) 16(20)pts
3 Pip Harris (UK) 14pts
Manufacturers' title: BMW

1961

SPANISH GRAND PRIX

Montjuich, Barcelona, 23 April
250cc: Gary Hocking (SRho), MV Agusta, 70.19mph/
112.96kph
125cc: Tom Phillis (Aus), Honda, 66.65mph/107.26kph
Sidecar: Helmut Fath/Alfred Wohlgemuth (FRG), BMW,
66.43mph/106.91kph

WEST GERMAN GRAND PRIX

Hockenheim, 14 May
500cc
1 Gary Hocking (SRho), MV Agusta, 120.27mph/
193.56kph
2 Frank Perris (UK), Norton
3 Hans-Gunter Jäger (FRG), BMW
Fastest lap: Hocking, 124.86mph/200.94kph
Other winners:
350cc: Frantisek Stastny (Cze), Jawa, 112.42mph/
180.92kph

250cc: Kunumitsu Takahashi (Jap), Honda, 115.84mph/186.43kph
125cc: Ernst Degner (GDR), MZ, 98.44mph/158.42kph
Sidecar: Max Deubel/Emil Hörner (FRG), BMW, 104.18mph/167.66kph

FRENCH GRAND PRIX

Clermont-Ferrand, 21 May
500cc
1 Gary Hocking (SRho), MV Agusta, 74.56mph/119.99kph
2 Mike Hailwood (UK), Norton
3 Antoine Paba (Fra), Norton
Fastest lap: Hocking, 76.38mph/122.92kph
Other winners:
250cc: Tom Phillis (Aus), Honda, 75.07mph/120.81kph
125cc: Tom Phillis (Aus), Honda, 70.11mph/112.83kph
Sidecar: Fritz Scheidegger (Swi)/Hans Burkhardt (FRG), BMW, 66.42mph/106.89kph

BRITISH GRAND PRIX (TOURIST TROPHY)

Isle of Man, 12–16 June
500cc
1 Mike Hailwood (UK), Norton, 100.60mph/161.90kph
2 Bob McIntyre (UK), Norton
3 Tom Phillis (Aus), Norton
Fastest lap: Gary Hocking (SRho), MV Agusta, 102.62mph/165.15kph
Other winners:
350cc: Phil Read (UK), Norton, 95.10mph/153.05kph
250cc: Mike Hailwood (UK), Honda, 98.38mph/158.33kph
125cc: Mike Hailwood (UK), Honda, 88.23mph/141.99kph
Sidecar: Max Deubel/Emil Hörner (FRG), BMW, 87.65mph/141.06kph

DUTCH TT

Assen, 24 June
500cc
1 Gary Hocking (SRho), MV Agusta, 87.49mph/140.80kph
2 Mike Hailwood (UK), Norton
3 Bob McIntyre (UK), Norton
Fastest lap: Hocking, 88.87mph/143.02kph
Other winners:
350cc: Gary Hocking (SRho), MV Agusta, 85.80mph/138.08kph
250cc: Mike Hailwood (UK), Honda, 86.25mph/138.81kph
125cc: Tom Phillis (Aus), Honda, 78.92mph/127.01kph
Sidecar: Max Deubel/Emil Hörner (FRG), BMW, 76.54mph/123.18kph

BELGIAN GRAND PRIX

Spa-Francorchamps, 2 July
500cc
1 Gary Hocking (SRho), MV Agusta, 119.69mph/192.68kph
2 Mike Hailwood (UK), Norton
3 Bob McIntyre (UK), Norton
Fastest lap: Hocking, 123.53mph/197.19kph

Other winners:
250cc: Jim Redman (SRho), Honda, 114.96mph/185.01kph
125cc: Luigi Taveri (Swi), Honda, 100.09mph/161.08kph
Sidecar: Fritz Scheidegger (Swi)/Hans Burkhardt (FRG), BMW, 104.63mph/169.39kph

EAST GERMAN GRAND PRIX

Sachsenring, 30 July
500cc
1 Gary Hocking (SRho), MV Agusta, 99.93mph/160.82kph
2 Mike Hailwood (UK), Norton
3 Bertie Schneider (Aut), Norton
Fastest lap: Hocking, 101.40mph/163.19kph
Other winners:
350cc: Gary Hocking (SRho), MV Agusta, 96.62mph/155.49kph
250cc: Mike Hailwood (UK), Honda, 97.63mph/157.12kph
125cc: Ernst Degner (GDR), MZ, 87.88mph/141.43kph

ULSTER GRAND PRIX

Dundrod Circuit, Belfast, 12 August
500cc
1 Gary Hocking (SRho), MV Agusta, 90.49mph/145.63kph
2 Mike Hailwood (UK), Norton
3 Alastair King (UK), Norton
Fastest lap: Hocking, 98.37mph/158.31kph
Other winners:
350cc: Gary Hocking (SRho), MV Agusta, 92.90mph/149.51kph
250cc: Bob McIntyre (UK), Honda, 95.44mph/153.60kph
125cc: Kunumitsu Takahashi (Jap), Honda, 87.51mph/83kph

ITALIAN GRAND PRIX (GRAND PRIX DES NATIONS)

Monza, 3 September
500cc
1 Mike Hailwood (UK), MV Agusta, 116.50mph/187.49kph
2 Alastair King (UK), Norton
3 Paddy Driver (SAf), Norton
Fastest lap: Gary Hocking (SRho), MV Agusta, 118.77mph/191.14kph
Other winners:
350cc: Gary Hocking (SRho), MV Agusta, 112.84mph/181.60kph
250cc: Jim Redman (SRho), Honda, 112.43mph/180.93kph
125cc: Ernst Degner (GDR), MZ, 98.77mph/158.95kph

SWEDISH TT

Kristianstadt, 17 September
500cc
1 Gary Hocking (SRho), MV Agusta, 97.49mph/156.89kph
2 Mike Hailwood (UK), MV Agusta
3 Frank Perris (UK), Norton
Fastest lap: Hocking, 102.76mph/165.38kph

Other winners:
350cc: Frantisek Stastny (Cze), Jawa, 94.19mph/
151.58kph
250cc: Mike Hailwood (UK), Honda, 94.34mph/
151.83kph
125cc: Luigi Taveri (Swi), Honda, 83.48mph/134.35kph

ARGENTINE GRAND PRIX

Buenos Aires, 15 October
500cc
1 Jorge Kissling (Arg), Matchless, 76.53mph/123.16kph

2 Juan Carlos Salatino (Arg), Norton
3 Frank Perris (UK), Norton
Fastest lap: Not recorded
Other winners:
250cc: Tom Phillis (Aus), Honda, 78.84mph/126.88kph
125cc: Tom Phillis (Aus), Honda, 71.00mph/114.26kph

LEADING CHAMPIONSHIP POSITIONS

500cc
Riders
1 Gary Hocking (SRho) 48(56)pts
2 Mike Hailwood (UK) 40(55)pts
3 Frank Perris (UK) 16pts
4 Bob McIntyre (UK) 14pts
5 Alastair King (UK) 13pts
6 Bertie Schneider (Aut) 9pts
Manufacturers
1 MV Agusta 48(64)pts
2 Norton 38(60)pts
3 Matchless 12pts

350cc
1 Gary Hocking (SRho) 32(38)pts
2 Frantisek Stastny (Cze) 30pts
3 Gustav Havel (Cze) 19pts
Manufacturers' title: MV Agusta

250cc
1 Mike Hailwood (UK) 44(54)pts
2 Tom Phillis (Aus) 38(45)pts
3 Jim Redman (SRho) 36(51)pts
Manufacturers' title: Honda

125cc
1 Tom Phillis (Aus) 44(48)pts
2 Ernst Degner (GDR) 42pts
3 Jim Redman (SRho) 28pts
Manufacturers' title: Honda

Sidecar
1 Max Deubel (FRG) 30pts
2 Fritz Scheidegger (Swi) 28pts
3 Edgar Strub (Swi) 14pts
Manufacturers' title: BMW

1962

SPANISH GRAND PRIX

Montjuich, Barcelona, 6 May
250cc: Jim Redman (SRho), Honda, 71.17mph/
114.54kph
125cc: Kunumitsu Takahashi (Jap), Honda, 63.56mph/
102.29kph
50cc: Hans-Georg Anscheidt (FRG), Kreidler, 60.55mph/
97.45kph
Sidecar: Max Deubel/Emil Hörner (FRG), BMW,
67.14mph/108.05kph

FRENCH GRAND PRIX

Clermont-Ferrand, 13 May
250cc: Jim Redman (SRho), Honda, 71.87mph/
115.66kph
125cc: Kunumitsu Takahashi (Jap), Honda, 67.29mph/
108.29kph
50cc: Jan Huberts (Hol), Kreidler, 60.15mph/96.80kph
Sidecar: Max Deubel/Emil Hörner (FRG), BMW,
67.36mph/108.41kph

BRITISH GRAND PRIX (TOURIST TROPHY)

Isle of Man, 4–8 June
500cc
1 Gary Hocking (SRho), MV Agusta, 103.51mph/
166.58kph

2 Ellis Boyce (UK), Norton
3 Fred Stevens (UK), Norton
Fastest lap: Hocking, 105.75mph/170.19kph
Other winners:
350cc: Mike Hailwood (UK), MV Agusta, 99.59mph/
160.27kph
250cc: Derek Minter (UK), Honda, 96.68mph/155.59kph
125cc: Luigi Taveri (Swi), Honda, 89.88mph/144.65kph
50cc: Ernst Degner (FRG), Suzuki, 75.13mph/120.89kph
Sidecar: Chris Vincent/Eric Bliss (UK), BSA, 83.57mph/
134.49kph

DUTCH TT

Assen, 30 June
500cc
1 Mike Hailwood (UK), MV Agusta, 87.35mph/140.58kph
2 Derek Minter (UK), Norton
3 Phil Read (UK), Norton
Fastest lap: Hailwood, 89.86mph/144.62kph
Other winners:
350cc: Jim Redman (SRho), Honda, 85.97mph/
138.36kph
250cc: Jim Redman (SRho), Honda, 82.95mph/
133.50kph
125cc: Luigi Taveri (Swi), Honda, 79.46mph/127.88kph
50cc: Ernst Degner (FRG), Suzuki, 69.77mph/112.28kph
Sidecar: Fritz Scheidegger (Swi)/John Robinson (UK),
BMW, 76.92mph/123.79kph

BELGIAN GRAND PRIX

Spa-Francorchamps, 8 July
500cc
1 Mike Hailwood (UK), MV Agusta, 119.35mph/
192.08kph
2 Alan Shepherd (UK), Matchless
3 Tony Godfrey (UK), Norton
Fastest lap: Hailwood, 120.30mph/193.60kph
Other winners:
250cc: Bob McIntyre (UK), Honda, 113.44mph/
182.56kph
125cc: Luigi Taveri (Swi), Honda, 102.23mph/164.52kph
50cc: Ernst Degner (FRG), Suzuki, 85.33mph/137.33kph
Sidecar: Florian Camathias (Swi)/Harry Winter (UK),
BMW, 105.60mph/169.95kph

WEST GERMAN GRAND PRIX

Solitude Circuit, Stuttgart, 15 July
250cc: Jim Redman (SRho), Honda, 90.47mph/
145.60kph
125cc: Luigi Taveri (Swi), Honda, 84.20mph/135.51kph
50cc: Ernst Degner (FRG), Suzuki, 74.52mph/119.93kph
Sidecar: Max Deubel/Emil Hörner (FRG), BMW,
87.99mph/141.61kph

ULSTER GRAND PRIX

Dundrod Circuit, Belfast, 11 August
500cc
1 Mike Hailwood (UK), MV Agusta, 96.55mph/155.38kph
2 Alan Shepherd (UK), Matchless
3 Phil Read (UK), Norton
Fastest lap: Hailwood, 99.99mph/160.92kph
Other winners:
350cc: Jim Redman (SRho), Honda, 93.76mph/150.89kph
250cc: Tommy Robb (UK), Honda, 88.39mph/142.25kph
125cc: Luigi Taveri (Swi), Honda, 83.30mph/134.06kph

EAST GERMAN GRAND PRIX

Sachsenring, 19 August
500cc
1 Mike Hailwood (UK), MV Agusta, 102.10mph/
164.31kph
2 Alan Shepherd (UK), Matchless
3 Bertie Schneider (Aut), Norton
Fastest lap: Hailwood, 104.43mph/168.06kph
Other winners:
350cc: Jim Redman (SRho), Honda, 98.12mph/
157.91kph
250cc: Jim Redman (SRho), Honda, 98.29mph/
158.18kph

125cc: Luigi Taveri (Swi), Honda, 88.83mph/142.96kph
50cc: Jan Huberts (Hol), Kreidler, 75.34mph/121.25kph

ITALIAN GRAND PRIX
(GRAND PRIX DES NATIONS)

Monza, 9 September
500cc
1 Mike Hailwood (UK), MV Agusta, 116.65mph/
187.73kph
2 Remo Venturi (Ita), MV Agusta
3 Silvio Grassetti (Ita), Bianchi
Fastest lap: Venturi, 118.98mph/191.48kph
Other winners:
350cc: Jim Redman (SRho), Honda, 112.37mph/
180.84kph
250cc: Jim Redman (SRho), Honda, 110.78mph/
178.28kph
125cc: Teisuke Tanaka (Jap), Honda, 97.11mph/
156.28kph
50cc: Hans-Georg Anscheidt (FRG), Kreidler, 83.64mph/
134.61kph

FINNISH GRAND PRIX

Tampere, 23 September
500cc
1 Alan Shepherd (UK), Matchless, 68.04mph/109.50kph
2 Sven Gunnarson (Swe), Norton
3 Frantisek Stastny (Cze), Jawa
Fastest lap: Shepherd, 72.02mph/115.90kph
Other winners:
350cc: Tommy Robb (UK), Honda, 66.42mph/106.89kph
125cc: Jim Redman (SRho), Honda, 65.24mph/
104.99kph
50cc: Luigi Taveri (Swi), Honda, 59.71mph/96.09kph

ARGENTINE GRAND PRIX

Buenos Aires, 14 October
500cc
1 Benedicto Caldarella (Arg), Matchless, 90.25mph/
145.24kph
2 Juan Carlos Salatino (Arg), Norton
3 Eduardo Salatino (Arg), Norton
Fastest lap: Not recorded
Other winners:
250cc: Arthur Wheeler (UK), Guzzi, 82.31mph/132.47kph
125cc: Hugh Anderson (NZ), Suzuki, 69.38mph/
111.66kph
50cc: Hugh Anderson (NZ), Suzuki, 65.78mph/105.86kph

LEADING CHAMPIONSHIP POSITIONS

500cc
Riders
1 Mike Hailwood (UK) 40pts
2 Alan Shepherd (UK) 29pts
3 Phil Read (UK) 11pts
4 Bertie Schneider (Aut) 10pts

5 Gary Hocking (SRho) 8pts
  Benedicto Caldarella (Arg) 8pts
Manufacturers
1 MV Agusta 40(48)pts
2 Norton 28(35)pts
3 Matchless 23pts

350cc
1 Jim Redman (SRho) 32(38)pts
2 Tommy Robb (UK) 22pts
3 Mike Hailwood (UK) 20pts
Manufacturers' title: Honda

250cc
1 Jim Redman (SRho) 48(66)pts
2 Bob McIntyre (UK) 32pts
3 Arthur Wheeler (UK) 19pts
Manufacturers' title: Honda

125cc
1 Luigi Taveri (Swi) 48(67)pts

2 Jim Redman (SRho) 38(47)pts
3 Tommy Robb (UK) 30(33)pts
Manufacturers' title: Honda

50cc
1 Ernst Degner* (FRG) 41pts
2 Hans-Georg Anscheidt (FRG)
  36(43)pts

3 Luigi Taveri (Swi) 29(33)pts
Manufacturers' title: Suzuki

Sidecar
1 Max Deubel (FRG) 34pts
2 Florian Camathias (Swi) 26pts
3 Fritz Scheidegger (Swi) 18pts
Manufacturers' title: BMW

* Ernst Degner was previously from GDR but he defected to West Germany at the end of 1961

1963

SPANISH GRAND PRIX ·

Montjuich, Barcelona, 5 May
250cc: Tarquinio Provini (Ita), Morini, 72.74mph/
117.06kph
125cc: Luigi Taveri (Swi), Honda, 68.27mph/109.87kph
50cc: Hans-Georg Anscheidt (FRG), Kreidler, 63.04mph/
101.45kph
Sidecar: Max Deubel/Emil Hörner (FRG), BMW,
66.41mph/106.88kph

FRENCH GRAND PRIX

Clermont-Ferrand, 2 June
125cc: Hugh Anderson (NZ), Suzuki, 72.59mph/
116.82kph
50cc: Hans-Georg Anscheidt (FRG), Kreidler, 60.41mph/
97.22kph

WEST GERMAN GRAND PRIX

Hockenheim, 26 May
350cc: Jim Redman (SRho), Honda, 121.85mph/
196.10kph
250cc: Tarquinio Provini (Ita), Morini, 116.26mph/
187.10kph
125cc: Ernst Degner (FRG), Suzuki, 105.63mph/
170.00kph
50cc: Hugh Anderson (NZ), Suzuki, 89.04mph/143.30kph
Sidecar: Florian Camathias/Alfred Herzig (Swi), FCS
BMW, 109.67mph/176.50kph

BRITISH GRAND PRIX (TOURIST TROPHY)

Isle of Man, 10–14 June
500cc
1 Mike Hailwood (UK), MV Agusta, 104.64mph/
168.40kph
2 John Hartle (UK), Gilera
3 Phil Read (UK), Gilera
Fastest lap: Hailwood, 106.41mph/171.25kph
Other winners:
350cc: Jim Redman (SRho), Honda, 94.91mph/
152.74kph
250cc: Jim Redman (SRho), Honda, 94.85mph/
152.65kph

125cc: Hugh Anderson (NZ), Suzuki, 89.27mph/
143.67kph
50cc: Mitsuo Itoh (Jap), Suzuki, 78.81mph/126.83kph
Sidecar: Florian Camathias/Alfred Herzig (Swi), FCS
BMW, 88.38mph/142.23kph

DUTCH TT

Assen, 29 June
500cc
1 John Hartle (UK), Gilera, 88.10mph/141.79kph
2 Phil Read (UK), Gilera
3 Alan Shepherd (UK), Matchless
Fastest lap: Hartle, 89.66mph/144.29kph
Other winners:
350cc: Jim Redman (SRho), Honda, 86.90mph/
139.85kph
250cc: Jim Redman (SRho), Honda, 86.15mph/
138.64kph
125cc: Hugh Anderson (NZ), Suzuki, 82.18mph/
132.26kph
50cc: Ernst Degner (FRG), Suzuki, 73.87mph/118.88kph
Sidecar: Max Deubel/Emil Hörner (FRG), BMW,
78.41mph/126.19kph

BELGIAN GRAND PRIX

Spa-Francorchamps, 7 July
500cc
1 Mike Hailwood (UK), MV Agusta, 123.99mph/
199.54kph
2 Phil Read (UK), Gilera
3 Alan Shepherd (UK), Matchless
Fastest lap: Hailwood, 125.61mph/202.15kph
Other winners:
250cc: Fumio Ito (Jap), Yamaha, 115.49mph/185.86kph
125cc: Bertie Schneider (Aut), Suzuki, 105.03mph/
169.03kph
50cc: Isao Morishita (Jap), Suzuki, 87.92mph/141.49kph
Sidecar: Fritz Scheidegger (Swi)/John Robinson (UK),
BMW, 107.13mph/172.41kph

ULSTER GRAND PRIX

Dundrod Circuit, Belfast, 10 August
500cc
1 Mike Hailwood (UK), MV Agusta, 99.27mph/159.76kph
2 John Hartle (UK), Gilera
3 Derek Minter (UK), Gilera
Fastest lap: Hailwood, 101.28mph/162.99kph

Other winners:
350cc: Jim Redman (SRho), Honda, 93.78mph/ 150.92kph
250cc: Jim Redman (SRho), Honda, 86.64mph/ 139.43kph
125cc: Hugh Anderson (NZ), Suzuki, 85.84mph/ 138.15kph

EAST GERMAN GRAND PRIX

Sachsenring, 18 August
500cc
1 Mike Hailwood (UK), MV Agusta, 103.15mph/ 166.03kph
2 Derek Minter (UK), Gilera
3 Alan Shepherd (UK), Matchless
Fastest lap: Hailwood, 104.72mph/168.53kph
Other winners:
350cc: Mike Hailwood (UK), MV Agusta, 99.54mph/ 160.19kph
250cc: Mike Hailwood (UK), MZ, 98.29mph/158.18kph
125cc: Hugh Anderson (NZ), Suzuki, 93.13mph/ 149.88kph

FINNISH GRAND PRIX

Tampere, 1 September
500cc
1 Mike Hailwood (UK), MV Agusta, 78.78mph/126.79kph
2 Alan Shepherd (UK), Matchless
3 Mike Duff (Can), Matchless
Fastest lap: Hailwood, 80.46mph/129.49kph
Other winners:
350cc: Mike Hailwood (UK), MV Agusta, 72.91mph/ 117.34kph
125cc: Hugh Anderson (NZ), Suzuki, 72.45mph/ 116.60kph
50cc: Hans-Georg Anscheidt (FRG), Kreidler, 63.36mph/ 101.97kph

ITALIAN GRAND PRIX (GRAND PRIX DES NATIONS)

Monza, 15 September
500cc
1 Mike Hailwood (UK), MV Agusta, 118.06mph/ 190.01kph
2 Jack Findlay (Aus), Matchless
3 Fred Stevens (UK), Norton
Fastest lap: Hailwood, 119.98mph/193.09kph
Other winners:
350cc: Jim Redman (SRho), Honda, 113.42mph/ 182.53kph
250cc: Tarquinio Provini (Ita), Morini, 111.60mph/ 179.60kph
125cc: Luigi Taveri (Swi), Honda, 97.22mph/156.46kph

ARGENTINE GRAND PRIX

Buenos Aires, 6 October
500cc
1 Mike Hailwood (UK), MV Agusta, 80.06mph/128.84kph
2 Jorg Kissling (Arg), Norton
3 Benedicto Caldarella (Arg), Matchless
Fastest lap: Hailwood, 81.79mph/131.63kph
Other winners:
250cc: Tarquinio Provini (Ita), Morini, 78.79mph/ 126.80kph
125cc: Jim Redman (SRho), Honda, 71.24mph/ 114.65kph
50cc: Hugh Anderson (NZ), Suzuki, 67.21mph/108.16kph

JAPANESE GRAND PRIX

Suzuka, 10 November
350cc: Jim Redman (SRho), Honda, 84.71mph/ 136.33kph
250cc: Jim Redman (SRho), Honda, 87.25mph/ 140.42kph
125cc: Frank Perris (UK), Suzuki, 84.15mph/135.43kph
50cc: Luigi Taveri (Swi), Honda, 76.42mph/122.99kph
The 350cc race did not count towards the World Championship because there were only three starters, three short of the minimum six required by the FIM

LEADING CHAMPIONSHIP POSITIONS

500cc
Riders
1 Mike Hailwood (UK) 40(56)pts
2 Alan Shepherd (UK) 21pts
3 John Hartle (UK) 20pts
4 Phil Read (UK) 16pts
5 Fred Stevens (UK) 13pts
6 Mike Duff (Can) 11pts
Manufacturers
1 MV Agusta 40(56)pts
2 Gilera 32pts
3 Matchless 24(34)pts

350cc
1 Jim Redman (SRho) 32(50)pts
2 Mike Hailwood (UK) 28pts
3 Luigi Taveri (Swi) 16pts
Manufacturers' title: Honda

250cc
1 Jim Redman (SRho) 44(58)pts
2 Tarquinio Provini (Ita) 42(49)pts
3 Fumio Ito (Jap) 26pts
Manufacturers' title: Honda

125cc
1 Hugh Anderson (NZ) 54(62)pts
2 Luigi Taveri (Swi) 38(47)pts
3 Jim Redman (SRho) 35pts
Manufacturers' title: Suzuki

50cc
1 Hugh Anderson (NZ) 34(47)pts
2 Hans-Georg Anscheidt (FRG) 32(36)pts
3 Ernst Degner (FRG) 30pts
Manufacturers' title: Suzuki

Sidecar
1 Max Deubel (FRG) 22(28)pts
2 Florian Camathias (Swi) 20(24)pts
3 Fritz Scheidegger (Swi) 20pts
Manufacturers' title: BMW

1964

UNITED STATES GRAND PRIX

Daytona, 1–2 February
500cc
1 Mike Hailwood (UK), MV Agusta, 100.17mph/161.21mph
2 Phil Read (UK), Matchless
3 John Hartle (UK), Norton
Fastest lap: Hailwood, 103.30mph/166.25kph
Other winners:
250cc: Alan Shepherd (UK), MZ, 91.19mph/146.76kph
125cc: Hugh Anderson (NZ), Suzuki, 88.50mph/142.43kph
50cc: Hugh Anderson (NZ) Suzuki, 78.93mph/127.03kph

SPANISH GRAND PRIX

Montjuich, Barcelona, 3 May
250cc: Tarquinio Provini (Ita), Benelli, 71.78mph/
115.51kph
125cc: Luigi Taveri (Swi), Honda, 69.87mph/112.44kph
50cc: Hans-Georg Anscheidt (FRG), Kreidler, 64.19mph/
103.30kph
Sidecar: Florian Camathias (Swi)/Roland Foll (FRG),
Gilera, 66.40mph/106.86kph

FRENCH GRAND PRIX

Clermont-Ferrand, 17 May
250cc: Phil Read (UK), Yamaha, 75.35mph/121.26kph
125cc: Luigi Taveri (Swi), Honda, 73.25mph/117.88kph
50cc: Hugh Anderson (NZ), Suzuki, 65.79mph/105.88kph
Sidecar: Fritz Scheidegger (Swi)/John Robinson (UK),
BMW, 67.65mph/108.87kph

BRITISH GRAND PRIX (TOURIST TROPHY)

Isle of Man, 8–12 June
500cc
1 Mike Hailwood (UK), MV Agusta, 100.95mph/
162.46kph
2 Derek Minter (UK), Norton
3 Fred Stevens (UK), Matchless
Fastest lap: Hailwood, 102.51mph/164.91kph
Other winners:
350cc: Jim Redman (SRho), Honda, 98.50mph/
158.52kph
250cc: Jim Redman (SRho), Honda, 97.45mph/
156.83kph
125cc: Luigi Taveri (Swi), Honda, 92.14mph/148.28kph
50cc: Hugh Anderson (NZ), Suzuki, 80.64mph/129.89kph
Sidecar: Max Deubel/Emil Hörner (FRG), BMW,
89.12mph/143.42kph

The 'Kings of the Little Bikes' in 1964 were Ralph Bryans, Hugh Anderson and Hans-Georg Anscheidt. In a great battle for the 50cc title, New Zealander Anderson managed to win, but only nine points separated the three riders

DUTCH TT

Assen, 27 June
500cc
1 Mike Hailwood (UK), MV Agusta, 87.53mph/140.87kph
2 Remo Venturi (Ita), Bianchi
3 Paddy Driver (SAf), Matchless
Fastest lap: Hailwood, 89.89mph/144.66kph
Other winners:
350cc: Jim Redman (SRho), Honda, 87.35mph/
140.58kph
250cc: Jim Redman (SRho), Honda, 88.38mph/
142.23kph
125cc: Jim Redman (SRho), Honda, 84.05mph/
135.27kph
50cc: Ralph Bryans (UK), Honda, 75.29mph/121.17kph
Sidecar: Colin Seeley/Ray Campbell (UK), FCS BMW,
78.70mph/126.66kph

BELGIAN GRAND PRIX

Spa-Francorchamps, 5 July
500cc
1 Mike Hailwood (UK), MV Agusta, 122.91mph/
197.80kph
2 Phil Read (UK), Matchless
3 Paddy Driver (SAf), Matchless
Fastest lap: Hailwood, 123.64mph/198.98kph
Other winners:
250cc: Mike Duff (Can), Yamaha, 118.43mph/190.59kph
50cc: Ralph Bryans (UK), Honda, 91.71mph/147.59kph
Sidecar: Max Deubel/Emil Hörner (FRG), BMW,
106.43mph/171.28kph

WEST GERMAN GRAND PRIX

Solitude Circuit, Stuttgart, 19 July
500cc
1 Mike Hailwood (UK), MV Agusta, 97.68mph/157.20kph
2 Jack Ahearn (Aus), Norton
3 Phil Read (UK), Matchless
Fastest lap: Hailwood, 99.64mph/160.36kph
Other winners:
350cc: Jim Redman (SRho), Honda, 94.90mph/
152.73kph
250cc: Phil Read (UK), Yamaha, 97.00mph/156.11kph
125cc: Jim Redman (SRho), Honda, 83.80mph/
134.86kph
50cc: Ralph Bryans (UK), Honda, 74.97mph/120.65kph
Sidecar: Fritz Scheidegger (Swi)/John Robinson (UK),
BMW, 87.58mph/140.95kph

EAST GERMAN GRAND PRIX

Sachsenring, 26 July
500cc
1 Mike Hailwood (UK), MV Agusta, 101.33mph/
163.07kph
2 Mike Duff (Can), Matchless
3 Paddy Driver (SAf), Matchless
Fastest lap: Hailwood, 103.32mph/166.28kph
Other winners:
350cc: Jim Redman (SRho), Honda, 96.80mph/155.78kph

250cc: Phil Read (UK), Yamaha, 99.64mph/160.36kph
125cc: Hugh Anderson (NZ), Suzuki, 94.27mph/
151.71kph

ULSTER GRAND PRIX

Dundrod Circuit, Belfast, 8 August
500cc
1 Phil Read (UK), Norton, 82.24mph/132.35kph
2 Dick Creith (UK), Norton
3 Jack Ahearn (Aus), Norton
Fastest lap: Read, 84.17mph/135.46kph
Other winners:
350cc: Jim Redman (SRho), Honda, 93.82mph/
150.99kph
250cc: Phil Read (UK), Yamaha, 85.91mph/138.26kph
125cc: Hugh Anderson (NZ), Suzuki, 91.53mph/
147.30kph

FINNISH GRAND PRIX

Imatra, 30 August
500cc
1 Jack Ahearn (Aus), Norton, 81.62mph/131.35kph
2 Mike Duff (Can), Matchless
3 Gyula Marsovszky (Swi), Matchless
Fastest lap: Duff, 82.64mph/133.00kph
Other winners:
350cc: Jim Redman (SRho), Honda, 83.88mph/
134.99kph
125cc: Luigi Taveri (Swi), Honda, 82.64mph/133.00kph
50cc: Hugh Anderson (NZ), Suzuki, 68.97mph/111.00kph

ITALIAN GRAND PRIX
(GRAND PRIX DES NATIONS)

Monza, 13 September
500cc
1 Mike Hailwood (UK), MV Agusta, 119.15mph/
191.75kph
2 Benedicto Caldarella (Arg), Gilera
3 Jack Ahearn (Aus), Norton
Fastest lap: Caldarella, 121.73mph/195.91kph
Other winners:
350cc: Jim Redman (SRho), Honda, 111.95mph/
180.17kph
250cc: Phil Read (UK), Yamaha, 113.91mph/183.32kph
125cc: Luigi Taveri (Swi), Honda, 105.17mph/169.25kph

JAPANESE GRAND PRIX

Suzuka, 1 November
350cc: Jim Redman (SRho), Honda, 86.15mph/
138.64kph
250cc: Jim Redman (SRho), Honda, 87.26mph/
140.43kph
125cc: Ernst Degner (FRG), Suzuki, 85.14mph/137.02kph
50cc: Ralph Bryans (UK), Honda, 76.71mph/123.45kph
*The 50cc race did not count towards the World
Championship because there were insufficient starters*

LEADING CHAMPIONSHIP POSITIONS

500cc
Riders
1 Mike Hailwood (UK) 40(56)pts
2 Jack Ahearn (Aus) 25(29)pts
3 Phil Read (UK) 25pts
4 Mike Duff (Can) 18pts
5 Paddy Driver (SAf) 16pts
6 Fred Stevens (UK) 8pts
Manufacturers
1 MV Agusta 40(56)pts
2 Norton 32(43)pts
3 Matchless 28(40)pts

350cc
1 Jim Redman (SRho) 40(64)pts
2 Bruce Beale (SRho) 24pts
3 Mike Duff (Can) 20pts
Manufacturers' title: Honda

250cc
1 Phil Read (UK) 46(50)pts
2 Jim Redman (SRho) 42(58)pts
3 Alan Shepherd (UK) 23pts
Manufacturers' title: Yamaha

125cc
1 Luigi Taveri (Swi) 46(64)pts
2 Jim Redman (SRho) 36(37)pts

3 Hugh Anderson (NZ) 34pts
Manufacturers' title: Honda

50cc
1 Hugh Anderson (NZ) 38(42)pts
2 Ralph Bryans (UK) 30pts
3 Hans-Georg Anscheidt (FRG) 29(38)pts
Manufacturers' title: Suzuki

Sidecar
1 Max Deubel (FRG) 28(34)pts
2 Fritz Scheidegger (Swi) 26pts
3 Colin Seeley (UK) 17pts
Manufacturers' title: BMW

1965

UNITED STATES GRAND PRIX

Daytona, 21 March
500cc
1 Mike Hailwood (UK), MV Agusta, 99.62mph/160.32kph
2 Buddy Parriot (USA), Norton
3 Roger Beaumont (Can), Norton
Fastest lap: Hailwood, 101.45mph/163.27kph
Other winners:
250cc: Phil Read (UK), Yamaha, 97.46mph/156.85kph
125cc: Hugh Anderson (NZ), Suzuki, 89.35mph/143.79kph
50cc: Ernst Degner (FRG), Suzuki, 77.55mph/124.80kph

WEST GERMAN GRAND PRIX

Nürburgring Süd, 25 April
500cc
1 Mike Hailwood (UK), MV Agusta, 86.18mph/138.70kph
2 Giacomo Agostini (Ita), MV Agusta
3 Walter Scheiman (FRG), Norton
Fastest lap: Hailwood, 89.73mph/144.41kph
Other winners:
350cc: Giacomo Agostini (Ita), MV Agusta, 84.71mph/136.33kph
250cc: Phil Read (UK), Yamaha, 84.01mph/135.20kph
125cc: Hugh Anderson (NZ), Suzuki, 78.17mph/125.80kph
50cc: Ralph Bryans (UK), Honda, 73.47mph/118.24kph
Sidecar: Fritz Scheidegger (Swi)/John Robinson (UK), BMW, 70.27mph/113.09kph

SPANISH GRAND PRIX

Montjuich, Barcelona, 9 May
250cc: Phil Read (UK), Yamaha, 72.81mph/117.18kph
125cc: Hugh Anderson (NZ), Suzuki, 69.94mph/112.56kph
50cc: Hugh Anderson (NZ), Suzuki, 64.59mph/103.95kph

Sidecar: Max Deubel/Emil Hörner (FRG), BMW, 66.05mph/106.30kph

FRENCH GRAND PRIX

Rouen, 16 May
250cc: Phil Read (UK), Yamaha, 96.07mph/154.61kph
125cc: Hugh Anderson (NZ), Suzuki, 92.11mph/148.24kph
50cc: Ralph Bryans (UK), Honda, 79.43mph/127.83kph
Sidecar: Florian Camathias/Franz Ducret (Swi), BMW, 87.96mph/141.56kph

BRITISH GRAND PRIX (TOURIST TROPHY)

Isle of Man, 14–18 June
500cc
1 Mike Hailwood (UK), MV Agusta, 91.69mph/147.56kph
2 Joe Dunphy (UK), Norton
3 Mike Duff (Can), Matchless
Fastest lap: Hailwood, 95.11mph/153.06kph
Other winners:
350cc: Jim Redman (SRho), Honda, 100.72mph/162.09kph
250cc: Jim Redman (SRho), Honda, 97.19mph/156.41kph
125cc: Phil Read (UK), Yamaha, 94.28mph/151.73kph
50cc: Luigi Taveri (Swi), Honda, 79.66mph/128.20kph
Sidecar: Max Deubel/Emil Hörner (FRG), BMW, 90.57mph/145.76kph

DUTCH TT

Assen, 26 June
500cc
1 Mike Hailwood (UK), MV Agusta, 88.39mph/142.25kph
2 Giacomo Agostini (Ita), MV Agusta
3 Paddy Driver (SAf), Matchless
Fastest lap: Hailwood, 90.23mph/145.21kph
Other winners:
350cc: Jim Redman (SRho), Honda, 88.22mph/141.98kph
250cc: Phil Read (UK), Yamaha, 87.28mph/140.46kph

Out in the country during the 1965 Belgian Grand Prix at Spa-Francorchamps, one of the fastest circuits on the Grand Prix calendar

125cc: Mike Duff (Can), Yamaha, 83.77mph/134.81kph
50cc: Ralph Bryans (UK), Honda, 76.11mph/122.49kph
Sidecar: Fritz Scheidegger (Swi)/John Robinson (UK), BMW, 78.81mph/126.83kph

BELGIAN GRAND PRIX

Spa-Francorchamps, 4 July
500cc
1 Mike Hailwood (UK), MV Agusta, 120.51mph/193.94kph
2 Giacomo Agostini (Ita), MV Agusta
3 Derek Minter (UK), Norton
Fastest lap: Hailwood, 123.04mph/198.01kph
Other winners:
250cc: Jim Redman (SRho), Honda, 120.19mph/193.43kph
50cc: Ernst Degner (FRG), Suzuki, 93,98mph/151.25kph
Sidecar: Fritz Scheidegger (Swi)/John Robinson (UK), BMW, 107.23mph/172.57kph

EAST GERMAN GRAND PRIX

Sachsenring, 18 July
500cc
1 Mike Hailwood (UK), MV Agusta, 93.68mph/150.76kph
2 Giacomo Agostini (Ita), MV Agusta

3 Paddy Driver (SAf), Matchless
Fastest lap: Hailwood, 95.63mph/153.90kph
Other winners:
350cc: Jim Redman (SRho), Honda, 98.74mph/158.91kph
250cc: Jim Redman (SRho), Honda, 91.57mph/147.37kph
125cc: Frank Perris (UK), Suzuki, 86.80mph/139.69kph

CZECHOSLOVAK GRAND PRIX

Brno, 25 July
500cc
1 Mike Hailwood (UK), MV Agusta, 95.01mph/152.90kph
2 Giacomo Agostini (Ita), MV Agusta
3 Jack Ahearn (Aus), Norton
Fastest lap: Hailwood, 96.31mph/155.00kph
Other winners:
350cc: Jim Redman (SRho), Honda, 94.64mph/152.31kph
250cc: Phil Read (UK), Yamaha, 95.32mph/153.40kph
125cc: Frank Perris (UK), Suzuki, 86.86mph/139.79kph

ULSTER GRAND PRIX

Dundrod Circuit, Belfast, 7 August
500cc
1 Dick Creith (UK), Norton, 86.20mph/138.73kph
2 Paddy Driver (SAf), Matchless
3 Chris Conn (UK), Norton
Fastest lap: Driver, 91.49mph/147.24kph
Other winners:
350cc: Frantisek Stastny (Cze), Jawa, 91.01mph/
146.47kph
250cc: Phil Read (UK), Yamaha, 86.04mph/138.47kph
125cc: Ernst Degner (FRG), Suzuki, 86.41mph/139.06kph

FINNISH GRAND PRIX

Imatra, 22 August
500cc
1 Giacomo Agostini (Ita), MV Agusta, 85.19mph/
137.10kph
2 Paddy Driver (SAf), Matchless
3 Fred Stevens (UK), Matchless
Fastest lap: Agostini, 87.67mph/141.11kph
Other winners:
350cc: Giacomo Agostini (Ita), MV Agusta, 84.31mph/
135.68kph
250cc: Mike Duff (Can), Yamaha, 82.88mph/133.38kph
125cc: Hugh Anderson (NZ), Suzuki, 80.16mph/
129.01kph

ITALIAN GRAND PRIX
(GRAND PRIX DES NATIONS)

Monza, 5 September
500cc
1 Mike Hailwood (UK), MV Agusta, 97.49mph/156.89kph
2 Giacomo Agostini (Ita), MV Agusta
3 Frantisek Stastny (Cze), Jawa
Fastest lap: Hailwood, 103.64mph/166.79kph
Other winners:
350cc: Giacomo Agostini (Ita), MV Agusta, 113.03mph/
181.90kph
250cc: Tarquinio Provini (Ita), Benelli, 94.53mph/
152.13kph
125cc: Hugh Anderson (NZ), Suzuki, 94.31mph/
151.78kph
Sidecar: Fritz Scheidegger (Swi)/John Robinson (UK),
BMW, 92.37mph/148.66kph

JAPANESE GRAND PRIX

Suzuka, 24 October
350cc: Mike Hailwood (UK), MV Agusta, 88.07mph/
141.73kph
250cc: Mike Hailwood (UK), Honda, 86.90mph/
139.85kph
125cc: Hugh Anderson (NZ), Suzuki, 85.56mph/
137.70kph
50cc: Luigi Taveri (Swi), Honda, 78.52mph/126.37kph

LEADING CHAMPIONSHIP POSITIONS

500cc
Riders
1 Mike Hailwood (UK) 48(64)pts
2 Giacomo Agostini (Ita) 38(44)pts
3 Paddy Driver (SAf) 26pts
4 Fred Stevens (UK) 15pts
5 Jack Ahearn (Aus) 9pts
6 Dick Creith (UK) 8pts
Manufacturers
1 MV Agusta 48(72)pts
2 Norton 32(38)pts
3 Matchless 27(36)pts

350cc
1 Jim Redman (SRho) 38pts
2 Giacomo Agostini (Ita) 32(34)pts
3 Mike Hailwood (UK) 20pts
Manufacturers' title: Honda

250cc
1 Phil Read (UK) 56(68)pts
2 Mike Duff (Can) 42(50)pts
3 Jim Redman (SRho) 34pts
Manufacturers' title: Yamaha

125cc
1 Hugh Anderson (NZ) 56(62)pts
2 Frank Perris (UK) 44(48)pts

3 Dennis Woodman (UK) 28(30)pts
Manufacturers' title: Suzuki

50cc
1 Ralph Bryans (UK) 36(38)pts
2 Luigi Taveri (Swi) 32(39)pts
3 Hugh Anderson (NZ) 32(37)pts
Manufacturers' title: Honda

Sidecar
1 Fritz Scheidegger (Swi) 32(50)pts
2 Max Deubel (FRG) 26pts
3 Georg Auerbacher (FRG) 15pts
Manufacturers' title: BMW

1966

SPANISH GRAND PRIX

Montjuich, Barcelona, 8 May
250cc: Mike Hailwood (UK), Honda, 73.51mph/
118.32kph
125cc: Bill Ivy (UK), Yamaha, 69.95mph/112.57kph
50cc: Luigi Taveri (Swi), Honda, 67.81mph/109.13kph

WEST GERMAN GRAND PRIX

Hockenheim, 22 May
500cc
1 Jim Redman (SRho), Honda, 110.42mph/177.70kph
2 Giacomo Agostini (Ita), MV Agusta
3 Gyula Marsovszky (Swi), Matchless
Fastest lap: Redman, 112.99mph/181.84kph
Other winners:
350cc: Mike Hailwood (UK), Honda, 107.37mph/172.80kph
250cc: Mike Hailwood (UK), Honda, 109.23mph/
175.80kph

125cc: Luigi Taveri (Swi), Honda, 100.97mph/162.50kph
50cc: Hans-Georg Anscheidt (FRG), Suzuki, 89.97mph/144.80kph
Sidecar: Fritz Scheidegger (Swi)/John Robinson (UK), BMW, 96.45mph/155.70kph

FRENCH GRAND PRIX

Clermont-Ferrand, 29 May
350cc: Mike Hailwood (UK), Honda, 79.33mph/127.66kph
250cc: Mike Hailwood (UK), Honda, 79.66mph/128.20kph
Sidecar: Fritz Scheidegger (Swi)/John Robinson (UK), BMW, 71.15mph/114.50kph

DUTCH TT

Assen, 25 June
500cc
1 Jim Redman (SRho), Honda, 89.10mph/143.39kph
2 Giacomo Agostini (Ita), MV Agusta
3 Frantisek Stastny (Cze), Jawa-CZ
Fastest lap: Mike Hailwood (UK), Honda, 92.31mph/148.60kph
Other winners:
350cc: Mike Hailwood (UK), Honda, 82.73mph/133.14kph
250cc: Mike Hailwood (UK), Honda, 83.33mph/134.11kph
125cc: Bill Ivy (UK), Yamaha, 84.64mph/136.21kph
50cc: Luigi Taveri (Swi), Honda, 77.54mph/124.78kph
Sidecar: Fritz Scheidegger (Swi)/John Robinson (UK), BMW, 79.32mph/127.65kph

BELGIAN GRAND PRIX

Spa-Francorchamps, 3 July
500cc
1 Giacomo Agostini (Ita), MV Agusta, 98.91mph/159.19kph
2 Stuart Graham (UK), Matchless
3 Jack Ahearn (Aus), Norton
Fastest lap: Mike Hailwood (UK), Honda, 105.35mph/169.54kph
Other winners:
250cc: Mike Hailwood (UK), Honda, 122.33mph/196.87kph
Sidecar: Fritz Scheidegger (Swi)/John Robinson (UK), BMW, 103.86/167.15kph

EAST GERMAN GRAND PRIX

Sachsenring, 17 July
500cc
1 Frantisek Stastny (Cze), Jawa-CZ, 98.80mph/159.01kph
2 Jack Findlay (Aus), Matchless
3 Jack Ahearn (Aus), Norton
Fastest lap: Giacomo Agostini (Ita), MV Agusta, 107.77mph/173.40kph
Other winners:
350cc: Giacomo Agostini (Ita), MV Agusta, 104.19mph/

167.70kph
250cc: Mike Hailwood (UK), Honda, 103.82mph/167.10kph
125cc: Luigi Taveri (Swi), Honda, 96.58mph/103.37kph

CZECHOSLOVAK GRAND PRIX

Brno, 24 July
500cc
1 Mike Hailwood (UK), Honda, 88.98mph/143.20kph
2 Giacomo Agostini (Ita), MV Agusta
3 Gyula Marsovszky (Swi), Matchless
Fastest lap: Hailwood, 91.71mph/147.60kph
Other winners:
350cc: Mike Hailwood (UK), Honda, 96.87mph/155.89kph
250cc: Mike Hailwood (UK), Honda, 92.40mph/148.70kph
125cc: Luigi Taveri (Swi), Honda, 86.37mph/139.00kph

FINNISH GRAND PRIX

Imatra, 7 August
500cc
1 Giacomo Agostini (Ita), MV Agusta, 86.99mph/140.00kph
2 Mike Hailwood (UK), Honda
3 Jack Findlay (Aus), Matchless
Fastest lap: Agostini, 89.18mph/143.52kph
Other winners:
350cc: Mike Hailwood (UK), Honda, 89.16mph/143.50kph
250cc: Mike Hailwood (UK), Honda, 82.49mph/132.76kph
125cc: Phil Read (UK), Yamaha, 83.26mph/134.00kph

ULSTER GRAND PRIX

Dundrod Circuit, Belfast, 20 August
500cc
1 Mike Hailwood (UK), Honda, 102.44mph/164.90kph
2 Giacomo Agostini (Ita), MV Agusta
3 Frantisek Stastny (Cze), Jawa-CZ
Fastest lap: Hailwood, 105.03mph/169.03kph
Other winners:
350cc: Mike Hailwood (UK), Honda, 95.50mph/153.70kph
250cc: Ginger Molloy (NZ), Bultaco 87.03mph/140.10kph
125cc: Luigi Taveri (Swi), Honda, 92.38mph/148.70kph

BRITISH GRAND PRIX (TOURIST TROPHY)

Isle of Man, 28 August–2 September
500cc
1 Mike Hailwood (UK), Honda, 103.11mph/165.94kph
2 Giacomo Agostini (Ita), MV Agusta
3 Chris Conn (UK), Norton
Fastest lap: Hailwood, 107.70mph/172.17kph
Other winners:
350cc: Giacomo Agostini (Ita), MV Agusta, 100.87mph/162.33kph
250cc: Mike Hailwood (UK), Honda, 101.79mph/163.82kph

125cc: Bill Ivy (UK), Yamaha, 97.66mph/157.17kph
50cc: Ralph Bryans (UK), Honda, 85.66mph/139.47kph
Sidecar: Fritz Scheidegger (Swi)/John Robinson (UK), BMW, 90.76mph/146.06kph

ITALIAN GRAND PRIX
(GRAND PRIX DES NATIONS)

Monza, 11 September
500cc
1 Giacomo Agostini (Ita), MV Agusta, 118.97mph/ 191.46kph
2 Peter Williams (UK), Matchless
3 Jack Findlay (Aus), Matchless
Fastest lap: Mike Hailwood (UK), Honda, 123.68mph/ 199.04kph
Other winners:
350cc: Giacomo Agostini (Ita), MV Agusta, 118.97mph/

191.50kph
250cc: Mike Hailwood (UK), Honda, 113.65mph/ 182.91kph
125cc: Luigi Taveri (Swi), Honda, 110.39mph/177.60kph
50cc: Hans-Georg Anscheidt (FRG), Suzuki, 94.57mph/ 152.20kph

JAPANESE GRAND PRIX

Fuji, 17 October
350cc: Phil Read (UK), Yamaha, 103.52mph/166.60kph
250cc: Hiroshi Hasegawa (Jap), Yamaha, 104.53mph/ 168.23kph
125cc: Bill Ivy (UK), Yamaha, 100.98mph/162.50kph
50cc: Hoshimi Katayama (Jap), Suzuki, 90.03mph/ 144.90kph

One of Britain's best-known and best-loved racers, Stanley Michael Bailey Hailwood, known affectionately as 'Mike the Bike'. He won nine world titles at 250, 350 and 500cc between 1961 and 1967, and in a 17-year career won 76 Grand Prix races altogether

LEADING CHAMPIONSHIP POSITIONS

500cc
Riders
1 Giacomo Agostini (Ita) 36(54)pts
2 Mike Hailwood (UK) 30pts
3 Jack Findlay (Aus) 20(21)pts
4 Frantisek Stastny (Cze) 17pts
5 Jim Redman (SRho) 16pts
6 Jack Ahearn (Aus) 13pts
  Gyula Marsovszky (Swi) 13pts
Manufacturers
1 Honda 40(46)pts
2 MV Agusta 36(54)pts
3 Matchless 26(38)pts

350cc
1 Mike Hailwood (UK) 48pts
2 Giacomo Agostini (Ita) 42pts
3 Renzo Pasolini (Ita) 15pts
Manufacturers' title: Honda

250cc
1 Mike Hailwood (UK) 56(80)pts
2 Phil Read (UK) 34pts
3 Jim Redman (SRho) 20pts
Manufacturers' title: Honda

125cc
1 Luigi Taveri (Swi) 44pts
2 Bill Ivy (UK) 40pts

3 Ralph Bryans (UK) 32pts
Manufacturers' title: Honda

50cc
1 Hans-Georg Anscheidt (FRG) 28pts
2 Luigi Taveri (Swi) 26pts
3 Ralph Bryans (UK) 26pts
Manufacturers' title: Honda

Sidecar
1 Fritz Scheidegger (Swi) 24pts
2 Max Deubel (FRG) 18pts
3 Georg Auerbacher (FRG) 12pts
Manufacturers' title: BMW

1967

SPANISH GRAND PRIX

Montjuich, Barcelona, 30 April
250cc: Phil Read (UK), Yamaha, 73.34mph/118.03kph
125cc: Bill Ivy (UK), Yamaha, 72.44mph/116.59kph
50cc: Hans-Georg Anscheidt (FRG), Suzuki, 66.90mph/107.67kph
Sidecar: Georg Auerbacher/Eduard Dein (FRG), BMW, 68.14mph/109.65kph

WEST GERMAN GRAND PRIX

Hockenheim, 7 May
500cc
1 Giacomo Agostini (Ita), MV Agusta, 112.34mph/180.80kph
2 Peter Williams (UK), Matchless
3 Jack Findlay (Aus), Matchless
Fastest lap: Agostini, 117.19mph/188.60kph
Other winners:
350cc: Mike Hailwood (UK), Honda, 111.22mph/179.00kph
250cc: Ralph Bryans (UK), Honda, 107.34mph/172.74kph
125cc: Hoshimi Katayama (Jap), Suzuki, 101.90mph/164.00kph
50cc: Hans-Georg Anscheidt (FRG), Suzuki, 89.23mph/143.60kph
Sidecar: Klaus Enders/Rolf Engelhardt (FRG), BMW, 96.87mph/155.00kph

FRENCH GRAND PRIX

Clermont-Ferrand, 21 May
250cc: Bill Ivy (UK), Yamaha, 78.07mph/125.64kph
125cc: Bill Ivy (UK), Yamaha, 77.20mph/124.24kph
50cc: Hoshimi Katayama (Jap), Suzuki, 70.14mph/112.88kph

Sidecar: Klaus Enders/Rolf Engelhardt (FRG), BMW, 71.08mph/114.39kph

BRITISH GRAND PRIX (TOURIST TROPHY)

Isle of Man, 12–16 June
500cc
1 Mike Hailwood (UK), Honda, 105.62mph/169.98kph
2 Peter Williams (UK), Matchless
3 Steve Spencer (UK), Norton
Fastest lap: Hailwood, 108.77mph/175.01kph
Other winners:
350cc: Mike Hailwood (UK), Honda, 104.68mph/168.47kph
250cc: Mike Hailwood (UK), Honda, 103.08mph/165.89kph
125cc: Phil Read (UK), Yamaha, 97.48mph/156.88kph
50cc: Stuart Graham (UK), Suzuki, 82.89mph/135.01kph
Sidecar: Siegfried Schauzu/Horst Schneider (FRG), BMW, 90.96mph/146.39kph

DUTCH TT

Assen, 24 June
500cc
1 Mike Hailwood (UK), Honda, 90.87mph/146.24kph
2 Giacomo Agostini (Ita), MV Agusta
3 Peter Williams (UK), Matchless
Fastest lap: Hailwood, 92.96mph/149.60kph
Other winners:
350cc: Mike Hailwood (UK), Honda, 87.93mph/141.52kph
250cc: Mike Hailwood (UK), Honda, 89.66mph/144.29kph
125cc: Phil Read (UK), Yamaha, 84.80mph/136.48kph
50cc: Hoshimi Katayama (Jap), Suzuki, 71.53mph/115.12kph
Sidecar: Klaus Enders/Rolf Engelhardt (FRG), BMW, 79.58mph/128.08kph

BELGIAN GRAND PRIX

Spa-Francorchamps, 2 July
500cc
1 Giacomo Agostini (Ita), MV Agusta, 123.95mph/
199.47kph
2 Mike Hailwood (UK), Honda
3 Fred Stevens (UK), Paton
Fastest lap: Agostini, 128.58mph/206.93kph
Other winners:
250cc: Bill Ivy (UK), Yamaha, 122.25mph/196.73kph
50cc: Hans-Georg Anscheidt (FRG), Suzuki, 98.54mph/
158.55kph
Sidecar: Klaus Enders/Rolf Engelhardt (FRG), BMW,
109.43mph/176.18kph

EAST GERMAN GRAND PRIX

Sachsenring, 16 July
500cc
1 Giacomo Agostini (Ita), MV Agusta, 106.05mph/
170.67kph
2 John Hartle (UK), Matchless
3 Jack Findlay (Aus), Matchless
Fastest lap: Agostini, 109.36mph/175.99kph
Other winners:
350cc: Mike Hailwood (UK), Honda, 94.82mph/
158.39kph
250cc: Phil Read (UK), Yamaha, 103.20mph/166.09kph
125cc: Bill Ivy (UK), Yamaha, 97.20mph/156.43kph

CZECHOSLOVAK GRAND PRIX

Brno, 23 July
500cc
1 Mike Hailwood (UK), Honda, 101.53mph/163.40kph
2 Giacomo Agostini (Ita), MV Agusta
3 John Cooper (UK), Norton
Fastest lap: Hailwood, 103.77mph/167.00kph
Other winners:
350cc: Mike Hailwood (UK), Honda, 98.18mph/
158.00kph
250cc: Phil Read (UK), Yamaha, 97.31mph/156.60kph
125cc: Bill Ivy (UK), Yamaha, 92.02mph/148.10kph

FINNISH GRAND PRIX

Imatra, 6 August
500cc
1 Giacomo Agostini (Ita), MV Agusta, 74.00mph/
119.06kph
2 John Hartle (UK), Norton
3 Billie Nelson (UK), Norton
Fastest lap: Not recorded
Other winners:
250cc: Mike Hailwood (UK), Honda, 79.72mph/
128.30kph
125cc: Stuart Graham (UK), Suzuki, 81.20mph/130.68kph
Sidecar: Klaus Enders/Rolf Engelhardt (FRG), BMW,
74.40mph/119.74kph

ULSTER GRAND PRIX

Dundrod Circuit, Belfast, 19 August
500cc
1 Mike Hailwood (UK), Honda, 102.88mph/165.60kph
2 John Hartle (UK), Matchless
3 Jack Findlay (Aus), Matchless
Fastest lap: Hailwood, 106.71mph/171.73kph
Other winners:
350cc: Giacomo Agostini (Ita), MV Agusta, 103.31mph/
166.26kph
250cc: Mike Hailwood (UK), Honda, 104.31mph/
167.87kph
125cc: Bill Ivy (UK), Yamaha, 94.81mph/152.58kph

ITALIAN GRAND PRIX
(GRAND PRIX DES NATIONS)

Monza, 3 September
500cc
1 Giacomo Agostini (Ita), MV Agusta, 124.45mph/
200.28kph
2 Mike Hailwood (UK), Honda
3 Angelo Bergamonti (Ita), Paton
Fastest lap: Hailwood, 126.85mph/204.14kph
Other winners:
350cc: Ralph Bryans (UK), Honda, 118.95mph/
191.79kph
250cc: Phil Read (UK), Yamaha, 119.79mph/192.77kph
125cc: Bill Ivy (UK), Yamaha, 103.66mph/166.82kph
Sidecar: Georg Auerbacher (FRG)/Billie Nelson (UK),
BMW, 101.04mph/162.62kph

CANADIAN GRAND PRIX

Mosport, 24 September
500cc
1 Mike Hailwood (UK), Honda, 80.29mph/129.21kph
2 Giacomo Agostini (Ita), MV Agusta
3 Mike Duff (Can), Matchless
Fastest lap: Hailwood, 85.95mph/138.29kph
Other winners:
250cc: Mike Hailwood (UK), Honda, 89.86mph/
144.61kph
125cc: Bill Ivy (UK), Yamaha, 79.07mph/127.22kph

JAPANESE GRAND PRIX

Fuji, 14 October
350cc: Mike Hailwood (UK), Honda, 98.55mph/
158.59kph
250cc: Ralph Bryans (UK), Honda, 100.99mph/
162.53kph
125cc: Bill Ivy (UK), Yamaha, 96.50mph/155.30kph
50cc: Mitsuo Itoh (Jap), Suzuki, 85.44mph/137.50kph

LEADING CHAMPIONSHIP POSITIONS

500cc
Riders
1 Giacomo Agostini (Ita) 46(58)pts
2 Mike Hailwood (UK) 46(52)pts
3 John Hartle (UK) 22pts
4 Peter Williams (UK) 16pts
5 Jack Findlay (Aus) 15pts
6 Fred Stevens (UK) 11pts
Manufacturers
1 MV Agusta 46(58)pts
2 Honda 46(52)pts
3 Matchless 32(42)pts

350cc
1 Mike Hailwood (UK) 40(48)pts
2 Giacomo Agostini (Ita) 36pts
3 Ralph Bryans (UK) 12pts
Manufacturers' title: Honda

250cc
1 Mike Hailwood (UK) 50(54)pts
2 Phil Read (UK) 50(56)pts
3 Bill Ivy (UK) 46(51)pts
Manufacturers' title: Honda
The riders' championship was decided on the most race wins. Hailwood took the title with 5 wins to Read's 4

125cc
1 Bill Ivy (UK) 56(76)pts
2 Phil Read (UK) 46pts
3 Stuart Graham (UK) 38(48)pts
Manufacturers' title: Yamaha

50cc
1 Hans-Georg Anscheidt (FRG) 30(42)pts
2 Hoshimi Katayama (Jap) 28pts
3 Stuart Graham (UK) 22pts
Manufacturers' title: Suzuki

Sidecar
1 Klaus Enders (FRG) 40(52)pts
2 Georg Auerbacher (FRG) 32pts
3 Siegfried Schauzu (FRG) 28(32)pts
Manufacturers' title: BMW

1968

WEST GERMAN GRAND PRIX

Nürburgring Süd, 21 April
500cc
1 Giacomo Agostini (Ita), MV Agusta, 89.42mph/143.91kph
2 Dan Shorey (UK), Norton
3 Peter Williams (UK), Matchless
Fastest lap: Agostini, 91.84mph/147.80kph
Other winners:
350cc: Giacomo Agostini (Ita), MV Agusta, 90.97mph/146.40kph
250cc: Bill Ivy (UK), Yamaha, 87.86mph/141.40kph
125cc: Phil Read (UK), Yamaha, 84.75mph/136.40kph
50cc: Hans-Georg Anscheidt (FRG), Suzuki, 74.19mph/119.40kph
Sidecar: Helmut Fath/Wolfgang Kalauch (FRG), URS Fath, 78.97mph/127.10kph

SPANISH GRAND PRIX

Montjuich, Barcelona, 5 May
500cc
1 Giacomo Agostini (Ita), MV Agusta, 74.09mph/119.24kph
2 Jack Findlay (Aus), Norton
3 John Dodds (Aus), Norton
Fastest lap: Agostini, 75.62mph/121.77kph
Other winners:
250cc: Phil Read (UK), Yamaha, 73.48mph/118.25kph
125cc: Salvador Canellas (Spa), Bultaco, 69.29mph/111.52kph
50cc: Hans-Georg Anscheidt (FRG), Suzuki, 63.28mph/101.84kph

BRITISH GRAND PRIX (TOURIST TROPHY)

Isle of Man, 10–14 June
500cc
1 Giacomo Agostini (Ita), MV Agusta, 101.63mph/163.56kph
2 Brian Ball (UK), Seeley
3 Barry Randall (UK), Norton
Fastest lap: Agostini, 104.91mph/168.84kph
Other winners:
350cc: Giacomo Agostini (Ita), MV Agusta, 104.78mph/168.63kph
250cc: Bill Ivy (UK), Yamaha, 99.58mph/160.26kph
125cc: Phil Read (UK), Yamaha, 99.12mph/159.52kph
50cc: Barry Smith (Aus), Derbi, 72.90mph/117.32kph
Sidecar: Siegfried Schauzu/Horst Schneider (FRG), BMW, 91.09mph/146.60kph

DUTCH TT

Assen, 29 June
500cc
1 Giacomo Agostini (Ita), MV Agusta, 87.88mph/141.43kph
2 Jack Findlay (Aus), Matchless
3 John Cooper (UK), Seeley
Fastest lap: Agostini, 90.60mph/145.82kph
Other winners:
350cc: Giacomo Agostini (Ita), MV Agusta, 87.87mph/141.41kph
250cc: Bill Ivy (UK), Yamaha, 88.14mph/141.85kph
125cc: Phil Read (UK), Yamaha, 82.67mph/133.04kph
50cc: Paul Lodewijkx (Hol), Jamathi, 72.87mph/117.28kph
Sidecar: Johann Attenberger/Josef Schillinger (FRG), BMW, 80.83mph/130.09kph

THE WORLD ROAD RACE CHAMPIONSHIPS **1968**

BELGIAN GRAND PRIX

Spa-Francorchamps, 7 July
500cc
1 Giacomo Agostini (Ita), MV Agusta, 124.78mph/
200.87kph
2 Jack Findlay (Aus), Matchless
3 Derek Woodman (UK), Seeley
Fastest lap: Agostini, 129.58mph/208.55kph
Other winners:
250cc: Phil Read (UK), Yamaha, 116.40mph/187.34kph
50cc: Hans-Georg Anscheidt (FRG), Suzuki, 93.53mph/
150.52kph
Sidecar: Georg Auerbacher/Hermann Hahn (FRG), BMW,
108.74mph/175.07kph

EAST GERMAN GRAND PRIX

Sachsenring, 14 July
500cc
1 Giacomo Agostini (Ita), MV Agusta, 105.87mph/
170.38kph
2 Alberto Pagani (Ita), Linto
3 Jack Findlay (Aus), Matchless
Fastest lap: Agostini, 109.86mph/176.80kph
Other winners:
350cc: Giacomo Agostini (Ita), MV Agusta, 102.99mph/
165.74kph
250cc: Bill Ivy (UK), Yamaha, 103.05mph/165.85kph
125cc: Phil Read (UK), Yamaha, 97.34mph/156.65kph

CZECHOSLOVAK GRAND PRIX

Brno, 21 July
500cc
1 Giacomo Agostini (Ita), MV Agusta, 86.49mph/
139.19kph
2 Jack Findlay (Aus), Matchless
3 Gyula Marsovszky (Swi), Matchless
Fastest lap: Agostini, 98.05mph/157.80kph
Other winners:
350cc: Giacomo Agostini (Ita), MV Àgusta, 88.98mph/
143.20kph
250cc: Phil Read (UK), Yamaha, 92.34mph/148.61kph
125cc: Phil Read (UK), Yamaha, 85.25mph/137.20kph

FINNISH GRAND PRIX

Imatra, 4 August
500cc
1 Giacomo Agostini (Ita), MV Agusta, 89.35mph/
143.80kph
2 Jack Findlay (Aus), Matchless
3 Derek Woodman (UK), Seeley
Fastest lap: Agostini, 93.33mph/150.20kph
Other winners:
250cc: Phil Read (UK), Yamaha, 79.60mph/128.20kph
125cc: Phil Read (UK), Yamaha, 85.38mph/137.40kph
Sidecar: Helmut Fath/Wolfgang Kalauch (FRG), URS
Fath, 77.98mph/125.50kph

ULSTER GRAND PRIX

Dundrod Circuit, Belfast, 17 August
500cc
1 Giacomo Agostini (Ita), MV Agusta, 94.89mph/
152.71kph
2 Bob Fitton (UK), Norton
3 John Hartle (UK), Metisse
Fastest lap: Agostini, 95.57mph/153.80kph
Other winners:
350cc: Giacomo Agostini (Ita), MV Agusta, 102.74mph/
165.34kph
250cc: Bill Ivy (UK), Yamaha, 97.48mph/156.88kph
125cc: Bill Ivy (UK), Yamaha, 99.65mph/160.37kph

ITALIAN GRAND PRIX
(GRAND PRIX DES NATIONS)

Monza, 15 September
500cc
1 Giacomo Agostini (Ita), MV Agusta, 110.76mph/
178.25kph
2 Renzo Pasolini (Ita), Benelli
3 Angelo Bergamonti (Ita), Paton
Fastest lap: Agostini, 113.59mph/182.80kph
Other winners:
350cc: Giacomo Agostini (Ita), MV Agusta, 106.33mph/
171.12kph
250cc: Phil Read (UK), Yamaha, 110.73mph/178.21kph
125cc: Bill Ivy (UK), Yamaha, 106.40mph/171.23kph

LEADING CHAMPIONSHIP POSITIONS

500cc
Riders
1 Giacomo Agostini (Ita) 48(80)pts
2 Jack Findlay (Aus) 34(36)pts
3 Gyula Marsovszky (Swi) 10pts
4 Bob Fitton (UK) 9pts
5 Alberto Pagani (Ita) 9pts
6 Peter Williams (UK) 9pts
Manufacturers
1 MV Agusta 48(80)pts
2 Matchless 32(39)pts
3 Norton 28(34)pts

350cc
1 Giacomo Agostini (Ita) 32(56)pts

2 Renzo Pasolini (Ita) 18pts
3 Kel Carruthers (Aus) 17pts
Manufacturers' title: MV Agusta

250cc
1 Phil Read (UK) 46(52)pts
2 Bill Ivy (UK) 46(52)pts
3 Heinz Rosner (GDR) 32(39)pts
Manufacturers' title: Yamaha
*Riders' championship decided by
aggregate times of Read and Ivy in
the four races they both completed*

125cc
1 Phil Read (UK) 40(60)pts

2 Bill Ivy (UK) 34pts
3 Ginger Molloy (NZ) 15pts
Manufacturers' title: Yamaha

50cc
1 Hans-Georg Anscheidt (FRG) 30pts
2 Paul Lodewijkx (FRG) 17pts
3 Barry Smith (Aus) 15pts
Manufacturers' title: Suzuki

Sidecar
1 Helmut Fath (FRG) 21pts
2 Johann Attenberger (FRG) 17pts
3 Siegfried Schauzu (FRG) 16pts
Manufacturers' title: BMW

1969

SPANISH GRAND PRIX

Jarama, 4 May
500cc
1 Giacomo Agostini (Ita), MV Agusta, 69.37mph/
111.64kph
2 Angelo Bergamonti (Ita), Paton
3 Ginger Molloy (NZ), Bultaco
Fastest lap: Agostini, 71.96mph/115.81kph
Other winners:
350cc: Giacomo Agostini (Ita), MV Agusta, 61.71mph/
99.32kph
250cc: Santiago Herrero (Spa), Ossa, 57.57mph/92.65kph
125cc: Cees van Dongen (Hol), Suzuki, 56.24mph/90.51kph
50cc: Aalt Toersen (Hol), Kreidler, 45.05mph/72.50kph

WEST GERMAN GRAND PRIX

Hockenheim, 11 May
500cc
1 Giacomo Agostini (Ita), MV Agusta, 112.78mph/
181.51kph
2 Karl Hoppe (FRG), Metisse
3 Jack Findlay (Aus), Linto
Fastest lap: Agostini, 116.58mph/187.62kph
Other winners:
350cc: Giacomo Agostini (Ita), MV Agusta, 111.72mph/
179.79kph
250cc: Kent Andersson (Swe), Yamaha, 101.29mph/
163.02kph
125cc: Dave Simmonds (UK), Kawasaki, 96.93mph/
155.99kph
50cc: Aalt Toersen (Hol), Kreidler, 85.05mph/136.87kph
Sidecar: Klaus Enders/Rolf Engelhardt (FRG), BMW,
97.24mph/156.49kph

FRENCH GRAND PRIX

Le Mans, 18 May
500cc
1 Giacomo Agostini (Ita), MV Agusta, 78.04mph/
125.59kph
2 Billie Nelson (UK), Paton
3 Karl Auer (Aut), Matchless
Fastest lap: Agostini, 83.81mph/134.07kph
Other winners:
250cc: Santiago Herrero (Spa), Ossa, 81.60mph/
131.32kph
125cc: Jean Aureal (Fra), Yamaha, 73.38mph/118.09kph
50cc: Aalt Toersen (Hol), Kreidler, 69.41mph/111.70kph
Sidecar: Helmut Fath/Wolfgang Kalauch (FRG), URS
Fath, 76.68mph/123.40kph

BRITISH GRAND PRIX (TOURIST TROPHY)

Isle of Man, 9–13 June
500cc
1 Giacomo Agostini (Ita), MV Agusta, 104.75mph/

168.58kph
2 Alan Barnett (UK), Metisse
3 Tom Dickie (UK), Seeley
Fastest lap: Agostini, 106.25mph/170.99kph
Other winners:
350cc: Giacomo Agostini (Ita), MV Agusta, 101.81mph/
163.85kph
250cc: Kel Carruthers (Aus), Benelli, 95.95mph/
154.42kph
125cc: Dave Simmonds (UK), Kawasaki, 91.08mph/
146.58kph
Sidecar: Klaus Enders/Rolf Engelhardt (FRG), BMW,
92.48mph/148.83kph

DUTCH TT

Assen, 28 June
500cc
1 Giacomo Agostini (Ita), MV Agusta, 89.09mph/
143.75kph
2 Peter Williams (UK), Matchless
3 Alan Barnett (UK), Metisse
Fastest lap: Agostini, 90.96mph/146.38kph
Other winners:
350cc: Giacomo Agostini (Ita), MV Agusta, 89.22mph/
143.58kph
250cc: Renzo Pasolini (Ita), Benelli, 86.26mph/138.83kph
125cc: Dave Simmonds (UK), Kawasaki, 81.65mph/
131.26kph
50cc: Barry Smith (Aus), Derbi, 74.37mph/119.69kph
Sidecar: Helmut Fath/Wolfgang Kalauch (FRG), URS
Fath, 80.46mph/129.49kph

BELGIAN GRAND PRIX

Spa-Francorchamps, 6 July
500cc
1 Giacomo Agostini (Ita), MV Agusta, 125.85mph/
202.53kph
2 Percy Tait (UK), Triumph
3 Alan Barnett (UK), Metisse
Fastest lap: Agostini, 130.66mph/210.28kph
Other winners:
250cc: Santiago Herrero (Spa), Ossa, 117.96mph/
189.84kph
125cc: Dave Simmonds (UK), Kawasaki, 106.89mph/
172.02kph
50cc: Barry Smith (Aus), Derbi, 89.91mph/144.70kph
Sidecar: Helmut Fath/Wolfgang Kalauch (FRG), URS
Fath, 111.79mph/179.91kph

EAST GERMAN GRAND PRIX

Sachsenring, 13 July
500cc
1 Giacomo Agostini (Ita), MV Agusta, 94.23mph/
151.65kph
2 Billie Nelson (UK), Paton
3 Steve Ellis (UK), Linto
Fastest lap: Agostini, 95.44mph/153.59kph
Other winners:
350cc: Giacomo Agostini (Ita), MV Agusta, 92.52mph/
148.90kph

250cc: Renzo Pasolini (Ita), Benelli, 93.14mph/149.90kph
125cc: Dave Simmonds (UK), Kawasaki, 88.61mph/142.60kph
50cc: Angel Nieto (Spa), Derbi, 79.28mph/127.59kph

CZECHOSLOVAK GRAND PRIX

Brno, 20 July
500cc
1 Giacomo Agostini (Ita), MV Agusta, 96.18mph/154.78kph
2 Gyula Marsovszky (Swi), Linto
3 Bohumil Stasa (Cze), CZ
Fastest lap: Agostini, 101.80mph/163.83kph
Other winners:
350cc: Giacomo Agostini (Ita), MV Agusta, 95.80mph/154.17kph
250cc: Renzo Pasolini (Ita), Benelli, 92.58mph/148,99kph
125cc: Dave Simmonds (UK), Kawasaki, 87.60mph/140.98kph
50cc: Paul Lodewijkx (Hol), Jamathi, 74.90mph/120.54kph

FINNISH GRAND PRIX

Imatra, 3 August
500cc
1 Giacomo Agostini (Ita), MV Agusta, 89.35mph/143.80kph
2 Billie Nelson (UK), Paton
3 Godfrey Nash (UK), Norton
Fastest lap: Agostini, 93.76mph/150.89kph
Other winners:
350cc: Giacomo Agostini (Ita), MV Agusta, 89.23mph/143.60kph
250cc: Kent Andersson (Swe), Yamaha, 86.69mph/139.51kph
125cc: Dave Simmonds (UK), Kawasaki, 79.60mph/128.10kph
Sidecar: Klaus Enders/Rolf Engelhardt (FRG), BMW, 78.10mph/125.69kph

ULSTER GRAND PRIX

Dundrod Circuit, Belfast, 16 August
500cc
1 Giacomo Agostini (Ita), MV Agusta, 103.74mph/
166.95kph
2 Brian Steenson (Ire), Seeley
3 Malcolm Uphill (UK), Norton
Fastest lap: Agostini, 107.66mph/173.26kph
Other winners:
350cc: Giacomo Agostini (Ita), MV Agusta, 99.01mph/159.34kph
250cc: Kel Carruthers (Aus), Benelli, 93.61mph/150.65kph
50cc: Angel Nieto (Spa), Derbi, 80.20mph/129.07kph
Sidecar: Klaus Enders/Rolf Engelhardt (FRG), BMW, 88.94mph/143.14kph

ITALIAN GRAND PRIX
(GRAND PRIX DES NATIONS)

Imola, 7 September
500cc
1 Alberto Pagani (Ita), Linto, 93.48mph/150.44kph
2 Gilberto Milani (Ita), Aermacchi
3 John Dodds (Aus), Linto
Fastest lap: Dodds, 95.65mph/153.93kph
Other winners:
350cc: Phil Read (UK), Yamaha, 93.89mph/151.10kph
250cc: Phil Read (UK), Yamaha, 94.28mph/151.73kph
125cc: Dave Simmonds (UK), Kawasaki, 87.01mph/140.17kph
50cc: Paul Lodewijkx (Hol), Jamathi, 76.24mph/122.70kph

YUGOSLAV GRAND PRIX

Opatija, 14 September
500cc
1 Godfrey Nash (UK), Norton, 79.61mph/128.12kph
2 Franco Trabalzini (Ita), Norton
3 Steve Ellis (UK), Linto
Fastest lap: Nash, 81.65mph/131.40kph
Other winners:
350cc: Silvio Grassetti (Ita), Jawa, 87.92mph/141.49kph
250cc: Kel Carruthers (Aus), Benelli, 81.27mph/130.80kph
125cc: Dieter Braun (FRG), Suzuki, 76.49mph/123.10kph
50cc: Paul Lodewijkx (Hol), Jamathi, 74.13mph/119.30kph

LEADING CHAMPIONSHIP POSITIONS

500cc
Riders
1 Giacomo Agostini (Ita) 105(150)pts
2 Gyula Marsovszky (Swi) 47pts
3 Godfrey Nash (UK) 45pts
4 Billie Nelson (UK) 42pts
5 Alan Barnett (UK) 32pts
6 Steve Ellis (UK) 26pts
Manufacturers
1 MV Agusta 105(150)pts
2 Linto 73(86)pts
3 Norton 61(77)pts

350cc
1 Giacomo Agostini (Ita) 90(120)pts
2 Silvio Grassetti (Ita) 47pts
3 Giuseppe Visenzi (Ita) 45pts
Manufacturers' title: MV Agusta

250cc
1 Kel Carruthers (Aus) 89(103)pts
2 Kent Andersson (Swe) 84(108)pts
3 Santiago Herrero (Spa) 83(88)pts
Manufacturers' title: Benelli

125cc
1 Dave Simmonds (UK) 90(144)pts
2 Dieter Braun (FRG) 59pts

3 Cees van Dongen (Hol) 51pts
Manufacturers' title: Kawasaki

50cc
1 Angel Nieto (Spa) 76pts
2 Aalt Toersen (Hol) 75(93)pts
3 Barry Smith (Aus) 69(73)pts
Manufacturers' title: Derbi

Sidecar
1 Klaus Enders (FRG) 60(72)pts
2 Helmut Fath (FRG) 55pts
3 Georg Auerbacher (FRG) 40pts
Manufacturers' title: BMW

1970

WEST GERMAN GRAND PRIX

Nürburgring, 3 May
500cc
1 Giacomo Agostini (Ita), MV Agusta, 78.82mph/
126.86kph
2 Alan Barnett (UK), Seeley
3 Tommy Robb (UK), Seeley
Fastest lap: Agostini, 79.59mph/128.09kph
Other winners:
350cc: Giacomo Agostini (Ita), MV Agusta, 75.25mph/
121.10kph
250cc: Kel Carruthers (Aus), Yamaha, 73.38mph/
118.10kph
125cc: John Dodds (Aus), Aermacchi, 67.85mph/
109.19kph
50cc: Angel Nieto (Spa), Derbi, 64.62mph/104.00kph
Sidecar: Georg Auerbacher/Hermann Hahn (FRG), BMW,
74.69mph/120.20kph

FRENCH GRAND PRIX

Le Mans, 17 May
500cc
1 Giacomo Agostini (Ita), MV Agusta, 83.40mph/
134.22kph
2 Ginger Molloy (NZ), Kawasaki
3 Alberto Pagani (Ita), Linto
Fastest lap: Agostini, 86.13mph/136.61kph
Other winners:
250cc: Rod Gould (UK), Yamaha, 82.18mph/132.25kph
125cc: Dieter Braun (FRG), Suzuki, 76.30mph/122.79kph
50cc: Angel Nieto (Spa), Derbi, 70.59mph/113.60kph
Sidecar: Klaus Enders/Wolfgang Kalauch (FRG), BMW,
77.73mph/125.09kph

YUGOSLAV GRAND PRIX

Opatija, 24 May
500cc
1 Giacomo Agostini (Ita), MV Agusta, 92.21mph/
148.40kph
2 Angelo Bergamonti (Ita), Aermacchi
3 Robert Gallina (Ita), Paton
Fastest lap: Agostini, 95.44mph/153.59kph
Other winners:
350cc: Giacomo Agostini (Ita), MV Agusta, 92.58mph/
148.99kph
250cc: Santiago Herrero (Spa), Ossa, 89.17mph/
143.50kph
125cc: Dieter Braun (FRG), Suzuki, 84.07mph/135.30kph
50cc: Angel Nieto (Spa), Derbi, 76.62mph/123.31kph

BRITISH GRAND PRIX (TOURIST TROPHY)

Isle of Man, 8–12 June
500cc
1 Giacomo Agostini (Ita), MV Agusta, 101.52mph/
163.38kph

2 Peter Williams (UK), Matchless
3 Bill Smith (UK), Kawasaki
Fastest lap: Agostini, 105.29mph/169.44kph
Other winners:
350cc: Giacomo Agostini (Ita), MV Agusta, 101.77mph/
163.78kph
250cc: Kel Carruthers (Aus), Yamaha, 96.13mph/
154.71kph
125cc: Dieter Braun (FRG), Suzuki, 89.27mph/143.67kph
Sidecar: Klaus Enders/Wolfgang Kalauch (FRG), BMW,
92.93mph/149.56kph

DUTCH TT

Assen, 27 June
500cc
1 Giacomo Agostini (Ita), MV Agusta, 88.95mph/
143.16kph
2 Angelo Bergamonti (Ita), Aermacchi
3 Alberto Pagani (Ita), Linto
Fastest lap: Agostini, 90.97mph/146.40kph
Other winners:
350cc: Giacomo Agostini (Ita), MV Agusta, 90.35mph/
145.40kph
250cc: Rod Gould (UK), Yamaha, 86.35mph/138.97kph
125cc: Dieter Braun (FRG), Suzuki, 81.38mph/130.97kph
50cc: Angel Nieto (Spa), Derbi, 75.56mph/121.60kph
Sidecar: Georg Auerbacher/Hermann Hahn (FRG), BMW,
80.72mph/129.91kph

BELGIAN GRAND PRIX

Spa-Francorchamps, 5 July
500cc
1 Giacomo Agostini (Ita), MV Agusta, 111.06mph/
178.74kph
2 Christian Ravel (Fra), Kawasaki
3 Tommy Robb (UK), Seeley
Fastest lap: Agostini, 112.84mph/181.60kph
Other winners:
250cc: Rod Gould (UK), Yamaha, 106.85mph/171.96kph
125cc: Angel Nieto (Spa), Derbi, 101.09mph/162.69kph
50cc: Aalt Toersen (Hol), Jamathi, 90.04mph/144.91kph
Sidecar: Arsenius Butscher/Josef Hüber (FRG), BMW,
102.59mph/165.10kph

EAST GERMAN GRAND PRIX

Sachsenring, 12 July
500cc
1 Giacomo Agostini (Ita), MV Agusta, 105.79mph/
170.25kph
2 John Dodds (Aus), Linto
3 Martin Carney (UK), Kawasaki
Fastest lap: Agostini, 107.50mph/173.00kph
Other winners:
350cc: Giacomo Agostini (Ita), MV Agusta, 105.76mph/
170.19kph
250cc: Rod Gould (UK), Yamaha, 100.36mph/161.52kph
125cc: Angel Nieto (Spa), Derbi, 94.95mph/152.81kph
50cc: Aalt Toersen (Hol), Jamathi, 82.27mph/132.40kph

CZECHOSLOVAK GRAND PRIX

Brno, 17 July
350cc: Giacomo Agostini (Ita), MV Agusta, 96.06mph/
154.59kph
250cc: Kel Carruthers (Aus), Yamaha, 92.81mph/
149.37kph
125cc: Gilberto Parlotti (Ita), Morbidelli, 84.75mph/
136.39kph
50cc: Aalt Toersen (Hol), Jamathi, 75.50mph/119.90kph
Sidecar: Klaus Enders/Wolfgang Kalauch (FRG), BMW,
85.00mph/136.79kph

FINNISH GRAND PRIX

Imatra, 2 August
500cc
1 Giacomo Agostini (Ita), MV Agusta, 90.02mph/
144.88kph
2 Ginger Molloy (NZ), Kawasaki
3 Alberto Pagani (Ita), Linto
Fastest lap: Agostini, 94.51mph/152.10kph
Other winners:
350cc: Giacomo Agostini (Ita), MV Agusta, 90.91mph/
146.31kph
250cc: Rod Gould (UK), Yamaha, 86.11mph/138.58kph
125cc: Dave Simmonds (UK), Kawasaki, 78.54mph/
126.40kph
Sidecar: Klaus Enders/Rolf Engelhardt (FRG), BMW,
79.39mph/127.77kph

ULSTER GRAND PRIX

Dundrod Circuit, Belfast, 15 August
500cc
1 Giacomo Agostini (Ita), MV Agusta, 101.88mph/
163.96kph
2 Ginger Molloy (NZ), Kawasaki
3 Percy Tait (UK), Seeley
Fastest lap: Agostini, 107.14mph/172.42kph
Other winners:
350cc: Giacomo Agostini (Ita), MV Agusta, 102.61mph/
165.13kph

250cc: Kel Carruthers (Aus), Yamaha, 100.03mph/
160.98kph
50cc: Angel Nieto (Spa), Derbi, 82.40mph/132.61kph
Sidecar: Klaus Enders/Rolf Engelhardt (FRG), BMW,
85.82mph/138.11kph

ITALIAN GRAND PRIX
(GRAND PRIX DES NATIONS)

Monza, 13 September
500cc
1 Giacomo Agostini (Ita), MV Agusta, 124.05mph/
199.64kph
2 Angelo Bergamonti (Ita), MV Agusta
3 Silvano Bertarelli (Ita), Kawasaki
Fastest lap: Renzo Pasolini (Ita), Benelli, 124.45mph/
200.28kph
Other winners:
350cc: Giacomo Agostini (Ita), MV Agusta, 121.10mph/
194.89kph
250cc: Rod Gould (UK), Yamaha, 115.42mph/185.76kph
125cc: Angel Nieto (Spa), Derbi, 104.26mph/167.79kph
50cc: Jan de Vries (Hol), Kreidler, 91.96mph/148.00kph

SPANISH GRAND PRIX

Montjuich, Barcelona, 27 September
500cc
1 Angelo Bergamonti (Ita), MV Agusta, 75.14mph/
120.92kph
2 Ginger Molloy (NZ), Kawasaki
3 Giuseppe Mandolini (Ita), Guzzi
Fastest lap: Bergamonti, 77.36mph/124.50kph
Other winners:
350cc: Angelo Bergamonti (Ita), MV Agusta, 75.18mph/
120.99kph
250cc: Kent Andersson (Swe), Yamaha, 72.38mph/
116.49kph
125cc: Angel Nieto (Spa), Derbi, 70.34mph/113.20kph
50cc: Salvador Canellas (Spa), Derbi, 65.74mph/
105.80kph

LEADING CHAMPIONSHIP POSITIONS

500cc
Riders
1 Giacomo Agostini (Ita) 90(150)pts
2 Ginger Molloy (NZ) 62(71)pts
3 Angelo Bergamonti (Ita) 59pts
4 Tommy Robb (UK) 36pts
5 Alberto Pagani (Ita) 30pts
6 Alan Barnett (UK) 24pts
Manufacturers
1 MV Agusta 90(165)pts
2 Kawasaki 70(106)pts
3 Seeley 56(82)pts

350cc
1 Giacomo Agostini (Ita) 90(135)pts
2 Kel Carruthers (Aus) 58pts
3 Renzo Pasolini (Ita) 46pts
Manufacturers' title: MV Agusta

250cc
1 Rod Gould (UK) 102(124)pts
2 Kel Carruthers (Aus) 84pts
3 Kent Andersson (Swe) 67pts
Manufacturers' title: Yamaha

125cc
1 Dieter Braun (FRG) 84(92)pts
2 Angel Nieto (Spa) 72pts
3 Borge Jansson (Swe) 62(73)pts
Manufacturers' title: Suzuki

50cc
1 Angel Nieto (Spa) 87(105)pts
2 Aalt Toersen (Hol) 75(84)pts
3 Rudi Kunz (FRG) 66(88)pts
Manufacturers' title: Derbi

Sidecar
1 Klaus Enders (FRG) 75pts
2 Georg Auerbacher (FRG) 62(67)pts
3 Siegfried Schauzu (FRG) 56(66)pts
Manufacturers' title: BMW

1971

AUSTRIAN GRAND PRIX

Salzburgring, 9 May
500cc
1 Giacomo Agostini (Ita), MV Agusta, 107.13mph/
172.41kph
2 Keith Turner (NZ), Suzuki
3 Eric Offenstadt (Fra), Kawasaki
Fastest lap: Agostini, 110.10mph/177.19kph
Other winners:
350cc: Giacomo Agostini (Ita), MV Agusta, 106.38mph/
171.20kph
250cc: Silvio Grassetti (Ita), MZ, 104.28mph/167.83kph
125cc: Angel Nieto (Spa), Derbi, 97.53mph/156.96kph
50cc: Jan de Vries (Hol), Kreidler, 87.13mph/140.22kph
Sidecar: Arsenius Butscher/Josef Hüber (FRG), BMW,
96.52mph/155.33kph

WEST GERMAN GRAND PRIX

Hockenheim, 16 May
500cc
1 Giacomo Agostini (Ita), MV Agusta, 100.86mph/
162.32kph
2 Rob Bron (Hol), Suzuki
3 Ron Chandler (UK), Kawasaki
Fastest lap: Agostini, 102.71mph/165.30kph
Other winners:
350cc: Giacomo Agostini (Ita), MV Agusta, 99.79mph/
160.60kph
250cc: Phil Read (UK), Yamaha, 95.94mph/154.40kph
125cc: Dave Simmonds (UK), Kawasaki, 90.84mph/
146.19kph
50cc: Jan de Vries (Hol), Kreidler, 82.95mph/133.50kph
Sidecar: Georg Auerbacher/Hermann Hahn (FRG), BMW,
90.41mph/145.50kph

BRITISH GRAND PRIX (TOURIST TROPHY)

Isle of Man, 9–12 June
500cc
1 Giacomo Agostini (Ita), MV Agusta, 102.59mph/
165.10kph
2 Peter Williams (UK), Matchless
3 Frank Perris (UK), Suzuki
Fastest lap: Agostini, 104.87mph/168.77kph
Other winners:
350cc: Tony Jefferies (UK), Yamsel, 89.91mph/
144.70kph
250cc: Phil Read (UK), Yamaha, 98.02mph/157.75kph
125cc: Charles Mortimer (UK), Yamaha, 83.96mph/
135.12kph
Sidecar: Siegfried Schauzu/Wolfgang Kalauch (FRG),
BMW, 86.21mph/138.74kph

DUTCH TT

Assen, 26 June
500cc
1 Giacomo Agostini (Ita), MV Agusta, 87.61mph/
140.99kph
2 Rob Bron (Hol), Suzuki
3 Dave Simmonds (UK), Kawasaki
Fastest lap: Agostini, 90.66mph/145.90kph
Other winners:
350cc: Giacomo Agostini (Ita), MV Agusta, 88.62mph/
142.62kph
250cc: Phil Read (UK), Yamaha, 85.61mph/137.78kph
125cc: Angel Nieto (Spa), Derbi, 83.41mph/134.24kph
50cc: Angel Nieto (Spa), Derbi, 75.86mph/122.08kph
Sidecar: Horst Owesle/Julius Kremer (FRG), Münch URS,
75.15mph/120.94kph

BELGIAN GRAND PRIX

Spa-Francorchamps, 4 July
500cc
1 Giacomo Agostini (Ita), MV Agusta, 123.51mph/
198.78kph
2 Eric Offenstadt (Fra), Kawasaki
3 Jack Findlay (Aus), Suzuki
Fastest lap: Agostini, 127.38mph/205.00kph
Other winners:
250cc: Silvio Grassetti (Ita), MZ, 119.55mph/192.40kph
125cc: Barry Sheene (UK), Suzuki, 110.31mph/
177.53kph
50cc: Jan de Vries (Hol), Kreidler, 97.86mph/157.49kph
Sidecar: Siegfried Schauzu/Wolfgang Kalauch (FRG),
BMW, 110.85mph/178.40kph

EAST GERMAN GRAND PRIX

Sachsenring, 11 July
500cc
1 Giacomo Agostini (Ita), MV Agusta, 104.21mph/
167.71kph
2 Keith Turner (NZ), Suzuki
3 Ernst Hiller (FRG), Kawasaki
Fastest lap: Agostini, 106.94mph/172.10kph
Other winners:
350cc: Giacomo Agostini (Ita), MV Agusta, 104.21mph/
167.71kph .
250cc: Dieter Braun (FRG), Yamaha, 102.20mph/
164.47kph
125cc: Angel Nieto (Spa), Derbi, 96.07mph/154.61kph
50cc: Angel Nieto (Spa), Derbi, 85.48mph/137.57kph

CZECHOSLOVAK GRAND PRIX

Brno, 18 July
350cc: Jarno Saarinen (Fin), Yamaha, 80.29mph/
129.21kph
250cc: Janos Drapal (Hun), Yamaha, 81.26mph/
130.36kph
125cc: Angel Nieto (Spa), Derbi, 76.90mph/123.76kph
50cc: Barry Sheene (UK), Kreidler, 67.17mph/108.10kph
Sidecar: Siegfried Schauzu/Wolfgang Kalauch (FRG),
BMW, 78.40mph/126.17kph

SWEDISH TT

Anderstorp, 25 July
500cc
1 Giacomo Agostini (Ita), MV Agusta, 70.29mph/
113.13kph
2 Keith Turner (NZ), Suzuki
3 Tommy Robb (UK), Seeley
Fastest lap: Agostini, 73.06mph/117.58kph
Other winners:
350cc: Giacomo Agostini (Ita), MV Agusta, 79.90mph/
128.59kph
250cc: Rod Gould (UK), Yamaha, 79.53mph/128.00kph
125cc: Barry Sheene (UK), Suzuki, 75.97mph/122.26kph
50cc: Angel Nieto (Spa), Derbi, 71.46mph/115.00kph

FINNISH GRAND PRIX

Imatra, 1 August
500cc
1 Giacomo Agostini (Ita), MV Agusta, 90.17mph/
145.12kph
2 Dave Simmonds (UK), Kawasaki
3 Rob Bron (Hol), Suzuki
Fastest lap: Agostini, 94.07mph/151.39kph
Other winners:
350cc: Giacomo Agostini (Ita), MV Agusta, 89.16mph/
143.49kph
250cc: Rod Gould (UK), Yamaha, 87.44mph/140.72kph
125cc: Barry Sheene (UK), Suzuki, 81.58mph/131.29kph
Sidecar: Horst Owesle (FRG)/Peter Rutterford (UK),
Münch URS, 79.97mph/128.70kph

ULSTER GRAND PRIX

Dundrod Circuit, Belfast, 14 August
500cc
1 Jack Findlay (Aus), Suzuki, 95.01mph/152.90kph
2 Rob Bron (Hol), Suzuki
3 Tommy Robb (UK), Seeley
Fastest lap: Findlay, 97.00mph/156.11kph

Other winners:
350cc: Peter Williams (UK), MZ, 88.31mph/142.12kph
250cc: Ray McCullough (Ire), Yamsel, 92.74mph/
149.25kph
Sidecar: Horst Owesle (FRG)/Peter Rutterford (UK),
Münch URS, 91.13mph/146.66kph

ITALIAN GRAND PRIX
(GRAND PRIX DES NATIONS)

Monza, 12 September
500cc
1 Alberto Pagani (Ita), MV Agusta, 117.99mph/189.89kph
2 Gianpiero Zubani (Ita), Kawasaki
3 Dave Simmonds (UK), Kawasaki
Fastest lap: Giacomo Agostini (Ita), MV Agusta,
127.09mph/204.53kph
Other winners:
350cc: Jarno Saarinen (Fin), Yamaha, 116.19mph/
186.99kph
250cc: Gyula Marsovszky (Swi), Yamaha, 115.24mph/
185.46kph
125cc: Gilberto Parlotti (Ita), Morbidelli, 108.23mph/
174.18kph
50cc: Jan de Vries (Hol), Kreidler, 95.57mph/153.81kph

SPANISH GRAND PRIX

Jarama, 26 September
500cc
1 Dave Simmonds (UK), Kawasaki, 67.80mph/109.11kph
2 Kaarlo Koivuniemi (Fin), Seeley
3 Eric Offenstadt (Fra), Kawasaki
Fastest lap: Kurt-Ivan Carlsson (Swe), Yamaha,
70.58mph/113.59kph
Other winners:
350cc: Teppi Länsivuori (Fin), Yamaha, 68.51mph/
110.26kph
250cc: Jarno Saarinen (Fin), Yamaha, 69.99mph/
112.64kph
125cc: Angel Nieto (Spa), Derbi, 67.51mph/108.65kph
50cc: Jan de Vries (Hol), Kreidler, 62.10mph/99.94kph

LEADING CHAMPIONSHIP POSITIONS

500cc
Riders
1 Giacomo Agostini (Ita) 90(120)pts
2 Keith Turner (NZ) 58(67)pts
3 Rob Bron (Hol) 57pts
4 Dave Simmonds (UK) 52pts
5 Jack Findlay (Aus) 50(51)pts
6 Eric Offenstadt (Fra) 32pts
Manufacturers
1 MV Agusta 90(135)pts
2 Suzuki 75(117)pts
3 Kawasaki 71(99)pts

350cc
1 Giacomo Agostini (Ita) 90pts
2 Jarno Saarinen (Fin) 63pts
3 Karl-Ivan Carlsson (Swe) 39pts
Manufacturers' title: MV Agusta

250cc
1 Phil Read (UK) 73pts
2 Rod Gould (UK) 68pts
3 Jarno Saarinen (Fin) 64(67)pts
Manufacturers' title: Yamaha

125cc
1 Angel Nieto (Spa) 87pts
2 Barry Sheene (UK) 79(109)pts
3 Borje Jansson (Swe) 39pts
Manufacturers' title: Derbi

50cc
1 Jan de Vries (Hol) 75(97)pts
2 Angel Nieto (Spa) 69(89)pts
3 Jos Schurgers (Hol) 42pts
Manufacturers' title: Kreidler

Sidecar
1 Horst Owesle (FRG) 69(75)pts
2 Siegfried Schauzu (FRG) 57pts
3 Arsenius Butscher (FRG) 57(68)pts
Manufacturers' title: BMW

1972

WEST GERMAN GRAND PRIX

Nürburgring, 30 April
500cc
1 Giacomo Agostini (Ita), MV Agusta, 87.77mph/
141.25kph
2 Alberto Pagani (Ita), MV Agusta
3 Kim Newcombe (NZ), König
Fastest lap: Agostini, 89.47mph/143.99kph
Other winners:
350cc: Jarno Saarinen (Fin), Yamaha, 87.61mph/
140.99kph
250cc: Hideo Kanaya (Jap), Yamaha, 85.51mph/
137.61kph
125cc: Gilberto Parlotti (Ita), Morbidelli, 82.39mph/
132.59kph
50cc: Jan de Vries (Hol), Kreidler, 72.02mph/115.90kph
Sidecar: Siegfried Schauzu/Wolfgang Kalauch (FRG),
BMW, 80.16mph/129.01kph

FRENCH GRAND PRIX

Clermont-Ferrand, 7 May
500cc
1 Giacomo Agostini (Ita), MV Agusta, 77.60mph/
124.89kph
2 Christian Bourgeois (Fra), Yamaha
3 Rob Bron (Hol), Suzuki
Fastest lap: Agostini, 78.42mph/126.20kph
Other winners:
350cc: Jarno Saarinen (Fin), Yamaha, 72.38mph/
116.48kph
250cc: Phil Read (UK), Yamaha, 78.24mph/125.92kph
125cc: Gilberto Parlotti (Ita), Morbidelli, 73.57mph/
118.40kph
Sidecar: Heinz Luthringhauser/Jurgen Cusnick (FRG),
BMW, 70.83mph/113.99kph

AUSTRIAN GRAND PRIX

Salzburgring, 14 May
500cc
1 Giacomo Agostini (Ita), MV Agusta, 107.60mph/
173.16kph
2 Guido Mandracci (Ita), Suzuki
3 Bo Granath (Swe), Husqvarna
Fastest lap: Agostini, 113.25mph/182.26kph
Other winners:
350cc: Giacomo Agostini (Ita), MV Agusta, 110.34mph/
177.58kph
250cc: Borje Jansson (Swe), Derbi, 105.31mph/
169.48kph
125cc: Angel Nieto (Spa), Derbi, 99.16mph/159.58kph
Sidecar: Klaus Enders/Rolf Engelhardt (FRG), BMW,
97.33mph/156.64kph

ITALIAN GRAND PRIX
(GRAND PRIX DES NATIONS)

Imola, 21 May
500cc
1 Giacomo Agostini (Ita), MV Agusta, 106.79mph/
171.86kph
2 Alberto Pagani (Ita), MV Agusta
3 Bruno Spaggiari (Ita), Ducati
Fastest lap: Agostini, 109.36mph/176.00kph
Other winners:
350cc: Giacomo Agostini (Ita), MV Agusta, 101.12mph/
162.74kph
250cc: Renzo Pasolini (Ita), Aermacchi, 97.77mph/
157.34kph
125cc: Angel Nieto (Spa), Derbi, 92.02mph/148.09kph
50cc: Jan de Vries (Hol), Kreidler, 87.95mph/131.89kph

BRITISH GRAND PRIX (TOURIST TROPHY)

Isle of Man, 3–9 June
500cc
1 Giacomo Agostini (Ita), MV Agusta, 104.02mph/
167.40kph
2 Alberto Pagani (Ita), MV Agusta
3 Mick Grant (UK), Kawasaki
Fastest lap: Agostini, 105.39mph/169.61kph
Other winners:
350cc: Giacomo Agostini (Ita), MV Agusta, 102.03mph/
164.20kph
250cc: Phil Read (UK), Yamaha, 99.68mph/160.42kph
125cc: Charles Mortimer (UK), Yamaha, 87.49mph/
140.80kph
Sidecar: Siegfried Schauzu/Wolfgang Kalauch (FRG),
BMW, 91.85mph/147.82kph

YUGOSLAV GRAND PRIX

Opatija, 18 June
500cc
1 Alberto Pagani (Ita), MV Agusta, 90.22mph/145.20kph
2 Charles Mortimer (UK), Yamaha
3 Paul Eickelberg (FRG), König
Fastest lap: Giacomo Agostini (Ita), MV Agusta, no *official*
speed recorded
Other winners:
350cc: Janos Drapal (Hun), Yamaha, 91.73mph/
147.63kph
250cc: Renzo Pasolini (Ita), Aermacchi, 89.85mph/
144.60kph
125cc: Kent Andersson (Swe), Yamaha, 83.88mph/
134.99kph
50cc: Jan Bruins (Hol), Kreidler, 72.42mph/116.55kph

DUTCH TT

Assen, 24 June
500cc
1 Giacomo Agostini (Ita), MV Agusta, 90.39mph/
145.47kph
2 Alberto Pagani (Ita), MV Agusta
3 Bruno Kneubühler (Swi), Yamaha
Fastest lap: Agostini, 92.06mph/148.16kph

Other winners:
350cc: Giacomo Agostini (Ita), MV Agusta, 91.15mph/
146.69kph
250cc: Rod Gould (UK), Yamaha, 90.22mph.145.20kph
125cc: Angel Nieto (Spa), Derbi, 83.60mph/134.54kph
50cc: Angel Nieto (Spa), Derbi, 78.18mph/125.82kph
Sidecar: Klaus Enders/Rolf Engelhardt (FRG), BMW,
82.81mph/133.27kph

BELGIAN GRAND PRIX

Spa-Francorchamps, 2 July
500cc
1 Giacomo Agostini (Ita), MV Agusta, 121.86mph/
196.12kph
2 Alberto Pagani (Ita), MV Agusta
3 Rod Gould (UK), Yamaha
Fastest lap: Agostini, 126.16mph/203.03kph
Other winners:
250cc: Jarno Saarinen (Fin), Yamaha, 121.46mph/
195.46kph
125cc: Angel Nieto (Spa), Derbi, 113.38mph/182.47kph
50cc: Angel Nieto (Spa), Derbi, 96.17mph/154.77kph
Sidecar: Klaus Enders/Rolf Engelhardt (FRG), BMW,
110.27mph/177.46kph

EAST GERMAN GRAND PRIX

Sachsenring, 8–9 July
500cc
1 Giacomo Agostini (Ita), MV Agusta, 106.06mph/
170.69kph
2 Rod Gould (UK), Yamaha
3 Kim Newcombe (NZ), König
Fastest lap: Agostini, 107.76mph/173.42kph
Other winners:
350cc: Phil Read (UK), Yamaha, 105.77mph/170.22kph
250cc: Jarno Saarinen (Fin), Yamaha, 104.03mph/
167.42kph
125cc: Borje Jansson (Swe), Maico, 96.53mph/
155.35kph
50cc: Theo Timmer (Hol), Jamathi, 83.40mph/134.22kph

CZECHOSLOVAK GRAND PRIX

Brno, 16 July
500cc
1 Giacomo Agostini (Ita), MV Agusta, 99.64mph/
160.35kph
2 Jack Findlay (Aus), Jada
3 Bruno Kneubühler (Swi), Yamaha
Fastest lap: Agostini, 101.84mph/163.90kph
Other winners:
350cc: Jarno Saarinen (Fin), Yamaha, 99.58mph/
160.26kph
250cc: Jarno Saarinen (Fin), Yamaha, 96.12mph/
154.69kph
125cc: Borje Jansson (Swe), Maico, 87.68mph/
141.11kph
Sidecar: Klaus Enders/Rolf Engelhardt (FRG), BMW,
89.08mph/143.36kph

SWEDISH TT

Anderstorp, 23 July
500cc
1 Giacomo Agostini (Ita), MV Agusta, 81.50mph/
131.15kph
2 Rod Gould (UK), Yamaha
3 Bo Granath (Swe), Husqvarna
Fastest lap: Agostini, 83.09mph/133.72kph
Other winners:
350cc: Giacomo Agostini (Ita), MV Agusta, 82.37mph/
132.56kph
250cc: Rod Gould (UK), Yamaha, 81.18mph/130.64kph
125cc: Angel Nieto (Spa), Derbi, 78.11mph/125.71kph
50cc: Jan de Vries (Hol), Kreidler, 73.39mph/118.11kph

FINNISH GRAND PRIX

Imatra, 30 July
500cc
1 Giacomo Agostini (Ita), MV Agusta, 91.68mph/
147.55kph
2 Alberto Pagani (Ita), MV Agusta
3 Rod Gould (UK), Yamaha
Fastest lap: Agostini, 95.81mph/154.19kph
Other winners:
350cc: Giacomo Agostini (Ita), MV Agusta, 93.33mph/
150.20kph
250cc: Jarno Saarinen (Fin), Yamaha, 88.06mph/
141.73kph
125cc: Kent Andersson (Swe), Yamaha, 82.83mph/
133.30kph
Sidecar: Chris Vincent/Mike Casey (UK), Münch URS,
81.52mph/131.19kph

SPANISH GRAND PRIX

Montjuich, Barcelona, 23 September
500cc
1 Charles Mortimer (UK), Yamaha, 74.06mph/119.19kph
2 Dave Simmonds (UK), Kawasaki
3 Jack Findlay (Aus), Jada
Fastest lap: Mortimer, 75.95mph/122.23kph
Other winners:
350c: Bruno Kneubühler (Swi), Yamaha, 74.23mph/
119.46kph
250cc: Renzo Pasolini (Ita), Aermacchi, 75.28mph/
121.15kph
125cc: Kent Andersson (Swe), Yamaha, 73.13mph/
117.69kph
50cc: Angel Nieto (Spa), Derbi, 68,19mph/109.74kph

LEADING CHAMPIONSHIP POSITIONS

500cc
Riders
1 Giacomo Agostini (Ita) 105(165)pts
2 Alberto Pagani (Ita) 87pts
3 Bruno Kneubühler (Swi) 54(57)pts
4 Rod Gould (UK) 52pts
5 Bo Granath (Swe) 47(51)pts
6 Charles Mortimer (UK) 42pts
Manufacturers
1 MV Agusta 105(180)pts
2 Yamaha 83(116)pts
3 Kawasaki 52(70)pts

350cc
1 Giacomo Agostini (Ita) 102(110)pts
2 Jarno Saarinen (Fin) 89(97)pts
3 Renzo Pasolini (Ita) 78(102)pts
Manufacturers' title: MV Agusta

250cc
1 Jarno Saarinen (Fin) 94(122)pts
2 Renzo Pasolini (Ita) 93(103)pts
3 Rod Gould (UK) 88(101)pts
Manufacturers' title: Yamaha

125cc
1 Angel Nieto (Spa) 97pts
2 Kent Andersson (Swe) 87(103)pts

3 Charles Mortimer (UK) 87(121)pts
Manufacturers' title: Derbi

50cc
1 Angel Nieto (Spa) 69(81)pts
2 Jan de Vries (Hol) 69(81)pts
3 Theo Timmer (Hol) 50pts
Manufacturers' title: Kreidler

Sidecar
1 Klaus Enders (FRG) 72pts
2 Heinz Luthringhauser (FRG) 63pts
3 Siegfried Schauzu (FRG) 62(80)pts
Manufacturers' title: BMW

1973

FRENCH GRAND PRIX

Paul Ricard, 22 April
500cc
1 Jarno Saarinen (Fin), Yamaha, 94.27mph/151.71kph
2 Phil Read (UK), MV Agusta
3 Hideo Kanaya (Jap), Yamaha
Fastest lap: Saarinen, 96.41mph/155.16kph
Other winners:
350cc: Giacomo Agostini (Ita), MV Agusta, 92.65mph/149.11kph
250cc: Jarno Saarinen (Fin), Yamaha, 90.72mph/146.01kph
125cc: Kent Andersson (Swe), Yamaha, 85.49mph/137.58kph
Sidecar: Klaus Enders/Rolf Engelhardt (FRG), BMW, 87.55mph/140.90kph

AUSTRIAN GRAND PRIX

Salzburgring, 6 May
500cc
1 Jarno Saarinen (Fin), Yamaha, 104.73mph/168.55kph
2 Hideo Kanaya (Jap), Yamaha
3 Kim Newcombe (NZ), König
Fastest lap: Saarinen, 106.81mph/171.89kph
Other winners:
350cc: Janos Drapal (Hun), Yamaha, 98.13mph/149.88kph
250cc: Jarno Saarinen (Fin), Yamaha, 97.69mph/157.22kph
125cc: Kent Andersson (Swe), Yamaha, 91.96mph/148.00kph
Sidecar: Klaus Enders/Rolf Engelhardt (FRG), BMW, 93.86mph/151.05kph

WEST GERMAN GRAND PRIX

Hockenheim, 13 May
500cc
1 Phil Read (UK), MV Agusta, 106.14mph/170.81kph
2 Werner Giger (Swi), Yamaha
3 Ernst Hiller (FRG), König
Fastest lap: Jarno Saarinen (Fin), Yamaha, 109.08mph/175.55kph
Other winners:
350cc: Teppi Länsivuori (Fin), Yamaha, 102.53mph/165.01kph
250cc: Jarno Saarinen (Fin), Yamaha, 99.17mph/159.60kph
125cc: Kent Andersson (Swe), Yamaha, 90.72mph/146.00kph
50cc: Theo Timmer (Hol), Jamathi, 79.54mph/128.01kph
Sidecar: Klaus Enders/Rolf Engelhardt (FRG), BMW, 94.20mph/151.60kph

ITALIAN GRAND PRIX (GRAND PRIX DES NATIONS)

Monza, 20 May
350cc: Giacomo Agostini (Ita), MV Agusta, 122.23mph/196.71kph
125cc: Kent Andersson (Swe), Yamaha, 106.56mph/171.49kph
50cc: Jan de Vries (Hol), Kreidler, 94.96mph/152.82kph

BRITISH GRAND PRIX (TOURIST TROPHY)

Isle of Man, 4-8 June
500cc
1 Jack Findlay (Aus), Suzuki, 101.55mph/163.43kph
2 Peter Williams (UK), Matchless
3 Charlie Sanby (UK), Suzuki
Fastest lap: Mick Grant (UK), Yamaha, 104.41mph/168.03kph
Other winners:
350cc: Tony Rutter (UK), Yamaha, 101.99mph/164.14kph
250cc: Charlie Williams (UK), Yamaha, 100.05mph/161.01kph
125cc: Tommy Robb (UK), Yamaha, 88.90mph/143.07kph

Sidecar: Klaus Enders/Rolf Engelhardt (FRG), BMW, 94.93mph/152.78kph

YUGOSLAV GRAND PRIX

Opatija, 16–17 June
500cc
1 Kim Newcombe (NZ), König, 90.60mph/145.80kph
2 Steve Ellis (UK), Yamaha
3 Gianfranco Bonera (Ita), Harley-Davidson
Fastest lap: Newcombe, 93.89mph/151.10kph
Other winners:
350cc: Janos Drapal (Hun), Yamaha, 94.40mph/151.92kph
250cc: Dieter Braun (FRG), Yamaha, 91.59mph/147.40kph
125cc: Kent Andersson (Swe), Yamaha, 85.30mph/137.28kph
50cc: Jan de Vries (Hol), Kreidler, 75.93mph/122.20kph

DUTCH TT

Assen, 23 June
500cc
1 Phil Read (UK), MV Agusta, 90.88mph/146.26kph
2 Kim Newcombe (NZ), König
3 Christian Bourgeois (Fra), Yamaha
Fastest lap: Giacomo Agostini (Ita), MV Agusta, 93.97mph/151.23kph
Other winners:
350cc: Giacomo Agostini (Ita), MV Agusta, 91.43mph/147.14kph
250cc: Dieter Braun (FRG), Yamaha, 88.52mph/142.45kph
125cc: Eugenio Lazzarini (Ita), Piovaticci, 82.74mph/133.16kph
50cc: Bruno Kneubühler (Swi), Kreidler, 76.59mph/123.26kph
Sidecar: Klaus Enders/Rolf Engelhardt (FRG), BMW, 83.89mph/135.01kph

BELGIAN GRAND PRIX

Spa-Francorchamps, 1 July
500cc
1 Giacomo Agostini (Ita), MV Agusta, 128.51mph/206.81kph
2 Phil Read (UK), MV Agusta
3 Jack Findlay (Aus), Suzuki
Fastest lap: Agostini, 130.93mph/210.71kph
Other winners:
250cc: Teppi Länsivuori (Fin), Yamaha, 122.35mph/196.91kph
125cc: Jos Schurgers (Hol), Bridgestone, 111.58mph/179.57kph
50cc: Jan de Vries (Hol), Kreidler, 99.95mph/160.85kph
Sidecar: Klaus Enders/Rolf Engelhardt (FRG), BMW, 113.53mph/182.71kph

CZECHOSLOVAK GRAND PRIX

Brno, 15 July
500cc
1 Giacomo Agostini (Ita), MV Agusta, 98.87mph/

159.11kph
2 Phil Read (UK), MV Agusta
3 Bruno Kneubühler (Swi), Yamaha
Fastest lap: Agostini, 100.79mph/162.21kph
Other winners:
350cc: Teppi Länsivuori (Fin), Yamaha, 99.05mph/159.41kph
250cc: Dieter Braun (FRG), Yamaha, 99.59mph/155.61kph
125cc: Otello Buscherini (Ita), Malanca, 87.10mph/140.17kph
Sidecar: Klaus Enders/Rolf Engelhardt (FRG), BMW, 86.68mph/139.50kph

SWEDISH TT

Anderstorp, 21 July
500cc
1 Phil Read (UK), MV Agusta, 82.87mph/133.36kph
2 Giacomo Agostini (Ita), MV Agusta
3 Kim Newcombe (NZ), König
Fastest lap: Agostini, 83.09mph/133.72kph
Other winners:
350cc: Teppi Länsivuori (Fin), Yamaha, 83.64mph/134.61kph
250cc: Dieter Braun (FRG), Yamaha, 80.76mph/129.98kph
125cc: Borje Jansson (Swe), Maico, 77.64mph/124.95kph
50cc: Jan de Vries (Hol), Kreidler, 72.37mph/116.47kph

FINNISH GRAND PRIX

Imatra, 29 July
500cc
1 Giacomo Agostini (Ita), MV Agusta, 91.73mph/147.63kph
2 Phil Read (UK), MV Agusta
3 Bruno Kneubühler (Swi), Yamaha
Fastest lap: Agostini, 93.35mph/150.23kph
Other winners:
350cc: Giacomo Agostini (Ita), MV Agusta, 92.21mph/148.40kph
250cc: Teppi Länsivuori (Fin), Yamaha, 88.42mph/142.30kph
125cc: Otello Buscherini (Ita), Malanca, 82.52mph/132.80kph
Sidecar: Kalvevi Rahko/Kari Laatikainen (Fin), Honda, 65.99mph/106.20kph

SPANISH GRAND PRIX

Jarama, 23 September
500cc
1 Phil Read (UK), MV Agusta, 72.05mph/115.96kph
2 Bruno Kneubühler (Swi), Yamaha
3 Werner Giger (Swi), Yamaha
Fastest lap: Read, 73.86mph/118.87kph
Other winners:
350cc: Adu Celso-Santos (Bra), Yamaha, 72.18mph/116.16kph
250cc: John Dodds (Aus), Yamaha, 71.30mph/114.75kph
125cc: Charles Mortimer (UK), Yamaha, 68.41mph/110.10kph
50cc: Jan de Vries (Hol), Kreidler, 65.21mph/104.95kph

LEADING CHAMPIONSHIP POSITIONS

500cc
Riders
1 Phil Read (UK) 84(108)pts
2 Kim Newcombe (NZ) 63(69)pts
3 Giacomo Agostini (Ita) 57pts
4 Werner Giger (Swi) 44(48)pts
5 Jack Findlay (Aus) 38pts
6 Bruno Kneubühler (Swi) 34pts
Manufacturers
1 MV Agusta 90(117)pts
2 Yamaha 76(115)pts
3 König 65(79)pts

350cc
1 Giacomo Agostini (Ita) 84pts
2 Teppi Länsivuori (Fin) 77pts
3 Phil Read (UK) 56pts
Manufacturers' title: Yamaha

250cc
1 Dieter Braun (FRG) 80pts
2 Teppi Länsivuori (Fin) 64pts
3 John Dodds (Aus) 58(62)pts
Manufacturers' title: Yamaha

125cc
1 Kent Andersson (Swe) 99pts
2 Charles Mortimer (UK) 75pts

3 Jos Schurgers (Hol) 70pts
Manufacturers' title: Yamaha

50cc
1 Jan de Vries (Hol) 60pts
2 Bruno Kneubühler (Swi) 51pts
3 Theo Timmer (Hol) 47pts
Manufacturers' title: Kreidler

Sidecar
1 Klaus Enders (FRG) 75(105)pts
2 Werner Schwärzel (FRG) 48pts
3 Siegfried Schauzu (FRG) 45pts
Manufacturers' title: BMW

1974

FRENCH GRAND PRIX

Clermont-Ferrand, 21 April
500cc
1 Phil Read (UK), MV Agusta, 82.94mph/133.48kph
2 Barry Sheene (UK), Suzuki
3 Gianfranco Bonera (Ita), MV Agusta
Fastest lap: Giacomo Agostini (Ita), Yamaha, 84.83mph/
136.52kph
Other winners:
350cc: Giacomo Agostini (Ita), Yamaha, 82.48mph/
132.74kph
125cc: Kent Andersson (Swe), Yamaha, 76.91mph/
123.77kph
50cc: Henk van Kessel (Hol), Kreidler, 69.22mph/
111.40kph
Sidecar: Siegfried Schauzu/Wolfgang Kalauch (FRG),
BMW, 72.46mph/116.61kph

WEST GERMAN GRAND PRIX

Nürburgring, 28 April
500cc
1 Edmond Czihak (FRG), Yamaha, 82.44mph/132.68kph
2 Helmut Kassner (FRG), Yamaha
3 W Kaletsch (FRG), Yamaha
Fastest lap: Czihak, 83.26mph/133.99kph
Other winners:
350cc: Helmut Kassner (FRG), Yamaha, 85.81mph/
138.10kph
250cc: Helmut Kassner (FRG), Yamaha, 83.41mph/
134.24kph
125cc: Fritz Reitmaier (FRG), Maico, 85.87mph/
122.10kph
50cc: Ingo Emmerich (FRG), Kreidler, 68.10mph/
109.60kph
Sidecar: Werner Schwärzel/Karl Kleis (FRG), König,
84.11mph/135.36kph

AUSTRIAN GRAND PRIX

Salzburgring, 5 May
500cc
1 Giacomo Agostini (Ita), Yamaha, 97.64mph/157.14kph
2 Gianfranco Bonera (Ita), MV Agusta
3 Barry Sheene (UK), Suzuki
Fastest lap: Bonera, 99.24mph/159.71kph
Other winners:
350cc: Giacomo Agostini (Ita), Yamaha, 93.02mph/
149.70kph
125cc: Kent Andersson (Swe), Yamaha, 90.53mph/
145.69kph
Sidecar: Siegfried Schauzu/Wolfgang Kalauch (FRG),
BMW, 85.06mph/136.89kph

ITALIAN GRAND PRIX
(GRAND PRIX DES NATIONS)

Imola, 19 May
500cc
1 Gianfranco Bonera (Ita), MV Agusta, 94.47mph/
152.04kph
2 Teppi Länsivuori (Fin), Yamaha
3 Phil Read (UK), MV Agusta
Fastest lap: Giacomo Agostini (Ita), Yamaha, 96.44mph/
155.20kph
Other winners:
350cc: Giacomo Agostini (Ita), Yamaha, 91.51mph/
147.27kph
250cc: Walter Villa (Ita), Harley-Davidson, 89.81mph/
144.53kph
125cc: Angel Nieto (Spa), Derbi, 83.45mph/134.30kph
50cc: Henk van Kessel (Hol), Kreidler, 74.41mph/
119.75kph
Sidecar: Klaus Enders/Rolf Engelhardt (FRG), Busch
Enders, 83.04mph/133.64kph

BRITISH GRAND PRIX (TOURIST TROPHY)

Isle of Man, 1–7 June
500cc
1 Phil Carpenter (UK), Yamaha, 96.99mph/156.09kph

2 Charlie Williams (UK), Yamaha
3 Tony Rutter (UK), Yamaha
Fastest lap: Williams, 101.92mph/164.02kph
Other winners:
350cc: Tony Rutter (UK), Yamaha, 104.44mph/168.08kph
250cc: Charlie Williams (UK), Yamaha, 94.16mph/
151.54kph
Sidecar: Heinz Luthringshauser/Hermann Hahn (FRG),
BMW, 92.27mph/148.49kph

DUTCH TT

Assen, 29 June
500cc
1 Giacomo Agostini (Ita), Yamaha, 93.96mph/151.21kph
2 Teppi Länsivuori (Fin), Yamaha
3 Phil Read (UK), MV Agusta
Fastest lap: Agostini, 95.85mph/154.25kph
Other winners:
350cc: Giacomo Agostini (Ita), Yamaha, 92.65mph/
149.11kph
250cc: Walter Villa (Ita), Harley-Davidson, 91.21mph/
146.97kph

125cc: Bruno Kneubühler (Swi), Yamaha, 86.62mph/
139.40kph
50cc: Herbert Rittberger (FRG), Kreidler, 77.85mph/
125.29kph
Sidecar: Klaus Enders/Rolf Engelhardt (FRG), Busch
Enders, 83.95mph/135.10kph

BELGIAN GRAND PRIX

Spa-Francorchamps, 7 July
500cc
1 Phil Read (UK), MV Agusta, 131.98mph/212.41kph
2 Giacomo Agostini (Ita), Yamaha
3 Dieter Braun (FRG), Yamaha
Fastest lap: Read, 133.42mph/214.72kph
Other winners:
250cc: Kent Andersson (Swe), Yamaha, 124.52mph/
200.40kph
125cc: Angel Nieto (Spa), Derbi, 115.01mph/185.09kph
50cc: Gerhard Throw (FRG), Kreidler, 100.35mph/
161.50kph
Sidecar: Rolf Steinhausen/Joseph Hüber (FRG), König,
116.80mph/187.97kph

The start of the 1974 Finnish Grand Prix (250cc). The eventual winner was Walter Villa on a Harley-Davidson

THE WORLD ROAD RACE CHAMPIONSHIPS 1974

SWEDISH TT

Anderstorp, 20–21 July
500cc
1 Teppi Länsivuori (Fin), Yamaha, 84.96mph/136.73kph
2 Phil Read (UK), MV Agusta
3 Pentti Korhonen (Fin), Yamaha
Fastest lap: Länsivuori, 86.13mph/138.62kph
Other winners:
350cc: Teppi Länsivuori (Fin), Yamaha, 85.00mph/
136.79kph
250cc: Takazumi Katayama (Jap), Yamaha, 82.92mph/
133.45kph
125cc: Kent Andersson (Swe), Yamaha, 78.11mph/
125.71kph
50cc: Henk van Kessel (Hol), Kreidler, 73.51mph/
118.30kph

FINNISH GRAND PRIX

Imatra, 27–28 July
500cc
1 Phil Read (UK), MV Agusta, 96.18mph/154.78kph
2 Gianfranco Bonera (Ita), MV Agusta
3 Teppi Länsivuori (Fin), Yamaha
Fastest lap: Länsivuori, 98.24mph/158.11kph
Other winners:
350cc: John Dodds (Aus), Yamaha, 90.36mph/145.42kph
250cc: Walter Villa (Ita), Harley-Davidson, 90.24mph/
145.22kph
50cc: Julien van Zeebroeck (Bel), Kreidler, 71.54mph/
115.13kph

CZECHOSLOVAK GRAND PRIX

Brno, 25 August
500cc
1 Phil Read (UK), MV Agusta, 102.30mph/164.64kph

2 Gianfranco Bonera (Ita), MV Agusta
3 Teppi Länsivuori (Fin), Yamaha
Fastest lap: Bonera, 103.86mph/167.15kph
Other winners:
250cc: Walter Villa (Ita), Harley-Davidson, 95.87mph/
154.29kph
125cc: Kent Andersson (Swe), Yamaha, 91.03mph/
146.50kph
50cc: Henk van Kessel (Hol), Kreidler, 79.72mph/
128.30kph
Sidecar: Werner Schwärzel/Karl Kleis (FRG), König,
92.27mph/148.49kph

YUGOSLAV GRAND PRIX

Opatija, 8 September
350cc: Giacomo Agostini (Ita), Yamaha, 96.56mph/
155.40kph
250cc: Charles Mortimer (UK), Yamaha, 92.01mph/
148.07kph
125cc: Kent Andersson (Swe), Yamaha, 87.30mph/
140.50kph
50cc: Henk van Kessel (Hol), Kreidler, 79.53mph/
127.99kph

SPANISH GRAND PRIX

Montjuich, Barcelona, 21–22 September
350cc: Victor Palomo (Spa), Yamaha, 78.16mph/
125.79kph
250cc: John Dodds (Aus), Yamaha, 78.06mph/125.63kph
125cc: Benjamin Grau (Spa), Derbi, 75.74mph/121.89kph
50cc: Henk van Kessel (Hol), Kreidler, 69.16mph/
111.30kph

LEADING CHAMPIONSHIP POSITIONS

500cc
Riders
1 Phil Read (UK) 82(92)pts
2 Gianfranco Bonera (Ita) 69(78)pts
3 Teppi Länsivuori (Fin) 67pts
4 Giacomo Agostini (Ita) 47pts
5 Jack Findlay (Aus) 34pts
6 Barry Sheene (UK) 30pts
Manufacturers
1 Yamaha 87(127)pts
2 MV Agusta 87(109)pts
3 Suzuki 52pts

350cc
1 Giacomo Agostini (Ita) 75pts
2 Dieter Braun (FRG) 62pts
3 Patrick Pons (Fra) 47pts
Manufacturers' title: Yamaha

250cc
1 Walter Villa (Ita) 77pts
2 Dieter Braun (FRG) 58pts
3 Patrick Pons (Fra) 50pts
Manufacturers' title: Yamaha

125cc:
1 Kent Andersson (Swe) 87(117)pts
2 Bruno Kneubühler (Swi) 63pts
3 Angel Nieto (Spa) 60pts
Manufacturers' title: Yamaha

50cc
1 Henk van Kessel (Hol) 90(114)pts
2 Herbert Rittberger (FRG) 65pts
3 Julien van Zeebroeck (Bel) 59pts
Manufacturers' title: Kreidler

Sidecar
1 Klaus Enders (FRG) 66pts
2 Werner Schwärzel (FRG) 64(70)pts
3 Siegfried Schauzu (FRG) 60(70)pts
Manufacturers' title: Busch

1975

FRENCH GRAND PRIX

Paul Ricard, 30 March
500cc
1 Giacomo Agostini (Ita), Yamaha, 95.00mph/152.88kph
2 Hideo Kanaya (Jap), Yamaha
3 Phil Read (UK), MV Agusta
Fastest lap: Kanaya, 97.13mph/156.32kph
Other winners:
350cc: Johnny Cecotto (Ven), Yamaha, 94.57mph/152.20kph
250cc: Johnny Cecotto (Ven), Yamaha, 93.22mph/150.03kph
125cc: Kent Andersson (Swe), Yamaha, 84.21mph/135.52kph
Sidecar: Hermann Schmid/Jean-Petit Matile (Swi), König, 85.02mph/136.83kph

SPANISH GRAND PRIX

Jarama, 20 April
350cc: Giacomo Agostini (Ita), Yamaha, 74.96mph/120.64kph
250cc: Walter Villa (Ita), Harley-Davidson, 72.82mph/117.19kph
125cc: Paolo Pileri (Ita), Morbidelli, 67.93mph/109.32kph
50cc: Angel Nieto (Spa), Kreidler, 62.95mph/101.31kph

AUSTRIAN GRAND PRIX

Salzburgring, 4 May
500cc
1 Hideo Kanaya (Jap), Yamaha, 113.44mph/182.57kph
2 Teppi Länsivuori (Fin), Suzuki
3 Phil Read (UK), MV Agusta
Fastest lap: Giacomo Agostini (Ita), Yamaha, 115.92mph/186.56kph
Other winners:
350cc: Hideo Kanaya (Jap), Yamaha, 110.42mph/177.70kph
125cc: Paolo Pileri (Ita), Morbidelli, 99.72mph/160.48kph
Sidecar: Rolf Steinhausen/Joseph Hüber (FRG), Busch König, 100.58mph/161.87kph

WEST GERMAN GRAND PRIX

Hockenheim, 11 May
500cc
1 Giacomo Agostini (Ita), Yamaha, 108.77mph/175.04kph
2 Phil Read (UK), MV Agusta
3 Teppi Länsivuori (Fin), Suzuki
Fastest lap: Agostini, 111.00mph/178.63kph
Other winners:
350cc: Johnny Cecotto (Ven) Yamaha, 105.69mph/170.09kph
250cc: Walter Villa (Ita), Harley-Davidson, 101.91mph/164.02kph
125cc: Paolo Pileri (Ita), Morbidelli, 97.03mph/156.15kph
50cc: Angel Nieto (Spa), Kreidler, 85.51mph/137.62kph

Sidecar: Rolf Biland/Freddy Freiburghaus (Swi), Seymaz Yamaha, 96.87mph/155.90kph

ITALIAN GRAND PRIX (GRAND PRIX DES NATIONS)

Imola, 18 May
500cc
1 Giacomo Agostini (Ita), Yamaha, 94.79mph/152.55kph
2 Phil Read (UK), MV Agusta
3 Hideo Kanaya (Jap), Yamaha
Fastest lap: Agostini, 96.20mph/154.81kph
Other winners:
350cc: Johnny Cecotto (Ven), Yamaha, 91.28mph/146.90kph
250cc: Walter Villa (Ita), Harley-Davidson, 89.43mph/143.93kph
125cc: Paolo Pileri (Ita), Morbidelli, 85.30mph/137.28kph
50cc: Angel Nieto (Spa), Kreidler, 75.36mph/121.28kph

BRITISH GRAND PRIX (TOURIST TROPHY)

Isle of Man, 2–6 June
500cc
1 Mick Grant (UK), Kawasaki, 100.27mph/161.37kph
2 John Williams (UK), Yamaha
3 Charles Mortimer (UK), Yamaha
Fastest lap: Grant, 102.93mph/165.65kph
Other winners:
350cc: Charlie Williams (UK), Yamaha, 104.38mph/167.98kph
250cc: Charles Mortimer (UK), Yamaha, 101.78mph/163.80kph
Sidecar: Rolf Steinhausen/Joseph Hüber (FRG), Busch König, 95.94mph/154.40kph

DUTCH TT

Assen, 28 June
500cc
1 Barry Sheene (UK), Suzuki, 95.71mph/154.03kph
2 Giacomo Agostini (Ita), Yamaha
3 Phil Read (UK), MV Agusta
Fastest lap: Sheene, 98.20mph/158.03kph
Other winners:
350cc: Dieter Braun (FRG), Yamaha, 93.32mph/150.18kph
250cc: Walter Villa (Ita), Harley-Davidson, 91.86mph/147.84kph
125cc: Paolo Pileri (Ita), Morbidelli, 86.99mph/140.00kph
50cc: Angel Nieto (Spa), Kreidler, 78.97mph/127.09kph
Sidecar: Werner Schwärzel/Andreas Hüber (FRG), König, 83.40mph/134.22kph

BELGIAN GRAND PRIX

Spa-Francorchamps, 6 July
500cc
1 Phil Read (UK), MV Agusta, 133.22mph/214.40kph
2 John Newbold (UK), Suzuki
3 Jack Findlay (Aus), Yamaha
Fastest lap: Barry Sheene (UK), Suzuki, 135.83mph/218.60kph

Other winners:
250cc: Johnny Cecotto (Ven), Yamaha, 125.17mph/201.45kph
125cc: Paolo Pileri (Ita), Morbidelli, 117.89mph/189.73kph
50cc: Julien van Zeebroeck (Bel), Kreidler, 101.72mph/163.70kph
Sidecar: Rolf Steinhausen/Joseph Hüber (FRG), Busch König, 116.39mph/187.31kph

SWEDISH TT

Anderstorp, 20 July
500cc
1 Barry Sheene (UK), Suzuki, 86.46mph/139.15kph
2 Phil Read (UK), MV Agusta
3 John Williams (UK), Yamaha
Fastest lap: Sheene, 88.25mph/142.02kph
Other winners:
250cc: Walter Villa (Ita), Harley-Davidson, 83.29mph/134.04kph
125cc: Paolo Pileri (Ita), Morbidelli, 80.98mph/130.32kph
50cc: Eugenio Lazzarini (Ita), Piovaticci, 74.58mph/120.02kph

FINNISH GRAND PRIX

Imatra, 27 July
500cc
1 Giacomo Agostini (Ita), Yamaha, 97.48mph/156.89kph
2 Teppi Länsivuori (Fin), Suzuki
3 Jack Findlay (Aus), Yamaha
Fastest lap: Agostini, 99.15mph/160.21kph
Other winners:
350cc: Johnny Cecotto (Ven), Yamaha, 94.76mph/152.50kph

250cc: Michel Rougerie (Fra), Harley-Davidson, 92.23mph/148.43kph
50cc: Angel Nieto (Spa), Kreidler, 77.90mph/125.37kph

CZECHOSLOVAK GRAND PRIX

Brno, 24 August
500cc
1 Phil Read (UK), MV Agusta, 107.47mph/172.96kph
2 Giacomo Agostini (Ita), Yamaha
3 Alex George (UK), Yamaha
Fastest lap: Teppi Länsivuori (Fin), Suzuki, 110.28mph/177.48kph
Other winners:
350cc: Otello Buscherini (Ita), Yamaha, 103.42mph/166.44kph
250cc: Michel Rougerie (Fra), Harley-Davidson, 103.22mph/166.11kph
125cc: Leif Gustavsson (Swe), Yamaha, 89.08mph/143.36kph
Sidecar: Werner Schwärzel/Andreas Hüber (FRG), König, 98.01mph/157.73kph

YUGOSLAV GRAND PRIX

Opatija, 21 September
350cc: Pentti Korhonen (Fin), Yamaha, 95.03mph/152.94kph
250cc: Dieter Braun (FRG), Yamaha, 94.05mph/151.36kph
125cc: Dieter Braun (FRG), Morbidelli, 90.63mph/145.85kph
50cc: Angel Nieto (Spa), Kreidler, 80.15mph/128.99kph

LEADING CHAMPIONSHIP POSITIONS

500cc
Riders
1 Giacomo Agostini (Ita) 84pts
2 Phil Read (UK) 76(96)pts
3 Hideo Kanaya (Jap) 45pts
4 Teppi Länsivuori (Fin) 40pts
5 John Williams (UK) 32pts
6 Barry Sheene (UK) 30pts
Manufacturers
1 Yamaha 87(131)pts
2 MV Agusta 78(98)pts
3 Suzuki 76(86)pts

350cc
1 Johnny Cecotto (Ven) 78pts
2 Giacomo Agostini (Ita) 59pts
3 Pentti Korhonen (Fin) 48(49)pts
Manufacturers' title: Yamaha

250cc
1 Walter Villa (Ita) 85pts
2 Michel Rougerie (Fra) 76(91)pts
3 Dieter Braun (FRG) 56(62)pts
Manufacturers' title: Harley-Davidson

125cc
1 Paolo Pileri (Ita) 90(115)pts
2 Pier Paolo Bianchi (Ita) 72(80)pts
3 Kent Andersson (Swe) 67(83)pts
Manufacturers' title: Morbidelli

50cc
1 Angel Nieto (Spa) 75(114)pts
2 Eugenio Lazzarini (Ita) 61(79)pts
3 Julien van Zeebroeck (Bel) 43pts
Manufacturers' title: Kreidler

Sidecar
1 Rolf Steinhausen (FRG) 57(75)pts
2 Werner Schwärzel (FRG) 54pts
3 Rolf Biland (Swi) 30pts
Manufacturers' title: Busch König

Right *Giacomo Agostini, the most successful Grand Prix rider of all time, in a familiar position – out in front*

1976

FRENCH GRAND PRIX

Le Mans, 25 April
500cc
1 Barry Sheene (UK), Suzuki, 91.64mph/147.48kph
2 Johnny Cecotto (Ven), Yamaha
3 Marco Lucchinelli (Ita), Suzuki
Fastest lap: Lucchinelli, 93.55mph/150.55kph
Other winners:
350cc: Walter Villa (Ita), Harley-Davidson, 89.91mph/
144.70kph
250cc: Walter Villa (Ita), Harley-Davidson, 86.72mph/
139.56kph
50cc: Herbert Rittberger (FRG), Kreidler, 69.60mph/
112.02kph
Sidecar: Rolf Biland (Swi)/Kenny Williams (UK), Seymaz
Yamaha, 82.53mph/132.81kph

AUSTRIAN GRAND PRIX

Salzburgring, 2 May
500cc
1 Barry Sheene (UK), Suzuki, 110.79mph/178.30kph

2 Marco Lucchinelli (Ita), Suzuki
3 Phil Read (UK), Suzuki
Fastest lap: Sheene, 113.01mph/181.89kph
Other winners:
350cc: Johnny Cecotto (Ven), Yamaha, 107.84mph/
173.55kph
125cc: Pier Paolo Bianchi (Ita), Morbidelli, 98.40mph/
158.36kph
Sidecar: Rolf Steinhausen/Joseph Hüber (FRG), Busch
König, 97.92mph/157.58kph

ITALIAN GRAND PRIX
(GRAND PRIX DES NATIONS)

Mugello, 16 May
500cc
1 Barry Sheene (UK), Suzuki, 90.60mph/145.81kph
2 Phil Read (UK), Suzuki
3 Virginio Ferrari (Ita), Suzuki
Fastest lap: Sheene and Read, 91.95mph/147.98kph
Other winners:
350cc: Johnny Cecotto (Ven), Yamaha, 88.84mph/
142.97kph
250cc: Walter Villa (Ita), Harley-Davidson, 86.96mph/
139.94kph
125cc: Pier Paolo Bianchi (Ita), Morbidelli, 83.38mph/
134.19kph
50cc: Angel Nieto (Spa), Bultaco, 76.11mph/122.48kph

YUGOSLAV GRAND PRIX

Opatija, 23 May
350cc: Oliver Chevallier (Fra), Yamaha, 93.63mph/
150.68kph
250cc: Dieter Braun (FRG), Yamaha, 93.34mph/
150.21kph
125cc: Pier Paolo Bianchi (Ita), Morbidelli, 89.69mph/
144.35kph
50cc: Ulrich Graf (Swi), Kreidler, 79.61mph/128.11kph

BRITISH GRAND PRIX (TOURIST TROPHY)

Isle of Man, 6–11 June
500cc
1 Tom Herron (UK), Yamaha, 105.16mph/169.24kph
2 Ian Richards (UK), Yamaha
3 Bill Guthrie (UK), Yamaha
Fastest lap: John Williams (UK), Suzuki, 112.27mph/
180.69kph
Other winners:
350cc: Charles Mortimer (UK), Yamaha, 106.78mph/
171.85kph
250cc: Tom Herron (UK), Yamaha, 103.55mph/
166.65kph
Sidecar: Rolf Steinhausen/Joseph Hüber (FRG), Busch
König, 96.42mph/155.18kph

DUTCH TT

Assen, 26 June
500cc
1 Barry Sheene (UK), Suzuki, 94.44mph/151.99kph
2 Pat Hennen (USA), Suzuki
3 Wil Hartog (Hol), Suzuki
Fastest lap: Sheene, 96.13mph/154.70kph
Other winners:
350cc: Giacomo Agostini (Ita), MV Agusta, 92.99mph/
149.66kph
250cc: Walter Villa (Ita), Harley-Davidson, 90.82mph/
146.16kph
125cc: Pier Paolo Bianchi (Ita), Morbidelli, 86.38mph/
139.02kph
50cc: Angel Nieto (Spa), Bultaco, 78.07mph/125.64kph
Sidecar: Hermann Schmid/Jean-Petit Matile (Swi),
Yamaha, 82.89mph/133.40kph

BELGIAN GRAND PRIX

Spa-Francorchamps, 4 July
500cc
1 John Williams (UK), Suzuki, 133.49mph/214.83kph
2 Barry Sheene (UK), Suzuki
3 Marcel Ancone (Hol), Suzuki
Fastest lap: Williams, 135.60mph/218.23kph
Other winners:
250cc: Walter Villa (Ita), Harley-Davidson, 126.08mph/
202.90kph
125cc: Angel Nieto (Spa), Bultaco, 117.38mph/
188.90kph
50cc: Herbert Rittberger (FRG), Kreidler, 100.62mph/
161.94kph
Sidecar: Rolf Steinhausen/Joseph Hüber (FRG), Busch
König, 118.45mph/190.63kph

SWEDISH TT

Anderstorp, 25 July
500cc
1 Barry Sheene (UK), Suzuki, 86.76mph/139.63kph
2 Jack Findlay (Aus), Suzuki
3 Charles Mortimer (UK), Suzuki
Fastest lap: Teppi Länsivuori (Fin), Suzuki, 88.43mph/
142.31kph
Other winners:
250cc: Takazumi Katayama (Jap), Yamaha, 83.06mph/
133.67kph
125cc: Pier Paolo Bianchi (Ita), Morbidelli, 81.06mph/
130.43kph
50cc: Angel Nieto (Spa), Bultaco, 74.54mph/119.95kph

FINNISH GRAND PRIX

Imatra, 1 August
500cc
1 Pat Hennen (USA), Suzuki, 97.44mph/156.82kph
2 Teppi Länsivuori (Fin), Suzuki
3 Philippe Coulon (Swi), Suzuki
Fastest lap: John Newbold (UK), Suzuki, 99.77mph/
160.56kph
Other winners:
350cc: Walter Villa (Ita), Harley-Davidson, 94.03mph/
151.32kph
250cc: Walter Villa (Ita), Harley-Davidson, 91.35mph/
147.02kph
125cc: Pier Paolo Bianchi (Ita), Morbidelli, 87.09mph/
140.16kph
50cc: Julien van Zeebroeck (Bel), Kreidler, 73.30kph/
117.97kph

CZECHOSLOVAK GRAND PRIX

Brno, 22 August
500cc
1 John Newbold (UK), Suzuki, 107.25mph/172.60kph
2 Teppi Länsivuori (Fin), Suzuki
3 Philippe Coulon (Swi), Suzuki
Fastest lap: Länsivuori, 109.95mph/176.95kph
Other winners:
350cc: Walter Villa (Ita), Harley-Davidson, 105.56mph/
169.89kph
250cc: Walter Villa (Ita), Harley-Davidson, 104.25mph/
167.77kph
Sidecar: Herman Schmid/Jean-Petit Matile (Swi),
Yamaha, 99.21mph/159.66kph

WEST GERMAN GRAND PRIX

Nürburgring, 29 August
500cc
1 Giacomo Agostini (Ita), MV Agusta, 89.81mph/
144.53kph
2 Marco Lucchinelli (Ita), Suzuki
3 Pat Hennen (USA), Suzuki
Fastest lap: Marcel Ancone (Hol), Suzuki, 94.61mph/
152.26kph
Other winners:
350cc: Walter Villa (Ita), Harley-Davidson, 93.02mph/
147.90kph

250cc: Walter Villa (Ita), Harley-Davidson, 91.90mph/
147.91kph
125cc: Anton Mang (FRG), Morbidelli, 80.74mph/
129.93kph
50cc: Angel Nieto (Spa), Bultaco, 80.55mph/129.64kph
Sidecar: Werner Schwärzel/Andreas Hüber (Swi), König,
76.16mph/122.58kph

SPANISH GRAND PRIX

Montjuich, Barcelona, 19 September
350cc: Kork Ballington (SAf), Yamaha, 81.08mph/
130.49kph
250cc: Gianfranco Bonera (Ita), Harley-Davidson,
79.35mph/127.71kph
125cc: Pier Paolo Bianchi (Ita), Morbidelli, 76.42mph/
122.98kph
50cc: Angel Nieto (Spa), Bultaco, 70.61mph/113.64kph

LEADING CHAMPIONSHIP POSITIONS

500cc
Riders
1 Barry Sheene (UK) 72(87)pts
2 Teppi Länsivuori (Fin) 48(54)pts
3 Pat Hennen (USA) 46pts
4 Marco Lucchinelli (Ita) 40pts
5 John Newbold (UK) 31(34)pts
6 Philippe Coulon (Swi) 28pts
Manufacturers
1 Suzuki 90(136)pts
2 Yamaha 48(55)pts
3 MV Agusta 26pts

350cc
1 Walter Villa (Ita) 76(81)pts
2 Johnny Cecotto (Ven) 65pts
3 Charles Mortimer (UK) 54pts
Manufacturers' title: Yamaha

250cc
1 Walter Villa (Ita) 90(117)pts
2 Takazumi Katayama (Jap) 73(87)pts
3 Gianfranco Bonera (Ita) 61(77)pts
Manufacturers' title: Not officially
recognised by FIM

125cc
1 Pier Paolo Bianchi (Ita) 90(105)pts
2 Angel Nieto (Spa) 67pts

3 Paolo Pileri (Ita) 64(74)pts
Manufacturers' title: Morbidelli

50cc
1 Angel Nieto (Spa) 85(97)pts
2 Herbert Rittberger (FRG) 76(92)pts
3 Ulrich Graf (Swi) 69(80)pts
Manufacturers' title: Bultaco

Sidecar
1 Rolf Steinhausen (FRG) 65(68)pts
2 Werner Schwärzel (FRG) 51(59)pts
3 Hermann Schmid (Swi) 38pts
Manufacturers' title: Not officially
recognised by FIM

1977

VENEZUELAN GRAND PRIX

San Carlos, 20 March
500cc
1 Barry Sheene (UK), Suzuki, 94.48mph/152.06kph
2 Steve Baker (USA), Yamaha
3 Pat Hennen (USA), Suzuki
Fastest lap: Sheene and Baker, 96.55mph/155.39kph
Other winners:
350cc: Johnny Cecotto (Ven), Yamaha, 92.49mph/
148.85kph
250cc: Walter Villa (Ita), Harley-Davidson, 90.05mph/
144.92kph
125cc: Angel Nieto (Spa), Bultaco, 82.63mph/132.98kph

AUSTRIAN GRAND PRIX

Salzburgring, 1 May
500cc
1 Jack Findlay (Aus), Suzuki, 107.74mph/173.39kph
2 Max Wiener (Aut), Suzuki
3 Alex George (UK), Suzuki
Fastest lap: Findlay, 110.32mph/177.55kph
Other winners:
125cc: Eugenio Lazzarini (Ita), Morbidelli, 98.21mph/
158.05kph

Sidecar: Rolf Biland/Kurt Waltisperg (Swi), Yamaha,
100.80mph/162.22kph

WEST GERMAN GRAND PRIX

Hockenheim, 8 May
500cc
1 Barry Sheene (UK), Suzuki, 110.99mph/178.63kph
2 Pat Hennen (USA), Suzuki
3 Steve Baker (USA), Yamaha
Fastest lap: Sheene, 112.98mph/181.82kph
Other winners:
350cc: Takazumi Katayama (Jap), Yamaha, 104.33mph/
167.90kph
250cc: Christian Sarron (Fra), Yamaha, 96.94mph/
156.01kph
125cc: Pier Paolo Bianchi (Ita), Morbidelli, 88.31mph/
142.12kph
50cc: Herbert Rittberger (FRG), Kreidler, 78.87mph/
126.93kph
Sidecar: Rolf Biland/Kurt Waltisperg (Swi), Yamaha,
86.57mph/139.32kph

ITALIAN GRAND PRIX
(GRAND PRIX DES NATIONS)

Imola, 15 May
500cc
1 Barry Sheene (UK), Suzuki, 94.16mph/151.54kph
2 Virginio Ferrari (Ita), Suzuki

3 Armando Toracca (Ita), Suzuki
Fastest lap: Sheene, 96.36mph/155.08kph
Other winners:
350cc: Alan North (SAf), Yamaha, 91.77mph/147.69kph
250cc: Franco Unicini (Ita), Harley-Davidson, 89.81mph/
144.54kph
125cc: Pier Paolo Bianchi (Ita), Morbidelli, 85.77mph/
138.03kph
50cc: Eugenio Lazzarini (Ita), Kreidler, 77.07mph/
124.03kph

SPANISH GRAND PRIX

Jarama, 22 May
350cc: Michel Rougerie (Fra), Yamaha, 73.80mph/
118.77kph
250cc: Takazumi Katayama (Jap), Yamaha, 75.06mph/
120.80kph
125cc: Pier Paolo Bianchi (Ita), Morbidelli, 70.64mph/
113.68kph
50cc: Angel Nieto (Spa), Bultaco, 68.74mph/110.63kph

FRENCH GRAND PRIX

Paul Ricard, 29 May
500cc
1 Barry Sheene (UK), Suzuki, 99.25mph/159.73kph
2 Giacomo Agostini (Ita), Yamaha
3 Steve Baker (USA), Yamaha
Fastest lap: Agostini, 101.28mph/163.00kph
Other winners:
350cc: Takazumi Katayama (Jap), Yahama, 98.92mph/
159.20kph
250cc: Jon Ekerold (SAf), Yamaha, 93.19mph/149.98kph
125cc: Pier Paolo Bianchi (Ita), Morbidelli, 90.32mph/
145.36kph
Sidecar: Alain Michel/Gerard Lecorre (Fra), Yamaha,
91.50mph/147.25kph

YUGOSLAV GRAND PRIX

Opatija, 19 June
350cc: Takazumi Katayama (Jap), Yamaha, 98.28mph/
139.32kph
250cc: Mario Lega (Ita), Morbidelli, 95.18mph/153.18kph
125cc: Pier Paolo Bianchi (Ita), Morbidelli, 91.50mph/
147.25kph
50cc: Angel Nieto (Spa), Bultaco, 82.20mph/132.29kph

DUTCH TT

Assen, 25 June
500cc
1 Wil Hartog (Hol), Suzuki, 87.84mph/141.36kph
2 Barry Sheene (UK), Suzuki
3 Pat Hennen (USA), Suzuki
Fastest lap: Sheene, 93.98mph/151.25kph
Other winners:
350cc: Kork Ballington (SAf), Yamaha, 93.10mph/
149.83kph
250cc: Mick Grant (UK), Kawasaki, 90.33mph/145.38kph
125cc: Angel Nieto (Spa), Bultaco, 86.61mph/139.39kph

50cc: Angel Nieto (Spa), Bultaco, 79.64mph/128.17kph
Sidecar: Rolf Biland (Swi)/Kenny Williams (UK), Yamaha,
89.06mph/143.33kph

BELGIAN GRAND PRIX

Spa-Francorchamps, 3 July
500cc
1 Barry Sheene (UK), Suzuki, 135.07mph/217.37kph
2 Steve Baker (USA), Yamaha
3 Pat Hennen (USA), Suzuki
Fastest lap: Sheene, 137.15mph/220.72kph
Other winners:
250cc: Walter Villa (Ita), Harley-Davidson, 127.03mph/
204.43kph
125cc: Pier Paolo Bianchi (Ita), Morbidelli, 118.54mph/
190.77kph
50cc: Eugenio Lazzarini (Ita), Kreidler, 101.16mph/
162.80kph
Sidecar: Werner Schwärzel/Andreas Hüber (FRG), ARO
Fath, 122.73mph/197.51kph

SWEDISH TT

Anderstorp, 24 July
500cc
1 Barry Sheene (UK), Suzuki, 88.57mph/142.55kph
2 Johnny Cecotto (Ven), Yamaha
3 Steve Baker (USA), Yamaha
Fastest lap: Sheene, 94.23mph/151.65kph
Other winners:
350cc: Takazumi Katayama (Jap), Yamaha, 86.62mph/
139.40kph
250cc: Mick Grant (UK), Kawasaki, 83.09mph/133.72kph
125cc: Angel Nieto (Spa), Bultaco, 70.79mph/113.93kph
50cc: Ricardo Tormo (Spa), Bultaco, 65.02mph/
104.64kph

FINNISH GRAND PRIX

Imatra, 31 July
500cc
1 Johnny Cecotto (Ven), Yamaha, 105.61mph/169.96kph
2 Marco Lucchinelli (Ita), Suzuki
3 Gianfranco Bonera (Ita), Suzuki
Fastest lap: Cecotto, 107.14mph/172.42kph
Other winners:
350cc: Takazumi Katayama (Jap), Yamaha, 97.87mph/
157.51kph
250cc: Walter Villa (Ita), Harley-Davidson, 97.20mph/
156.45kph
125cc: Pier Paolo Bianchi (Ita), Morbidelli, 92.53mph/
148.91kph

CZECHOSLOVAK GRAND PRIX

Brno, 7 August
500cc
1 Johnny Cecotto (Ven), Yamaha, 114.45mph/184.19kph
2 Giacomo Agostini (Ita), Yamaha
3 Michel Rougerie (Fra), Suzuki
Fastest lap: Cecotto, 116.49mph/187.48kph

Other winners:
350cc: Johnny Cecotto (Ven), Yamaha, 109.85mph/
176.70kph
250cc: Franco Uncini (Ita), Harley-Davidson, 105.94mph/
170.21kph
Sidecar: Rolf Steinhausen/Joseph Hüber (FRG), Busch
Yamaha, 100.06mph/161.03kph

BRITISH GRAND PRIX

Silverstone, 14 August
500cc
1 Pat Hennen (USA), Suzuki, 108.00mph/173.81kph

2 Steve Baker (USA), Yamaha
3 Teppi Länsivuori (Fin), Suzuki
Fastest lap: Steve Parrish (UK), Suzuki, 117.78mph/
179.92kph
Other winners:
350cc: Kork Ballington (SAf), Yamaha, 107.99mph/
173.79kph
250cc: Kork Ballington (SAf), Yamaha, 104.69mph/
168.49kph
125cc: Pier Luigi Conforti (Ita), Morbidelli, 98.53mph/
158.57kph
Sidecar: Werner Schwärzel/Andreas Hüber (FRG), ARO
Fath, 87.97mph/141.57kph

LEADING CHAMPIONSHIP POSITIONS

500cc
Riders
1 Barry Sheene (UK) 107pts
2 Steve Baker (USA) 80pts
3 Pat Hennen (USA) 67pts
4 Johnny Cecotto (Ven) 50pts
5 Steve Parrish (UK) 39pts
6 Giacomo Agostini (Ita) 37pts
  Gianfranco Bonera (Ita) 37pts
Manufacturers
1 Suzuki 157pts
2 Yamaha 114pts
Only two manufacturers scored points

350cc
1 Takazumi Katayama (Jap) 95pts
2 Tom Herron (UK) 56pts
3 Jon Ekerold (SAf) 54pts
Manufacturers' title: Yamaha

250cc
1 Mario Lega (Ita) 85pts
2 Franco Uncini (Ita) 72pts
3 Walter Villa (Ita) 67pts
Manufacturers' title: Yamaha

125cc
1 Pier Paolo Bianchi (Ita) 131pts
2 Eugenio Lazzarini (Ita) 105pts

3 Angel Nieto (Spa) 80pts
Manufacturers' title: Morbidelli

50cc
1 Angel Nieto (Spa) 87pts
2 Eugenio Lazzarini (Ita) 72pts
3 Ricardo Tormo (Spa) 69pts
Manufacturers' title: Bultaco

Sidecar
1 George O'Dell (UK) 64pts
2 Rolf Biland (Swi) 56pts
3 Werner Schwärzel (FRG) 46pts
Manufacturers' title: Yamaha

Britain's last world 500cc champion, Barry Sheene, seen here in an uncharacteristic pose

1978

VENEZUELAN GRAND PRIX

San Carlos, 19 March
500cc
1 Barry Sheene (UK), Suzuki, 97.20mph/156.43kph
2 Pat Hennen (USA), Suzuki
3 Steve Baker (USA), Suzuki
Fastest lap: Sheene, 97.78mph/157.36kph
Other winners:
350cc: Takazumi Katayama (Jap), Yamaha, 93.50mph/
150.47kph
250cc: Kenny Roberts (USA), Yamaha, 91.66mph/
147.51kph
125cc: Pier Paolo Bianchi (Ita), Morbidelli, 87.47mph/
140.77kph

SPANISH GRAND PRIX

Jarama, 16 April
500cc
1 Pat Hennen (USA), Suzuki, 79.56mph/128.04kph
2 Kenny Roberts (USA), Yamaha
3 Takazumi Katayama (Jap), Yamaha
Fastest lap: Roberts, 81.05mph/130.44kph
Other winners:
250cc: Gregg Hansford (Aus), Kawasaki, 77.44mph/
124.63kph
125cc: Eugenio Lazzarini (Ita), Morbidelli, 71.94mph/
115.78kph
50cc: Eugenio Lazzarini (Ita), Kreidler, 66.07mph/
106.33kph

AUSTRIAN GRAND PRIX

Salzburgring, 30 April
500cc
1 Kenny Roberts (USA), Yamaha, 114.08mph/183.59kph
2 Johnny Cecotto (Ven), Yamaha
3 Barry Sheene (UK), Suzuki
Fastest lap: Roberts, 116.78mph/187.94kph
Other winners:
350cc: Kork Ballington (SAf), Kawasaki, 109.79mph/
176.69kph
125cc: Eugenio Lazzarini (Ita), MBA, 100.66mph/
162.00kph
Sidecar: Rolf Biland (Swi)/Kenny Williams (UK), Yamaha,
102.93mph/165.65kph

FRENCH GRAND PRIX

Nogaro, 7 May
500cc
1 Kenny Roberts (USA), Yamaha, 82.53mph/132.82kph
2 Pat Hennen (USA), Yamaha
3 Barry Sheene (UK), Suzuki
Fastest lap: Roberts, 84.78mph/136.44kph
Other winners:
350cc: Gregg Hansford (Aus), Kawasaki, 70.20mph/
112.98kph

250cc: Gregg Hansford (Aus), Kawasaki, 79.82mph/
128.46kph
125cc: Pier Paolo Bianchi (Ita), Morbidelli, 74.35mph/
119.65kph
Sidecar: Rolf Biland (Swi)/Kenny Williams (UK), Yamaha,
75.61mph/121.68kph

ITALIAN GRAND PRIX
(GRAND PRIX DES NATIONS)

Mugello, 14 May
500cc
1 Kenny Roberts (USA), Yamaha, 92.89mph/149.49kph
2 Pat Hennen (USA), Suzuki
3 Marco Lucchinelli (Ita), Suzuki
Fastest lap: Roberts, 97.32mph/156.62kph
Other winners:
350cc: Kork Ballington (SAf), Kawasaki, 90.83mph/
146.18kph
250cc: Kork Ballington (SAf), Kawasaki, 89.77mph/
144.47kph
125cc: Eugenio Lazzarini (Ita), Morbidelli, 87.20mph/
140.33kph
50cc: Ricardo Tormo (Spa), Bultaco, 79.48mph/
127.91kph
Sidecar: Rolf Biland (Swi)/Kenny Williams (UK), Yamaha,
86.13mph/138.61kph

DUTCH TT

Assen, 24 June
500cc
1 Johnny Cecotto (Ven), Yamaha, 93.35mph/150.23kph
2 Kenny Roberts (USA), Yamaha
3 Barry Sheene (UK), Suzuki
Fastest lap: Roberts, 97.88mph/157.52kph
Other winners:
350cc: Kork Ballington (SAf), Kawasaki, 84.80mph/
136.47kph
250cc: Kenny Roberts (USA), Yamaha, 87.69mph/
141.12kph
125cc: Eugenio Lazzarini (Ita), Morbidelli, 86.30mph/
138.89kph
50cc: Eugenio Lazzarini (Ita), Kreidler, 79.96mph/
128.68kph
Sidecar: Werner Schwärzel/Andreas Hüber (FRG), ARO
Fath, 87.67mph/141.09kph

BELGIAN GRAND PRIX

Spa-Francorchamps, 2 July
500cc
1 Wil Hartog (Hol), Suzuki, 132.90mph/213.88kph
2 Kenny Roberts (USA), Yamaha
3 Barry Sheene (UK), Suzuki
Fastest lap: Michel Rougerie (Fra), Suzuki, 137.11mph/
220.66kph
Other winners:
250cc: Paolo Pileri (Ita), Morbidelli, 116.74mph/
187.87kph
125cc: Pier Paolo Bianchi (Ita), Morbidelli, 110.17mph/
177.30kph
50cc: Ricardo Tormo (Spa), Bultaco, 99.04mph/
159.39kph

Sidecar: Bruno Holzer/Karl Meierhans (Swi), Yamaha, 99.62mph/160.32kph

SWEDISH TT

Karlskoga, 23 July
500cc
1 Barry Sheene (UK), Suzuki, 84.16mph/135.44kph
2 Wil Hartog (Hol), Suzuki
3 Takazumi Katayama (Jap), Yamaha
Fastest lap: Johnny Cecotto (Ven), Yamaha, 85.90mph/138.24kph
Other winners:
350cc: Gregg Hansford (Aus), Kawasaki, 84.01mph/135.20kph
250cc: Gregg Hansford (Aus), Kawasaki, 83.52mph/134.66kph
125cc: Pier Paolo Bianchi (Ita), Morbidelli, 78.05mph/125.61kph

FINNISH GRAND PRIX

Imatra, 30 July
500cc
1 Wil Hartog (Hol), Suzuki, 103.23mph/166.13kph
2 Takazumi Katayama (Jap)
3 Johnny Cecotto (Ven), Yamaha
Fastest lap: Cecotto, 104.81mph/168.67kph
Other winners:
350cc: Kork Ballington (SAf), Kawasaki, 98.51mph/158.54kph
250cc: Kork Ballington (SAf), Kawasaki, 97.27mph/156.54kph
125cc: Angel Nieto (Spa), Minarelli, 92.09mph/148.20kph

BRITISH GRAND PRIX

Silverstone, 6 August
500cc
1 Kenny Roberts (USA), Yamaha, 87.89mph/141.45kph
2 Steve Manship (UK), Suzuki
3 Barry Sheene (UK), Suzuki
Fastest lap: Roberts, 115.32mph/185.59kph
Other winners:
350cc: Kork Ballington (SAf), Kawasaki, 109.84mph/176.93kph

250cc: Anton Mang (FRG), Kawasaki, 106.06mph/170.69kph
125cc: Angel Nieto (Spa), Minarelli, 93.97mph/151.23kph
Sidecar: Alain Michel (Fra)/Stu Collins (UK), Seymaz Yamaha, 96.58mph/155.43kph

WEST GERMAN GRAND PRIX

Nürburgring, 20 August
500cc
1 Virginio Ferrari (Ita), Suzuki, 99.45mph/160.05kph
2 Johnny Cecotto (Ven), Yamaha
3 Kenny Roberts (USA), Yamaha
Fastest lap: Ferrari, 100.26mph/161.35kph
Other winners:
350cc: Takazumi Katayama (Jap), Yamaha, 97.33mph/156.64kph
250cc: Kork Ballington (SAf), Kawasaki, 95.25mph/153.29kph
125cc: Angel Nieto (Spa), Minarelli, 90.93mph/146.34kph
50cc: Ricardo Tormo (Spa), Bultaco, 82.32mph/132.48kph
Sidecar: Werner Schwärzel/Andreas Hüber (FRG), ARO Fath, 91.83mph/147.79kph

CZECHOSLOVAK GRAND PRIX

Brno, 27 August
350cc: Kork Ballington (SAf), Kawasaki, 102.97mph/165.71kph
250cc: Kork Ballington (SAf), Kawasaki, 98.85mph/159.08kph
50cc: Ricardo Tormo (Spa), Bultaco, 83.93mph/135.07kph
Sidecar: Alain Michel (Fra)/Stu Collins (UK), Seymaz Yamaha, 96.51mph/155.32kph

YUGOSLAV GRAND PRIX

Rijeka, 17 September
350cc: Gregg Hansford (Aus), Kawasaki, 93.16mph/149.93kph
250cc: Gregg Hansford (Aus), Kawasaki, 91.03mph/146.50kph
125cc: Angel Nieto (Spa), Minarelli, 87.22mph/140.37kph
50cc: Ricardo Tormo (Spa), Bultaco, 81.21mph/130.69kph

LEADING CHAMPIONSHIP POSITIONS

500cc
Riders
1 Kenny Roberts (USA) 110pts
2 Barry Sheene (UK) 100pts
3 Johnny Cecotto (Ven) 66pts
4 Wil Hartog (Hol) 65pts
5 Takazumi Katayama (Jap) 53pts
6 Pat Hennen (USA) 51pts
Manufacturers
1 Suzuki 146pts
2 Yamaha 139pts
Only two manufacturers scored points

350cc
1 Kork Ballington (SAf) 134pts
2 Takazumi Katayama (Jap) 77pts
3 Gregg Hansford (Aus) 76pts
Manufacturers' title: Kawasaki

250cc
1 Kork Ballington (SAf) 124pts
2 Gregg Hansford (Aus) 118pts
3 Patrick Fernandez (Fra) 55pts
Manufacturers' title: Kawasaki

125cc
1 Eugenio Lazzarini (Ita) 114pts

2 Angel Nieto (Spa) 88pts
3 Pier Paolo Bianchi (Ita) 70pts
Manufacturers' title: Not awarded

50cc
1 Ricardo Tormo (Spa) 99pts
2 Eugenio Lazzarini (Ita) 64pts
3 Patrick Plisson (Fra) 48pts
Manufacturers' title: Bultaco

Sidecar
1 Rolf Biland (Swi) 99pts
2 Alain Michel (Fra) 76pts
3 Bruno Holzer (Swi) 49pts
Manufacturers' title: Yamaha

1979

VENEZUELAN GRAND PRIX

San Carlos, 18 March
500cc
1 Barry Sheene (UK), Suzuki, 96.59mph/155.45kph
2 Virginio Ferrari (Ita), Suzuki
3 Tom Herron (UK), Suzuki
Fastest lap: Sheene, 98.31mph/158.21kph
Other winners:
350cc: Carlos Lavado (Ven), Yamaha, 95.51mph/
153.71kph
250cc: Walter Villa (Ita), Yamaha, 93.38mph/150.28kph
125cc: Angel Nieto (Spa), Minarelli, 87.79mph/141.29kph

AUSTRIAN GRAND PRIX

Salzburgring, 29 April
500cc
1 Kenny Roberts (USA), Yamaha, 114.33mph/183.99kph
2 Virginio Ferrari (Ita), Suzuki
3 Wil Hartog (Hol), Suzuki
Fastest lap: Roberts, 116.12mph/186.88kph
Other winners:
350cc: Kork Ballington (SAf), Kawasaki, 109.70mph/
176.54kph
125cc: Angel Nieto (Spa), Minarelli, 100.48mph/
161.71kph
Sidecar* B2a: Gote Brodin/Billy Gallros (Swe), Yamaha,
100.15mph/161.18kph
Sidecar B2b: Rolf Biland/Kurt Waltisperg (Swi), LCR
Yamaha, 100.12mph/161.12kph

WEST GERMAN GRAND PRIX

Hockenheim, 6 May
500cc
1 Wil Hartog (Hol), Suzuki, 112.97mph/181.80kph
2 Kenny Roberts (USA), Yamaha
3 Virginio Ferrari (Ita), Suzuki
Fastest lap: Roberts, 114.68mph/184.57kph
Other winners:
350cc: Jon Ekerold (SAf), Yamaha, 108.18mph/
174.10kph
250cc: Kork Ballington (SAf), Kawasaki, 104.95mph/
168.90kph
125cc: Angel Nieto (Spa), Minarelli, 99.48mph/160.10kph
50cc: Gerhard Waibel (FRG), Kreidler, 84.01mph/
135.20kph
Sidecar B2a: Rolf Steinhausen (FRG)/Kenny Arthur (UK),
KSA Yamaha, 100.72mph/162.10kph

** The FIM ran two sidecar championships in 1979, one for traditional
outfits (B2a) and one for outfits containing innovations (B2b) as
introduced by Rolf Biland in 1978*

ITALIAN GRAND PRIX
(GRAND PRIX DES NATIONS)

Imola, 13 May
500cc
1 Kenny Roberts (USA), Yamaha, 95.89mph/154.32kph
2 Virginio Ferrari (Ita), Suzuki
3 Tom Herron (UK), Suzuki
Fastest lap: Roberts, 97.19mph/156.41kph
Other winners:
350cc: Gregg Hansford (Aus), Kawasaki, 92.68mph/
149.16kph
250cc: Kork Ballington (SAf), Kawasaki, 92.00mph/
148.06kph
125cc: Angel Nieto (Spa), Minarelli, 85.89mph/138.23kph
50cc: Eugenio Lazzarini (Ita), Kreidler, 77.15mph/
124.16kph

SPANISH GRAND PRIX

Jarama, 20 May
500cc
1 Kenny Roberts (USA), Yamaha, 79.91mph/128.59kph
2 Wil Hartog (Hol), Suzuki
3 Mike Baldwin (USA), Suzuki
Fastest lap: Roberts, 81.10mph/130.52kph
Other winners:
350cc: Kork Ballington (SAf), Kawasaki, 78.22mph/
125.88kph
250cc: Kork Ballington (SAf), Kawasaki, 77.63mph/
124.93kph
125cc: Angel Nieto (Spa), Minarelli, 72.52mph/116.71kph
50cc: Eugenio Lazzarini (Ita), Kreidler, 66.44mph/
106.93kph

YUGOSLAV GRAND PRIX

Rijeka, 17 June
500cc
1 Kenny Roberts (USA), Yamaha, 96.64mph/155.53kph
2 Virginio Ferrari (Ita), Suzuki
3 Franco Uncini (Ita), Suzuki
Fastest lap: Not recorded
Other winners:
350cc: Kork Ballington (SAf), Kawasaki, 94.85mph/
152.64kph
250cc: Graziano Rossi (Ita), Morbidelli, 92.42mph/
148.73kph
125cc: Angel Nieto (Spa), Minarelli, 87.27mph/140.45kph
50cc: Eugenio Lazzarini (Ita), Kreidler, 79.88mph/
128.55kph

DUTCH TT

Assen, 23 June
500cc
1 Virginio Ferrari (Ita), Suzuki, 97.94mph/157.63kph
2 Barry Sheene (UK), Suzuki
3 Will Hartog (Hol), Suzuki
Fastest lap: Ferrari, 98.93mph/159.22kph
Other winners:
350cc: Gregg Hansford (Aus), Kawasaki, 94.57mph/
152.19kph

250cc: Graziano Rossi (Ita), Morbidelli, 93.41mph/150.34kph
125cc: Angel Nieto (Spa), Minarelli, 87.96mph/141.56kph
50cc: Eugenio Lazzarini (Ita), Kreidler, 79.25mph/127.54kph
Sidecar B2a: Rolf Biland/Kurt Waltisperg (Swi), Yamaha, 89.42mph/143.91kph

BELGIAN GRAND PRIX

Spa-Francorchamps, 1 July
500cc
1 Dennis Ireland (NZ), Suzuki, 90.62mph/145.84kph
2 Kenny Blake (Aus), Yamaha
3 Gary Lingham (UK), Suzuki
Fastest lap: Blake, 91.82mph/147.77kph
Other winners:
250cc: Ed Stöllinger (Aut), Kawasaki, 89.18mph/143.52kph
125cc: Barry Smith (Aus), MBA, 82.69mph/133.07kph
50cc: Henk van Kessel (Hol), Kreidler, 75.32mph/121.21kph
Sidecar B2a: Rolf Steinhausen (FRG)/Kenny Arthur (UK), KSA Yamaha, 90.68mph/145.93kph

SWISS GRAND PRIX

Paul Ricard, 15 July
Sidecar B2b: Rolf Biland/Kurt Waltisperg (Swi), LCR Yamaha, 82.35mph/132.53kph

SWEDISH TT

Karlskoga, 22 July
500cc
1 Barry Sheene (UK), Suzuki, 84.89mph/136.61kph
2 Jack Middelburg (Hol), Suzuki
3 Boet van Dulmen (Hol), Suzuki
Fastest lap: Wil Hartog (Hol), Suzuki, 86.64mph/139.44kph
Other winners:
250cc: Graziano Rossi (Ita), Morbidelli, 84.93mph/136.68kph
125cc: Pier Paolo Bianchi (Ita), Minarelli, 76.76mph/123.53kph
Sidecar B2a: Jock Taylor (UK)/Benga Johansson (Swe), Yamaha, 77.40mph/124.57kph

FINNISH GRAND PRIX

Imatra, 29 July
500cc
1 Boet van Dulmen (Hol), Suzuki, 91.47mph/147.20kph
2 Randy Mamola (USA), Suzuki
3 Barry Sheene (UK), Suzuki
Fastest lap: Jack Middelburg (Hol), Suzuki, 94.63mph/152.30kph

Other winners:
350cc: Gregg Hansford (Aus), Kawasaki, 78.17mph/125.80kph
250cc: Kork Ballington (SAf), Kawasaki, 81.21mph/130.70kph
125cc: Ricardo Tormo (Spa), Bultaco, 73.94mph/119.00kph

BRITISH GRAND PRIX

Silverstone, 12 August
500cc
1 Kenny Roberts (USA), Yamaha, 114.50mph/184.27kph
2 Barry Sheene (UK), Suzuki
3 Wil Hartog (Hol), Suzuki
Fastest lap: Sheene, 117.10mph/188.45kph
Other winners:
350cc: Kork Ballington (SAf), Kawasaki, 110.43mph/177.72kph
250cc: Kork Ballington (SAf), Kawasaki, 108.13mph/174.02kph
125cc: Angel Nieto (Spa), Minarelli, 101.12mph/162.74kph
Sidecar B2a: Rolf Biland/Kurt Waltisperg (Swi), Yamaha, 104.35mph/167.94kph
Sidecar B2b: Alain Michel (Fra)/Michael Burkhard (FRG), Seymaz Yamaha, 93.89mph/151.10kph

CZECHOSLOVAK GRAND PRIX

Brno, 19 August
350cc: Kork Ballington (SAf), Kawasaki, 106.11mph/170.77kph
250cc: Kork Ballington (SAf), Kawasaki, 102.62mph/165.16kph
125cc: Guy Bertin (Fra), Motobecane, 96.82mph/155.81kph
Sidecar B2a: Rolf Biland/Kurt Waltisperg (Swi), Yamaha, 99.92mph/160.81kph

FRENCH GRAND PRIX

Le Mans, 2 September
500cc
1 Barry Sheene (UK), Suzuki, 95.31mph/153.39kph
2 Randy Mamola (USA), Suzuki
3 Kenny Roberts (USA), Yamaha
Fastest lap: Virginio Ferrari (Ita), Suzuki, 96.89mph/155.93kph
Other winners:
350cc: Patrick Fernandez (Fra), Yamaha, 85.28mph/137.24kph
250cc: Kork Ballington (SAf), Kawasaki, 90.60mph/145.81kph
125cc: Guy Bertin (Fra), Motobecane, 84.85mph/136.55kph
50cc: Eugenio Lazzarini (Ita), Kreidler, 72.56mph/116.77kph
Sidecar B2b: Rolf Biland/Kurt Waltisperg (Swi), LCR Yamaha, 86.41mph/139.07kph

LEADING CHAMPIONSHIP POSITIONS

500cc
Riders
1 Kenny Roberts (USA) 113pts
2 Virginio Ferrari (Ita) 89pts
3 Barry Sheene (UK) 87pts
4 Wil Hartog (Hol) 66pts
5 Franco Uncini (Ita) 51pts
6 Boet van Dulmen (Hol) 50pts
Manufacturers
1 Suzuki 165pts
2 Yamaha 138pts
3 Morbidelli 2pts

350cc
1 Kork Ballington (SAf) 141pts
2 Patrick Fernandez (Fra) 90pts
3 Gregg Hansford (Aus) 77pts
Manufacturers' title: Kawasaki

250cc
1 Kork Ballington (SAf), 141pts
2 Gregg Hansford (Aus) 81pts
3 Graziano Rossi (Ita) 67pts
Manufacturers' title: Kawasaki

125cc
1 Angel Nieto (Spa) 120pts
2 Maurizio Massimiani (Ita) 53pts
3 Hans Muller (Swi) 50pts
Manufacturers' title: Minarelli

50cc
1 Eugenio Lazzarini (Ita) 75pts
2 Rolf Blatter (Swi) 62pts
3 Patrick Plisson (Fra) 32pts
Manufacturers' title: Kreidler

Sidecar B2a
1 Rolf Biland (Swi) 67pts
2 Rolf Steinhausen (FRG) 58pts
2 Dick Greasley (UK) 58pts

Sidecar B2b
1 Bruno Holzer (Swi) 72pts
2 Rolf Biland (Swi) 60pts
3 Masao Kumano (Jap) 41pts
Manufacturers' title: Yamaha *(only one sidecar title)*

1980

ITALIAN GRAND PRIX (GRAND PRIX DES NATIONS)

Misano, 11 May
500cc
1 Kenny Roberts (USA), Yamaha, 92.95mph/149.59kph
2 Franco Uncini (Ita), Suzuki
3 Graziano Rossi (Ita), Suzuki
Fastest lap: Roberts, 94.69mph/152.39kph
Other winners:
350cc: Johnny Cecotto (Ven), Yamaha, 90.74mph/146.03kph
250cc: Anton Mang (FRG), Kawasaki, 88.70mph/142.75kph
125cc: Pier Paolo Bianchi (Ita), MBA, 85.30mph/137.28kph
50cc: Eugenio Lazzarini (Ita), Iprem, 76.24mph/122.70kph

SPANISH GRAND PRIX

Jarama, 18 May
500cc
1 Kenny Roberts (USA), Yamaha, 79.34mph/127.69kph
2 Marco Lucchinelli (Ita), Suzuki
3 Randy Mamola (USA), Suzuki
Fastest lap: Roberts, 80.87mph/130.15kph
Other winners:
250cc: Kork Ballington (SAf), Kawasaki, 76.04mph/122.37kph
125cc: Pier Paolo Bianchi (Ita), MBA, 73.06mph/117.58kph
50cc: Eugenio Lazzarini (Ita), Iprem, 65.76mph/105.83kph

FRENCH GRAND PRIX

Paul Ricard, 25 May
500cc
1 Kenny Roberts (USA), Yamaha, 102.84mph/165.50kph
2 Randy Mamola (USA), Suzuki
3 Marco Lucchinelli (Ita), Suzuki
Fastest lap: Roberts, 104.15mph/167.61kph
Other winners:
350cc: Jon Ekerold (SAf), Yamaha, 99.16mph/159.58kph
250cc: Kork Ballington (SAf), Kawasaki, 96.10mph/154.65kph
125cc: Angel Nieto (Spa), Minarelli, 91.94mph/147.96kph
Sidecar: Rolf Biland/Kurt Waltisperg (Swi), Yamaha, 95.55mph/153.77kph

YUGOSLAV GRAND PRIX

Rijeka, 15 June
250cc: Anton Mang (FRG), Kawasaki, 93.46mph/150.41kph
125cc: Guy Bertin (Fra), Motobecane, 89.38mph/143.84kph
50cc: Ricardo Tormo (Spa), Kreidler, 81.49mph/131.15kph
Sidecar: Rolf Biland/Kurt Waltisperg (Swi), Yamaha, 92.58mph/148.99kph

DUTCH TT

Assen, 28 June
500cc
1 Jack Middelburg (Hol), Yamaha, 95.19mph/153.19kph
2 Graziano Rossi (Ita), Suzuki
3 Franco Uncini (Ita), Suzuki
Fastest lap: Randy Mamola (USA), Suzuki, 97.21mph/156.45kph
Other winners:
350cc: Jon Ekerold (SAf), Yamaha, 94.48mph/152.05kph
250cc: Carlos Lavado (Ven), Yamaha, 88.37mph/142.22kph

125cc: Angel Nieto (Spa), Minarelli, 85.67mph/137.87kph
50cc: Ricardo Tormo (Spa), Kreidler, 76.61mph/
123.29kph
Sidecar: Jock Taylor (UK)/Benga Johansson (Swe),
Yamaha, 92.42mph/148.74kph

BELGIAN GRAND PRIX

Zolder, 6 July
500cc
1 Randy Mamola (USA), Suzuki, 93.25mph/150.07kph
2 Marco Lucchinelli (Ita), Suzuki
3 Kenny Roberts (USA), Yamaha
Fastest lap: Lucchinelli, 94.56mph/152.18kph
Other winners:
250cc: Anton Mang (FRG), Kawasaki, 89.16mph/
143.49kph
125cc: Angel Nieto (Spa), Minarelli, 84.89mph/136.62kph
50cc: Stefan Dörflinger (Swi), Kreidler, 75.24mph/
121.09kph
Sidecar: Jock Taylor (UK)/Benga Johansson (Swe),
Yamaha, 88.05mph/141.70kph

FINNISH GRAND PRIX

Imatra, 27 July
500cc
1 Wil Hartog (Hol), Suzuki, 94.33mph/151.82kph
2 Kenny Roberts (USA), Yamaha
3 Franco Uncini (Ita), Suzuki
Fastest lap: Hartog, 96.57mph/155.41kph
Other winners:
250cc: Kork Ballington (SAf), Kawasaki, 88.78mph/
142.88kph
125cc: Angel Nieto (Spa), Bultaco, 84.02mph/135.22kph
Sidecar: Jock Taylor (UK)/Benga Johansson (Swe),
Yamaha, 85.14mph/137.02kph

BRITISH GRAND PRIX

Silverstone, 10 August
500cc
1 Randy Mamola (USA), Suzuki, 114.68mph/184.54kph

2 Kenny Roberts (USA), Yamaha
3 Marco Lucchinelli (Ita), Suzuki
Fastest lap: Roberts, 116.16mph/186.95kph
Other winners:
350cc: Anton Mang (FRG), Kawasaki, 111.04mph/
178.70kph
250cc: Kork Ballington (SAf), Kawasaki, 108.88mph/
175.22kph
125cc: Loris Reggiani (Ita), Minarelli, 101.76mph/
163.77kph
Sidecar: Derek Jones/Bryan Ayres (UK), Yamaha,
109.26mph/175.84kph

CZECHOSLOVAK GRAND PRIX

Brno, 17 August
350cc: Anton Mang (FRG), Kawasaki, 107.91mph/
173.66kph
250cc: Anton Mang (FRG), Kawasaki, 104.11mph/
167.55kph
125cc: Guy Bertin (Fra), Motobecane, 97.30mph/
156.59kph
Sidecar: Rolf Biland/Kurt Waltisperg (Swi), Yamaha,
102.81mph/165.46kph

WEST GERMAN GRAND PRIX

Nürburgring, 24 August
500cc
1 Marco Lucchinelli (Ita), Suzuki, 100.88mph/162.34kph
2 Graeme Crosby (NZ), Suzuki
3 Wil Hartog (Hol), Suzuki
Fastest lap: Lucchinelli, 101.70mph/163.68kph
Other winners:
350cc: Jon Ekerold (SAf), Yamaha, 99.60mph/160.29kph
250cc: Kork Ballington (SAf), Kawasaki, 88.91mph/
143.09kph
125cc: Guy Bertin (Fra), Motobecane, 90.27mph/
145.28kph
50cc: Stefan Dörflinger (Swi), Kreidler, 72.27mph/
116.31kph
Sidecar: Jock Taylor (UK)/Benga Johansson (Swe),
Yamaha, 92.98mph/148.51kph

LEADING CHAMPIONSHIP POSITIONS

500cc
Riders
1 Kenny Roberts (USA) 87pts
2 Randy Mamola (USA) 72pts
3 Marco Lucchinelli (Ita) 59pts
4 Franco Uncini (Ita) 50pts
5 Graziano Rossi (Ita) 38pts
6 Wil Hartog (Hol) 31pts
Manufacturers
1 Suzuki 108pts
2 Yamaha 102pts
3 Kawasaki 13pts

350cc
1 Jon Ekerold (SAf) 63pts
2 Anton Mang (FRG) 60pts
3 Jean-François Baldé (Fra) 38pts
Manufacturers' title: Yamaha

250cc
1 Anton Mang (FRG) 128pts
2 Kork Ballington (SAf) 87pts
3 Jean-François Baldé (Fra) 59pts
Manufacturers' title: Kawasaki

125cc
1 Pier Paolo Bianchi (Ita) 90pts
2 Guy Bertin (Fra) 81pts
3 Angel Nieto (Spa) 78pts
Manufacturers' title: Minarelli

50cc
1 Eugenio Lazzarini (Ita) 74pts
2 Stefan Dörflinger (Swi) 72pts
3 Hans Hummel (Aut) 37pts
Manufacturers: Kreidler

Sidecar
1 Jock Taylor (UK) 94pts
2 Rolf Biland (Swi) 63pts
3 Alain Michel (Fra) 63pts
Manufacturers' title: Yamaha

1981

ARGENTINE GRAND PRIX

Buenos Aires, 22 March
350cc: Jon Ekerold (SAf), Yamaha, 80.47mph/129.50kph
250cc: Jean-François Baldé (Fra), Kawasaki, 78.41mph/126.19kph
125cc: Angel Nieto (Spa), Minarelli, 74.92mph/120.57kph

AUSTRIAN GRAND PRIX

Salzburgring, 26 April
500cc
1 Randy Mamola (USA), Suzuki, 114.99mph/185.07kph
2 Graeme Crosby (NZ), Suzuki
3 Hiroyuki Kawasaki (Jap), Suzuki
Fastest lap: Mamola, 117.47mph/189.05kph
Other winners:
350cc: Patrick Fernandez (Fra), Yamaha, 110.49mph/177.82kph
125cc: Angel Nieto (Spa), Minarelli, 100.42mph/161.61kph
Sidecar: Jock Taylor (UK)/Benga Johansson (Swe), Yamaha, 106.76mph/171.81kph

WEST GERMAN GRAND PRIX

Hockenheim, 3 May
500cc
1 Kenny Roberts (USA), Yamaha, 114.27mph/183.90kph
2 Randy Mamola (USA), Suzuki
3 Marco Lucchinelli (Ita), Suzuki
Fastest lap: Roberts, 116.31mph/187.18kph
Other winners:
350cc: Anton Mang (FRG), Kawasaki, 108.85mph/175.18kph
250cc: Anton Mang (FRG), Kawasaki, 106.05mph/170.67kph
125cc: Angel Nieto (Spa), Minarelli, 98.74mph/158.91kph
50cc: Stefan Dörflinger (Swi), Kreidler, 86.91mph/139.87kph
Sidecar: Alain Michel (Fra)/Michael Burkhard (FRG), Seymaz Yamaha, 105.39mph/169.61kph

ITALIAN GRAND PRIX (GRAND PRIX DES NATIONS)

Monza, 10 May
500cc
1 Kenny Roberts (USA), Yamaha, 99.73mph/160.51kph
2 Graeme Crosby (NZ), Suzuki
3 Barry Sheene (UK), Yamaha
Fastest lap: Marco Lucchinelli (Ita), Suzuki, 102.24mph/164.54kph
Other winners:
350cc: Jon Ekerold (SAf), Yamaha, 107.60mph/173.16kph
250cc: Eric Saul (Fra), Yamaha, 93.54mph/150.54kph

125cc: Guy Bertin (Fra), Sanvenero, 88.10mph/121.78kph
50cc: Ricardo Tormo (Spa), Bultaco, 87.25mph/140.41kph

FRENCH GRAND PRIX

Paul Ricard, 17 May
500cc
1 Marco Lucchinelli (Ita), Suzuki, 102.94mph/165.67kph
2 Randy Mamola (USA), Suzuki
3 Graeme Crosby (NZ), Suzuki
Fastest lap: Lucchinelli, 104.38mph/167.99kph
Other winners:
250cc: Anton Mang (FRG), Kawasaki, 97.56mph/157.01kph
125cc: Angel Nieto (Spa), Minarelli, 91.85mph/147.82kph
Sidecar: Rolf Biland/Kurt Waltisperg (Swi), Yamaha, 97.97mph/157.67kph

SPANISH GRAND PRIX

Jarama, 24 May
250cc: Anton Mang (FRG), Kawasaki, 76.53mph/123.16kph
125cc: Angel Nieto (Spa), Minarelli, 73.02mph/117.51kph
50cc: Ricardo Tormo (Spa), Bultaco, 55.96mph/67.12kph
Sidecar: Rolf Biland/Kurt Waltisperg (Swi), Yamaha, 76.57mph/123.23kph

YUGOSLAV GRAND PRIX

Rijeka, 31 May
500cc
1 Randy Mamola (USA), Suzuki, 97.72mph/157.27kph
2 Marco Lucchinelli (Ita), Suzuki
3 Kenny Roberts (USA), Yamaha
Fastest lap: Lucchinelli, 98.68mph/158.81kph
Other winners:
350cc: Anton Mang (FRG), Kawasaki, 94.98mph/152.86kph
125cc: Loris Reggiani (Ita), Minarelli, 89.80mph/144.52kph
50cc: Ricardo Tormo (Spa), Bultaco, 82.50mph/132.77kph

DUTCH TT

Assen, 27 June
500cc
1 Marco Lucchinelli (Ita), Suzuki, 91.19mph/146.76kph
2 Boet van Dulmen (Hol), Yamaha
3 Kork Ballington (SAf), Kawasaki
Fastest lap: Ballington, 93.24mph/150.05kph
Other winners:
350cc: Anton Mang (FRG), Kawasaki, 95.87mph/154.29kph
250cc: Anton Mang (FRG), Kawasaki, 94.21mph/151.62kph
125cc: Angel Nieto (Spa), Minarelli, 89.17mph/143.50kph
50cc: Ricardo Tormo (Spa), Bultaco, 80.82mph/130.07kph
Sidecar: Alain Michel (Fra)/Michael Burkhard (FRG), Seymaz Yamaha, 93.70mph/150.80kph

BELGIAN GRAND PRIX

Spa-Francorchamps, 5 July
500cc
1 Marco Lucchinelli (Ita), Suzuki, 95.40mph/153.53kph
2 Kenny Roberts (USA), Yamaha
3 Randy Mamola (USA), Suzuki
Fastest lap: Lucchinelli, 98.68mph/158.81kph
Other winners:
250cc: Anton Mang (FRG), Kawasaki, 92.41mph/148.72kph
50cc: Ricardo Tormo (Spa), Bultaco, 78.55mph/126.41kph
Sidecar: Rolf Biland/Kurt Waltisperg (Swi), Yamaha, 92.52mph/148.90kph

SAN MARINO GRAND PRIX

Imola, 12 July
500cc
1 Marco Lucchinelli (Ita), Suzuki, 93.21mph/150.01kph
2 Barry Sheene (UK), Yamaha
3 Graeme Crosby (NZ), Suzuki
Fastest lap: Sheene, 95.84mph/154.23kph
Other winners:
250cc: Anton Mang (FRG), Kawasaki, 90.40mph/145.48kph
125cc: Loris Reggiani (Ita), Minarelli, 85.49mph/137.58kph
50cc: Ricardo Tormo (Spa), Bultaco, 76.99mph/123.90kph

BRITISH GRAND PRIX

Silverstone, 2 August
500cc
1 Jack Middelburg (Hol), Suzuki, 113.29mph/182.32kph
2 Kenny Roberts (USA), Yamaha
3 Randy Mamola (USA), Suzuki
Fastest lap: Mamola and Kork Ballington (SAf), Kawasaki, 115.27mph/185.51kph
Other winners:
350cc: Anton Mang (FRG), Kawasaki, 110.87mph/178.43kph
250cc: Anton Mang (FRG), Kawasaki, 109.35mph/175.99kph

125cc: Angel Nieto (Spa), Minarelli, 101.85mph/163.91kph
Sidecar: Rolf Biland/Kurt Waltisperg (Swi), Yamaha, 110.10mph/177.19kph

FINNISH GRAND PRIX

Imatra, 9 August
500cc
1 Marco Lucchinelli (Ita), Suzuki, 95.94mph/154.40kph
2 Randy Mamola (USA), Suzuki
3 Kork Ballington (SAf), Kawasaki
Fastest lap: Lucchinelli, 97.13mph/156.32kph
Other winners:
250cc: Anton Mang (FRG), Kawasaki, 89.32mph/143.74kph
125cc: Angel Nieto (Spa), Minarelli, 84.19mph/135.49kph
Sidecar: Rolf Biland/Kurt Waltisperg (Swi), Yamaha, 88.61mph/142.60kph

SWEDISH TT

Anderstorp, 16 August
500cc
1 Barry Sheene (UK), Yamaha, 87.44mph/140.72kph
2 Boet van Dulmen (Hol), Yamaha
3 Jack Middelburg (Hol), Suzuki
Fastest lap: Sheene, 87.54mph/140.90kph
Other winners:
250cc: Anton Mang (FRG), Kawasaki, 85.41mph/137.46kph
125cc: Ricardo Tormo (Spa), Sanvenero, 72.99mph/117.47kph
Sidecar: Rolf Biland/Kurt Waltisperg (Swi), Yamaha, 85.77mph/138.03kph

CZECHOSLOVAK GRAND PRIX

Brno, 30 August
350cc: Anton Mang (FRG), Kawasaki, 108.70mph/174.93kph
250cc: Anton Mang (FRG), Kawasaki, 104.83mph/168.71kph
50cc: Theo Timmer (Hol), Bultaco, 84.26mph/135.61kph
Sidecar: Rolf Biland/Kurt Waltisperg (Swi), Yamaha, 103.94mph/167.27kph

LEADING CHAMPIONSHIP POSITIONS

500cc
Riders
1 Marco Lucchinelli (Ita) 105pts
2 Randy Mamola (USA) 94pts
3 Kenny Roberts (USA) 74pts
4 Barry Sheene (UK) 72pts
5 Graeme Crosby (NZ) 68pts
6 Boet van Dulmen (Hol) 64pts
Manufacturers
1 Suzuki 154pts
2 Yamaha 124pts
3 Kawasaki 43pts

350cc
1 Anton Mang (FRG) 103pts
2 Jon Ekerold (SAf) 52pts
3 Jean-François Baldé (Fra) 49pts
Manufacturers' title: Kawasaki

250cc
1 Anton Mang (FRG) 160pts
2 Jean-François Baldé (Fra) 95pts
3 Roland Freymond (Swi) 72pts
Manufacturers' title: Kawasaki

125cc
1 Angel Nieto (Spa) 140pts
2 Loris Reggiani (Ita) 95pts

3 Pier Paolo Bianchi (Ita) 84pts
Manufacturers' title: Minarelli

50cc
1 Ricardo Tormo (Spa) 90pts
2 Theo Timmer (Hol) 65pts
3 Stefan Dörflinger (Swi) 51pts
Manufacturers' title: Bultaco

Sidecar
1 Rolf Biland (Swi) 127pts
2 Alain Michel (Fra) 106pts
3 Jock Taylor (UK) 87pts
Manufacturers' title: Yamaha

1982

ARGENTINE GRAND PRIX

Buenos Aires, 28 March
500cc
1 Kenny Roberts (USA), Yamaha, 93.66mph/150.73kph
2 Barry Sheene (UK), Yamaha
3 Freddie Spencer (USA), Honda
Fastest lap: Roberts, 95.68mph/153.99kph
Other winners:
350cc: Carlos Lavado (Ven), Yamaha, 90.95mph/
146.37kph
125cc: Angel Nieto (Spa), Garelli, 84.80mph/136.47kph

AUSTRIAN GRAND PRIX

Salzburgring, 2 May
500cc
1 Franco Uncini (Ita), Suzuki, 115.26mph/185.43kph
2 Barry Sheene (UK), Yamaha
3 Kenny Roberts (USA), Yamaha
Fastest lap: Marco Lucchinelli (Ita), Honda, 118.87mph/
191.30kph
Other winners:
350cc: Eric Saul (Fra), Yamaha, 110.84mph/178.38kph
125cc: Angel Nieto (Spa), Garelli, 100.92mph/162.41kph
Sidecar: Rolf Biland/Kurt Waltisperg (Swi), LCR Yamaha,
109.16mph/175.68kph

FRENCH GRAND PRIX

Nogaro, 9 May
500cc
1 Michel Frutschi (Swi), Sanvenero, 81.10mph/130.51kph
2 Frank Gross (Fra), Suzuki
3 Steve Parrish (UK), Yamaha
Fastest lap: Frutschi, 82.15mph/132.20kph
Other winners:
350cc: Jean-Francois Baldé (Fra), Kawasaki, 80.58mph/
129.68kph
250cc: Jean-Louis Tournadre (Fra), Yamaha, 79.59mph/
128.08kph
125cc: Jean-Claude Selini (Fra), MBA, 76.38mph/
122.92kph

SPANISH GRAND PRIX

Jarama, 23 May
500cc
1 Kenny Roberts (USA), Yamaha, 79.97/128.70kph
2 Barry Sheene (UK), Yamaha
3 Franco Uncini (Ita), Suzuki
Fastest lap: Roberts, 81.35mph/130.92kph
Other winners:
250cc: Carlos Lavado (Ven), Yamaha, 76.60mph/
123.28kph
125cc: Angel Nieto (Spa), Garelli, 73.31mph/117.98kph
50cc: Stefan Dörflinger (Swi), Kreidler, 68.86mph/
110.82kph

ITALIAN GRAND PRIX
(GRAND PRIX DES NATIONS)

Misano, 30 May
500cc
1 Franco Uncini (Ita), Suzuki, 93.74mph/150.85kph
2 Freddie Spencer (USA), Honda
3 Graeme Crosby (NZ), Yamaha
Fastest lap: Spencer, 95.12mph/153.08kph
Other winners:
350cc: Didier de Radigues (Bel), Yamaha, 91.14mph/
146.68kph
250cc: Anton Mang (FRG), Kawasaki, 89.41mph/
143.90kph
125cc: Angel Nieto (Spa), Garelli, 86.22mph/138.76kph
50cc: Stefan Dörflinger (Swi), Kreidler, 77.37mph/
124.51kph

DUTCH TT

Assen, 26 June
500cc
1 Franco Uncini (Ita), Suzuki, 98.78mph/158.97kph
2 Kenny Roberts (USA), Yamaha
3 Barry Sheene (UK), Yamaha
Fastest lap: Freddie Spencer (USA), Honda, 100.90mph/
162.38kph
Other winners:
350cc: Jean-Francois Baldé (Fra), Kawasaki, 95.04mph/
152.95kph
250cc: Anton Mang (FRG), Kawasaki, 94.15mph/
152.10kph
125cc: Angel Nieto (Spa), Garelli, 90.16mph/145.10kph
50cc: Stefan Dörflinger (Swi), Kreidler, 80.52mph/129.58kph
Sidecar: Rolf Biland/Kurt Waltisperg (Swi), LCR Yamaha,
85.25mph/137.20kph

BELGIAN GRAND PRIX

Spa-Francorchamps, 4 July
500cc
1 Freddie Spencer (USA), Honda, 98.15mph/157.87kph
2 Barry Sheene (UK), Yamaha
3 Franco Uncini (Ita), Suzuki
Fastest lap: Spencer, 99.43mph/160.02kph
Other winners:
250cc: Anton Mang (FRG), Kawasaki, 93.10mph/
149.83kph
125cc: Ricardo Tormó (Spa), Sanvenero, 88.46mph/
142.36kph
Sidecar: Rolf Biland/Kurt Waltisperg (Swi), LCR Yamaha,
92.95mph/149.59kph

YUGOSLAV GRAND PRIX

Rijeka, 18 July
500cc
1 Franco Uncini (Ita) Suzuki, 98.41mph/158.36kph
2 Graeme Crosby (NZ), Yamaha
3 Barry Sheene (UK), Yamaha
Fastest lap: Uncini, 99.51mph/160.14kph
Other winners:
250cc: Didier de Radigues (Bel), Yamaha, 93.40mph/
150.31kph

125cc: Eugenio Lazzarini (Ita), Garelli, 91.46mph/147.19kph
50cc: Eugenio Lazzarini (Ita), Garelli, 83.62mph/134.57kph

BRITISH GRAND PRIX

Silverstone, 1 August
500cc
1 Franco Uncini (Ita), Suzuki, 114.62mph/184.46kph
2 Freddie Spencer (USA), Honda
3 Graeme Crosby (NZ), Yamaha
Fastest lap: Crosby, 116.42mph/187.36kph
Other winners:
350cc: Jean-Francois Baldé (Fra), Kawasaki, 109.68mph/176.51kph
250cc: Martin Wimmer (FRG), Yamaha, 109.44mph/176.13kph
125cc: Angel Nieto (Spa), Garelli, 105.04mph/169.05kph
Sidecar: Egbert Streuer/Bernie Schneiders (Hol), LCR Yamaha, 109.91mph/176.88kph

SWEDISH TT

Anderstorp, 7–8 August
500cc
1 Takazumi Katayama (Jap), Honda, 89.31mph/143.72kph
2 Randy Mamola (USA), Suzuki
3 Graeme Crosby (NZ), Yamaha
Fastest lap: Mamola, 91.72mph/147.61kph
Other winners:
250cc: Roland Freymond (Swi), MBA, 86.51mph/139.23kph
125cc: Ivan Palazzese (Ven), MBA, 82.16mph/132.22kph
Sidecar: Rolf Biland/Kurt Waltisperg (Swi), LCR Yamaha, 86.12mph/138.60kph

FINNISH GRAND PRIX

Imatra, 15 August
350cc: Anton Mang (FRG), Kawasaki, 78.68mph/126.62kph
250cc: Christian Sarron (Fra), Yamaha, 79.09mph/127.28kph
125cc: Ivan Palazzese (Ven), MBA, 75.37mph/121.30kph
Sidecar: Rolf Biland/Kurt Waltisperg (Swi), LCR Yamaha, 76.44mph/123.02kph

CZECHOSLOVAK GRAND PRIX

Brno, 29 August
350cc: Didier de Radigues (Bel), Yamaha, 107.63mph/173.21kph
250cc: Carlos Lavado (Ven), Yamaha, 104.31mph/167.87kph
125cc: Eugenio Lazzarini (Ita), Garelli, 99.24mph/149.71kph
Sidecar: Alain Michel (Fra)/Michael Burkhard (FRG), Seymaz Yamaha, 102.84mph/165.50kph

SAN MARINO GRAND PRIX

Mugello, 5 September
500cc
1 Freddie Spencer (USA), Honda, 93.36mph/150.25kph
2 Randy Mamola (USA), Suzuki
3 Graeme Crosby (NZ), Yamaha
Fastest lap: Takazumi Katayama (Jap), Honda, 94.86mph/152.66kph
Other winners:
250cc: Anton Mang (FRG), Kawasaki, 89.29mph/143.71kph
50cc: Eugenio Lazzarini (Ita), Garelli, 73.51mph/118.30kph
Sidecar: Alain Michel (Fra)/Michael Burkhard (FRG), Seymaz Yamaha, 89.49mph/144.02kph

WEST GERMAN GRAND PRIX

Hockenheim, 26 September
500cc
1 Randy Mamola (USA), Suzuki, 116.03mph/186.73kph
2 Virginio Ferrari (Ita), Suzuki
3 Loris Reggiani (Ita), Suzuki
Fastest lap: Freddie Spencer (USA), Honda, 117.56mph/171.80kph
Other winners:
350cc: Manfred Herweh (FRG), Yamaha, 98.08mph/157.84kph
250cc: Anton Mang (FRG), Kawasaki, 106.75mph/171.80kph
50cc: Eugenio Lazzarini (Ita), Garelli, 88.26mph/142.04kph
Sidecar: Rolf Biland/Kurt Waltisperg (Swi), LCR Yamaha, 95.85mph/154.26kph

LEADING CHAMPIONSHIP POSITIONS

500cc
Riders
1 Franco Uncini (Ita) 103pts
2 Graeme Crosby (NZ) 76pts
3 Freddie Spencer (USA) 72pts
4 Kenny Roberts (USA) 68pts
5 Barry Sheene (UK) 68pts
6 Randy Mamola (USA) 65pts
Manufacturers
1 Suzuki 154pts
2 Yamaha 133pts
3 Honda 106pts

350cc
1 Anton Mang (FRG) 81pts
2 Didier de Radigues (Bel) 64pts
3 Jean-Francois Baldé (Fra) 59pts
Manufacturers' title: Kawasaki

250cc
1 Jean-Louis Tournadre (Fra) 118pts
2 Anton Mang (FRG) 117pts
3 Roland Freymond (Swi) 72pts
Manufacturers' title: Yamaha

125cc
1 Angel Nieto (Spa) 111pts
2 Eugenio Lazzarini (Ita) 95pts
3 Ivan Palazzese (Ven) 75pts
Manufacturers' title: Garelli

50cc
1 Stefan Dörflinger (Swi) 81pts
2 Eugenio Lazzarini (Ita) 69pts
3 Claudio Lusuardi (Ita) 43pts
Manufacturers' title: not awarded

Sidecar
1 Werner Schwärzel (FRG) 86pts
2 Rolf Biland (Swi) 82½pts
3 Alain Michel (Fra) 68pts
Manufacturers' title: LCR Yamaha

1983

SOUTH AFRICAN GRAND PRIX

Kyalami, 19 March
500cc
1 Freddie Spencer (USA), Honda, 104.38mph/167.99kph
2 Kenny Roberts (USA), Yamaha
3 Ron Haslam (UK), Honda
Fastest lap: Spencer, 106.22mph/170.94kph
Other winners:
250cc: Jean-Francois Baldé (Fra), Chevalier, 98.60mph/
158.67kph

FRENCH GRAND PRIX

Le Mans, 3 April
500cc
1 Freddie Spencer (USA), Honda, 95.91mph/154.35kph
2 Marco Lucchinelli (Ita), Honda
3 Ron Haslam (UK), Honda
Fastest lap: Spencer, 97.28mph/156.55kph
Other winners:
250cc: Alan Carter (UK), Yamaha, 89.27mph/143.67kph
125cc: Ricardo Tormo (Spa), MBA, 81.99mph/131.94kph
50cc: Stefan Dörflinger (Swi), Krauser Kreidler,
64.81mph/104.30kph
Sidecar: Rolf Biland/Kurt Waltisperg (Swi), LCR Yamaha,
87.97mph/141.60kph

ITALIAN GRAND PRIX
(GRAND PRIX DES NATIONS)

Monza, 24 April
500cc
1 Freddie Spencer (USA), Honda, 113.38mph/182.45kph
2 Randy Mamola (USA), Suzuki
3 Eddie Lawson (USA), Yamaha
Fastest lap: Kenny Roberts (USA), Yamaha, 115.02mph/
185.11kph
Other winners:
250cc: Carlos Lavado (Ven), Yamaha, 105.39mph/
169.61kph
125cc: Angel Nieto (Spa), Garelli, 85.17mph/137.07kph
50cc: Eugenio Lazzarini (Ita), Garelli, 85.55mph/
137.68kph

WEST GERMAN GRAND PRIX

Hockenheim, 8 May
500cc
1 Kenny Roberts (USA), Yamaha, 115.18mph/185.37kph
2 Takazumi Katayama (Jap), Honda
3 Marco Lucchinelli (Ita), Honda
Fastest lap: Katayama 116.38mph/187.29kph
Other winners:
250cc: Carlos Lavado (Ven), Yamaha, 102.80mph/
165.44kph
125cc: Angel Nieto (Spa), Garelli, 101.57mph/163.46kph
50cc: Stefan Dörflinger (Swi), Krauser Kreidler,
88.67mph/142.71kph

Sidecar: Egbert Streuer/Bernie Schneiders (Hol), LCR
Yamaha, 98.00mph/157.71kph

SPANISH GRAND PRIX

Jarama, 22 May
500cc
1 Freddie Spencer (USA), Honda, 81.16mph/130.62kph
2 Kenny Roberts (USA), Yamaha
3 Takazumi Katayama (Jap), Honda
Fastest lap: Roberts, 82.71mph/133.12kph
Other winners:
250cc: Hervé Guilleux (Fra), Kawasaki, 78.15mph/
125.77kph
125cc: Angel Nieto (Spa), Garelli, 74.02mph/119.11kph
50cc: Eugenio Lazzarini (Ita), Garelli, 67.31mph/
108.32kph

AUSTRIAN GRAND PRIX

Salzburgring, 29 May
500cc
1 Kenny Roberts (USA), Yamaha, 118.24mph/190.28kph
2 Eddie Lawson (USA), Yamaha
3 Randy Mamola (USA), Suzuki
Fastest lap: Mamola, 121.42mph/195.42kph
Other winners:
250cc: Manfred Herweh (FRG), Rotax Real, 106.53mph/
171.44kph
125cc: Angel Nieto (Spa), Garelli, 103.94mph/167.27kph
Sidecar: Rolf Biland/Kurt Waltisperg (Swi), LCR Yamaha,
108.33mph/174.34kph

YUGOSLAV GRAND PRIX

Rijeka, 12 June
500cc
1 Freddie Spencer (USA), Honda, 98.80mph/159.00kph
2 Randy Mamola (USA), Suzuki
3 Eddie Lawson (USA), Yamaha
Fastest lap: Spencer, 99.89mph/160.72kph
Other winners:
250cc: Carlos Lavado (Ven), Yamaha, 94.85mph/
152.64kph
125cc: Bruno Kneubühler (Swi), MBA, 90.26mph/
145.26kph
50cc: Stefan Dörflinger (Swi), Krauser Kreidler,
81.77mph/131.60kph

DUTCH TT

Assen, 25 June
500cc
1 Kenny Roberts (USA), Yamaha, 100.79mph/162.20kph
2 Takazumi Katayama (Jap), Honda
3 Freddie Spencer (USA), Honda
Fastest lap: Roberts, 102.65mph/165.20kph
Other winners:
250cc: Carlos Lavado (Ven), Yamaha, 95.02mph/
152.92kph
125cc: Angel Nieto (Spa), Garelli, 90.98mph/146.41kph
50cc: Eugenio Lazzarini (Ita), Garelli, 82.07mph/
132.08kph

The thrill of the start of a sidecar race is captured here at a crowded Spa-Francorchamps in 1983

Sidecar: Rolf Biland/Kurt Waltisperg (Swi), LCR Yamaha, 93.39mph/105.29kph

BELGIAN GRAND PRIX

Spa-Francorchamps, 3 July
500cc
1 Kenny Roberts (USA), Yamaha, 101.24mph/162.93kph
2 Freddie Spencer (USA), Honda
3 Randy Mamola (USA), Suzuki
Fastest lap: Roberts, 102.33mph/164.67kph
Other winners:
250cc: Didier de Radigues (Bel), Chevalier, 95.86mph/154.26kph
125cc: Eugenio Lazzarini (Ita), Garelli, 91.35mph/147.01kph
Sidecar: Rolf Biland/Kurt Waltisperg (Swi), LCR Yamaha, 94.98mph/152.85kph

BRITISH GRAND PRIX

Silverstone, 31 July
500cc
1 Kenny Roberts (USA), Yamaha, 116.20mph/187.00kph
2 Freddie Spencer (USA), Honda
3 Randy Mamola (USA), Suzuki
Fastest lap: Roberts, 119.46mph/192.25kph
Other winners:
250cc: Jacques Bolle (Fra), Pernod, 109.83mph/176.76kph
125cc: Angel Nieto (Spa), Garelli, 103.69mph/166.86kph
Sidecar: Egbert Streuer/Bernie Schneiders (Hol), LCR Yamaha, 110.78mph/178.28kph

SWEDISH TT

Anderstorp, 6 August
500cc
1 Freddie Spencer (USA), Honda, 91.46mph/147.20kph
2 Kenny Roberts (USA), Yamaha
3 Takazumi Katayama (Jap), Honda
Fastest lap: Roberts, 92.86mph/149,44kph
Other winners:
250cc: Christian Sarron (Fra), Yamaha, 77.99mph/125.51kph
125cc: Bruno Kneubühler (Swi), MBA, 82.57mph/132.88kph
Sidecar: Rolf Biland/Kurt Waltisperg (Swi), LCR Yamaha, 87.12mph/140.21kph

SAN MARINO GRAND PRIX

Imola, 4 September
500cc
1 Kenny Roberts (USA), Yamaha, 97.31mph/156.60kph
2 Freddie Spencer (USA), Honda
3 Eddie Lawson (USA), Yamaha
Fastest lap: Roberts, 99.46mph/160.07kph
Other winners:
125cc: Maurizio Vitali (Ita), MBA, 86.96mph/139.94kph
50cc: Ricardo Tormo (Spa), Garelli, 78.52mph/126.36kph
Sidecar: Rolf Biland/Kurt Waltisperg (Swi), LCR Yamaha, 89.23mph/143.59kph

LEADING CHAMPIONSHIP POSITIONS

500cc
Riders
1 Freddie Spencer (USA) 144pts
2 Kenny Roberts (USA) 142pts
3 Randy Mamola (USA) 89pts
4 Eddie Lawson (USA) 78pts
5 Takazumi Katayama (Jap) 77pts
6 Marc Fontan (Fra) 64pts
Manufacturers
1 Honda 158pts
2 Yamaha 154pts
3 Suzuki 98pts

250cc
1 Carlos Lavado (Ven) 100pts
2 Christian Sarron (Fra) 73pts
3 Didier de Radigues (Bel) 68pts
Manufacturers' title: Yamaha

125cc
1 Angel Nieto (Spa) 102pts
2 Bruno Kneubühler (Swi) 76pts
3 Eugenio Lazzarini (Ita) 67pts
Manufacturers' title: MBA

50cc
1 Stefan Dörflinger (Swi) 81pts
2 Eugenio Lazzarini (Ita) 69pts
3 Claudio Lusuardi (Ita) 38pts
Manufacturers' title: Garelli

Sidecar
1 Rolf Biland (Swi) 98pts
2 Egbert Streuer (Hol) 72pts
3 Alain Michel (Fra) 55pts
Manufacturers' title: LCR Yamaha

1984

SOUTH AFRICAN GRAND PRIX

Kyalami, 24 March
500cc
1 Eddie Lawson (USA), Yamaha, 85.94mph/138.31kph
2 Raymond Roche (Fra), Honda
3 Barry Sheene (UK), Suzuki
Fastest lap: Sheene, 89.94mph/144.74kph
Other winners:
250cc: Patrick Fernandez (Fra), Yamaha, 90.83mph/146.17kph

ITALIAN GRAND PRIX
(GRAND PRIX DES NATIONS)

Misano, 15 April
500cc
1 Freddie Spencer (USA), Honda, 93.99mph/151.26kph
2 Eddie Lawson (USA), Yamaha
3 Raymond Roche (Fra), Honda
Fastest lap: Spencer, 95.92mph/154.37kph
Other winners:
250cc: Fausto Ricci (Ita), Yamaha, 91.13mph/146.65kph
125cc: Angel Nieto (Spa), Garelli, 87.64mph/141.05kph
80cc: Pier Paolo Bianchi (Ita), Casal, 81.08mph/130.49kph

SPANISH GRAND PRIX

Jarama, 6 May
500cc
1 Eddie Lawson (USA), Yamaha, 80.03mph/128.79kph
2 Randy Mamola (USA), Honda
3 Raymond Roche (Fra), Honda
Fastest lap: Lawson, 81.56mph/131.26kph
Other winners:
250cc: Sito Pons (Spa), Cobas, 78.04mph/125.59kph
125cc: Angel Nieto (Spa), Garelli, 71.48mph/115.04kph
80cc: Pier Paolo Bianchi (Ita), Casal, 67.89mph/109.26kph

AUSTRIAN GRAND PRIX

Salzburgring, 20 May
500cc
1 Eddie Lawson (USA), Yamaha, 118.33mph/190.44kph
2 Freddie Spencer (USA), Honda
3 Randy Mamola (USA), Honda
Fastest lap: Mamola, 120.11mph/193.30kph
Other winners:
250cc: Christian Sarron (Fra), Yamaha, 110.05mph/177.11kph
80cc: Stefan Dörflinger (Swi), Zündapp, 96.89mph/155.93kph
Sidecar: Egbert Streuer/Bernie Schneiders (Hol), LCR Yamaha, 110.37mph/177.63kph

WEST GERMAN GRAND PRIX

Nürburgring, 27 May
500cc
1 Freddie Spencer (USA), Honda, 96.52mph/155.33kph
2 Eddie Lawson (USA), Yamaha
3 Randy Mamola (USA), Honda
Fastest lap: Spencer, 98.23mph/158.09kph
Other winners:
250cc: Christian Sarron (Fra), Yamaha, 91.63mph/147.46kph
125cc: Angel Nieto (Spa), Garelli, 87.04mph/140.07kph
80cc: Stefan Dörflinger (Swi), Zündapp, 81.91mph/131.82kph
Sidecar: Egbert Streuer/Bernie Schneiders (Hol), LCR Yamaha, 96.52mph/155.33kph

FRENCH GRAND PRIX

Paul Ricard, 11 June
500cc
1 Freddie Spencer (USA), Honda, 104.50mph/168.17kph
2 Eddie Lawson (USA), Yamaha
3 Randy Mamola (USA), Honda
Fastest lap: Spencer, 106.56mph/171.49kph
Other winners:
250cc: Anton Mang (FRG), Yamaha, 99.19mph/159.62kph
125cc: Angel Nieto (Spa), Garelli, 94.64mph/152.31kph
Sidecar: Rolf Biland/Kurt Waltisperg (Swi), LCR Yamaha, 100.29mph/161.40kph

YUGOSLAV GRAND PRIX

Rijeka, 17 June
500cc
1 Freddie Spencer (USA), Honda, 99.43mph/160.02kph
2 Randy Mamola (USA), Honda
3 Raymond Roche (Fra), Honda
Fastest lap: Spencer, 100.98mph/162.51kph
Other winners:
250cc: Manfred Herweh (FRG), Real, 95.44mph/153.6kph
80cc: Stefan Dörflinger (Swi), Zündapp, 88.04mph/
141.69kph

DUTCH TT

Assen, 30 June
500cc
1 Randy Mamola (USA), Honda, 99.84mph/160.67kph
2 Raymond Roche (Fra), Honda
3 Eddie Lawson (USA), Yamaha
Fastest lap: Lawson, 101.67mph/162.67kph
Other winners:
250cc: Carlos Lavado (Ven), Yamaha, 90.70mph/
145.96kph
125cc: Angel Nieto (Spa), Garelli, 89.87mph/144.63kph
80cc: Jorge Martinez (Spa), Derbi, 84.41mph/135.84kph
Sidecar: Rolf Biland/Kurt Waltisperg (Swi), LCR Yamaha,
94.44mph/151.99kph

BELGIAN GRAND PRIX

Spa-Francorchamps, 8 July
500cc
1 Freddie Spencer (USA), Honda, 100.38mph/161.54kph
2 Randy Mamola (USA), Honda
3 Raymond Roche (Fra), Honda
Fastest lap: Spencer, 101.61mph/163.53kph
Other winners:
250cc: Manfred Herweh (FRG), Real, 95.67mph/
152.96kph
80cc: Stefan Dörflinger (Swi), Zündapp, 85.78mph/
138.05kph
Sidecar: Alain Michel/Jean-Marc Fresc (Fra), LCR
Yamaha, 95.48mph/153.66kph

BRITISH GRAND PRIX

Silverstone, 5 August
500cc
1 Randy Mamola (USA), Honda, 116.22mph/187.04kph
2 Eddie Lawson (USA), Yamaha
3 Ron Haslam (UK), Honda
Fastest lap: Mamola 117.64mph/189.32kph
Other winners:
250cc: Christian Sarron (Fra), Yamaha, 110.72mph/
178.18kph
125cc: Angel Nieto (Spa), Garelli, 104.14mph/167.60kph
Sidecar: Egbert Streuer/Bernie Schneiders (Hol), LCR
Yamaha, 112.68mph/181.34kph

SWEDISH TT

Anderstorp, 12 August
500cc
1 Eddie Lawson (USA), Yamaha, 90.15mph/145.08kph
2 Raymond Roche (Fra), Honda
3 Wayne Gardner (Aus), Honda
Fastest lap: Lawson, 91.41mph/147.10kph
Other winners:
250cc: Manfred Herweh (FRG), Real, 86.43mph/
139.10kph
125cc: Fausto Gresini (Ita), Garelli, 83.17mph/133.85kph
Sidecar: Rolf Biland/Kurt Waltisperg (Swi), LCR Yamaha,
87.79mph/141.28kph

SAN MARINO GRAND PRIX

Mugello, 2 September
500cc
1 Randy Mamola (USA), Honda, 93.97mph/151.23kph
2 Raymond Roche (Fra), Honda
3 Ron Haslam (UK), Honda
Fastest lap: Mamola, 94.81mph/152.58kph
Other winners:
250cc: Manfred Herweh (FRG), Real, 90.79mph/
146.11kph
125cc: Maurizio Vitali (Ita), MBA, 88.79mph/142.89kph
80cc: Gerhard Waibel (FRG), Real, 84.12mph/135.37kph

LEADING CHAMPIONSHIP POSITIONS

500cc
Riders
1 Eddie Lawson (USA) 142pts
2 Randy Mamola (USA) 111pts
3 Raymond Roche (Fra) 99pts
4 Freddie Spencer (USA) 87pts
5 Ron Haslam (UK) 77pts
6 Barry Sheene (UK) 34pts
Manufacturers
1 Honda 168pts
2 Yamaha 142pts
3 Suzuki 64pts

250cc
1 Christian Sarron (Fra) 109pts
2 Manfred Herweh (FRG) 100pts
3 Carlos Lavado (Ven) 77pts
Manufacturers' title: Yamaha

125cc
1 Angel Nieto (Spa) 90pts
2 Eugenio Lazzarini (Ita) 68pts
3 Fausto Gresini (Ita) 51pts
Manufacturers' title: Garelli

80cc
1 Stefan Dörflinger (Swi) 82pts
2 Hubert Abold (FRG) 75pts
3 Pier Paolo Bianchi (Ita) 68pts
Manufacturers' title: Zündapp

Sidecar
1 Egbert Streuer (Hol) 75pts
2 Werner Schwärzel (Swi) 72pts
3 Alain Michel (Fra) 65pts
Manufacturers' title: LCR Yamaha

1985

SOUTH AFRICAN GRAND PRIX

Kyalami, 23 March
500cc
1 Eddie Lawson (USA), Yamaha, 106.83mph/171.93kph
2 Freddie Spencer (USA), Honda
3 Wayne Gardner (Aus), Honda
Fastest lap: Spencer, 108.12mph/174.00kph
Other winners:
250cc: Freddie Spencer (USA), Honda, 102.15mph/
164.39kph

SPANISH GRAND PRIX

Jarama, 5 May
500cc
1 Freddie Spencer (USA), Honda, 81.47mph/131.11kph
2 Eddie Lawson (USA), Yamaha
3 Christian Sarron (Fra), Yamaha
Fastest lap: Spencer, 83.25mph/133.98kph
Other winners:
250cc: Carlos Lavado (Ven), Yamaha, 79.49mph/
127.92kph
125cc: Pier Paolo Bianchi (Ita), MBA, 75.84mph/
122.05kph
80cc: Jorge Martinez (Spa), Derbi, 71.62mph/115.26kph

WEST GERMAN GRAND PRIX

Hockenheim, 19 May
500cc
1 Christian Sarron (Fra), Yamaha, 106.65mph/171.63kph
2 Freddie Spencer (USA), Honda
3 Ron Haslam (UK), Honda
Fastest lap: Sarron, 108.71mph/174.95kph
Other winners:
250cc: Martin Wimmer (FRG), Yamaha, 101.36mph/
163.13kph
125cc: August Auinger (Aut), Monnet, 93.19mph/
149.98kph
80cc: Stefan Dörflinger (Swi), Krauser, 88.65mph/
142.67kph
Sidecar: Werner Schwärzel/Fritz Buck (FRG), LCR
Yamaha, 100.73mph/162.11kph

ITALIAN GRAND PRIX
(GRAND PRIX DES NATIONS)

Mugello, 26 May
500cc
1 Freddie Spencer (USA), Honda, 94.77mph/152.52kph
2 Eddie Lawson (USA), Yamaha
3 Wayne Gardner (Aus), Honda
Fastest lap: Spencer, 96.00mph/154.49kph
Other winners:
250cc: Freddie Spencer (USA), Honda, 92.52mph/
148.89kph

125cc: Pier Paolo Bianchi (Ita), MBA, 88.28mph/
142.07kph
80cc: Jorge Martinez (Spa), Derbi, 85.07mph/136.90kph

AUSTRIAN GRAND PRIX

Salzburgring, 2 June
500cc
1 Freddie Spencer (USA), Honda, 116.59mph/187.64kph
2 Eddie Lawson (USA), Yamaha
3 Christian Sarron (Fra), Yamaha
Fastest lap: Spencer, 121.32mph/195.24kph
Other winners:
250cc: Freddie Spencer (USA), Honda, 112.03mph/
180.29kph
125cc: Fausto Gresini (Ita), Garelli, 105.62mph/
169.97kph
Sidecar: Rolf Biland/Kurt Waltisperg (Swi), Krauser,
101.26mph/162.96kph

YUGOSLAV GRAND PRIX

Rijeka, 16 June
500cc
1 Eddie Lawson (USA), Yamaha, 99.90mph/160.77kph
2 Freddie Spencer (USA), Honda
3 Wayne Gardner (Aus), Honda
Fastest lap: Lawson, 101.59mph/163.49kph
Other winners:
250cc: Freddie Spencer (USA), Honda, 97.46mph/
156.85kph
80cc: Stefan Dörflinger (Swi), Krauser, 88.48mph/
142.39kph

DUTCH TT

Assen, 29 June
500cc
1 Randy Mamola (USA), Honda, 90.06mph/144.94kph
2 Ron Haslam (UK), Honda
3 Wayne Gardner (Aus), Honda
Fastest lap: Gardner, 92.30mph/148.54kph
Other winners:
250cc: Freddie Spencer (USA), Honda, 90.99mph/
146.43kph
125cc: Pier Paolo Bianchi (Ita), MBA, 83.50mph/
134.38kph
80cc: Gerd Kafka (Aut), Seel, 81.76mph/131.58kph
Sidecar: Rolf Biland/Kurt Waltisperg (Swi), Krauser,
93.76mph/150.90kph

BELGIAN GRAND PRIX

Spa-Francorchamps, 7 July
500cc
1 Freddie Spencer (USA), Honda, 103.78mph/167.02kph
2 Eddie Lawson (USA), Yamaha
3 Christian Sarron (Fra), Yamaha
Fastest lap: Lawson, 104.65mph/168.41kph
Other winners:
250cc: Freddie Spencer (USA), Honda, 98.34mph/
158.27kph
125cc: Fausto Gresini (Ita), Garelli, 92.19mph/148.36kph

Sidecar: Egbert Streuer/Bernie Schneiders (Hol), LCR Yamaha, 97.47mph/156.87kph

FRENCH GRAND PRIX

Le Mans, 21 July
500cc
1 Freddie Spencer (USA), Honda, 99.72mph/160.48kph
2 Raymond Roche (Fra), Yamaha
3 Randy Mamola (USA), Honda
Fastest lap: Sarron, 100.99mph/162.52kph
Other winners:
250cc: Freddie Spencer (USA), Honda, 94.82mph/152.59kph
125cc: Ezio Gianolo (Ita), Garelli, 88.74mph/142.81kph
80cc: Angel Nieto (Spa), Derbi, 82.12mph/132.17kph
Sidecar: Egbert Streuer/Bernie Schneiders (Hol), LCR Yamaha, 93.74mph/150.86kph

BRITISH GRAND PRIX

Silverstone, 4 August
500cc
1 Freddie Spencer (USA), Honda, 99.66mph/160.39kph
2 Eddie Lawson (USA), Yamaha
3 Christian Sarron (Fra), Yamaha
Fastest lap: Spencer, 101.77mph/163.78kph
Other winners:
250cc: Anton Mang (FRG), Honda, 96.75mph/155.70kph

125cc: August Auinger (Aut), Monnet, 90.12mph/145.56kph

SWEDISH TT

Anderstorp, 11 August
500cc
1 Freddie Spencer (USA), Honda, 91.18mph/146.74kph
2 Eddie Lawson (USA), Yamaha
3 Ron Haslam (UK), Honda
Fastest lap: Spencer, 92.67mph/149.14kph
Other winners:
250cc: Anton Mang (FRG), Honda, 87.85mph/141.38kph
125cc: August Auinger (Aut), Monnet, 77.00mph/123.92kph
Sidecar: Egbert Streuer/Bernie Schneiders (Hol), LCR Yamaha, 87.83mph/141.35kph

SAN MARINO GRAND PRIX

Misano, 1 September
500cc
1 Eddie Lawson (USA), Yamaha, 95.67mph/153.97kph
2 Wayne Gardner (Aus), Honda
3 Randy Mamola (USA), Honda
Fastest lap: Lawson, 96.97mph/156.06kph
Other winners:
250cc: Carlos Lavado (Ven), Yamaha, 92.96mph/149.61kph
125cc: Fausto Gresini (Ita), Garelli, 89.24mph/143.62kph
80cc: Jorge Martinez (Spa), Derbi, 84.15mph/135.42kph

LEADING CHAMPIONSHIP POSITIONS

500cc
Riders
1 Freddie Spencer (USA) 141pts
2 Eddie Lawson (USA) 133pts
3 Christian Sarron (Fra) 80pts
4 Wayne Gardner (Aus) 73pts
5 Ron Haslam (UK) 73pts
6 Randy Mamola (USA) 72pts
Manufacturers
1 Honda 168pts
2 Yamaha 144pts
3 Suzuki 26pts

250cc
1 Freddie Spencer (USA) 127pts
2 Anton Mang (FRG) 124pts
3 Carlos Lavado (Ven) 94pts
Manufacturers' title: Honda

125cc
1 Fausto Gresini (Ita) 109pts
2 Pier Paolo Bianchi (Ita) 99pts
3 August Auinger (Aut) 78pts
Manufacturers' title: MBA

80cc
1 Stefan Dörflinger (Swi) 86pts
2 Jorge Martinez (Spa) 67pts
3 Gerd Kafka (Aut) 48pts
Manufacturers' title: Krauser

Sidecar
1 Egbert Streuer (Hol) 73pts
2 Werner Schwärzel (FRG) 73pts
3 Rolf Biland (Swi) 50pts
Manufacturers' title: LCR Yamaha

1986

SPANISH GRAND PRIX

Jarama, 4 May
500cc
1 Wayne Gardner (Aus), Honda, 81.60mph/131.31kph
2 Eddie Lawson (USA), Yamaha
3 Mike Baldwin (USA), Yamaha
Fastest lap: Gardner, 82.97mph/133.53kph
Other winners:
250cc: Carlos Lavado (Ven), Yamaha, 80.07mph/

128.85kph
125cc: Fausto Gresini (Ita), Garelli, 76.02mph/122.34kph
80cc: Jorge Martinez (Spa), Derbi, 73.41mph/118.14kph

ITALIAN GRAND PRIX (GRAND PRIX DES NATIONS)

Monza, 18 May
500cc
1 Eddie Lawson (USA), Yamaha, 116.26mph/187.10kph
2 Randy Mamola (USA), Yamaha
3 Mike Baldwin (USA), Yamaha
Fastest lap: Baldwin, 118.69mph/191.02kph

Other winners:
250cc: Anton Mang (FRG), Honda, 109.34mph/
175.97kph
125cc: Fausto Gresini (Ita), Garelli, 102.81mph/
165.46kph
80cc: Stefan Dörflinger (Swi), Krauser, 97.12mph/
156.30kph

WEST GERMAN GRAND PRIX

Nürburgring, 25 May
500cc
1 Eddie Lawson (USA), Yamaha, 97.33mph/156.63kph
2 Wayne Gardner (Aus), Honda
3 Mike Baldwin (USA), Yamaha
Fastest lap: Lawson, 99.91mph/158.38kph
Other winners:
250cc: Carlos Lavado (Ven), Yamaha, 93.97mph/
151.23kph
125cc: Luca Cadalora (Ita), Garelli, 89.37mph/143.83kph
80cc: Manuel Herreros (Spa), Derbi, 84.40mph/
135.83kph
Sidecar: Egbert Streuer/Bernie Schneiders (Hol), LCR
Yamaha, 92.36mph/148.64kph

AUSTRIAN GRAND PRIX

Salzburgring, 8 June
500cc
1 Eddie Lawson (USA), Yamaha, 113.73mph/183.02kph
2 Wayne Gardner (Aus), Honda
3 Randy Mamola (USA), Yamaha
Fastest lap: Lawson, 115.19mph/183.37kph
Other winners:
250cc: Carlos Lavado (Ven), Yamaha, 107.24mph/
172.58kph
125cc: Luca Cadalora (Ita), Garelli, 95.61mph/153.86kph
80cc: Jorge Martinez (Spa), Derbi, 94.81mph/152.58kph
Sidecar: Egbert Streuer/Bernie Schneiders (Hol), LCR
Yamaha, 105.84mph/170.33kph

YUGOSLAV GRAND PRIX

Rijeka, 15 June
500cc
1 Eddie Lawson (USA), Yamaha, 99.59mph/160.28kph
2 Randy Mamola (USA), Yamaha
3 Wayne Gardner (Aus), Honda
Fastest lap: Lawson, 101.21mph/162.88kph
Other winners:
250cc: Sito Pons (Spa), Honda, 95.96mph/154.44kph
80cc: Jorge Martinez (Spa), Derbi, 89.78mph/144.48kph

DUTCH TT

Assen, 28 June
500cc
1 Wayne Gardner (Aus), Honda, 100.98mph/162.50kph
2 Randy Mamola (USA), Yamaha
3 Mike Baldwin (USA), Yamaha
Fastest lap: Gardner, 102.19mph/164.45kph
Other winners:
250cc: Carlos Lavado (Ven), Yamaha, 97.50mph/156.91kph

125cc: Luca Cadalora (Ita), Garelli, 92.63mph/149.08kph
80cc: Jorge Martinez (Spa), Derbi, 88.38mph/141.23kph
Sidecar: Alain Michel/Jean-Marc Fresc (Fra), LCR
Yamaha, 94.45mph/151.99kph

BELGIAN GRAND PRIX

Spa-Francorchamps, 6 July
500cc
1 Randy Mamola (USA), Yamaha, 90.13mph/145.04kph
2 Eddie Lawson (USA), Yamaha
3 Christian Sarron (Fra), Yamaha
Fastest lap: Mamola, 91.87mph/147.84kph
Other winners:
250cc: Sito Pons (Spa), Honda, 86.76mph/139.60kph
125cc: Domenico Brigaglia (Ita), MBA, 83.54mph/
134.45kph
Sidecar: Steve Webster/Tony Hewitt (UK), LCR Yamaha,
86.07mph/138.52kph

FRENCH GRAND PRIX

Paul Ricard, 20 July
500cc
1 Eddie Lawson (USA), Yamaha, 105.91mph/170.44kph
2 Randy Mamola (USA), Yamaha
3 Christian Sarron (Fra), Yamaha
Fastest lap: Lawson, 106.95mph/170.12kph
Other winners:
250cc: Carlos Lavado (Ven), Yamaha, 101.03mph/
162.59kph
125cc: Luca Cadalora (Ita), Garelli, 95.88mph/154.30kph
Sidecar: Egbert Streuer/Bernie Schneiders (Hol), LCR
Yamaha, 100.39mph/161.57kph

BRITISH GRAND PRIX

Silverstone, 2–3 August
500cc
1 Wayne Gardner (Aus), Honda, 95.66mph/153.94kph
2 Didier de Radigues (Bel), Honda
3 Eddie Lawson (USA), Yamaha
Fastest lap: Gardner, 101.11mph/162.69kph
Other winners:
250cc: Dominique Sarron (Fra), Honda, 94.30mph/
151.74kph
125cc: August Auinger (Aut), MBA, 94.27mph/145.26kph
80cc: Ian McConnachie (UK), Krauser, 99.99mph/
160.90kph
Sidecar: Egbert Streuer/Bernie Schneiders (Hol), LCR
Yamaha, 112.40mph/180.88kph

SWEDISH TT

Anderstorp, 9–10 August
500cc
1 Eddie Lawson (USA), Yamaha, 91.97mph/148.10kph
2 Wayne Gardner (Aus), Honda
3 Mike Baldwin (USA), Yamaha
Fastest lap: Lawson, 93.35mph/150.24kph
Other winners:
250cc: Carlos Lavado (Ven), Yamaha, 84.30mph/
135.67kph
125cc: Fausto Gresini (Ita), Garelli, 84.89mph/136.70kph

Sidecar: Alain Michel/Jean-Marc Fresc (Fra), LCR Yamaha, 87.80mph/141.40kph

125cc: August Auinger (Aut), MBA, 90.70mph/145.97kph
80cc: Pier Paolo Bianchi (Ita), Seel, 85.63mph/137.81kph

SAN MARINO GRAND PRIX

Misano, 24 August
500cc
1 Eddie Lawson (USA), Yamaha, 95.79mph/154.16kph
2 Wayne Gardner (Aus), Honda
3 Randy Mamola (USA), Yamaha
Fastest lap: Lawson, 97.29mph/156.57kph
Other winners:
250cc: Tadahiko Taira (Jap), Yamaha, 93.16mph/149.92kph

WEST GERMAN GRAND PRIX

Hockenheim, 28 September
125cc: Fausto Gresini (Ita), Garelli, 104.92mph/168.85kph
80cc: Gerhard Waibel (FRG), Krauser, 99.52mph/160.16kph
Sidecar: Egbert Streuer/Bernie Schneiders (Hol), LCR Yamaha, 111.29mph/179.09kph
There were two West German Grands Prix in 1986

LEADING CHAMPIONSHIP POSITIONS

500cc
Riders
1 Eddie Lawson (USA) 139pts
2 Wayne Gardner (Aus) 117pts
3 Randy Mamola (USA) 105pts
4 Mike Baldwin (USA) 78pts
5 Rob McElnea (UK) 60pts
6 Christian Sarron (Fra) 58pts
Manufacturers
1 Yamaha 154pts
2 Honda 123pts
3 Suzuki 27pts

250cc
1 Carlos Lavado (Ven) 114pts
2 Sito Pons (Spa) 108pts
3 Dominique Sarron (Fra) 72pts
Manufacturers' title: Honda

125cc
1 Luca Cadalora (Ita) 122pts
2 Fausto Gresini (Ita) 114pts
3 Domenico Brigaglia (Ita) 80pts
Manufacturers' title: Garelli

80cc
1 Jorge Martinez (Spa) 94pts
2 Manuel Herreros (Spa) 85pts
3 Stefan Dörflinger (Swi) 82pts
Manufacturers' title: Derbi

Sidecar
1 Egbert Streuer (Hol) 75pts
2 Alain Michel (Fra) 75pts
3 Steve Webster (UK) 71pts
Manufacturers' title: LCR Yamaha

1987

JAPANESE GRAND PRIX

Suzuka, 29 March
500cc
1 Randy Mamola (USA), Yamaha, 84.51mph/136.00kph
2 Wayne Gardner (Aus), Honda
3 Takumi Ito (Jap), Suzuki
Fastest lap: Mamola 85.54mph/137.67kph
Other winners:
250cc: Masaru Kobayashi (Jap), Honda, 86.00mph/138.40kph

SPANISH GRAND PRIX

Jerez, 26 April
500cc
1 Wayne Gardner (Aus), Honda, 84.19mph/135.49kph
2 Eddie Lawson (USA), Yahama
3 Ron Haslam (UK), Elf-Honda
Fastest lap: Gardner 84.94mph/136.70kph
Other winners:
250cc: Martin Wimmer (FRG), Yamaha, 82.45mph/132.69kph
125cc: Fausto Gresini (Ita), Garelli, 79.65mph/128.19kph
80cc: Jorge Martinez (Spa), Derbi, 75.94mph/122.21kph
Sidecar: Steve Webster/Tony Hewitt (UK), LCR Yamaha, 81.43mph/131.05kph

WEST GERMAN GRAND PRIX

Hockenheim, 17 May
500cc
1 Eddie Lawson (USA), Yamaha, 119.14mph/191.73kph
2 Randy Mamola (USA), Yamaha
3 Ron Haslam (UK), Elf-Honda
Fastest lap: Wayne Gardner (Aus), Honda, 120.99mph/194.72kph
Other winners:
250cc: Anton Mang (FRG), Honda, 112.20mph/180.56kph
125cc: Fausto Gresini (Ita), Garelli, 105.23mph/169.35kph
80cc: Gerhard Waibel (FRG), Krauser, 98.94mph/159.23kph
Sidecar: Steve Webster/Tony Hewitt (UK), LCR Yamaha, 110.96mph/178.56kph

ITALIAN GRAND PRIX (GRAND PRIX DES NATIONS)

Monza, 24 May
500cc
1 Wayne Gardner (Aus), Honda, 117.74mph/189.47kph
2 Eddie Lawson (USA), Yamaha
3 Christian Sarron (Fra), Yamaha
Fastest lap: Gardner, 119.03mph/191.56kph
Other winners:
250cc: Anton Mang (FRG), Honda, 110.65mph/178.07kph

Eddie Lawson dominated the 500cc Grand Prix scene in the latter part of the eighties, winning the world title four times between 1984 and 1989; three times for Yamaha and in 1989 for Honda

125cc: Fausto Gresini (Ita), Garelli, 104.09mph/ 167.51kph
80cc: Jorge Martinez (Spa), Derbi, 97.65mph/157.15kph

AUSTRIAN GRAND PRIX

Salzburgring, 7 June
500cc
1 Wayne Gardner (Aus), Honda, 114.79mph/184.73kph
2 Randy Mamola (USA), Yamaha
3 Niall Mackenzie (UK), Honda
Fastest lap: Didier de Radigues (Bel), Cagiva, 117.96mph/189.84kph
Other winners:
250cc: Anton Mang (FRG), Honda, 108.41mph/ 174.47kph
125cc: Fausto Gresini (Ita), Garelli, 102.50mph/ 164.95kph
80cc: Jorge Martinez (Spa), Derbi, 93.35mph/153.44kph
Sidecar: Rolf Biland/Kurt Waltisperg (Swi), LCR Krauser, 107.89mph/173.63kph

YUGOSLAV GRAND PRIX

Rijeka, 14 June
500cc
1 Wayne Gardner (Aus), Honda, 100.23mph/161.31kph
2 Randy Mamola (USA), Yamaha
3 Eddie Lawson (USA), Yamaha
Fastest lap: Gardner, 101.35mph/163.10kph
Other winners:
250cc: Carlos Lavado (Ven), Yamaha, 97.56mph/ 157.01kph
80cc: Jorge Martinez (Spa), Derbi, 90.55mph/145.73kph

DUTCH TT

Assen, 27 June
500cc
1 Eddie Lawson (USA), Yamaha, 91.09mph/146.58kph
2 Wayne Gardner (Aus), Honda
3 Randy Mamola (USA), Yamaha
Fastest lap: Lawson, 100.86mph/162.31kph
Other winners:
250cc: Anton Mang (FRG), Honda, 98.51mph/158.54kph

125cc: Fausto Gresini (Ita), Garelli, 93.78mph/150.93kph
80cc: Jorge Martinez (Spa), Derbi, 88.41mph/142.27kph
Sidecar: Egbert Streuer/Bernie Schneiders (Hol), LCR Yamaha, 88.75mph/148.82kph

FRENCH GRAND PRIX

Le Mans, 19 July
500cc
1 Randy Mamola (USA), Yamaha, 78.06mph/125.63kph
2 Pier Francesco Chili (Ita), Honda
3 Christian Sarron (Fra), Yamaha
Fastest lap: Mamola, 80.02mph/128.77kph
Other winners:
250cc: Reinhold Roth (FRG), Honda, 76.22mph/122.67kph
125cc: Fausto Gresini (Ita), Garelli, 73.48mph/118.25kph
Sidecar: Rolf Biland/Kurt Waltisperg (Swi), LCR Krauser, 76.44mph/123.02kph

BRITISH GRAND PRIX

Donington Park, 2 August
500cc
1 Eddie Lawson (USA), Yamaha, 89.70mph/144.36kph
2 Wayne Gardner (Aus), Honda
3 Randy Mamola (USA), Yamaha
Fastest lap: Tadahiko Taira (Jap), Yamaha, 90.56mph/145.75kph
Other winners:
250cc: Anton Mang (FRG), Honda, 86.84mph/139.76kph
125cc: Fausto Gresini (Ita), Garelli, 81.98mph/131.93kph
80cc: Jorge Martinez (Spa), Derbi, 78.60mph/126.48kph
Sidecar: Steve Webster/Tony Hewitt (UK), LCR Yamaha, 87.28mph/140.45kph

SWEDISH TT

Anderstorp, 9 August
500cc
1 Wayne Gardner (Aus), Honda, 92.44mph/148.77kph
2 Eddie Lawson (USA), Yamaha
3 Randy Mamola (USA), Yamaha
Fastest lap: Gardner, 93.57mph/150.58kph
Other winners:
250cc: Anton Mang (FRG), Honda, 89.11mph/143.41kph
125cc: Fausto Gresini (Ita), Garelli, 85.50mph/137.60kph
Sidecar: Rolf Biland/Kurt Waltisperg (Swi), LCR Krauser, 88.93mph/143.12kph

CZECHOSLOVAK GRAND PRIX

Brno, 23 August
500cc
1 Wayne Gardner (Aus), Honda, 93.05mph/149.75kph
2 Eddie Lawson (USA), Yamaha
3 Tadahiko Taira (Jap), Yamaha
Fastest lap: Gardner, 94.12mph/151.47kph
Other winners:
250cc: Anton Mang (FRG), Honda, 89.55mph/144.12kph
125cc: Fausto Gresini (Ita), Garelli, 86.28mph/138.86kph
80cc: Stefan Dörflinger (Swi), Krauser, 82.23mph/132.34kph

Sidecar: Rolf Biland/Kurt Waltisperg (Swi), LCR Krauser, 90.90mph/146.28kph

SAN MARINO GRAND PRIX

Misano, 30 August
500cc
1 Randy Mamola (USA), Yamaha, 97.68mph/157.19kph
2 Eddie Lawson (USA), Yamaha
3 Wayne Gardner (Aus), Honda
Fastest lap: Mamola 98.79mph/158.99kph
Other winners:
250cc: Loris Reggiani (Ita), Aprilia, 94.32mph/151.80kph
125cc: Fausto Gresini (Ita), Garelli, 90.95mph/146.38kph
80cc: Manuel Herreros (Spa), Derbi, 85.10mph/136.96kph

PORTUGUESE GRAND PRIX

Jarama (Spain), 13 September
500cc
1 Eddie Lawson (USA), Yamaha, 82.55mph/132.85kph
2 Randy Mamola (USA), Yamaha
3 Kevin Magee (Aus), Yamaha
Fastest lap: Wayne Gardner (Aus), Honda, 84.20mph/135.51kph
Other winners:
250cc: Anton Mang (FRG), Honda, 80.55mph/129.63kph
125cc: Paolo Casoli (Ita), AGV, 77.90mph/125.36kph
80cc: Jorge Martinez (Spa), Derbi, 74.13mph/119.30kph

BRAZILIAN GRAND PRIX

Goiania, 27 September
500cc
1 Wayne Gardner (Aus), Honda, 96.00mph/154.50kph
2 Eddie Lawson (USA), Yamaha
3 Randy Mamola (USA), Yamaha
Fastest lap: Gardner, 96.68mph/155.59kph
Other winners:
250cc: Dominique Sarron (Fra), Honda, 93.31mph/150.17kph

ARGENTINE GRAND PRIX

Buenos Aires, 4 October
500cc
1 Eddie Lawson (USA), Yamaha, 93.38mph/150.27kph
2 Randy Mamola (USA), Yamaha
3 Wayne Gardner (Aus), Honda
Fastest lap: Not recorded
Other winners:
250cc: Sito Pons (Spa), Honda, 89.48mph/144.00kph

LEADING CHAMPIONSHIP POSITIONS

500cc
Riders
1 Wayne Gardner (Aus) 178pts
2 Randy Mamola (USA) 158pts
3 Eddie Lawson (USA) 157pts
4 Ron Haslam (UK) 72pts
5 Niall Mackenzie (UK) 61pts
6 Tadahiko Taira (Jap) 56pts
Manufacturers
1 Yamaha 204pts
2 Honda 186pts
3 Elf-Honda/Elf 72pts

250cc
1 Anton Mang (FRG) 136pts
2 Reinhold Roth (FRG) 108pts
3 Sito Pons (Spa) 108pts
Manufacturers' title: Honda

125cc
1 Fausto Gresini (Ita) 150pts
2 Bruno Casanova (Ita) 88pts
3 Paolo Casoli (Ita) 61pts
Manufacturers' title: Garelli

80cc
1 Jorge Martinez (Spa) 129pts
2 Manuel Herreros (Spa) 86pts
3 Gerhard Waibel (FRG) 84pts
Manufacturers' title: Derbi

Sidecar
1 Steve Webster (UK) 97pts
2 Egbert Streuer (Hol) 75pts
3 Rolf Biland (Swi) 68pts
Manufacturers' title: LCR Yamaha

1988

JAPANESE GRAND PRIX

Suzuka, 27 March
500cc
1 Kevin Schwantz (USA), Suzuki, 95.99mph/154.48kph
2 Wayne Gardner (Aus), Honda
3 Eddie Lawson (USA), Yamaha
Fastest lap: Schwantz, 96.92mph/155.99kph
Other winners:
250cc: Anton Mang (FRG), Honda, 92.48mph/148.84kph

UNITED STATES GRAND PRIX

Laguna Seca, 10 April
500cc
1 Eddie Lawson (USA), Yamaha, 88.68mph/139.50kph
2 Wayne Gardner (Aus), Honda
3 Niall Mackenzie (UK), Honda
Fastest lap: Lawson, 87.88mph/141.42kph
Other winners:
250cc: Jim Filice (USA), Honda, 84.43mph/135.88kph

SPANISH GRAND PRIX

Jarama, 24 April
500cc
1 Kevin Magee (Aus), Yamaha, 83.26mph/133.99kph
2 Eddie Lawson (USA), Yamaha
3 Wayne Gardner (Aus), Honda
Fastest lap: Magee, 84.10mph/135.35kph
Other winners:
250cc: Sito Pons (Spa), Honda, 81.50mph/131.08kph
125cc: Jorge Martinez (Spa), Derbi, 76.08mph/122.44kph
80cc: Stefan Dörflinger (Swi), Krauser, 73.34mph/118.03kph

PORTUGUESE GRAND PRIX

Jerez (Spain), 1 May
500cc
1 Eddie Lawson (USA), Yamaha, 84.77mph/136.42kph
2 Wayne Rainey (USA), Yamaha

3 Kevin Magee (Aus), Yamaha
Fastest lap: Lawson, 86.33mph/138.94kph
Other winners:
250cc: Juan Garriga (Spa), Yamaha, 82.98mph/133.54km
80cc: Jorge Martinez (Spa), Derbi, 75.22mph/121.13kph
Sidecar: Rolf Biland/Kurt Waltisperg (Swi), LCR Krauser, 70.43mph/113.35kph

ITALIAN GRAND PRIX (GRAND PRIX DES NATIONS)

Imola, 22 May
500cc
1 Eddie Lawson (USA), Yamaha, 97.67mph/157.19kph
2 Wayne Gardner (Aus), Honda
3 Wayne Rainey (USA), Yamaha
Fastest lap: Lawson, 98.93mph/159.22kph
Other winners:
250cc: Dominique Sarron (Fra), Honda, 94.41mph/151.94kph
125cc: Jorge Martinez (Spa), Derbi, 84.46mph/139.15kph
80cc: Jorge Martinez (Spa), Derbi, 82.93mph/133.45kph

WEST GERMAN GRAND PRIX

Nürburgring, 29 May
500cc
1 Kevin Schwantz (USA), Suzuki, 82.11mph/132..14kph
2 Wayne Rainey (USA), Yamaha
3 Christian Sarron (Fra), Yamaha
Fastest lap: Schwantz, 85.32mph/137.31kph
Other winners:
250cc: Luca Cadalora (Ita), Yamaha, 82.66mph/133.3kph
125cc: Ezio Gianola (Ita), Honda, 75.65mph/121.75kph
80cc: Jorge Martinez (Spa), Derbi, 72.98mph/117.45kph
Sidecar: Rolf Biland/Kurt Waltisperg (Swi), LCR Krauser, 93.08mph/149.80kph

AUSTRIAN GRAND PRIX

Salzburgring, 12 June
500cc
1 Eddie Lawson (USA), Yamaha, 115.62mph/186.07kph
2 Didier de Radigues (Bel), Yamaha
3 Wayne Rainey (USA), Yamaha
Fastest lap: de Radigues, 117.74mph/189.49kph

Other winners:
250cc: Jacques Cornu (Swi), Honda, 110.08mph/
177.16kph
125cc: Jorge Martinez (Spa), Derbi, 99.26mph/159.50kph
Sidecar: Rolf Biland/Kurt Waltisperg (Swi), LCR Krauser,
108.04mph/173.87kph

DUTCH TT

Assen, 25 June
500cc
1 Wayne Gardner (Aus), Honda, 103.34mph/166.32kph
2 Eddie Lawson (USA), Yamaha
3 Christian Sarron (Fra), Yamaha
Fastest lap: Gardner, 104.52mph/168.21kph
Other winners:
250cc: Juan Garriga (Spa), Yamaha, 99.64mph/
160.36kph
125cc: Jorge Martinez (Spa), Derbi, 92.16mph/148.32kph
80cc: Jorge Martinez (Spa), Derbi, 87.47mph/140.77kph
Sidecar: Rolf Biland/Kurt Waltisperg (Swi), LCR Krauser,
98.36mph/158.30kph

BELGIAN GRAND PRIX

Spa-Francorchamps, 3 July
500cc
1 Wayne Gardner (Aus), Honda, 93.75mph/150.87kph
2 Eddie Lawson (USA), Yamaha
3 Randy Mamola (USA), Cagiva
Fastest lap: Christian Sarron (Fra), Yamaha, 96.56mph/
155.39kph
Other winners:
250cc: Sito Pons (Spa), Honda, 100.02mph/160.96kph
125cc: Jorge Martinez (Spa), Derbi, 87.14mph/140.24kph
Sidecar: Rolf Biland/Kurt Waltisperg (Swi), LCR Krauser,
92.70mph/149.19kph

YUGOSLAV GRAND PRIX

Rijeka, 17 July
500cc
1 Wayne Gardner (Aus), Honda, 101.93mph/164.04kph
2 Christian Sarron (Fra), Yamaha
3 Wayne Rainey (USA), Yamaha
Fastest lap: Sarron, 102.94mph/165.67kph
Other winners:
250cc: Sito Pons (Spa), Honda, 100.11mph/161.12kph
125cc: Jorge Martinez (Spa), Derbi, 92.27mph/148.49kph
80cc: Jorge Martinez (Spa), Derbi, 89.41mph/143.89kph

FRENCH GRAND PRIX

Paul Ricard, 24 July
500cc
1 Eddie Lawson (USA), Yamaha, 107.64mph/173.23kph
2 Christian Sarron (Fra), Yamaha
3 Kevin Schwantz (USA), Suzuki
Fastest lap: Wayne Gardner (Aus), Honda, 108.97mph/
175.37kph
Other winners:
250cc: Jacques Cornu (Swi), Honda, 104.25mph/
167.78kph

125cc: Jorge Martinez (Spa), Derbi, 95.33mph/153.42kph
Sidecar: Rolf Biland/Kurt Waltisperg (Swi), LCR Krauser,
102.49mph/164.94kph

BRITISH GRAND PRIX

Donington Park, 7 August
500cc
1 Wayne Rainey (USA), Yamaha, 92.66mph/149.12kph
2 Wayne Gardner (Aus), Honda
3 Christian Sarron (Fra), Yamaha
Fastest lap: Sarron, 95.54mph/150.53kph
Other winners:
250cc: Luca Cadalora (Ita), Yamaha, 90.12mph/
145.03kph
125cc: Ezio Gianola (Ita), Honda, 84.29mph/135.65kph
Sidecar: Steve Webster/Tony Hewitt (UK), LCR Krauser,
88.54mph/142.49kph

SWEDISH TT

Anderstorp, 14 August
500cc
1 Eddie Lawson (USA), Yamaha, 93.95mph/151.20kph
2 Wayne Gardner (Aus), Honda
3 Christian Sarron (Fra), Yamaha
Fastest lap: Lawson, 95.49mph/153.68kph
Other winners:
250cc: Sito Pons (Spa), Honda, 91.85mph/147.82kph
125cc: Jorge Martinez (Spa), Derbi, 83.53mph/134.43kph
Sidecar: Steve Webster/Tony Hewitt (UK), LCR Krauser,
88.74mph/142.81kph

CZECHOSLOVAK GRAND PRIX

Brno, 28 August
500cc
1 Wayne Gardner (Aus), Honda, 94.04mph/151.34kph
2 Eddie Lawson (USA), Yamaha
3 Wayne Rainey (USA), Yamaha
Fastest lap: Gardner, 95.58mph/153.82kph
Other winners:
250cc: Juan Garriga (Spa), Yamaha, 91.59mph/
147.40kph
125cc: Jorge Martinez (Spa), Derbi, 85.97mph/138.07kph
80cc: Jorge Martinez (Spa), Derbi, 82.30mph/132.45kph
Sidecar: Steve Webster/Gavin Simmons (UK), LCR
Krauser, 91.78mph/147.71kph

BRAZILIAN GRAND PRIX

Goiania, 17 September
500cc
1 Eddie Lawson (USA), Yamaha, 97.13mph/156.31kph
2 Wayne Gardner (Aus), Honda
3 Kevin Schwantz (USA), Suzuki
Fastest lap: Lawson, 97.70mph/157.23kph
Other winners:
250cc: Dominique Sarron (Fra), Honda, 93.99mph/
151.26kph

LEADING CHAMPIONSHIP POSITIONS

500cc
Riders
1 Eddie Lawson (USA) 252pts
2 Wayne Gardner (Aus) 229pts
3 Wayne Rainey (USA) 189pts
4 Christian Sarron (Fra) 149pts
5 Kevin Magee (Aus) 138pts
6 Niall Mackenzie (UK) 125pts
Manufacturers
1 Yamaha 280pts
2 Honda 242pts
3 Suzuki 157pts

250cc
1 Sito Pons (Spa) 231pts
2 Juan Garriga (Spa) 221pts
3 Jacques Cornu (Swi) 166pts
Manufacturers' title: Honda

125cc
1 Jorge Martinez (Spa) 197pts
2 Ezio Gianola (Ita) 168pts
3 Hans Spaan (Hol) 110pts
Manufacturers' title: Derbi

80cc
1 Jorge Martinez (Spa) 137pts
2 Alex Criville (Spa) 90pts
3 Stefan Dörflinger (Swi) 77pts
Manufacturers' title: Derbi

Sidecar
1 Steve Webster (UK) 156pts
2 Rolf Biland (Swi) 154pts
3 Egbert Streuer (Hol) 97pts
Manufacturers' title: LCR Krauser

1989

JAPANESE GRAND PRIX

Suzuka, 26 March
500cc
1 Kevin Schwantz (USA), Suzuki, 98.47mph/158.47kph
2 Wayne Rainey (USA), Yamaha
3 Eddie Lawson (USA), Honda
Fastest lap: Schwantz, 98.93mph/159.22kph
Other winners:
250cc: John Kocinski (USA), Yamaha, 94.83mph/
152.62kph
125cc: Ezio Gianola (Ita), Honda, 88.84mph/142.97kph

AUSTRALIAN GRAND PRIX

Phillip Island, 9 April
500cc
1 Wayne Gardner (Aus), Honda, 103.12mph/165.96kph
2 Wayne Rainey (USA), Yamaha
3 Christian Sarron (Fra), Yamaha
Fastest lap: Pier Francesco Chili (Ita), Honda,
104.47mph/168.14kph
Other winners:
250cc: Sito Pons (Spa), Honda, 99.68mph/160.41kph
125cc: Alex Criville (Spa), Cobas, 92.01mph/148.08kph

UNITED STATES GRAND PRIX

Laguna Seca, 16 April
500cc
1 Wayne Rainey (USA), Yamaha, 85.45mph/137.52kph
2 Kevin Schwantz (USA), Suzuki
3 Eddie Lawson (USA), Honda
Fastest lap: Wayne Gardner (Aus), Honda, 89.83mph/
144.57kph
Other winners:
250cc: John Kocinski (USA), Yamaha, 87.24mph/
140.39kph
Sidecar: Steve Webster/Tony Hewitt (UK), LCR Krauser,
85.45mph/137.53kph

SPANISH GRAND PRIX

Jerez, 30 April
500cc
1 Eddie Lawson (USA), Honda, 85.49mph/137.57kph
2 Wayne Rainey (USA), Yamaha
3 Niall Mackenzie (UK), Yamaha
Fastest lap: Kevin Schwantz (USA), Suzuki, 86.06mph/
139.58kph
Other winners:
250cc: Luca Cadalora (Ita), Yamaha, 84.05mph/
135.27kph
125cc: Alex Criville (Spa), Cobas, 79.25mph/127.54kph
80cc: Herri Torrontegui (Spa), Krauser, 76.07mph/
122.43kph

ITALIAN GRAND PRIX
(GRAND PRIX DES NATIONS)

Misano, 14 May
500cc
1 Pier Francesco Chili (Ita), Honda, 72.30mph/116.36kph
2 Simon Buckmaster (UK), Honda
3 Michael Rudroff (FRG), Honda
Fastest lap: Eddie Lawson (USA), Honda, 98.55mph/
158.61kph
Other winners:
250cc: Sito Pons (Spa), Honda, 96.15mph/154.74kph
125cc: Ezio Gianola (Ita), Honda, 90.22mph/145.20kph
80cc: Jorge Martinez (Spa), Derbi, 85.32mph/137.31kph

WEST GERMAN GRAND PRIX

Hockenheim, 28 May
500cc
1 Wayne Rainey (USA), Yamaha, 122.54mph/197.20kph
2 Eddie Lawson (USA), Honda
3 Michael Doohan (Aus), Honda
Fastest lap: Kevin Schwantz (USA), Suzuki, 123.79mph/
199.22kph
Other winners:
250cc: Sito Pons (Spa), Honda, 114.11mph/183.65kph
125cc: Alex Criville (Spa), Cobas, 104.35mph/167.93kph
80cc: Peter Öttl (FRG), Krauser, 98.33mph/158.25kph
Sidecar: Steve Webster/Tony Hewitt (UK), LCR Krauser,
112.86mph/181.62kph

AUSTRIAN GRAND PRIX

Salzburgring, 4 June
500cc
1 Kevin Schwantz (USA), Suzuki, 118.69mph/191.01kph
2 Eddie Lawson (USA), Honda
3 Wayne Rainey (USA), Yamaha
Fastest lap: Schwantz, 119.92mph/192.99kph
Other winners:
250cc: Sito Pons (Spa), Honda, 110.09mph/177.17kph
125cc: Hans Spaan (Hol), Honda, 93.62mph/150.67kph
Sidecar: Rolf Biland/Kurt Waltisperg (Swi), LCR Krauser,
109.48mph/176.19kph

YUGOSLAV GRAND PRIX

Rijeka, 11 June
500cc
1 Kevin Schwantz (USA), Suzuki, 103.18mph/166.05kph
2 Wayne Rainey (USA), Yamaha
3 Eddie Lawson (USA), Honda
Fastest lap: Rainey, 104.42mph/168.05kph
Other winners:
250cc: Sito Pons (Spa), Honda, 99.47mph/160.08kph
80cc: Peter Öttl (FRG), Krauser, 90.61mph/145.82kph

DUTCH TT

Assen, 24 June
500cc
1 Wayne Rainey (USA), Yamaha, 106.18mph/170.88kph
2 Eddie Lawson (USA), Honda
3 Christian Sarron (Fra), Yamaha
Fastest lap: Kevin Schwantz (USA), Suzuki, 106.24mph/
170.97kph
Other winners:
250cc: Reinhold Roth (FRG), Honda, 101.06mph/
162.63kph
125cc: Hans Spaan (Hol), Honda, 94.64mph/151.14kph
80cc: Peter Öttl (FRG), Krauser, 89.37mph/143.82kph
Sidecar: Steve Webster/Tony Hewitt (UK), LCR Krauser,
99.27mph/159.76kph

BELGIAN GRAND PRIX

Spa-Francorchamps, 2 July
500cc
1 Eddie Lawson (USA), Honda, 104.69mph/168.49kph
2 Kevin Schwantz (USA), Suzuki
3 Wayne Rainey (USA), Yamaha
Fastest lap: Schwantz, 106.25mph/170.99kph
Other winners:
250cc: Jacques Cornu (Swi), Honda, 98.54mph/
158.59kph
125cc: Hans Spaan (Hol), Honda, 87.05mph/140.09kph
Sidecar: Egbert Streuer/Geral de Haas (Hol), LCR
Yamaha, 89.05mph/143.31kph
*Rain interrupted the 500cc race, which consequently
carried only half the normal points*

FRENCH GRAND PRIX

Le Mans, 16 July
500cc
1 Eddie Lawson (USA), Honda, 95.25mph/153.30kph
2 Kevin Schwantz (USA), Suzuki
3 Wayne Rainey (USA), Yamaha
Fastest lap: Schwantz, 96.24mph/154.88kph
Other winners:
250cc: Carlos Cardus (Spa), Honda, 91.43mph/
147.15kph
125cc: Jorge Martinez (Spa), Derbi, 85.23mph/137.16kph
Sidecar: Rolf Biland/Kurt Waltisperg (Swi), LCR Krauser,
88.65mph/142.67kph

BRITISH GRAND PRIX

Donington Park, 6 August
500cc
1 Kevin Schwantz (USA), Suzuki, 94.21mph/151.61kph
2 Eddie Lawson (USA), Honda
3 Wayne Rainey (USA), Yamaha
Fastest lap: Lawson, 95.22mph/153.24kph
Other winners:
250cc: Sito Pons (Spa), Honda, 90.22mph/145.20kph
125cc: Hans Spaan (Hol), Honda, 85.35mph/137.35kph
Sidecar: Steve Webster/Tony Hewitt (UK), LCR Krauser,
89.22mph/143.57kph

SWEDISH TT

Anderstorp, 13 August
500cc
1 Eddie Lawson (USA), Honda, 96.89mph/155.93kph
2 Christian Sarron (Fra), Yamaha
3 Wayne Gardner (Aus), Honda
Fastest lap: Sarron, 98.02mph/157.75kph
Other winners:
250cc: Sito Pons (Spa), Honda, 92.48mph/148.83kph
125cc: Alex Criville (Spa), Cobas, 86.55mph/139.30kph
Sidecar: Rolf Biland/Kurt Waltisperg (Swi), LCR Krauser,
91.25mph/146.85kph

CZECHOSLOVAK GRAND PRIX

Brno, 27 August
500cc
1 Kevin Schwantz (USA), Suzuki, 95.67mph/153.97kph
2 Eddie Lawson (USA), Honda
3 Wayne Rainey (USA), Yamaha
Fastest lap: Schwantz, 99.99mph/156.09kph
Other winners:
250cc: Reinhold Roth (FRG), Honda, 92.32mph/
148.58kph
125cc: Alex Criville (Spa), Cobas, 86.60mph/139.38kph
80cc: Herri Torrontegui (Spa), Krauser, 82.98mph/
133.54kph
Sidecar: Egbert Streuer/Geral de Haas (Hol), LCR
Yamaha, 91.01mph/146.47kph

Wayne Rainey in action during the 1989 British Grand Prix at Donington

BRAZILIAN GRAND PRIX

Goiania, 17 September
500cc
1 Kevin Schwantz (USA), Suzuki, 97.89mph/157.54kph

2 Eddie Lawson (USA), Honda
3 Wayne Rainey (USA), Yamaha
Fastest lap: Lawson, 98.63mph/158.73kph
Other winners:
250cc: Luca Cadalora (Ita), Yamaha, 94.69mph/
152.39kph

LEADING CHAMPIONSHIP POSITIONS

500cc
Riders
1 Eddie Lawson (USA) 228pts
2 Wayne Rainey (USA) 210.5pts
3 Christian Sarron (Fra) 165.5pts
4 Kevin Schwantz (USA) 162.5pts
5 Kevin Magee (Aus) 138.5pts
6 Pier Francesco Chili (Ita) 122pts
Manufacturers
1 Honda 257pts
2 Yamaha 227.5pts
3 Suzuki 211.5pts

250cc
1 Sito Pons (Spa) 262pts
2 Reinhold Roth (FRG) 190pts
3 Jacques Cornu (Swi) 187pts
Manufacturers' title: Honda

125cc
1 Alex Criville (Spa) 166pts
2 Hans Spaan (Hol) 152pts
3 Ezio Gianola (Ita) 138pts
Manufacturers' title: Honda

80cc
1 Manuel Herreros (Spa) 92pts
2 Stefan Dörflinger (Swi) 80pts
3 Peter Öttl (FRG) 75pts
Manufacturers' title: Krauser

Sidecar
1 Steve Webster (UK) 145pts
2 Egbert Streuer (Hol) 136pts
3 Alain Michel (Fra) 109pts
Manufacturers' title: LCR Krauser

1990

JAPANESE GRAND PRIX

Suzuka, 25 March
500cc
1 Wayne Rainey (USA), Yamaha, 98.27mph/
158.15kph

2 Wayne Gardner (Aus), Honda
3 Kevin Schwantz (USA), Suzuki
Fastest lap: Rainey, 99.78mph/160.58kph
Other winners:
250cc: Luca Cadalora (Ita), Yamaha, 95.13mph/
153.10kph
125cc: Hans Spaan (Hol), Honda, 89.31mph/
143.73kph

UNITED STATES GRAND PRIX

Laguna Seca, 8 April
500cc
1 Wayne Rainey (USA), Yamaha, 90.56mph/145.74kph
2 Michael Doohan (Aus), Honda
3 Pier Francisco Chili (Ita), Honda
Fastest lap: Kevin Schwantz (USA), Suzuki, 92.10mph/
148.22kph
Other winners:
250cc: John Kocinski (USA), Yamaha, 87.85mph/
141.38kph
Sidecar: Alain Michel (Fra)/Simon Birchall (UK), LCR
Krauser, 83.60mph/134.54kph

SPANISH GRAND PRIX

Jerez, 6 May
500cc
1 Wayne Gardner (Aus), Honda, 86.10mph/138.56kph
2 Wayne Rainey (USA), Yamaha
3 Kevin Schwantz (USA), Suzuki
Fastest lap: Michael Doohan (Aus), Honda, 87.62mph/
141.01kph
Other winners:
250cc: John Kocinski (USA), Yamaha, 85.38mph/137.41kph
125cc: Jorge Martinez (Spa), JJ Cobas, 80.72mph/
129.91kph
Sidecar: Steve Webster/Gavin Simmons (UK), LCR
Krauser, 81.91mph/131.82kph

ITALIAN GRAND PRIX
(GRAND PRIX DES NATIONS)

Misano, 19–20 May
500cc
1 Wayne Rainey (USA), Yamaha, 101.58mph/163.48kph
2 Kevin Schwantz (USA), Suzuki
3 Michael Doohan (Aus), Honda
Fastest lap: Rainey, 103.38mph/166.37kph
Other winners:
250cc: John Kocinski (USA), Yamaha, 99.19mph/
159.63kph
125cc: Jorge Martinez (Spa), JJ Cobas, 91.15mph/
146.69kph
Sidecar: Rolf Biland/Kurt Waltisperg (Swi), LCR Krauser,
95.89mph/154.32kph

WEST GERMAN GRAND PRIX

Nürburgring, 27 May
500cc
1 Kevin Schwantz (USA), Suzuki, 99.46mph/160.07kph
2 Wayne Rainey (USA), Yamaha
3 Niall Mackenzie (UK), Suzuki
Fastest lap: Schwantz, 101.03mph/162.59kph
Other winners:
250cc: Wilco Zeelemberg (Hol), Honda, 97.46mph/
156.85kph
125cc: Doriano Romboni (Ita), Honda, 90.11mph/
145.02kph
Sidecar: Steve Webster/Gavin Simmons (UK), LCR
Krauser, 93.11mph/149.85kph

AUSTRIAN GRAND PRIX

Salzburgring, 10 June
500cc
1 Kevin Schwantz (USA), Suzuki, 119.53mph/192.36kph
2 Wayne Rainey (USA), Yamaha
3 Michael Doohan (Aus), Honda
Fastest lap: Schwantz, 121.08mph/194.86kph
Other winners:
250cc: Luca Cadalora (Ita), Yamaha, 111.22mph/
178.99kph
125cc: Jorge Martinez (Spa), JJ Cobas, 96.35mph/
155.06kph
Sidecar: Egbert Streuer/Geral de Haas (Hol), LCR
Yamaha, 96.17mph/154.77kph

YUGOSLAV GRAND PRIX

Rijeka, 10 June
500cc
1 Wayne Rainey (USA), Yamaha, 103.21mph/166.10kph
2 Kevin Schwantz (USA), Suzuki
3 Niall Mackenzie (UK), Suzuki
Fastest lap: Rainey, 104.50mph/168.18kph
Other winners:
250cc: Carlos Cardus (Spa), Honda, 99.90mph/
160.78kph
125cc: Stefan Prein (FRG), Honda, 93.39mph/150.29kph
Sidecar: Alain Michel (Fra)/Simon Birchall (UK), LCR
Krauser, 97.80mph/157.39kph

DUTCH TT

Assen, 30 June
500cc
1 Kevin Schwantz (USA), Suzuki, 108.62mph/174.81kph
2 Wayne Rainey (USA), Yamaha
3 Eddie Lawson (USA), Yamaha
Fastest lap: Schwantz, 109.51mph/176.24kph
Other winners:
250cc: John Kocinski (USA), Yamaha, 103.39mph/
166.39kph
125cc: Doriano Romboni (Ita), Honda, 95.62mph/
153.89kph
Sidecar: Alain Michel (Fra)/Simon Birchall (UK), LCR
Krauser, 100.45mph/161.66kph

BELGIAN GRAND PRIX

Spa-Francorchamps, 8 July
500cc
1 Wayne Rainey (USA), Yamaha, 92.19mph/148.37kph
2 Jean-Phillippe Ruggia (Fra), Yamaha
3 Eddie Lawson (USA), Yamaha
Fastest lap: Rainey, 93.58mph/150.60kph
Other winners:
250cc: John Kocinski (USA), Yamaha, 90.46mph/
145.58kph
125cc: Hans Spaan (Hol), Honda, 85.70mph/137.92kph
Sidecar: Egbert Streuer/Geral de Haas (Hol), LCR
Yamaha, 87.09mph/140.16kph

FRENCH GRAND PRIX

Le Mans, 22 July
500cc
1 Kevin Schwantz (USA), Suzuki, 96.11mph/138.66kph
2 Wayne Gardner (Aus), Honda
3 Wayne Rainey (USA), Yamaha
Fastest lap: Schwantz, 97.14mph/156.33kph
Other winners:
250cc: Carlos Cardus (Spa), Honda, 92.23mph/
148.52kph
125cc: Hans Spaan (Hol), Honda, 86.10mph/138.66kph
Sidecar: Steve Webster/Gavin Simmons (UK), LCR
Krauser, 88.98mph/143.20kph

BRITISH GRAND PRIX

Donington Park, 5 August
500cc
1 Kevin Schwantz (USA), Suzuki, 95.15mph/153.13kph
2 Wayne Rainey (USA), Yamaha
3 Eddie Lawson (USA), Yamaha
Fastest lap: Schwantz, 95.92mph/154.37kph
Other winners:
250cc: Luca Cadalora (Ita), Yamaha, 91.37mph/
147.14kph
125cc: Loris Capirossi (Ita), Honda, 85.19mph/137.10kph
Sidecar: Egbert Streuer/Geral de Haas (Hol), LCR
Yamaha, 89.30mph/143.71kph

SWEDISH TT

Anderstorp, 12 August
500cc
1 Wayne Rainey (USA), Yamaha, 97.80mph/157.40kph
2 Eddie Lawson (USA), Yamaha
3 Wayne Gardner (Aus), Honda
Fastest lap: Rainey, 98.76mph/158.94kph
Other winners:
250cc: Carlos Cardus (Spa), Honda, 93.65mph/
150.71kph
125cc: Hans Spaan (Hol), Honda, 87.23mph/140.39kph
Sidecar: Alain Michel (Fra)/Simon Birchall (UK), LCR
Krauser, 91.44mph/147.16kph

CZECHOSLOVAK GRAND PRIX

Brno, 26 August
500cc
1 Wayne Rainey (USA), Yamaha, 96.61mph/155.48kph
2 Wayne Gardner (Aus), Honda
3 Eddie Lawson (USA), Yamaha
Fastest lap: Rainey, 97.46mph/156.86kph
Other winners:
250cc: Carlos Cardus (Spa), Honda, 93.90mph/
151.12kph
125cc: Hans Spaan (Hol), Honda, 87.34mph/140.56kph
Sidecar: Alain Michel (Fra)/Simon Birchall (UK), LCR
Krauser, 91.35mph/147.01kph

HUNGARIAN GRAND PRIX

Budapest, 2 September
500cc
1 Michael Doohan (Aus), Honda, 84.59mph/136.13kph
2 Eddie Lawson (USA), Yamaha
3 Kevin Schwantz (USA), Suzuki
Fastest lap: Doohan, 85.52mph/137.63kph
Other winners:
250cc: John Kocinski (USA), Yamaha, 83.26mph/
133.99kph
125cc: Loris Capirossi (Ita), Honda, 77.91mph/125.38kph
Sidecar: Paul Guedel/Charly Guedel (Swi), LCR Yamaha,
80.97mph/130.31kph

AUSTRALIAN GRAND PRIX

Phillip Island, 16 September
500cc
1 Wayne Gardner (Aus), Honda, 104.79mph/168.64kph
2 Michael Doohan (Aus), Honda
3 Wayne Rainey (USA), Yamaha
Fastest lap: Gardner, 105.83mph/170.32kph
Other winners:
250cc: John Kocinski (USA), Yamaha, 101.69mph/
163.65kph
125cc: Loris Capirossi (Ita), Honda, 94.91mph/152.74kph

LEADING CHAMPIONSHIP POSITIONS

500cc
Riders
1 Wayne Rainey (USA) 255pts
2 Kevin Schwantz (USA) 188pts
3 Michael Doohan (Aus) 179pts
4 Niall Mackenzie (UK) 140pts
5 Wayne Gardner (Aus) 138pts
6 Juan Garriga (Spa) 121pts
Manufacturers
1 Yamaha 272pts
2 Honda 233pts
3 Suzuki 223pts

250cc
1 John Kocinski (USA) 223pts
2 Carlos Cardus (Spa) 208pts
3 Luca Cadalora (Ita) 184pts
Manufacturers' title: Yamaha

125cc
1 Loris Capirossi (Ita) 182pts
2 Hans Spaan (Hol) 173pts
3 Stefan Prein (FRG) 169pts
Manufacturers' title: Honda

Sidecar
1 Alain Michel (Fra) 178pts
2 Egbert Streuer (Hol) 167pts
3 Steve Webster (UK) 166pts
Manufacturers' title: LCR Krauser

WORLD CHAMPIONSHIP RECORDS

RIDERS' RECORDS

MOST TITLE WINS BY CLASS

500cc
8 Giacomo Agostini 1966–75; 4 Mike Hailwood 1962–65, John Surtees 1956–60, Geoff Duke 1951–55, Eddie Lawson 1984–89; 3 Kenny Roberts 1978–80

350cc
7 Giacomo Agostini 1968–74; 4 Jim Redman 1962–65; 3 John Surtees 1958–60

250cc
4 Phil Read 1964–71; 3 Carlo Ubbiali 1956–60, Mike Hailwood 1961–67, Anton Mang 1980–87, Walter Villa 1974–76

125cc
7 Angel Nieto 1971–84; 6 Carlo Ubbiali 1958–60; 3 Luigi Taveri 1962–66, Pier Paolo Bianchi 1976–80

80cc
3 Jorge Martinez 1986–88

50cc
6 Angel Nieto 1969–77; 3 Hans-Georg Anscheidt 1966–68

Sidecar
6 Klaus Enders 1967–74; 4 Eric Oliver 1949–53, Max Deubel 1961–64; Rolf Biland 1978–83; 3 Egbert Streuer 1984–86, Steve Webster 1987–89

WINNERS OF TWO WORLD TITLES IN ONE YEAR

1951 Geoff Duke (350/500)
1953 Werner Haas (125/250)
1956 Carlo Ubbiali (125/250)
1958 John Surtees (350/500)
1959 Carlo Ubbiali (125/250)
    John Surtees (350/500)
1960 Carlo Ubbiali (125/250)
    John Surtees (350/500)
1961 Gary Hocking (350/500)

1962 Jim Redman (250/350)
1963 Hugh Anderson (50/125)
    Jim Redman (250/350)
1966 Mike Hailwood (250/350)
1967 Mike Hailwood (250/350)
1968 Phil Read (125/250)
    Giacomo Agostini (350/500)
1969 Giacomo Agostini (350/500)
1970 Giacomo Agostini (350/500)

1971 Giacomo Agostini (350/500)
1972 Angel Nieto (50/125)
    Giacomo Agostini (350/500)
1976 Walter Villa (250/350)
1978 Kork Ballington (250/350)
1979 Kork Ballington (250/350)
1981 Anton Mang (250/350)
1985 Freddie Spencer (250/500)
1988 Jorge Martinez (80/125)

WINNERS OF WORLD TITLES WITHOUT WINNING A RACE DURING CHAMPIONSHIP SEASON

1977 George O'Dell (Sidecar)
1982 Werner Schwärzel (Sidecar)
1989 Manuel Herreros (80cc)

OLDEST WORLD CHAMPION

46yr Herman-Peter Müller (FRG), when he won the 250cc title in 1955

YOUNGEST WORLD CHAMPION

17yr Loris Capirossi (Ita), when he won the 125cc title in 1990

MOST RACE WINS IN ONE SEASON

19 Mike Hailwood (1966)
    3 x 500cc, 6 x 350cc, 10 x 250cc
19 Giacomo Agostini (1970)
    10 x 500cc, 9 x 350cc
18 Giacomo Agostini (1969)
    10 x 500cc, 8 x 350cc

17 Giacomo Agostini (1968)
    10 x 500cc, 7 x 350cc
17 Giacomo Agostini (1972)
    11 x 500cc, 6 x 350cc

16 Mike Hailwood (1967)
    5 x 500cc, 6 x 350cc, 5 x 250cc
15 Jorge Martinez (1988)
    9 x 125cc, 6 x 80cc

MOST RACE WINS BY CLASS

500cc
68 Giacomo Agostini; **37** Mike Hailwood; **30** Eddie Lawson; **22** Geoff Duke, Kenny Roberts, John Surtees; **20** Freddie Spencer; **19** Barry Sheene; **17** Wayne Gardner; **13** Randy Mamola, Kevin Schwantz; **11** Phil Read

350cc
54 Giacomo Agostini; **21** Jim Redman; **16** Mike Hailwood; **15** John Surtees; **14** Kork Ballington; **11** Geoff Duke

250cc
33 Anton Mang; **27** Phil Read; **21** Mike Hailwood; **20** Walter Villa; **18** Jim Redman; **17** Kork Ballington, Carlos Lavado; **15** Sito Pons; **14** Tarquinio Provini; **13** Carlo Ubbiali; **10** Rod Gould

125cc
62 Angel Nieto; **26** Carlo Ubbiali; **24** Pier Paolo Bianchi; **22** Luigi Taveri; **18** Fausto Gresini; **17** Hugh Anderson; **14** Kent Andersson, Bill Ivy; **13** Jorge Martinez; **10** Phil Read, Dave Simmonds

80cc
22 Jorge Martinez; **9** Stefan Dörflinger; **3** Pier Paolo Bianchi, Gerhard Waibel, Peter Öttl

50cc
27 Angel Nieto; **18** Eugenio Lazzarini; **15** Ricardo Tormo; **14** Hans-Georg Anscheidt, Jan de Vries

Sidecar
56 Rolf Biland; **27** Klaus Enders; **20** Egbert Streuer; **17** Eric Oliver, Alain Michel; **16** Fritz Scheidegger; **14** Steve Webster; **12** Max Deubel; **11** Helmut Fath; **10** Werner Schwärzel, Rolf Steinhausen

MOST WINS IN A SEASON BY CLASS

500cc
11 Giacomo Agostini (1972)
10 Giacomo Agostini (1968, 1969, 1970)
8 Mike Hailwood (1965), Giacomo Agostini (1971)
7 John Surtees (1959), Gary Hocking (1961), Mike Hailwood (1963, 1964), Freddie Spencer (1985), Eddie Lawson (1986, 1988), Wayne Gardner (1987), Wayne Rainey (1990)

350cc
9 Giacomo Agostini (1970)
8 Jim Redman (1964), Giacomo Agostini (1969)
7 Giacomo Agostini (1968)

250cc
10 Mike Hailwood (1966), Anton Mang (1981)
8 Anton Mang (1987)
7 Phil Read (1965), Walter Villa (1976), Kork Ballington (1979), Freddie Spencer (1985), Sito Pons (1989), John Kocinski (1990)

125cc
10 Fausto Gresini (1987)
9 Jorge Martinez (1988)
8 Bill Ivy (1967), Angel Nieto (1979, 1981)

80cc
7 Jorge Martinez (1987)
6 Jorge Martinez (1988)
4 Stefan Dörflinger (1984), Jorge Martinez (1986)

50cc
6 Henk van Kessel (1974), Angel Nieto (1975), Ricardo Tormo (1981)
5 Jan de Vries (1971, 1973), Angel Nieto (1970, 1976), Ricardo Tormo (1978), Eugenio Lazzarini (1979)
4 Ernest Degner (1962), Hugh Anderson (1964)

Sidecar
7 Klaus Enders (1973), Rolf Biland (1981)
6 Rolf Biland (1982, 1983, 1988)
5 Fritz Scheidegger (1966), Klaus Enders (1967, 1970), Egbert Streuer (1986), Alain Michel (1990)

RIDERS WHO HAVE WON RACES IN THREE CLASSES IN ONE SEASON

Fergus Anderson
1953: 250cc, 230cc, 500cc
Bill Lomas
1955: 250cc, 350cc, 500cc
Gary Hocking
1961: 250cc, 350cc, 500cc

Mike Hailwood
1961: 125cc, 250cc, 500cc
1963: 250cc, 350cc, 500cc
1965: 250cc, 350cc, 500cc
1966: 250cc, 350cc, 500cc
1967: 250cc, 350cc, 500cc

Jim Redman
1962: 125cc, 250cc, 350cc
1963: 125cc, 250cc, 350cc
1964: 125cc, 250cc, 350cc
Dieter Braun
1975: 125cc, 250cc, 350cc

RIDERS WHO HAVE WON THREE RACES AT ONE GRAND PRIX MEETING

Mike Hailwood
1961 British GP (TT), 125cc, 250cc, 500cc
1963 East German GP, 250cc, 350cc, 500cc
1966 Czechoslovak GP, 250cc, 350cc, 500cc
1967 British GP (TT), 250cc, 350cc, 500cc
Dutch TT, 250cc, 350cc, 500cc

Jim Redman
1964 Dutch TT, 125cc, 250cc, 350cc

WORLD TITLES

Title wins (all classes)	Sidecar	50cc	80cc	125cc	250cc	350cc	500cc
15 Giacomo Agostini (Ita) 1966–75	–	–	–	–	–	7	8
13 Angel Nieto (Spa) 1969–84	–	6	–	7	–	–	–
9 Carlo Ubbiali (Ita) 1951–60	–	–	–	6	3	–	–
9 Mike Hailwood (UK) 1961–67	–	–	–	–	3	2	4
7 John Surtees (UK) 1956–60	–	–	–	–	–	3	4
7 Phil Read (UK) 1964–74	–	–	–	1	4	–	2
6 Geoff Duke (UK) 1951–55	–	–	–	–	–	2	4
6 Jim Redman (SRho) 1962–65	–	–	–	–	2	4	–
6 Klaus Enders (FRG) 1967–74	6	–	–	–	–	–	–
5 Anton Mang (FRG) 1980–87	–	–	–	–	3	2	–
4 Eric Oliver (UK) 1949–53	4	–	–	–	–	–	–
4 Max Deubel (FRG) 1961–64	4	–	–	–	–	–	–
4 Hugh Anderson (NZ) 1963–65	–	2	–	2	–	–	–
4 Walter Villa (Ita) 1974–76	–	–	–	–	3	1	–
4 Kork Ballington (SAf) 1978–79	–	–	–	–	2	2	–
4 Rolf Biland (Swi) 1978–83	4	–	–	–	–	–	–
4 Stefan Dörflinger (Swi) 1982–85	–	2	2	–	–	–	–
4 Jorge Martinez (Spa) 1986–88	–	–	3	1	–	–	–
4 Eddie Lawson (USA) 1984–89	–	–	–	–	–	–	4
3 Bruno Ruffo (Ita) 1949–51	–	–	–	1	2	–	–
3 Werner Haas (FRG) 1953–54	–	–	–	1	2	–	–
3 Luigi Taveri (Swi) 1962–66	–	–	–	3	–	–	–
3 Hans-Georg Anscheidt (FRG) 1966–68	–	3	–	–	–	–	–
3 Pier Paolo Bianchi (Ita) 1976–80	–	–	–	3	–	–	–
3 Eugenio Lazzarini (Ita) 1978–80	–	2	–	1	–	–	–
3 Kenny Roberts (USA) 1978–80	–	–	–	–	–	–	3
3 Freddie Spencer (USA) 1983–85	–	–	–	–	1	–	2
3 Egbert Streuer (Hol) 1984–86	3	–	–	–	–	–	–
3 Steve Webster (UK) 1987–89	3	–	–	–	–	–	–
2 Umberto Masetti (Ita) 1950–52	–	–	–	–	–	–	2
2 Fergus Anderson (UK) 1953–54	–	–	–	–	–	2	–
2 Wilhelm Noll (FRG) 1954–56	2	–	–	–	–	–	–
2 Bill Lomas (UK) 1955–56	–	–	–	–	–	2	–
2 Cecil Sandford (UK) 1952–57	–	–	–	1	1	–	–
2 Tarquinio Provini (Ita) 1957–58	–	–	–	1	1	–	–
2 Walter Schneider (FRG) 1958–59	2	–	–	–	–	–	–
2 Gary Hocking (SRho) 1961	–	–	–	–	–	1	1
2 Fritz Scheidegger (Swi) 1965–66	2	–	–	–	–	–	–
2 Helmut Fath (FRG) 1960–68	2	–	–	–	–	–	–
2 Dieter Braun (FRG) 1970–73	–	–	–	1	1	–	–
2 Jan de Vries (Hol) 1971–73	–	2	–	–	–	–	–
2 Kent Andersson (Swe) 1973–74	–	–	–	2	–	–	–
2 Rolf Steinhausen (FRG) 1975–76	2	–	–	–	–	–	–
2 Barry Sheene (UK) 1976–77	–	–	–	–	–	–	2
2 Ricardo Tormo (Spa) 1978–81	–	2	–	–	–	–	–
2 Carlos Lavado (Ven) 1983–86	–	–	–	–	2	–	–
2 Fausto Gresini (Ita) 1985–87	–	–	–	2	–	–	–
2 Sito Pons (Spa) 1988–89	–	–	–	–	2	–	–

The following have all won one world title:

500cc: Les Graham (UK) 1949, Libero Liberati (Ita) 1957, Marco Lucchinelli (Ita) 1981, Franco Uncini 1982, Wayne Gardner (Aus) 1987, Wayne Rainey (USA) 1990

350cc: Freddie Frith (UK) 1949, Bob Foster (UK) 1950, Keith Campbell (Aus) 1957, Johnny Cecotto (Ven) 1975, Takazumi Katayama (Jap) 1977, Jon Ekerold (SAf) 1980

250cc: Dario Ambrosini (Ita) 1950, Enrico Lorenzetti (Ita) 1952, Herman-Paul Müller (FRG) 1955, Kel Carruthers (Aus) 1969, Rod Gould (UK) 1970, Jarno Saarinen (Fin) 1972, Mario Lega (Ita) 1977, Jean-Louis Tournadre (Fra) 1982, Christian Sarron (Fra) 1984, John Kocinski (USA) 1990

125cc: Nello Pagani (Ita) 1949, Rupert Hollaus (Aut) 1954, Tom Phillis (Aus) 1961, Bill Ivy (UK) 1967, Dave Simmonds (UK) 1969, Paolo Pileri (Ita) 1975, Luca Cadalora (Ita) 1986, Alex Criville (Spa) 1989, Loris Capirossi (Ita) 1990

80cc: Manuel Herreros (Spa) 1989 **50cc:** Ernest Degner (FRG) 1962, Ralph Bryans (UK) 1965, Henk van Kessel (Hol) 1974

Sidecar: Cyril Smith (UK) 1952, Wilhelm Faust (FRG) 1955, Fritz Hillebrand (FRG) 1957, Horst Owesle (FRG) 1971,

George O'Dell (UK) 1977, Jock Taylor (UK) 1980, Werner Schwärzel (FRG) 1982, Alain Michel (Fra) 1990

Mike Hailwood and Phil Read are the only riders to have won world titles in three classes.

RACE WINS

Most wins (all classes)	Sidecar	50cc	80cc	125cc	250cc	350cc	500cc	Year
122 Giacomo Agostini (Ita)	–	–	–	–	–	54	68	1965–76
90 Angel Nieto (Spa)	–	27	1	62	–	–	–	1969–85
76 Mike Hailwood (UK)	–	–	–	2	21	16	37	1959–67
56 Rolf Biland (Swi)	56	–	–	–	–	–	–	1975–90
52 Phil Read (UK)	–	–	–	10	27	4	11	1961–75
45 Jim Redman (SRho)	–	–	–	4	18	21	2	1961–66
42 Anton Mang (FRG)	–	–	–	1	33	8	–	1976–88
39 Carlo Ubbiali (Ita)	–	–	–	26	13	–	–	1950–60
38 John Surtees (UK)	–	–	–	–	1	15	22	1955–60
35 Jorge Martinez (Spa)	–	–	22	13	–	–	–	1984–90
33 Geoff Duke (UK)	–	–	–	–	–	11	22	1950–58
31 Kork Ballington (SAf)	–	–	–	–	17	14	–	1976–80
30 Luigi Taveri (Swi)	–	6	–	22	2	–	–	1955–66
30 Eddie Lawson (USA)	–	–	–	–	–	–	30	1984–89
27 Klaus Enders (FRG)	27	–	–	–	–	–	–	1967–74
27 Pier Paolo Bianchi (Ita)	–	–	3	24	–	–	–	1976–86
27 Eugenio Lazzarini (Ita)	–	18	–	9	–	–	–	1973–83
27 Freddie Spencer (USA)	–	–	–	–	7	–	20	1982–85
25 Hugh Anderson (NZ)	–	8	–	17	–	–	–	1962–65
24 Kenny Roberts (USA)	–	–	–	–	2	–	22	1978–83
24 Walter Villa (Ita)	–	–	–	–	20	4	–	1974–79
23 Barry Sheene (UK)	–	1	–	3	–	–	19	1971–81
21 Bill Ivy (UK)	–	–	–	14	7	–	–	1966–68
20 Tarquinio Provini (Ita)	–	–	–	6	14	–	–	1954–64
20 Egbert Streuer (Hol)	20	–	–	–	–	–	–	1982–90
19 Gary Hocking (SRho)	–	–	–	–	5	6	8	1959–62
19 Ricardo Tormo (Spa)	–	15	–	4	–	–	–	1977–83
19 Carlos Lavado (Ven)	–	–	–	–	17	2	–	1979–87
18 Kent Andersson (Swe)	–	–	–	14	4	–	–	1972–75
18 Stefan Dörflinger (Swi)	–	9	9	–	–	–	–	1980–88
18 Fausto Gresini (Ita)	–	–	–	18	–	–	–	1984–87
17 Eric Oliver (UK)	17	–	–	–	–	–	–	1949–54
17 Wayne Gardner (Aus)	–	–	–	–	–	–	17	1986–90
17 Alain Michel (Fra)	17	–	–	–	–	–	–	1977–90
16 Fritz Scheidegger (Swi)	16	–	–	–	–	–	–	1959–66
15 Ernst Degner (GDR/FRG)	–	7	–	8	–	–	–	1959–65
15 Jarno Saarinen (Fin)	–	–	–	–	8	5	2	1971–73
15 Sito Pons (Spa)	–	–	–	–	15	–	–	1984–89
14 Hans-Georg Anscheidt (FRG)	–	14	–	–	–	–	–	1962–68
14 Dieter Braun (FRG)	–	–	–	6	7	1	–	1969–76
14 Johnny Cecotto (Ven)	–	–	–	–	2	9	3	1975–80
14 Jan de Vries (Hol)	–	14	–	–	–	–	–	1970–73
14 Steve Webster (UK)	14	–	–	–	–	–	–	1986–90
13 Randy Mamola (USA)	–	–	–	–	–	–	13	1980–87
13 Kevin Schwantz (USA)	–	–	–	–	–	–	13	1988–90
12 Max Deubel (FRG)	12	–	–	–	–	–	–	1961–65
12 Fergus Anderson (UK)	–	–	–	–	3	7	2	1951–54
11 Werner Haas (FRG)	–	–	–	4	7	–	–	1952–54
11 Takazumi Katayama (Jap)	–	–	–	–	3	7	1	1974–82
11 Dave Simmonds (UK)	–	–	–	10	–	–	1	1969–71
11 Helmut Fath (FRG)	11	–	–	–	–	–	–	1960–69
11 Luca Cadalora (Ita)	–	–	–	4	7	–	–	1986–90
11 Wayne Rainey (USA)	–	–	–	–	–	–	11	1988–90
10 Ralph Bryans (UK)	–	7	–	–	2	1	–	1964–66
10 Werner Schwärzel (FRG)	10	–	–	–	–	–	–	1974–85
10 Rolf Steinhausen (FRG)	10	–	–	–	–	–	–	1974–79
10 Rod Gould (UK)	–	–	–	–	10	–	–	1970–72
10 Gregg Hansford (Aus)	–	–	–	–	4	6	–	1978–79

Two of the American stars of present-day road racing in action, as Wayne Rainey (2) leads Eddie Lawson at the Swedish Grand Prix. Rainey went on to dethrone Lawson as the 500cc world champion in 1990.

Left *John Surtees with his trophies in 1960. The following year he quit bikes to take up car racing and more trophies followed in the four-wheeled branch of motor sport, including the Formula One world drivers' championship*

Right *The best-known name in British racing, Norton, returned to road racing in 1988. Trevor Nation was the spearhead of the John Player team which sought the return of the glory days of the early 1950s*

Bottom right *A picture that captures the thrill, severity and popularity of trials riding*

Below *Simon Webster and Gavin Simmons, Britain's top sidecar duo in the 1990 world championships*

Above *Brightly coloured livery – and, of course, advertising – plays a prominent part in road racing at the highest level*

Left *It can be lonely out in the desert! But these two are keeping each other company during the gruelling Paris–Dakar Rally*

Right *Mike Hailwood, the most successful British rider of all time*

Above *The 1990 world champion Wayne Rainey displays tremendous control over his Yamaha during the French Grand Prix*

Right *Eddie Lawson (left) seen talking to his Australian Rothmans Honda teammates Wayne Gardner and Michael Doohan*

Below *Christian Sarron of France takes a tumble during the British Grand Prix, and a few thousand pounds' worth of machinery heads for an expensive trip*

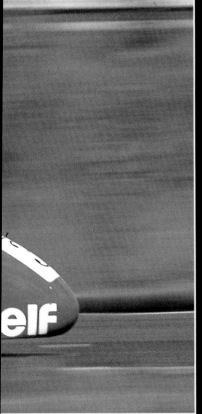

Left *Alain Michel of France, with his British passenger Simon Birchall, on their way to winning the 1990 Swedish Grand Prix. The combination then went on to capture the world title*

Bottom left *Jamie James, the 1989 AMA National Superbike champion*

Bottom *The successful Rothmans Honda, seen here in the hands of Australia's Wayne Gardner*

Below *Action from the 1987 Transatlantic Challenge at Brands Hatch*

Opposite page *Wayne Rainey (2) leads at the 1990 Spanish Grand Prix*

Left *Moto-cross action from the 1990 Belgian Grand Prix. The sport is very popular in Belgium and the country has produced many of the best known names in moto-cross: Harry Everts, Eric Geboers, Roger De Coster, André Malherbe and Georges Jobé*

Below *'Wheelie' fun during the 1989 US Grand Prix (250cc) at Laguna Seca. Number 19, the American John Kocinski, won the race*

Top *Steve Webster and Tony Hewitt, the British pair that won the world sidecar title three years in succession from 1987–89*

Above *Another of the talented American riders to have come to the fore in the 1980s, Kevin Schwantz. Fourth in the '00cc championship in 1989 and runner-up in 1990, he is certainly a potential world champion*

Left *Eric Geboers of Belgium regained his world 500cc moto-cross title in 1990*

Right *American world champion Eddie Lawson on his 1987 Marlboro Yamaha*

Bottom *The Isle of Man TT can be an isolated race at times, as this picture shows. Note, too, how it captures the coastline of the island*

Below *'What a waste of good champers!' Grand Prix winner Kevin Schwantz (centre), Wayne Rainey (left) and Britain's Niall Mackenzie celebrate by showering each other in bubbly at the Nürburgring in 1990*

Above *Kevin Schwantz is waiting for his Lucky Strike Suzuki to be reassembled before the start of the action at Laguna Seca in 1990. However, despite setting the fastest lap once the race got under way, he didn't finish in the first three*

Below *Australia has been the only nation to offer a convincing challenge to the Americans in the latter part of the 1980s and Kevin Magee is one of their top riders*

NATIONAL RECORDS

TOTAL GRAND PRIX RACE WINS, BY NATION

ARGENTINA (Total wins: 2)
500cc (2): Benedicto Caldarella (1), Jorge Kissling (1)

AUSTRALIA (Total wins: 62)
500cc (24): Wayne Gardner (17), Jack Findlay (3), Ken Kavanagh (1), Jack Ahearn (1), Kevin Magee (1), Michael Doohan (1)
350cc (14): Gregg Hansford (6), Ken Kavanagh (4), Keith Campbell (3), John Dodds (1)
250cc (15): Kel Carruthers (7), Gregg Hansford (4), Tom Phillis (2), John Dodds (2)
125cc (6): Tom Phillis (4), John Dodds (1), Barry Smith (1)
50cc (3): Barry Smith (3)

AUSTRIA (Total wins: 13)
250cc (2): Rupert Hollaus (1), Ed Stollinger (1)
125cc (10): August Auinger (5), Rupert Hollaus (4), Bertie Schneider (1)
80cc (1): Gerd Kafka (1)

BELGIUM (Total wins: 7)
350cc (2): Didier de Radigues (2)
250cc (2): Didier de Radigues (2)
50cc (3): Julien van Zeebroeck (3)

BRAZIL (Total wins: 1)
350cc (1): Santos Adu Celso (1)

CANADA (Total wins: 3)
250cc (2): Mike Duff (2)
125cc (1): Mike Duff (1)

CZECHOSLOVAKIA (Total wins: 4)
500cc (1): Frantisek Stastny (1)
350cc (3): Frantisek Stastny (3)

FINLAND (Total wins: 25)
500cc (3): Jarno Saarinen (2), Teppi Länsivuori (1)
350cc (11): Jarno Saarinen (5), Teppi Länsivuori (5), Pentti Korhonen (1)
250cc (10): Jarno Saarinen (8), Teppi Länsivuori (2)
Sidecar (1): Rahko Kalvevi (1)

FRANCE (Total wins: 55)
500cc (2): Christian Sarron (1), Pierre Monneret (1)
350cc (9): Jean-Francois Baldé (3), Patrick Fernandez (2), Michel Rougerie (1), Pierre Monneret (1), Eric Saul (1), Oliver Chevallier (1)
250cc (19): Christian Sarron (6), Dominique Sarron (4), Jean-Francois Baldé (2), Michel Rougerie (2), Patrick Fernandez (1), Eric Saul (1), Jacques Bolle (1), Herve Guilleux (1), Jean-Louis Tournadre (1)
125cc (8): Guy Bertin (6), Jean Auriel (1), Jean-Claude Selini (1)
Sidecar (17): Alain Michel (17)

**GERMAN DEMOCRATIC REPUBLIC, East Germany
(Total wins: 6)**
250cc (1): Horst Fügner (1)
125cc (5): Ernst Degner (5)*
See also FEDERAL REPUBLIC OF GERMANY

**FEDERAL REPUBLIC OF GERMANY, West Germany
(Total wins: 239)**
500cc (1): Edmund Czihak (1)
350cc (11): Anton Mang (8), Dieter Braun (1), Manfred Herweh (1), Helmut Kassner (1)
250cc (61): Anton Mang (33), Dieter Braun (7), Werner Haas (7), Manfred Herweh (5), Martin Wimmer (3), Reinhold Roth (3), Helmut Kassner (1), Rudi Felgenheier (1), Paul Hermann Müller (1)
125cc (16): Dieter Braun (6), Werner Haas (4), Ernst Degner (3)*, Anton Mang (1), Fritz Reitmaier (1), Stefan Prein (1)
80cc (6): Peter Öttl (3), Gerhard Waibel (3)
50cc (28): Hans-Georg Anscheidt (14), Ernst Degner (7)*, Herbert Rittberger (4), Ingo Emmerich (1), Gerhard Thurow (1), Gerhard Waibel (1)
Sidecar (116): Klaus Enders (27), Max Deubel (12), Helmut Fath (11), Werner Schwärzel (10), Rolf Steinhausen (10), Siegfried Schauzu (9), Wilhelm Noll (8), Walter Schneider (7), Georg Auerbacher (6), Fritz Hillebrand (5), Willy Faust (3), Horst Owesle (3), Arsenius Butscher (2), Heinz Luthringshauser (2), Johann Attenberger (1)
See also GERMAN DEMOCRATIC REPUBLIC

HOLLAND (Total wins: 77)
500cc (8): Wil Hartog (5), Jack Middelburg (2), Boet van Dulmen (1)
250cc (1): Wilco Zeelemberg (1)
125cc (11): Hans Spaan (9), Jos Schurgers (1), Cees van Dongen (1)
50cc (37): Jan de Vries (14), Henk van Kessell (7), Aalt Toersen (6), Paul Lodewijkx (4), Theo Timmer (3), Jan Huberts (2), Jan Bruins (1)
Sidecar (20): Egbert Streuer (20)

HUNGARY (Total wins: 4)
350cc (3): Janos Drapal (3)
250cc (1): Janos Drapal (1)

ITALY (Total wins: 417)
500cc (104): Giacomo Agostini (68), Marco Lucchinelli (6), Umberto Masetti (6), Franco Uncini (5), Libero Liberati (4), Alfredo Milani (3), Alberto Pagani (3), Nello Pagani (2), Virginio Ferrari (2), Giuseppe Colnago (1), Angelo Bergamonti (1), Gianfranco Bonera (1), Remo Venturi (1), Pier Francesco Chili (1)
350cc (66): Giacomo Agostini (54), Walter Villa (4), Enrico Lorenzetti (2), Libero Liberati (2), Duilio Agostini (1), Otello Buscherini (1), Silvio Grassetti (1), Angelo Bergamonti (1)

250cc (86): Walter Villa (20), Tarquinio Provini (14), Carlo Ubbiali (13), Luca Cadalora (7), Renzo Pasolini (6), Enrico Lorenzetti (5), Dario Ambrosini (5), Bruno Ruffo (3), Graziano Rossi (3), Silvio Grassetti (2), Franco Uncini (2), Emilio Mendogni (1), Gianfranco Bonera (1), Mario Lega (1), Fausto Ricci (1), Paolo Pileri (1), Loris Reggiani (1)
125cc (133): Carlo Ubbiali (26), Pier Paolo Bianchi (24), Fausto Gresini (18), Eugenio Lazzarini (9), Paolo Pileri (7), Tarquinio Provini (6), Ezio Gianola (5), Luca Cadalora (4), Gilberto Parlotti (3), Gianni Leoni (3), Loris Reggiani (3), Loris Capirossi (3), Alberto Gandossi (2), Maurizio Vitali (2), Nello Pagani (2), Otello Buscherini (2), Emilio Mendogni (2), Doriano Romboni (2), Domenico Brigaglia (1), Bruno Ruffo (1), Pierluigi Conforti (1), Angelo Copeta (1), Romolo Ferri (1), Guido Leoni (1), Guido Sala (1), Bruno Spaggiari (1), Paolo Casolini (1)
80cc (3): Pier Paolo Bianchi (3)
50cc (18): Eugenio Lazzarini (18)
Sidecar (7): Albino Milani (4), Ercole Frigerio (2), Ernesto Merlo (1)

JAPAN (Total wins: 30)
500cc (2): Takazumi Katayama (1), Hideo Kanaya (1)
350cc (8): Takazumi Katayama (7), Hideo Kanaya (1)
250cc (9): Takazumi Katayama (3), Kunumitsu Takahashi (1), Hideo Kanaya (1), Hiroshi Hasegawa (1), Fumio Ito (1), Tadahiko Taira (1), Masaru Kobayashi (1)
125cc (5): Kunumitsu Takahashi (3), Hoshimi Katayama (1), Teisuke Tanaka (1)
50cc (6): Hoshimi Katayama (3), Mitsuo Itoh (2), Morishita Isao (1)

NEW ZEALAND (Total wins: 30)
500cc (2): Dennis Ireland (1), Kim Newcombe (1)
350cc (2): Ken Mudford (1), Rod Coleman (1)
250cc (1): Ginger Molloy (1)
125cc (17): Hugh Anderson (17)
50cc (8): Hugh Anderson (8)

REPUBLIC OF IRELAND (Total wins: 9)
500cc (4): Reg Armstrong (4)
350cc (1): Reg Armstrong (1)
250cc (4): Reg Armstrong (2), Manliff Barrington (1), Ray McCullough (1)

SOUTH AFRICA (Total wins: 39)
350cc (21): Kork Ballington (14); Jon Ekerold (6), Alan North (1)
250cc (18): Kork Ballington (17), Jon Ekerold (1)

SOUTHERN RHODESIA (Total wins: 70)
500cc (12): Gary Hocking (8), Jim Redman (2), Ray Amm (2)
350cc (31): Jim Redman (21), Gary Hocking (6), Ray Amm (4)
250cc (23): Jim Redman (18), Gary Hocking (5)
125cc (4): Jim Redman (4)

SPAIN (Total wins: 179)
350cc (1): Victor Palomo (1)
250cc (27): Sito Pons (15), Carlos Cardus (5), Santiago Herrero (4), Juan Garriga (3)
125cc (81): Angel Nieto (62), Jorge Martinez (13),

Carlo Ubbiali is, after Giacomo Agostini, the most successful Italian rider ever, with nine world title wins between 1951 and 1960. He is seen here on his 125cc MV Agusta in 1956

Ricardo Tormo (4), Salvador Canellas (1), Benjamin Grau (1)
80cc (27): Jorge Martinez (22), Manuel Herreros (2), Herri Torrontegui (2), Angel Nieto (1)
50cc (43): Angel Nieto (27), Ricardo Tormo (15), Salvador Canellas (1)

SWEDEN (Total wins: 24)
250cc (5): Kent Andersson (4), Borje Jansson (1)
125cc (18): Kent Andersson (14), Borje Jansson (3), Leif Gustavsson (1)
Sidecar (1): Göte Brodin (1)

SWITZERLAND (Total wins: 145)
500cc (1): Michel Frutschi (1)
350cc (1): Bruno Kneubühler (1)
250cc (7): Jacques Cornu (3), Luigi Taveri (2), Roland Freymond (1), Gyula Marsovszky (1)
125cc (25): Luigi Taveri (22), Bruno Kneubühler (3)
80cc (9): Stefan Dörflinger (9)
50cc (17): Stefan Dörflinger (9), Luigi Taveri (6), Bruno Kneubühler (1), Ulrich Graf (1)
Sidecar (85): Rolf Biland (56), Fritz Scheidegger (16), Florian Camathias (8), Hermann Schmid (3), Bruno Holzer (1), Paul Geudel (1)

UNITED KINGDOM (Total wins: 423)
500cc (138): Mike Hailwood (37), John Surtees (22), Geoff Duke (22), Barry Sheene (19), Phil Read (11), Leslie Graham (5), John Hartle (3), Fergus Anderson (2), Dave Simmonds (1), Bill Lomas (1), Charles Mortimer (1), Bob McIntyre (1), Mick Grant (1), Dickie Dale (1), Bill Doran (1), Alan Shepherd (1), Jack Brett (1), Phil Carpenter (1), Harold Daniell (1), Cromie McCandless (1), John Newbold (1), Godfrey Nash (1), John Williams (1), Tom Herron (1), Dick Creith (1)
350cc (85): Mike Hailwood (16), John Surtees (15), Geoff Duke (11), Fergus Anderson (7), Bill Lomas (7), Freddie Frith (5), Phil Read (4), Bob Foster (3), Leslie Graham (2), Bob McIntyre (2), Tony Rutter (2), Charlie Williams (1), Charles Mortimer (1), John Hartle (1), Dickie Dale (1), Bill Doran (1), Tommy Wood (1), Tony Jefferies (1), Peter Williams (1), Tommy Robb (1), Ralph Bryans (1), Artie Bell (1)
250cc (94): Phil Read (27), Mike Hailwood (21), Rod Gould (10), Bill Ivy (7), Fergus Anderson (3), Maurice Cann (3), Charles Mortimer (2), Bob McIntyre (2), Cecil Sandford (2), Mick Grant (2), Charlie Williams (2), Arthur Wheeler (2), Ralph Bryans (2), John Surtees (1), Bill Lomas (1), John Hartle (1), Alan Shepherd (1), Tommy Wood (1), Alan Carter (1), Derek Minter (1), Tommy Robb (1), Tom Herron (1)
125cc (52): Bill Ivy (14), Phil Read (10), Dave Simmonds (10), Barry Sheene (3), Charles Mortimer (3), Cecil Sandford (3), Frank Perris (3), Mike Hailwood (2), Leslie Graham (1), Stuart Graham (1), Tommy Robb (1), Cromie McCandless (1)
80cc (1): Ian McConnachie (1)
50cc (9): Ralph Bryans (7), Barry Sheene (1), Stuart Graham (1)
Sidecar (44): Eric Oliver (17), Steve Webster (14), Jock Taylor (6), Cyril Smith (2), Chris Vincent (2), Derek Jones (1), Colin Seeley (1), Peter 'Pip' Harris (1)

UNITED STATES (Total wins: 131)
500cc (112): Eddie Lawson (30), Kenny Roberts (22), Freddie Spencer (20), Randy Mamola (13), Kevin Schwantz (13), Wayne Rainey (11), Pat Hennen (3)
250cc (19): John Kocinski (9), Freddie Spencer (7), Kenny Roberts (2), Jim Filice (1)

VENEZUELA (Total wins: 35)
500cc (3): Johnny Cecotto (3)
350cc (11): Johnny Cecotto (9), Carlos Lavado (2)
250cc (19): Carlos Lavado (17), Johnny Cecotto (2)
125cc (2): Ivan Palazzese (2)

MANUFACTURERS' RECORDS

RACE WINS Solo classes only

Manufacturer	50cc	80cc	125cc	250cc	350cc	500cc	Year
350 Yamaha	–	–	46	149	71	84	1963–90
273 MV Agusta	–	–	33	26	75	139	1952–76
256 Honda	13	–	52	98	35	58	1961–90
130 Suzuki	30	–	35	–	–	65	1962–90
85 Kawasaki	–	–	10	45	28	2	1969–83
70 Derbi	17	25	27	1	–	–	1968–89
69 Kreidler	69	–	–	–	–	–	1962–82
51 Garelli	7	–	44	–	–	–	1982–87
46 Guzzi	–	–	–	18	25	3	1949–62
41 Norton	–	–	–	–	20	21	1949–69
41 Morbidelli	–	–	36	5	–	–	1970–79
39 Gilera	–	–	1	–	4	34	1949–63
29 Bultaco	21	–	7	1	–	–	1966–81
28 Harley-Davidson	–	–	–	24	4	–	1974–77
27 Minarelli	–	–	27	–	–	–	1978–81

The first challenge to Honda's status as the top Japanese manufacturer came from Yamaha in the mid-1960s

20 NSU	–	–	8	12	–	–	1952–55
19 MBA	–	–	18	1	–	–	1978–86
18 Mondial	–	–	14	4	–	–	1949–57
13 Benelli	–	–	–	13	–	–	1949–69
13 MZ	–	–	5	7	1	–	1958–71
13 Krauser	–	13	–	–	–	–	1985–89
10 AJS	–	–	–	–	4	6	1949–54
9 Velocette	–	–	–	–	9	–	1949–51
9 Jamathi	9	–	–	–	–	–	1968–73
9 Cobas/JJ Cobas	–	–	8	1	–	–	1984–90
7 Morini	–	–	2	5	–	–	1952–63
6 Real/Real Rotax	–	1	–	5	–	–	1983–84
5 Motobecane	–	–	5	–	–	–	1979–80
4 Ducati	–	–	4	–	–	–	1958–59
4 Jawa	–	–	–	–	4	–	1961–69
4 Ossa	–	–	–	4	–	–	1969–70
4 Aermacchi	–	–	1	3	–	–	1970–72
4 Maico	–	–	4	–	–	–	1972–74
4 Sanvanero	–	–	3	–	–	1	1981–82
4 Zündapp	–	4	–	–	–	–	1984
3 Matchless	–	–	–	–	–	3	1961–62
3 Krauser-Kreidler	3	–	–	–	–	–	1983
3 Monnet	–	–	3	–	–	–	1985
2 Yamsel	–	–	–	1	1	–	1971
2 Malanca	–	–	2	–	–	–	1973
2 Piovaticci	1	–	1	–	–	–	1973–75
2 Iprem	2	–	–	–	–	–	1980
2 Chevalier	–	–	–	2	–	–	1983
2 Casal	–	2	–	–	–	–	1984
2 Seel	–	2	–	–	–	–	1985–86
1 DKW	–	–	–	1	–	–	1952
1 Jawa-CZ	–	–	–	–	–	1	1966
1 Linto	–	–	–	–	–	1	1969
1 Bridgestone	–	–	1	–	–	–	1973
1 König	–	–	–	–	–	1	1973
1 Pernod	–	–	–	1	–	–	1983
1 AGV	–	–	1	–	–	–	1987
1 Aprilia	–	–	–	1	–	–	1987

WORLD TITLES

Title wins (all solo classes, not Sidecar)

Manufacturer	50cc	80cc	125cc	250cc	350cc	500cc
37 MV Agusta	–	–	7	5	9	16
29 Yamaha	–	–	4	13	6	6
29 Honda	2	–	6	10	6	5
15 Suzuki	5	–	3	–	–	7
9 Kawasaki	–	–	1	4	4	–
8 Derbi	2	3	3	–	–	–
7 Kreidler	7	–	–	–	–	–
6 Guzzi	–	–	–	3	3	–
5 Norton	–	–	–	–	2	3
5 Mondial	–	–	4	1	–	–
5 Garelli	1	–	4	–	–	–
4 Gilera	–	–	–	–	1	3
4 Bultaco	4	–	–	–	–	–
3 Minarelli	–	–	3	–	–	–
3 Morbidelli	–	–	3	–	–	–
2 Velocette	–	–	–	–	2	–
2 Benelli	–	–	–	2	–	–
2 MBA	–	–	2	–	–	–
2 Krauser	–	2	–	–	–	–
1 AJS	–	–	–	–	–	1
1 Harley-Davidson	–	–	–	1	–	–
1 NSU	–	–	–	1	–	–
1 Zündapp	–	1	–	–	–	–

Honda is the only manufacturer to win world titles in five solo classes

MOST WORLD TITLES IN ONE YEAR

5 Honda, 1966
(50/125/250/350/500)

4 MV Agusta, 1958
(125/250/350/500)

4 MV Agusta, 1959
(125/250/350/500)

4 MV Agusta, 1960
(125/250/350/500)

4 Yamaha, 1974
(125/250/350/500)

3 MV Agusta, 1956
(125/250/500)

3 Honda, 1962
(125/250/350)

3 Yamaha, 1973
(125/250/350)

3 Honda, 1989
(125/250/500)

MOST RACE WINS IN A SEASON

29 Honda (1966) 3 x 50cc, 5 x 125cc, 10 x 250cc, 6 x 350cc, 5 x 500cc
27 Yamaha (1973) 7 x 125cc, 11 x 250cc, 7 x 350cc, 2 x 500cc
27 Yamaha (1974) 6 x 125cc, 6 x 250cc, 10 x 350cc, 5 x 500cc
25 Honda (1962) 1 x 50cc, 10 x 125cc, 9 x 250cc, 5 x 350cc
23 Honda (1989) 6 x 125cc, 11 x 250cc, 6 x 500cc
22 MV Agusta (1959) 5 x 125cc, 4 x 250cc, 6 x 350cc, 7 x 500cc
21 MV Agusta (1960) 4 x 125cc, 6 x 250cc,. 5 x 350cc, 6 x 500cc
21 Honda (1964) 3 x 50cc, 7 x 125cc, 3 x 250cc, 8 x 350cc
21 MV Agusta (1970) 10 x 350cc, 11 x 500cc
20 MV Agusta (1958) 4 x 125cc, 4 x 250cc, 6 x 350cc, 6 x 500cc
20 Yamaha (1972) 4 x 125cc, 9 x 250cc, 6 x 350cc, 1 x 500c
Honda (1966) is the only manufacturer to win races in five classes in one season

MOST TITLE WINS BY CLASS

500cc 16 MV Agusta; 7 Suzuki; 6 Yamaha; 5 Honda
350cc 9 MV Agusta; 6 Yamaha, Honda; 4 Kawasaki
250cc 13 Yamaha; 10 Honda; 5 MV Agusta
125cc 7 MV Agusta; 6 Honda; 4 Garelli, Mondial, Yamaha
80cc 3 Derbi; 2 Krauser; 1 Zündapp
50cc 7 Kreidler; 5 Suzuki; 4 Bultaco

MOST RACE WINS BY CLASS IN A SEASON

500cc
12 MV Agusta (1972)
11 MV Agusta (1970)
10 MV Agusta (1968, 1969)
 9 MV Agusta (1965, 1971), Suzuki (1977), Yamaha (1988)
 8 MV Agusta (1961), Honda (1984, 1985), Suzuki (1976, 1981), Yamaha (1986, 1987)
350cc
11 Yamaha (1977)
10 MV Agusta (1970), Yamaha (1974, 1975)
 9 Kawasaki (1978)
250cc
12 Honda (1987)
11 Yamaha (1970, 1973), Kawasaki (1981), Honda (1989)
10 Honda (1961, 1966, 1988), Yamaha (1968, 1990)
125cc
11 Honda (1990)
10 Honda (1962), Suzuki (1965), Yamaha (1967), Minarelli (1981), Garelli (1987)
 9 Suzuki (1963), Morbidelli (1977), Minarelli (1979), Derbi (1988)
80cc
 8 Derbi (1987)
 6 Derbi (1988)
 5 Derbi (1986), Krauser (1989)
50cc
10 Kreidler (1974)
 7 Suzuki (1967), Kreidler (1975, 1979), Bultaco (1981)
 6 Derbi (1970), Kreidler (1971, 1973)

MOST WINS AT ONE GRAND PRIX

The following have all provided machines for the winners of four races at one Grand Prix:

MV AGUSTA (10 times): 1956 Belgian GP; 1958 British GP (TT), Dutch TT, West German GP, Ulster GP; 1959 British GP (TT), West Germany GP; 1960 British GP (TT), Dutch TT, Italian GP

HONDA (3 times): 1964 Dutch TT; 1966 Dutch TT, Czechoslovak GP
YAMAHA (3 times): 1973 Austrian GP; 1974 Swedish GP; 1975 French GP

MOST RACE WINS BY CLASS

500cc
139 MV Agusta; **84** Yamaha; **65** Suzuki
350cc
75 MV Agusta; **71** Yamaha; **35** Honda
250cc
149 Yamaha; **98** Honda; **45** Kawasaki

125cc
52 Honda; **46** Yamaha; **44** Garelli
80cc
25 Derbi; **13** Krauser; **4** Zündapp
50cc
69 Kreidler; **30** Suzuki; **21** Bultaco

SIDECAR MANUFACTURERS' RECORDS

MOST WORLD TITLES

18 BMW, 1955–73
11 Yamaha/LCR Yamaha, 1977–87
5 Norton, 1949–53
3 LCR Krauser, 1988–90
2 Busch/Busch König, 1974–75

RACE WINS

110 BMW, 1954–74
   107 BMW, 1954–74
    3 FCS BMW, 1963–64
90 Yamaha, 1975–90
   47 LCR Yamaha, 1979–90
   31 Yamaha, 1976–81
    9 Seymaz Yamaha, 1975–82
    2 KSA Yamaha, 1979
    1 Busch Yamaha, 1977

31 Krauser, 1985–90
   29 LCR Krauser, 1987–90
    2 Krauser, 1985
19 Norton, 1949–54
13 König, 1975–76
    7 König, 1974–76
    6 Busch König, 1975–76
8 Gilera, 1949–64

6 URS, 1968–72
    4 Münch URS, 1971–72
    2 URS Fath, 1968–69
3 ARO Fath, 1977–78
2 Busch Enders, 1974
1 BSA, 1962
1 Honda, 1973

THE 1990 GRAND PRIX CIRCUITS

AUSTRALIA: Phillip Island, Victoria

Length: 2.78mile/4.47km
Lap record: 105.83mph/170.32kph Wayne Gardner (Aus), Honda, 1990
Year first used for World Championship Grand Prix and first 500cc winner:
1989 Wayne Gardner (Aus), Honda

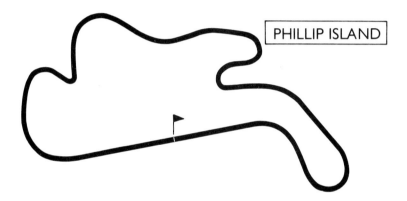

PHILLIP ISLAND

AUSTRIA: Salzburgring

Length: 2.63mile/4.2km
Lap record: 121.08mph/194.86kph Kevin Schwantz (USA), Suzuki, 1990
Year first used for World Championship Grand Prix and first 500cc winner:
1971 Giacomo Agostini (Ita), MV Agusta

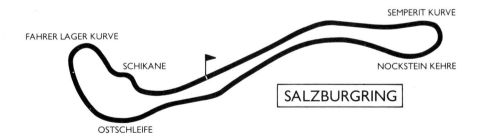

SEMPERIT KURVE

FAHRER LAGER KURVE

SCHIKANE

NOCKSTEIN KEHRE

SALZBURGRING

OSTSCHLEIFE

BELGIUM: Circuit de Spa-Francorchamps

Length: 4.31mile/6.94km
Lap record: 106.25mph/170.99kph Kevin Schwantz (USA), Suzuki, 1989
Year first used for World Championship Grand Prix and first 500cc winner:
1949 Bill Doran (UK), AJS

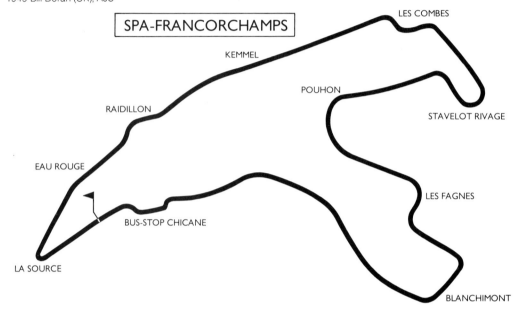

CZECHOSLOVAKIA: Autodromo Brno

Length: 3.35mile/5.39km
Lap record: 97.46mph/156.86kph Wayne Rainey (USA), Yamaha, 1990
Year first used for World Championship Grand Prix and first 500cc winner:
1965 Mike Hailwood (UK), MV Agusta

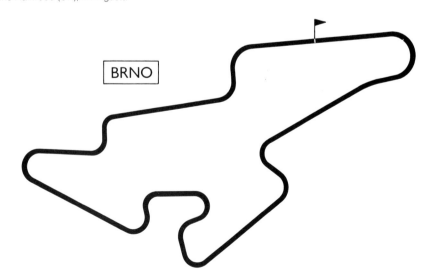

ENGLAND: Donington Park

Length: 2.50mile/4.00km
Lap record: 95.92mph/154.37kph Kevin Schwantz (USA), Suzuki, 1990
Year first used for World Championship Grand Prix and first 500cc winner:
1987 Eddie Lawson (USA), Yamaha

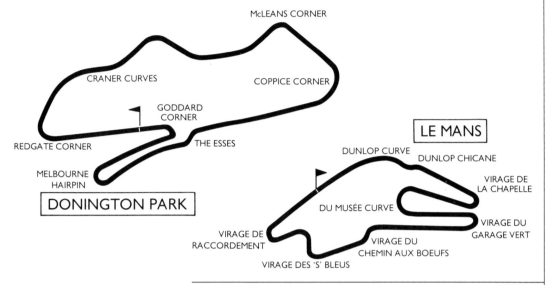

FRANCE: Circuit Bugatti, Le Mans

Length: 2.75mile/4.43km
Lap record: 97.14mph/156.33kph Kevin Schwantz (USA), Suzuki, 1990
Year first used for World Championship Grand Prix and first 500cc winner:
1969 Giacomo Agostini (Ita), MV Agusta

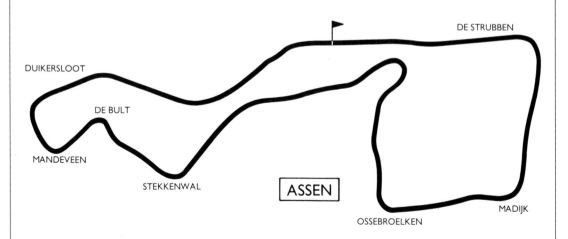

HOLLAND: Circuit van Drenthe, Assen

Length: 3.76mile/6.05km
Lap record: 109.51mph/176.24kph Kevin Schwantz (USA), Suzuki, 1990
Year first used for World Championship Grand Prix and first 500cc winner:
1949 Nello Pagani (Ita), Gilera

HUNGARY: Hungaroring, Budapest

Length: 2.48mile/3.99km
Lap record: 85.52mph/137.63kph Michael Doohan (Aus), Honda, 1990
Year first used for World Championship Grand Prix and first 500cc winner:
1990 Michael Doohan (Aus), Honda

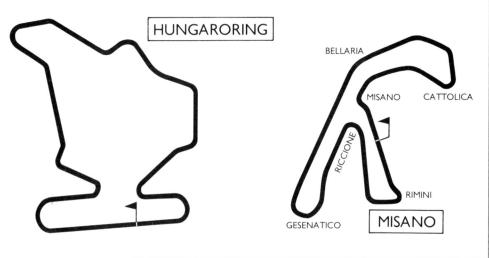

ITALY: Autodromo Santamonica, Misano

Length: 2.18mile/3.51km
Lap record: 103.38mph/166.37kph Wayne Rainey (USA), Yamaha, 1990
Year first used for World Championship Grand Prix and first 500cc winner:
1980 Kenny Roberts (USA), Yamaha

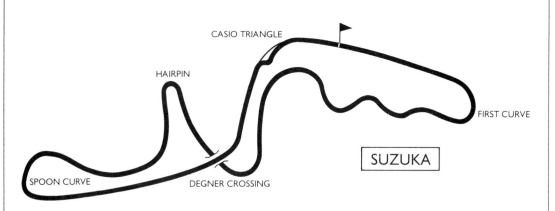

JAPAN: Suzuka Circuit

Length: 3.66mile/5.89km
Lap record: 99.78mph/160.58kph Wayne Rainey (USA), Yamaha, 1990
Year first used for World Championship Grand Prix: 1963
First 500cc race: 1987, won by Randy Mamola (USA), Yamaha

SPAIN: Circuito de Jerez

Length: 2.64mile/4.25km
Lap record: 87.62mph/141.01kph Michael Doohan (Aus), Honda, 1990
Year first used for World Championship Grand Prix and first 500cc winner:
1987 Wayne Gardner (Aus), Honda

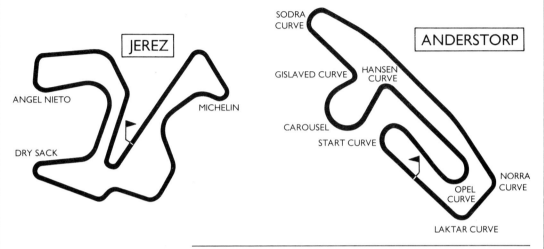

SWEDEN: Scandinavian Raceway, Anderstorp

Length: 2.51mile/4.03km
Lap record: 98.76mph/158.94kph Wayne Rainey (USA), Yamaha, 1990
Year first used for World Championship Grand Prix and first 500cc winner:
1971 Giacomo Agostini (Ita), MV Agusta

UNITED STATES: Laguna Seca Raceway, Monterey

Length: 2.20mile/3.53km
Lap record: 92.10mph/148.22kpm Kevin Schwantz (USA), Suzuki, 1990
Year first used for World Championship Grand Prix and first 500cc winner:
1988 Eddie Lawson (USA), Yamaha

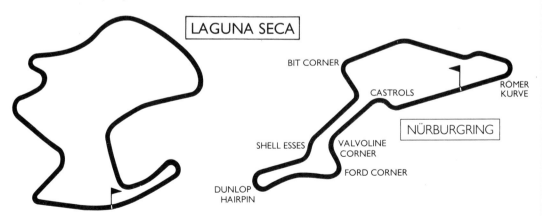

WEST GERMANY: Nürburgring

Length: 2.82mile/4.54km
Lap record: 101.03mph/162.59kph Kevin Schwantz (USA), Suzuki, 1990
Year first used for World Championship Grand Prix and first 500cc winner:
1955 Geoff Duke (UK), Gilera

YUGOSLAVIA: Rijeka

Length: 2.59mile/4.17km
Lap record: 104.50mph/168.18kph Wayne Rainey (USA), Yamaha, 1990
*Year first used for World Championship Grand Prix:*1978
First 500cc race: 1979, won by Kenny Roberts (USA), Yamaha

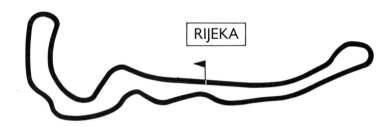

RIJEKA

OTHER CIRCUITS

ENGLAND: Silverstone

Length: 2.97mile/4.78km
Lap record: 119.47mph/192.27kph Kenny Roberts (USA), Yamaha, 1983
Year first used for World Championship Grand Prix and first 500cc winner:
1977 Pat Hennen (USA), Suzuki

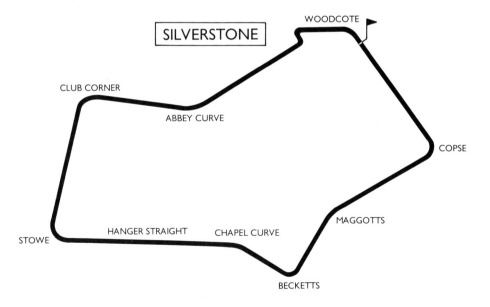

SILVERSTONE

NORTHERN IRELAND: Dundrod Circuit, Belfast

Length: 7.38mile/11.88km
Lap record: 123.72mph/199.11kph Steve Hislop (UK), Honda, 1990
Year first used for World Championship Grand Prix and first 500cc winner:
1953 (Ulster GP) Ken Kavanagh (Aus), Norton

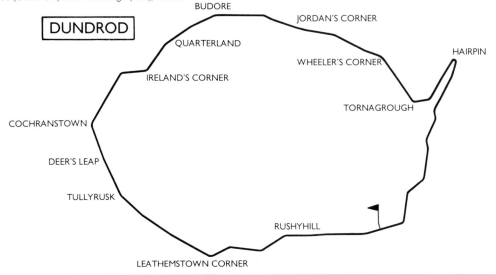

UNITED STATES: Daytona International Speedway, Florida

Length: 3.56mile/5.73km
Lap record: 111.87mph/180.04kph Thomas Stevens, Yamaha, 1990
Year first used for World Championship Grand Prix and first 500cc winner:
1964 Mike Hailwood (UK), MV Agusta

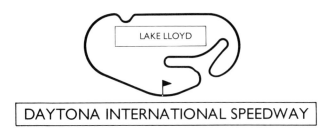

WEST GERMANY: Hockenheimring

Length: 4.22mile/6.79km
Lap record: 123.79mph/199.22kph Kevin Schwantz (USA), Suzuki, 1989
Year first used for World Championship Grand Prix and first 500cc winner:
1957 Libero Liberati (Ita), Gilera

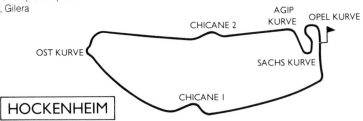

NB: Lap records set in practice are excluded

SUPERBIKE RACING

Superbike racing in Britain and Europe grew out of the popular Formula 750 racing in the United States, and the inaugural British Superbike Championship was held in 1971, known then as the *Motor Cycle News* Superbike Championship.

Perhaps inevitably, the concept of a world championship for Superbikes came from America, which in the 1980s had produced world champions and contenders such as Freddie Spencer, Eddie Lawson, Wayne Rainey and Kevin Schwantz who had all excelled at Superbike racing on home soil.

The FIM were eventually persuaded that there was room for a Superbike championship in the 1988 calendar, and in October 1987 a list of venues and dates for the new championship were duly accepted. Donington Park, England, staged the first World Superbike Championship race on 3 April 1988, as Production racing gained worldwide attention for the first time.

All superbikes must be standard production models available to the public who wish to acquire high-performance machines. They must have been manufactured within the last five years and be produced in quantity. Slight modifications to the catalogue bike are permitted, but the type of engine, number of cylinders, stroke etc, cannot be altered. The engine limits for Superbike racing are:

Over 400cc and up to 750cc: 4-stroke with 3 or 4 cylinders

Over 750cc and up to 1000cc: 4-stroke with 2 cylinders

Superbike racing was popularised in the United States and one of their most successful riders, at both superbike and Grand Prix racing, has been Eddie Lawson

1988

DONINGTON PARK, England, 3 April
Marco Lucchinelli (Ita), Ducati, 92.54mph/148.91kph
For the inaugural race, the aggretate times of two heats decided the overall places. But after this meeting, the FIM clarified the rules, which stated that in future all races would consist of two heats, each being run as separate races and with their own points classification counting towards the championship.

HUNGARORING, Hungary, 30 April
Heat 1: Fred Merkel (USA), Honda, 75.34mph/121.24kph
Heat 2: Adrien Morillas (Fra), Kawasaki, 75.36mph/
121.28kph

HOCKENHEIMRING, West Germany, 8 May
Heat 1: Davide Tardozzi (Ita), Bimota, 114.07mph/
183.58mph
Heat 2: Davide Tardozzi (Ita), Bimota, 113.72mph/
183.01kph

ÖSTERREICHRING, Austria, 3 July
Heat 1: Marco Lucchinelli (Ita), Ducati, 111.00mph/
178.64kph
Heat 2: Davide Tardozzi (Ita), Bimota, 111.16mph/
178.89kph

SUGO, Japan, 28 August
Heat 1: Gary Goodfellow (Can), Suzuki, 75.98mph/
122.28kph
Heat 2: Michael Doohan (Aus), Yamaha, 83.55mph/
134.47kph

LE MANS, France, 4 September
Heat 1: Fabrizio Pirovano (Ita), Yamaha, 77.87mph/
125.32kph
Meeting reduced to one race because of adverse weather

ESTORIL, Portugal, 11 September
Heat 1: Davide Tardozzi (Ita), Bimota, 88.37mph/
142.22kph
Heat 2: Stéphane Mertens (Bel), Bimota, 88.87mph/
143.03kph

ORAN PARK, Australia, 25 September
Heat 1: Michael Doohan (Aus), Yamaha, 79.16mph/
127.40kph
Heat 2: Michael Doohan (Aus), Yamaha, 79.29mph/
127.61kph

MANFEILD, New Zealand, 2 October
Heat 1: Fred Merkel (USA), Honda, 89.38mph/143.84kph
Heat 2: Stéphane Mertens (Bel), Bimota, 93.09mph/
149.81kph

LEADING CHAMPIONSHIP POSITIONS

1 Fred Merkel (USA), Honda, 272pts
2 Stéphane Mertens (Bel), Honda 265pts
3 Raymond Roche (Fra), Ducati 222pts

1989

DONINGTON PARK, England, 27 March
Heat 1: Fabrizio Pirovano (Ita), Yamaha, 94.60mph/
152.24kph
Heat 2: Giancarlo Falappa (Ita), Bimota, 94.51mph/
152.10kph

HUNGARORING, Hungary, 30 April
Heat 1: Fred Merkel (USA), Honda, 79.54mph/128.01kph
Heat 2: Fred Merkel (USA), Honda, 80.24mph/129.14kph

MOSPORT PARK, Canada, 4 June
Heat 1: Fred Merkel (USA), Honda, 100.79mph/
162.21kph
Heat 2: Giancarlo Falappa (Ita), Bimota, 101.56mph/
163.45kph

BRAINERD RACEWAY, United States, 11 June
Heat 1: Raymond Roche (Fra), Ducati, 102.44mph/
164.86kph
Heat 2: Raymond Roche (Fra), Ducati, 102.55mph/
165.04kph

ÖSTERREICHRING, Austria, 2 July
Heat 1: Alex Vieira (Fra), Ducati, 112.31mph/180.75kph
Heat 2: Stéphane Mertens (Bel), Honda, 92.25mph/
148.46kph

PAUL RICARD, France, 30 July
Heat 1: Stéphane Mertens (Bel), Honda, 88.66mph/
142.69kph
Heat 2: Giancarlo Falappa (Ita), Bimota, 88.92mph/
143.11kph

SUGO, Japan, 2 August
Heat 1: Doug Polen (USA), Suzuki, 73.95mph/119.01kph
Heat 2: Michael Dowson (Aus), Yamaha, 72.95mph/
117.40kph

HOCKENHEIMRING, West Germany, 17 September
Heat 1: Raymond Roche (Fra), Ducati, 116.10mph/
186.85kph
Heat 2: Raymond Roche (Fra), Ducati, 116.67mph/
187.76kph

PERGUSA, Italy, 24 September
Heat 1: Stéphane Mertens (Bel), Honda, 105.36mph/
169.57kph
Heat 2: Raymond Roche (Fra), Ducati, 105.00mph/
168.98kph

ORAN PARK, Australia, 8 October
Heat 1: Peter Goddard (Aus), Yamaha, 71.62mph/
115.26kph
Heat 2: Michael Dowson (Aus), Yamaha, 78.83mph/
126.86kph

MANFEILD, New Zealand, 15 October
Heat 1: Terry Rymer (UK), Yamaha, 90.10mph/145.00kph
Heat 2: Stéphane Mertens (Bel), Honda, 98.82mph/
159.04kph

LEADING CHAMPIONSHIP POSITIONS

1 Fred Merkel (USA), Honda, 99pts
2 Fabrizio Pirovano (Ita), Yamaha, 93½pts
3 Davide Tardozzi (Ita), Bimota, 91½pts

1990

JEREZ, Spain, 18 March
Heat 1: Raymond Roche (Fra), Ducati, 82.74mph/133.16kph
Heat 2: Raymond Roche (Fra), Ducati, 83.13mph/113.78kph

DONINGTON PARK, England, 16 April
Heat 1: Fred Merkel (USA), Honda, 89.76mph/144.45kph
Heat 2: Giancarlo Falappa (Ita), Ducati, 89.90mph/144.68kph

HUNGARORING, Hungary, 29 April
Heat 1: Fred Merkel (USA), Honda, 80.41mph/129.41kph
Heat 2: Raymond Roche (Fra), Ducati, 81.06mph/130.45kph

HOCKENHEIMRING, West Germany, 6 May
Heat 1: Fred Merkel (USA), Honda, 117.30mph/188.78kph
Heat 2: Stéphane Mertens (Bel), Honda, 117.46mph/189.03kph

MOSPORT PARK, Canada, 3 June
Heat 1: Raymond Roche (Fra), Ducati, 102.70mph/165.28kph
Heat 2: Raymond Roche (Fra), Ducati, 101.88mph/163.96kph

BRAINERD RACEWAY, United States, 10 June
Heat 1: Stéphane Mertens (Bel), Honda, 103.65mph/166.81kph
Heat 2: Doug Chandler (USA), Kawasaki, 102.06mph/164.25kph

ZELTWEG, Austria, 1 July
Heat 1: Fabrizio Pirovano (Ita), Yamaha, 94.84mph/152.63kph
Heat 2: Stéphane Mertens (Bel), Honda, 113.83mph/183.19kph

SUGO, Japan, 26 August
Heat 1: Raymond Roche (Fra), Ducati, 86.75mph/139.61kph
Heat 2: Doug Chandler (USA), Kawasaki, 87.20mph/140.33kph

LE MANS, France, 9 September
Heat 1: Raymond Roche (Fra), Ducati, 92.70mph/149.19kph
Heat 2: Raymond Roche (Fra), Ducati, 92.66mph/149.12kph

MISANO, Italy, 7 October
Heat 1: Fabrizio Pirovano (Ita), Yamaha, 104.32mph/167.89kph
Heat 2: Fabrizio Pirovano (Ita), Yamaha, 109.02mph/175.45kph

JOHOR, Shah Alam, Malaysia, 4 November
Heat 1: Fabrizio Pirovano (Ita), Yamaha, 86.89mph/139.84kph
Heat 2: Fabrizio Pirovano (Ita), Yamaha, 87.03mph/140.06kph

ORAN PARK, Australia, 11 November
Heat 1: Peter Goddard (Aus), Yamaha, 98.99mph/159.31kph
Heat 2: Rob Phillis (Aus), Yamaha, 99.21mph/159.66kph

MANFEILD, New Zealand, 18 November
Heat 1: Terry Rymer (Aus), Yamaha, 100.87mph/162.33kph
Heat 2: Rob Phillis (Aus), Kawasaki, 100.58mph/161.87kph

FINAL CHAMPIONSHIP POSITIONS

1 Raymond Roche (Fra), Ducati, 382pts
2 Fabrizio Pirovano (Ita), Yamaha, 325pts
3 Stéphane Mertens (Bel), Honda, 300pts

MOST RACE/HEAT WINS

9 Stéphane Mertens
8 Fred Merkel
7 Fabrizio Pirovano

ENDURANCE RACING

Long-distance or endurance racing is one of the earliest forms of motorcycle racing, reminiscent of the days at the turn of the century when races were from city to city. For many years it became the forgotten branch of motorcycle sport, but received a boost in 1960 when the long-distance classic, the Bol d'Or, received official recognition and returned to the racing calendar.

Since then, certain endurance races on closed tracks, such as the Liège 24-hours race at Spa and the Le Mans event, have become major motorcycling occasions. There is also a motorbike section in some of the world's great rallies, notably the Paris–Dakar event. However, the best known endurance race is still the Bol d'Or, first run near Paris in 1922 but for many years not featuring in the FIM Coupe d'Endurance calendar, because the Bol d'Or race organisers allowed bikes to be modified outside the regulations laid down by the governing body. However, FIM amendments to their rules were made so that the prestigious event could be classed as a championship race.

Long-distance racing grew in popularity in the 1970s and in 1975 the FIM introduced its Coupe d'Endurance; it became the World Endurance Championship, consisting of seven rounds, in 1980, and is now known as the FIM Endurance Cup. As in world championship road racing, race winners receive 20 points towards the championship, runners-up 17, and so on down to 1 point for finishing 15th; the points are doubled, however, in races of 24 hours.

For real endurance, there can be no race more demanding than the Paris–Dakar rally. Here Marc Joineau of Team Suzuki takes time out to reflect during the 1982 race

Above *The best known of motorcycling's long distance races, the Bol D'Or, which is run near Paris. This action is from the 1924 race, two years after its inception*
Below *By the 1970s the race had certainly grown in popularity, attracting this large crowd despite the bad weather*

FIM COUPE D'ENDURANCE

LEADING CHAMPIONSHIP POSITIONS

1975
1 Alain Genoud (Swi), Kawasaki 33pts & Georges Godier (Fra), Kawaski 33pts
3 Christian Huguet (Fra), Japauto 31pts & Roger Ruiz (Fra), Japauto 31pts

1976
1 Jean-Claude Chemarin (Fra), Honda 45pts
2 Christian Léon (Fra), Honda 42pts
3 Christian Huguet (Fra), Honda 35pts

1977
1 Jean-Claude Chemarin (Fra), Honda 49pts & Christian Léon (Fra), Honda 49pts
3 Charlie Williams (UK), Honda 47 pts & Stan Woods (UK), Honda 47pts

1978
1 Jean-Claude Chemarin (Fra), Honda 72pts & Christian Léon (Fra), Honda 72pts
3 Charlie Williams (UK), Honda 61pts

1979
1 Jean-Claude Chemarin (Fra), Honda 49pts & Christian Léon (Fra), Honda 49pts
3 Christian Huguet (Fra), Kawasaki 42pts

WORLD ENDURANCE CHAMPIONSHIP

LEADING CHAMPIONSHIP POSITIONS

1980
1 Marc Fontan (Fra), Honda 58pts & Hervé Moineau (Fra), Honda 58pts
3 Christian Huguet (Fra), Kawasaki 49pts

1981
1 Jean Lafond (Fra), Kawasaki 81pts & Raymond Roche (Fra), Kawasaki 81pts
3 Christian Huguet (Fra), Kawasaki 76pts

1982
1 Jean-Claude Chemarin (Fra), Kawasaki 60pts & Jacques Cornu (Swi), Kawasaki 60pts
3 Hervé Guilleux (Fra), Kawasaki 45pts & Jean Lafond (Fra), Kawasaki 45pts

1983
1 Richard Hubin (Bel), Suzuki 89pts & Hervé Moineau (Fra), Suzuki 89pts
3 Patrick Igoa (Fra), Kawasaki 84pts & Jean Lafond (Fra), Kawasaki 84pts

1984
1 Gérard Coudray (Fra), Honda 70pts & Patrick Igoa (Fra), Honda 70pts
3 Guy Bertin (Fra), Honda 46pts & Dominique Sarron, (Fra) Honda 46pts

1985
1 Gérard Coudray (Fra), Honda 96pts & Patrick Igoa (Fra), Honda 96pts
3 Jean-Pierre Oudin (Fra), Suzuki 76pts

1986
1 Patrick Igoa (Fra), Honda 105pts
2 Alex Vieira (Fra), Honda 90pts
3 Gérard Coudray (Fra), Honda 75pts

1987
1 Hervé Moineau (Fra), Suzuki 120pts & Bruno le Bihan (Fra), Suzuki 120pts
3 Johan van Vaerenbergh (Bel), Kawasaki 83pts

1988
1 Hervé Moineau (Fra), Suzuki 83pts & Thierry Crine (Fra), Suzuki 83pts
3 Alex Vieira (Fra), Honda 79pts & Christophe Bouheben (Fra), Honda 79pts

1989
1 Alex Vieira (Fra), Honda 140pts
2 Roger Burnett (UK), Honda 120pts
3 Jean-Michel Mattioli (Fra), Honda 80pts

1990
1 Alex Vieira (Fra), Honda 95pts
2 Jean-Michel Mattioli (Fra), Honda 80pts & Stéphane Mertens (Bel), Honda 80pts

MOST WORLD TITLES

4 Hervé Moineau (Fra)
3 Patrick Igoa (Fra)
2 Gérard Coudray (Fra), Alex Vieira (Fra)*

* Vieira was born in Portugal but is now a French citizen

TT FORMULA

TT Formula One, Two and Three were created by the ACU in 1977 to preserve the Isle of Man's status as one of the world's leading racing centres.

The previous year, after mounting criticism of the dangers of the Mountain Course and the subsequent drop in the number of top riders entering, the FIM withdrew the Isle of Man races from its Grand Prix calendar, but in order to maintain the island's prestige the FIM agreed to grant 'world championship' status to any alternative races the ACU could come up with, and so was born Formula One, Two and Three. Plans for Formula Four were also drawn up, but because of the lack of interest, no such races took place.

The new Formulae were based on street bikes that had sold at least 1000 models in the year to 1 March before the TT races, which were categorised as follows:

	Two-stroke	Four-stroke
Formula One	350–500cc	600–1000cc
Formula Two	250–350cc	400–600cc
Formula Three	125–250cc	200–400cc

(Formula Four was to have been for 50–125cc two-strokes and 50–200cc four-strokes)

In both 1977 and 1978 the Isle of Man round was the only one that counted towards the championship, but there were two rounds in 1979 and the number has grown steadily since then. The 1990 TT Formula One championship was over five rounds.

The Formula Three championship was scrapped at the end of the 1981 season and Formula Two ended in 1986.

Formula One machines are, essentially, quantity-produced bikes which are available to the public. Modifications to the type of engine or the number of cylinders and stroke are not permitted, and the current regulations concerning engines are:

2-stroke 350–500cc: max. 4 cylinders
4-stroke 600–750cc: max. 4 cylinders
4-stroke 600–1000cc: max. 2 cylinders

TT Formula One's most successful rider, winner of five successive world titles from 1982–86, Joey Dunlop

WORLD CHAMPIONSHIP POSITIONS

TT FORMULA ONE

1977
1 Phil Read (UK), Honda 15pts
2 Roger Nicholls (UK), Ducati 12pts
3 Ian Richards (UK), Honda 10pts
1978
1 Mike Hailwood (UK), Ducati 15pts
2 John Williams (UK), Honda 12pts
3 Ian Richards (UK), Honda 10pts
1979
1 Ron Haslam (UK), Honda 25pts
2 Alex George (UK), Honda 23pts
3 Graeme Crosby (NZ), Kawasaki
   18pts
1980
1 Graeme Crosby (NZ), Suzuki 27pts
2 Mick Grant (UK), Honda 25pts
3 Joey Dunlop (UK), Suzuki 12pts
1981
1 Graeme Crosby (NZ), Suzuki 27pts
2 Ron Haslam (UK), Honda 27pts
3 Joey Dunlop (UK), Honda 16pts

1982
1 Joey Dunlop (UK), Honda 36pts
2 Ron Haslam (UK), Honda 30pts
3 Dave Hiscock (NZ), Suzuki 26pts
1983
1 Joey Dunlop (UK), Honda 42pts
2 Rob McElnea (UK), Suzuki 35pts
3 Roger Marshall (UK), Honda 26pts
1984
1 Joey Dunlop (UK), Honda 66pts
2 Roger Marshall (UK), Honda 54pts
3 Tony Rutter (UK), Ducati 36pts
1985
1 Joey Dunlop (UK), Honda 90pts
2 Mick Grant (UK), Suzuki 40pts
3 Graeme McGregor (Aus), Suzuki
   32pts

1986
1 Joey Dunlop (UK), Honda 93pts
2 Paul Iddon (UK), Suzuki 61pts
3 Anders Andersson (Swe), Suzuki
   58pts
1987
1 Virginio Ferrari (Ita), Yamaha 49pts
2 Joey Dunlop (UK), Honda 46pts
3 Paul Iddon (UK), Suzuki 43pts
1988
1 Carl Fogarty (UK), Honda 84pts
2 Joey Dunlop (UK), Honda 63½pts
3 Roger Burnett (UK), Honda 52pts
1989
1 Carl Fogarty (UK), Honda 90pts
2 Steve Hislop (UK), Honda 82pts
3 Robert Dunlop (UK), Honda 54pts
1990
1 Carl Fogarty (UK), Honda 71pts
2 Joey Dunlop (UK), Honda 54pts
3 Robert Dunlop (UK), Honda 49pts

TT FORMULA TWO

1977
1 Alan Jackson (UK), Honda 15pts
2 Neil Tuxworth (UK), Honda 12pts
3 Denis Casement (UK), Honda
   10pts
1978
1 Alan Jackson (UK), Honda 15pts
2 David Mason (UK), Honda 12pts
3 Neil Tuxworth (UK), Honda 10pts
1979
1 Alan Jackson (UK), Honda 30pts
2 Roger Bowler (UK), Honda 22pts
3 Steve Ward (UK), Benelli 14pts
1980
1 Charlie Williams (UK), Yamaha
   30pts
2 Malcolm Lucas (UK), Honda 22pts
3 Phil Odlin (UK), Honda 14pts
1981
1 Tony Rutter (UK), Ducati 27pts
2 Phil Odlin (UK), Yamaha 22pts
3 Phil Mellor (UK), Yamaha 15pts

1982
1 Tony Rutter (UK), Ducati 45pts
2 Naigel Rainer (FRG), Ducati 16pts
   George Fogarty (UK), Ducati 16pts
   Phil Odlin (UK), Yamaha 16pts
1983
1 Tony Rutter (UK), Ducati 39pts
2 Phil Mellor (UK), Yamaha 35pts
3 Graeme McGregor (Aus), Ducati
   22pts
1984
1 Tony Rutter (UK), Ducati 43pts
2 Trevor Nation (UK), Ducati 28pts
3 Brian Reid (UK), Yamaha 25pts
1985
1 Brian Reid (UK), Yamaha 45pts
2 Tony Rutter (UK), Ducati 37pts
3 John Weeden (UK), Yamaha 24pts
1986
1 Brian Reid (UK), Yamaha 32pts
2 Eddie Laycock (UK), Yamaha 26pts
3 Graeme McGregor (Aus), Ducati
   18pts

TT FORMULA THREE

1977
1 John Kidson (UK), Honda 15pts
2 Derek Loan (UK), Suzuki 12pts
3 Brian Peters (UK), Suzuki 10pts
1978
1 Bill Smith (UK), Honda 15pts
2 Derek Mortimer (UK), Yamaha
   12pts
3 John Stephens (UK), Honda 10pts
1979
1 Barry Smith (Aus), Yamaha 30pts
2 Richard Hunter (UK), Honda 20pts
3 Bill Smith (UK), Honda 12pts
1980
1 Ron Haslam (UK), Honda 25pts
2 Chris Griffiths (UK), Aermacchi
   20pts
3 Denis Casement (UK), Yamaha
   18pts
1981
1 Barry Smith (Aus), Yamaha 30pts
2 Denis Casement (UK), Yamaha
   22pts
3 David Rayborn (UK), Yamaha 17pts

MOST TITLES

Formula One
5 Joey Dunlop; 3 Carl Fogarty;
2 Graeme Crosby

Formula Two
4 Tony Rutter; 3 Alan Jackson;
2 Brian Reid

Formula Three
2 Barry Smith

The Isle of Man Tourist Trophy races, known simply as the TT, are the ultimate test of man and machine over natural road racing conditions. Six laps of the Mountain Course take in over 226 miles of racing; approximately three times the length of the average Grand Prix.

With motorcycle racing becoming increasing popular at the turn of the century, largely on the Continent, it was apparent that the British riders and their machines were no match for their overseas counterparts in the International Cup Races. The 20mph (32.18kph) speed restriction on British roads, and

Parliament's refusal to close sections of roads for racing, did not help British riders at the time. However, the Manx Parliament was only too pleased to help out and a 15.81 mile (25.44km) section of Isle of Man roads was closed off and used to stage an elimination race for the 1905 'International'. The winner was J S Campbell, who covered the 11 laps on his 6hp Ariel-JAP at an average speed of over 40mph/64.28kph.

The International Cup was discontinued after the 1906

event, largely because of poor organisation. But the Auto-Cycle Club was still keen to host a major international event on home soil. However, Westminster would still not budge on speed limits and road closures The Isle of Man stepped in to help yet again and on 28 May 1907, staged its first TT meeting.

There was only one race, over ten laps of the St John's Circuit. The machines were divided into two categories, single and twin cylinders. There were 25 starters

Above *The Tourist Trophy, still one of the most sought after in motorcycle sport*

Right *An historic picture taken at Laxey Glen in 1907. Back row, left to right: F A Applebee; Harold Williamson, manager of the Rex company; J P Le Grand; W A Jacobs. Seated is Oliver Godfrey, winner of the first Senior TT.*

The start of the TT, 1928-style, as the riders make their final preparations

and the honour of getting the first TT under way fell to Frank Hulbert and Jack Marshall, who were the first pair of riders to be shown the starter's flag – starting in pairs was to become a feature of future TT races. Charlie Collier won the single-cylinder category while Rem Fowler took the twins' first prize.

Although the 1907 race was organised by the Auto-Cycle Union, who changed their name from the Auto-Cycle Club that year, the single-cylinder trophy was donated by the Marquis de Mouzilly St Mars, and the twin-cylinder trophy by Dr Hele-Shaw.

After Charlie Collier won at an average speed of 50.63mph/ 81.46kph in 1910, it was felt the 'short course' had become too fast and so the more demanding Mountain Course (then 37.5 miles/60.34km long) was first used the following year.

The change of course coincided with the introduction of the Senior and Junior TTs, which remain the most prestigious events of TT week. The first Senior TT was for single-cylinder machines with a capacity of 500cc, and up to 585cc for twins, while the Junior TT was restricted to 300cc for singles and 340cc for twins. The first Senior TT proved to be a disaster for the British manufacturers, as the Americans occupied the first three places with their Indian machine. But that was to be the last success for an overseas machine in the Senior TT until the 1930s.

The Isle of Man came close to losing the TT races in 1922 after a disagreement between the island's authorities and the ACU, and an offer to stage the races in Belgium was accepted.

However, the differences were patched up; racing remained on the island and that troubled year, 1922, saw the introduction of a new Lightweight class.

Sidecar racing was introduced in 1923 but it initially lasted just three years. Reappearing in 1954, it has since been a regular feature of TT week. The Ultra-lightweight class, which was introduced in 1924, didn't last as long; it disappeared after just two years.

During the 1930s the British domination of the Senior TT started to decline. Stanley Woods won the 1935 race on the Italian Moto Guzzi and in 1939 the German Georg Meier became the first overseas rider to win on a foreign machine, a BMW. But the banning of superchargers gave renewed hope to the British manufacturers in the post-war years and

Germany's Georg Meier takes the flag in 1939 to become the first overseas rider to win the Senior TT

Norton reasserted their authority on the Senior race.

Clubman's races became part of TT week in 1947 and were races for individual riders, or teams of three, providing they were members of clubs affiliated to the ACU and had not entered for any other TT race. The last Clubman's was staged in 1956.

Formula One had made its TT debut in 1959 when 500cc and 350cc classes were contested. When the FIM stripped the TT races of world championship status at the end of 1976, though, the ACU then ran its own Formula TT championships for Formulae One, Two and Three.

A 50cc class existed from 1962–68, and in 1967 the first of the Production races were launched with titles at 250, 500 and 750cc. They were discontinued in 1976 but re-appeared in 1984. However, with engine sizes soaring to 1500cc, and concern over the production

models' combination of greater power and smaller tyres, this category was eventually discontinued in 1989. Other events have made brief appearances at the TT races over the years but the ultimate ambition of all TT riders is still to win the Senior TT.

Because of smaller fields in such events as the Lightweight, Sidecar, and, in 1955, the 250cc race, a shorter course with a mass start was used. This circuit was known as the Clypse Circuit; measuring 10.79miles/ 17.36km, it took in part of the Mountain course. However, it was used only from 1954–59.

The demanding Mountain Course was extended to its present length of 37.73miles/ 60.71km in 1920 with the addition of the Governor's Bridge section. It contains over 200 bends and has all the natural hazards which go with road racing. It is often decried as too dangerous, but the riders know of its perils and are aware there is no room for human error. Sadly, more than 150 men have lost their lives since Victor Surridge was killed while practising for the 1911 race on his

Rudge.

Because of the increased power of machines, the ACU ruled after the 1989 races that the size of solo machines would be restricted to 750cc and 600cc for sidecars. So, it was goodbye to the monster 1500cc production models which roared around the island's roads.

Further efforts to make the TT races safer included a reduction in fields by 10 per cent and allowing riders to set off individually at 10-second intervals rather than in pairs.

From the beginning of the road racing World Championships in 1949, the Isle of Man TT races formed an important round in the event, but the TT lost its Grand Prix status in 1976 when many of the top riders boycotted the circuit because of its dangers and the FIM dropped it from its list of world championship races. But, despite no longer being one of the world's leading international events, its popularity with race fans has never waned and at the end of May or beginning of June each year, around fifty thousand enthusiasts still flock to the island for TT week.

SENIOR TT

Figures in brackets after dates indicate the course and length of the race. For example, 5M indicates 5 laps of Mountain Course; 9C indicates 9 laps of the Clypse Course and 10J indicates 10 laps of the original St John's Circuit. All winners from the United Kingdom unless otherwise stated.

1911 (5M) 1 Oliver Godfrey, Indian, 47.63mph/76.65kph
2 Charlie Franklin, Indian
3 Arthur Moorhouse, Indian

1912 (5M) 1 Frank Applebee, Scott, 48.69mph/78.36kph
2 Jack Haswell, Triumph
3 Harry Collier, Matchless

1913 (7M) 1 Tim Wood, Scott, 48.27mph/77.68kph
2 Ray Abbott, Rudge
3 Alfie Alexander, Indian

1914 (6M) 1 Cyril Pullin, Rudge, 49.49mph/79.65kph
2 Howard Davies, Sunbeam
Oliver Godfrey, Indian (dead-heat)

1920 (6M) 1 Tommy De La Hay, Sunbeam, 51.48mph/
82.85kph
2 Douggie Brown, Norton
3 Reg Brown, Sunbeam

1921 (6M) 1 Howard Davies, AJS, 54.50mph/87.71kph
2 Freddie Dixon, Indian
3 Bert Le Vack, Indian

1922 (6M) 1 Alec Bennett, Sunbeam, 58.31mph/93.64kph
2 Walter Brandish, Triumph
3 Harry Langman, Scott

1923 (6M) 1 Tom Sheard, Douglas, 55.55mph/89.40kph
2 Graham Black, Norton
3 Freddie Dixon, Indian

1924 (6M) 1 Alec Bennett, Norton, 61.64mph/104.03kph
2 Harry Langman, Scott
3 Freddie Dixon, Douglas

1925 (6M) 1 Howard Davies, HRD, 66.13mph/106.43kph
2 Frank Longman, AJS
3 Alec Bennett, Norton

1926 (7M) 1 Stanley Woods, Norton, 67.54mph/
108.70kph
2 Wal Handley, Rex Acme
3 Frank Longman, AJS

1927 (7M) 1 Alec Bennett, Norton, 68.41mph/110.10kph
2 Jimmy Guthrie, New Hudson
3 Tommy Simister, Triumph

1928 (7M) 1 Charlie Dodson, Sunbeam, 62.98mph/
101.36kph
2 George Rowley, AJS
3 Tommy Hatch, Scott

1929 (7M) 1 Charlie Dodson, Sunbeam, 72.05mph/
115.95kph
2 Alec Bennett, Sunbeam
3 HG Tyrell Smith, Rudge

1930 (7M) 1 Wal Handley, Rudge, 74.24mph/119.48kph
2 Graham Walker, Rudge
3 Jimmy Simpson, Norton

1931 (7M) 1 Tim Hunt, Norton, 77.90mph/125.37kph
2 Jimmy Guthrie, Norton
3 Stanley Woods, Norton

1932 (7M) 1 Stanley Woods, Norton, 79.38mph/
127.75kph
2 Jimmy Guthrie, Norton
3 Jimmy Simpson, Norton

1933 (7M) 1 Stanley Woods, Norton, 81.04mph/
130.42kph
2 Jimmy Simpson, Norton
3 Tim Hunt, Norton

1934 (7M) 1 Jimmy Guthrie, Norton, 78.01mph/
125.54kph
2 Jimmy Simpson, Norton
3 Walter Rusk, Velocette

1935 (7M) 1 Stanley Woods, Guzzi, 84.68mph/136.28kph
2 Jimmy Guthrie, Norton
3 Walter Rusk, Norton

Oliver Godfrey crosses the line on his Indian to win the first Senior TT in 1911

1936 (7M) 1 Jimmy Guthrie, Norton, 85.80mph/
138.08kph
2 Stanley Woods, Velocette
3 Freddie Frith, Norton
1937 (7M) 1 Freddie Frith, Norton, 88.21mph/141.96kph
2 Stanley Woods, Velocette
3 John White, Norton
1938 (7M) 1 Harold Daniell, Norton, 89.11mph/143.41kph
2 Stanley Woods, Velocette
3 Freddie Frith, Norton
1939 (7M) 1 Georg Meier (Ger), BMW, 89.38mph/
143.84kph
2 Jock West, BMW
3 Freddie Frith, Norton
1947 (7M) 1 Harold Daniell, Norton, 82.81mph/133.27kph
2 Artie Bell, Norton
3 Percy Goodman, Velocette
1948 (7M) 1 Artie Bell, Norton, 84.97mph/136.75kph
2 Bill Doran, Norton
3 Jock Weddell, Norton
1949 (7M) 1 Harold Daniell, Norton, 86.93mph/139.90kph
2 Johnny Lockett, Norton
3 Ernie Lyons, Velocette
1950 (7M) 1 Geoff Duke, Norton, 92.27mph/148.49kph
2 Artie Bell, Norton
3 Johnny Lockett, Norton
1951 (7M) 1 Geoff Duke, Norton, 93.83mph/151.00kph
2 Bill Doran, AJS
3 Cromie McCandless, Norton

1952 (7M) 1 Reg Armstrong, Norton, 92.97mph/
149.62kph
2 Leslie Graham, MV Agusta
3 Ray Amm (SRho), Norton
1953 (7M) 1 Ray Amm (SRho), Norton, 93.85mph/
151.04kph
2 Jack Brett, Norton
3 Reg Armstrong, Gilera
1954 (4M) 1 Ray Amm (SRho), Norton, 88.12mph/
141.82kph
2 Geoff Duke, Gilera
3 Jack Brett, Norton
1955 (7M) 1 Geoff Duke, Gilera, 97.93mph/157.60kph
2 Reg Armstrong, Gilera
3 Ken Kavanagh (Aus), Guzzi
1956 (7M) 1 John Surtees, MV Agusta, 96.57mph/
155.41kph
2 John Hartle, Norton
3 Jack Brett, Norton
1957 (8M) 1 Bob McIntyre, Gilera, 98.99mph/159.31kph
2 John Surtees, MV Agusta
3 Bob Brown (Aus), Gilera
1958 (7M) 1 John Surtees, MV Agusta, 98.63mph/
158.73kph
2 Bob Anderson, Norton
3 Bob Brown (Aus), Norton
1959 (7M) 1 John Surtees, MV Agusta, 87.94mph/
141.53kph
2 Alastair King, Norton

Giacomo Agostini of Italy on his way to winning the 1970 Senior TT. It was his third successive win in the race, and he went on to make it five in a row, all on an MV Agusta

3 Bob Brown (Aus), Norton
1960 (6M) 1 John Surtees, MV Agusta, 102.44mph/
164.86kph
2 John Hartle, MV Agusta
3 Mike Hailwood, Norton
1961 (6M) 1 Mike Hailwood, Norton, 100.60mph/
161.90kph
2 Bob McIntyre, Norton
3 Tom Phillis (Aus), Norton
1962 (6M) 1 Gary Hocking (SRho), MV Agusta,
103.51mph/166.58kph
2 Ellis Boyce, Norton
3 Fred Stevens, Norton
1963 (6M) 1 Mike Hailwood, MV Agusta, 104.64mph/
168.40kph
2 John Hartle, Gilera
3 Phil Read, Gilera
1964 (6M) 1 Mike Hailwood, MV Agusta, 100.95mph/
162.46kph
2 Derek Minter, Norton
3 Fred Stevens, Matchless
1965 (6M) 1 Mike Hailwood, MV Agusta, 91.69mph/
147.56kph
2 Joe Dunphy, Norton
3 Mike Duff (Can), Matchless
1966 (6M) 1 Mike Hailwood, Honda, 103.11mph/
165.94kph
2 Giacomo Agostini (Ita), MV Agusta
3 Chris Conn, Norton
1967 (6M) 1 Mike Hailwood, Honda, 105.62mph/
169.98kph
2 Peter Williams, Matchless
3 Steve Spencer, Norton
1968 (6M) 1 Giacomo Agostini (Ita), MV Agusta,
101.63mph/163.56kph
2 Brian Ball, Seeley
3 Barry Randle, Norton
1969 (6M) 1 Giacomo Agostini (Ita), MV Agusta,
104.75mph/168.58kph
2 Alan Barnett, Metisse
3 Tom Dickie, Seeley
1970 (6M) 1 Giacomo Agostini (Ita), MV Agusta,
101.52mph/163.38kph
2 Peter Williams, Matchless
3 Bill Smith, Kawasaki
1971 (6M) 1 Giacomo Agostini (Ita), MV Agusta,
102.59mph/165.10kph
2 Peter Williams, Matchless
3 Frank Perris (Can), Suzuki
1972 (6M) 1 Giacomo Agostini (Ita), MV Agusta,
104.02mph/167.40kph
2 Alberto Pagani (Ita), MV Agusta
3 Mick Grant, Kawasaki
1973 (6M) 1 Jack Findlay (Aus), Suzuki, 101.55mph/
163.43kph
2 Peter Williams, Matchless
3 Charlie Sanby, Suzuki
1974 (5M) 1 Phil Carpenter, Yamaha, 96.99mph/
156.09kph
2 Charlie Williams, Yamaha
3 Tony Rutter, Yamaha
1975 (6M) 1 Mick Grant, Kawasaki, 100.27mph/
161.37kph

2 John Williams, Yamaha
3 Charles Mortimer, Yamaha
1976 (6M) 1 Tom Herron, Yamaha, 105.16mph/
169.24kph
2 Ian Richards, Yamaha
3 Billy Guthrie, Yamaha
1977 (5M) 1 Phil Read, Suzuki, 106.98mph/172.17kph
2 Tom Herron, Yamaha
3 Eddie Roberts, Yamaha
1978 (6M) 1 Tom Herron, Suzuki, 111.74mph/179.83kph
2 Billy Guthrie, Suzuki
3 Charles Mortimer, Yamaha
1979 (6M) 1 Mike Hailwood, Suzuki, 111.75mph/
179.84kph
2 Tony Rutter, Suzuki
3 Dennis Ireland (NZ), Suzuki
1980 (6M) 1 Graeme Crosby (NZ), Suzuki, 109.65mph/
176.46kph
2 Steve Cull, Suzuki
3 Steve Ward, Suzuki
1981 (6M) 1 Mick Grant, Suzuki, 106.14mph/170.82kph
2 Donnie Robinson, Yamaha
3 John Newbold, Suzuki
1982 (6M) 1 Norman Brown, Suzuki, 110.98mph/
178.60kph
2 Jon Ekerold (SAf), Suzuki
3 Dennis Ireland (NZ), Suzuki
1983 *See* **Classic TT**
1984 (6M) 1 Rob McElnea, Suzuki, 115.66mph/
186.14kph
2 Roger Marshall, Honda
3 Trevor Nation, Suzuki
1985 (6M) 1 Joey Dunlop, Honda, 113.69mph/182.97kph
2 Roger Marshall, Honda
3 Mark Johns, Suzuki
1986 (6M) 1 Roger Burnett, Honda, 113.98mph/
183.43kph
2 Geoff Johnson, Honda
3 Barry Woodland, Suzuki
1987 (4M) 1 Joey Dunlop, Honda, 99.85mph/160.69kph
2 Geoff Johnson, Yamaha
3 Roger Marshall, Suzuki
1988 (6M) 1 Joey Dunlop, Honda, 117.38mph/188.90kph
2 Steve Hislop, Honda
3 Geoff Johnson, Yamaha
1989 (6M) 1 Steve Hislop, Honda, 118.23mph/190.27kph
2 Nick Jefferies, Yamaha
3 Graeme McGregor (Aus), Honda
1990 (6M) 1 Carl Fogarty, Honda, 110.95mph/178.56kph
2 Trevor Nation, Norton
3 Dave Leach, Yamaha

JUNIOR TT

1911 (4M) 1 Percy Evans, Humber, 41.45mph/66.71kph
2 Harry Collier, Matchless
3 Harold Cox, Forward
1912 (4M) 1 Harry Bashall, Douglas, 39.65mph/63.81kph
2 Eric Kickham, Douglas
3 Harold Cox, Forward
1913 (6M) 1 Hugh Mason, NUT, 43.75mph/70.41kph
2 Billy Newsome, Douglas
3 H C Newman, Ivy Green
1914 (5M) 1 Eric Williams, AJS, 45.58mph/73.35kph
2 Cyril Williams, AJS
3 Frank Walker, Royal Enfield
1920 (5M) **350cc**
1 Cyril Williams, AJS, 40.74mph/65.56kph
2 Jack Watson-Bourne, Blackburne
3 Jack Holroyd, Blackburne
250cc
1 Reg Clark, Levis, 38.30mph/61.64kph
2 Gus Kuhn, Levis
3 Frank Applebee, Levis
1921 (5M) **350cc**
1 Eric Williams, AJS, 52.11mph/83.86kph
2 Howard Davies, AJS
3 Tom Sheard, AJS
250cc
1 Doug Prentice, New Imperial, 44.61mph/
71.79kph
2 Geoff Davison, Levis
3 W G Harrison, Velocette
1922 (5M) 1 Tom Sheard, AJS, 54.75mph/88.11kph
2 George Grinton, AJS
3 Jack Thomas, Sheffield Henderson
1923 (6M) 1 Stanley Woods, Cotton, 55.73mph/89.69kph
2 Harry Harris, AJS
3 Alfie Alexander, Douglas
1924 (6M) 1 Ken Twemlow, New Imperial, 55.67mph/
89.59kph
2 Stanley Ollerhead, DOT
3 H R Scott (SAf), AJS
1925 (6M) 1 Wal Handley, Rex Acme, 65.02mph/
104.64kph
2 Howard Davies, HRD
3 Jimmy Simpson, AJS
1926 (7M) 1 Alec Bennett, Velocette, 66.70mph/
107.34kph
2 Jimmy Simpson, AJS
3 Wal Handley, Rex Acme
1927 (7M) 1 Freddie Dixon, HRD, 67.19mph/108.13kph
2 Harold Willis, Velocette
3 Jimmy Simpson, AJS
1928 (7M) 1 Alec Bennett, Velocette, 68.65mph/
110.48kph
2 Harold Willis, Velocette
3 Ken Twemlow, DOT
1929 (7M) 1 Freddie Hicks, Velocette, 69.71mph/
112.19kph
2 Wal Handley, AJS
3 Alec Bennett, Velocette
1930 (7M) 1 H G Tyrell-Smith, Rudge, 71.08mph/
114.39kph

2 Ernie Nott, Rudge
3 Graham Walker, Rudge
1931 (7M) 1 Tim Hunt, Norton, 73.94mph/118.99kph
2 Jimmy Guthrie, Norton
3 Ernie Nott, Rudge
1932 (7M) 1 Stanley Woods, Norton, 77.16mph/
124.18kph
2 Wal Handley, Rudge
3 H G Tyrell-Smith, Rudge
1933 (7M) 1 Stanley Woods, Norton, 78.08mph/
125.66kph
2 Tim Hunt, Norton
3 Jimmy Guthrie, Norton
1934 (7M) 1 Jimmy Guthrie, Norton, 79.16mph/
127.40kph
2 Jimmy Simpson, Norton
3 Ernie Nott, Husqvarna
1935 (7M) 1 Jimmy Guthrie, Norton, 79.14mph/
127.36kph
2 Walter Rusk, Norton
3 John White, Norton
1936 (7M) 1 Freddie Frith, Norton, 80.14mph/128.97kph
2 John White, Norton
3 Ted Mellors, Velocette
1937 (7M) 1 Jimmy Guthrie, Norton, 84.43mph/
135.88kph
2 Freddie Frith, Norton
3 John White, Norton
1938 (7M) 1 Stanley Woods, Velocette, 84.08mph/
135.25kph
2 Ted Mellors, Velocette
3 Freddie Frith, Norton
1939 (7M) 1 Stanley Woods, Velocette, 83.19mph/
133.88kph
2 Harold Daniell, Norton
3 Heiner Fleischmann (Ger), DKW
1947 (7M) 1 Albert Foster, Velocette, 80.31mph/
129.25kph
2 David Whitworth, Velocette
3 Jock Weddell, Velocette
1948 (7M) 1 Freddie Frith, Velocette, 81.45mph/
131.08kph
2 Bob Foster, Velocette
3 Artie Bell, Norton
1949 (7M) 1 Freddie Frith, Velocette, 83.15mph/
133.82kph
2 Ernie Lyons, Velocette
3 Artie Bell, Norton
1950 (7M) 1 Artie Bell, Norton, 86.33mph/138.93kph
2 Geoff Duke, Norton
3 Harold Daniell, Norton
1951 (7M) 1 Geoff Duke, Norton, 89.90mph/144.68kph
2 Johnny Lockett, Norton
3 Jack Brett, Norton
1952 (7M) 1 Geoff Duke, Norton, 90.29mph/145.31kph
2 Reg Armstrong, Norton
3 Rod Coleman (NZ), AJS
1953 (7M) 1 Ray Amm (SRho), Norton, 90.52mph/
145.68kph
2 Ken Kavanagh (Aus), Norton
3 Fergus Anderson, Guzzi
1954 (5M) 1 Rod Coleman (NZ), AJS, 91.51mph/
147.27kph
2 Derek Farrant, AJS

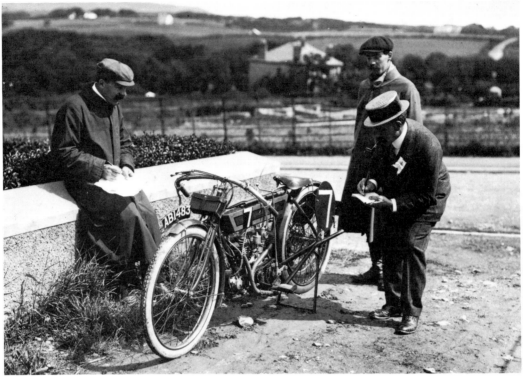

Officials examine Colver's Enfield before the start of the inaugural Junior TT in 1911

3 Bob Keeler, Norton
1955 (7M) 1 Bill Lomas, Guzzi, 92.33mph/148.59kph
2 Bob McIntyre, Norton
3 Cecil Sandford, Guzzi
1956 (7M) 1 Ken Kavanagh (Aus), Guzzi, 89.29mph/
143.70kph
2 Derek Ennett, AJS
3 John Hartle, Norton
1957 (7M) 1 Bob McIntyre, Gilera, 94.99mph/152.87kph
2 Keith Campbell (Aus), Guzzi
3 Bob Brown (Aus), Gilera
1958 (7M) 1 John Surtees, MV Agusta, 93.97mph/
151.23kph
2 Dave Chadwick, Norton
3 Geoff Tanner, Norton
1959 (7M) 1 John Surtees, MV Agusta, 95.38mph/
153.50kph
2 John Hartle, MV Agusta
3 Alastair King, Norton
1960 (6M) 1 John Hartle, MV Agusta, 96.70mph/
155.62kph
2 John Surtees, MV Agusta
3 Bob McIntyre, AJS
1961 (6M) 1 Phil Read, Norton, 95.10mph/153.05kph
2 Gary Hocking (SRho), MV Agusta
3 Ralph Rensen, Norton
1962 (6M) 1 Mike Hailwood, MV Agusta, 99.59mph/
160.27kph

2 Gary Hocking (SRho), MV Agusta
3 Frantisek Stastny (Cze), Jawa
1963 (6M) 1 Jim Redman (SRho), Honda, 94.91mph/
152.74kph
2 John Hartle, Gilera
3 Frantisek Stastny (Cze), Jawa
1964 (6M) 1 Jim Redman (SRho), Honda, 98.50mph/
158.52kph
2 Phil Read, AJS
3 Mike Duff (Can), AJS
1965 (6M) 1 Jim Redman (SRho), Honda, 100.72mph/
162.09kph
2 Phil Read, Yamaha
3 Giacomo Agostini (Ita), MV Agusta
1966 (6M) 1 Giacomo Agostini (Ita), MV Agusta,
100.87mph/162.33kph
2 Peter Williams, AJS
3 Chris Conn, Norton
1967 (6M) 1 Mike Hailwood, Honda, 104.68mph/
168.47kph
2 Giacomo Agostini (Ita), MV Agusta
3 Dennis Woodman, MZ
1968 (6M) 1 Giacomo Agostini (Ita), MV Agusta,
104.78mph/168.63kph
2 Renzo Pasolini (Ita), Benelli
3 Bill Smith, Honda
1969 (6M) 1 Giacomo Agostini (Ita), MV Agusta,
101.81mph/163.85kph
2 Brian Steenson, Aermacchi
3 Jack Findlay (Aus), Aermacchi
1970 (6M) 1 Giacomo Agostini (Ita), MV Agusta,
101.77mph/163.78kph

2 Alan Barnett, Aermacchi
3 Paul Smart, Yamaha

1971 (5M) 1 Tony Jefferies, Yamsel, 89.91mph/
144.70kph
2 Gordon Pantall, Yamaha
3 Bill Smith, Honda

1972 (5M) 1 Giacomo Agostini (Ita), MV Agusta,
102.03mph/164.20kph
2 Tony Rutter, Yamaha
3 Mick Grant, Yamaha

1973 (5M) 1 Tony Rutter, Yamaha, 101.99mph/
164.14kph
2 Ken Huggett, Yamaha
3 John Williams, Yamaha

1974 (5M) 1 Tony Rutter, Yamaha, 104.44mph/
168.08kph
2 Mick Grant, Yamaha
3 Paul Cott, Yamaha

1975 (5M) 1 Charlie Williams, Yamaha, 104.38mph/
167.98kph
2 Charles Mortimer, Yamaha
3 Tom Herron, Yamaha

1976 (5M) 1 Charles Mortimer, Yamaha, 106.78mph/
171.86kph
2 Tony Rutter, Yamaha
3 Billy Guthrie, Yamaha

1977 (3M) 1 Charlie Williams, Yamaha, 99.63mph/
160.34kph
2 Ian Richards, Yamaha
3 Tom Herron, Yamaha

1978 (5M) 1 Charles Mortimer, Yamaha, 100.63mph/
161.95kph
2 Charlie Williams, Yamaha
3 Tom Herron, Yamaha

1979 (6M) 1 Charlie Williams, Yamaha, 105.13mph/
169.19kph
2 Graeme McGregor (Aus), Yamaha
3 Ian Richards, Yamaha

1980 (4M) 1 Charlie Williams, Yamaha, 102.22mph/
164.51kph
2 Donnie Robinson, Yamaha
3 Steve Tonkin, Cotton

1981 (6M) 1 Steve Tonkin, Armstrong, 106.21mph/
170.93kph
2 Bob Jackson, Yamaha
3 Charlie Williams, Yamaha

1982 (6M) 1 Con Law, Waddon, 105.32mph/169.50kph
2 Norman Brown, Yamaha
3 Pete Wild, Yamaha

1983 (6M) 1 Con Law, EMC, 108.09mph/173.95kph
2 Graeme McGregor (Aus), Yamaha
3 Norman Brown, Yamaha

1984 (6M) 1 Graeme McGregor (Aus), EMC, 109.57mph/
176.34kph
2 Charlie Williams, Yamaha
3 Brian Reid, EMC

1985 (6M) 1 Joey Dunlop, Honda, 109.91mph/176.88kph
2 Steve Cull, Honda
3 Eddie Roberts, Kimoco

1986 (6M) 1 Steve Cull, Honda, 109.62mph/176.42kph
2 Phil Mellor, EMC
3 Graham Cannell, Honda

1987 (6M) 1 Eddie Laycock, EMC, 108.52mph/
174.65kph
2 Brian Reid, EMC
3 Graeme McGregor (Aus), Yamaha

1988 (4M) 1 Joey Dunlop, Honda, 111.87mph/180.04kph
2 Brian Reid, EMC
3 Eddie Laycock, EMC

1989 (4M) 1 Johnny Rea, Yamaha, 112.12mph/
180.44kph
2 Eddie Laycock, Yamaha
3 Steve Hazlett, EMC

1990 (4M) 1 Ian Lougher, Yamaha, 115.16mph/
185.33kph
2 Steve Hislop, Honda
3 Eddie Laycock, Yamaha

OTHER WINNERS

TOURIST TROPHY

1907 (10J) Twins: Harry 'Rem'
Fowler, Norton,
36.20mph/58.26
kph

1907 (10J) Singles: Charlie Collier,
Matchless,
38.20mph/61.48
kph

1908 (10J) Twins: Harry Reed,
DOT, 38.50mph/
61.96kph

1908 (10J) Singles: Jack Marshall,
Triumph,
40.49mph/65.16
kph

1909 (10J) Harry Collier, Matchless,
49.01mph/78.87kph

1910 (10J) Charlie Collier, Matchless,
50.63mph/81.46kph

LIGHTWEIGHT

1922 (5M) Geoff Davison, Levis,
49.89mph/80.29kph

1923 (6M) Jock Porter, New Gerrard,
51.93mph/83.57kph

1924 (6M) Edwin Twemlow, New
Imperial, 55.44mph/
89.22kph

1925 (6M) Edwin Twemlow, New
Imperial, 57.74mph/
92.92kph

1926 (7M) Paddy Johnston, Cotton,
60.24mph/96.95kph

1927 (7M) Wal Handley, Rex Acme,
63.30mph/101.87kph

1928 (7M) Frank Longman, OK
Supreme, 62.87mph/
101.18kph

1929 (7M) Syd Crabtree, Excelsior,
63.87mph/102.79kph

1930 (7M) Jimmy Guthrie, AJS,
64.71mph/104.14kph

1931 (7M) Graham Walker, Rudge,
68.98mph/112.62kph

1932 (7M) Leo Davenport, New
Imperial, 70.48mph/
113.43kph

1933 (7M) Syd Gleave, Excelsior,
71.59mph/115.21kph

J M West setting off in the 1939 Lightweight TT, won by Ted Mellors on a Benelli

1934 (7M) Jimmy Simpson, Rudge,
70.81mph/113.96kph
1935 (7M) Stanley Woods, Guzzi,
71.56mph/115.16kph
1936 (7M) Bob Foster, New Imperial,
74.28mph/119.54kph
1937 (7M) Omobono Tenni (Ita),
Guzzi, 74.72mph/
120.25kph
1938 (7M) Ewald Kluge (Ger), DKW,
78.48mph/126.30kph
1939 (7M) Ted Mellors, Benelli,
74.25mph/119.49kph
1947 (7M) Manliff Barrington, Guzzi,
73.22mph/117.84kph
1948 (7M) Maurice Cann, Guzzi,
75.18mph/120.99kph
1949 (7M) Manliff Barrington, Guzzi,
77.96mph/125.46kph
1950 (7M) Dario Ambrosini (Ita),
Benelli, 78.08mph/
125.66kph

ULTRA-LIGHTWEIGHT

1924 (3M) Jock Porter, New Gerrard,
51.20mph/82.40kph
1925 (4M) Wal Handley, Rex Acme,
53.45mph/86.02kph

CLUBMAN'S RACES

Senior Clubman's
1947 (4M) Eric Briggs, Norton,
78.67mph/126.61kph
1948 (4M) J Daniells, Vincent HRD,
80.51mph/129.57kph
1949 (3M) Geoff Duke, Norton,
82.97mph/133.53kph
1950 (4M) Peter Carter, Norton,
75.60mph/121.67kph
1951 (4M) Ivor Arber, Norton,
79.70mph/128.26kph
1952 (4M) Bernard Hargreaves,
Triumph, 82.45mph/
132.69km

1953 (3M) Bob Keeler, Norton,
84.14mph/135.41kph
1954 (4M) Alistair King, BSA,
85.76mph/138.02kph
1955 (9C) Eddie Dow, BSA,
70.73mph/113.83kph
1956 (3M) Bernard Codd, BSA,
86.33mph/138.93kph

Junior Clubman's
1947 (4M) Denis Parkinson, Norton,
70.74mph/113.84kph
1948 (4M) Bob Hazlehurst, Velocette,
70.33mph/113.19kph
1949 (3M) Harold Clark, Norton,
75.18mph/120.99kph
1950 (4M) Brian Jackson, BSA,
74.25mph/119.49kph
1951 (4M) Brian Purslow, BSA,
75.36mph/121.28kph
1952 (4M) Eric Houseley, BSA,
78.92mph/127.01kph

1953 (4M) Derek Powell, BSA,
  80.17mph/129.02kph
1954 (4M) Peter Palmer, BSA,
  81.83mph/131.69kph
1955 (9C) Jimmy Buchan, BSA,
  68.23mph/109.81kph
1956 (3M) Bernard Codd, BSA,
  82.02mph/132.00kph

Lightweight Clubman's
1947 (3M) Bill McVeigh, Triumph,
  64.27mph/103.43kph
1948 (3M) M Lockwood, Excelsior,
  64.93mph/104.49kph
1949 (2M) Cyril Taft, Excelsior,
  68.10mph/109.60kph
1950 (4M) Frank Fletcher, Excelsior,
  66.89mph/107.65kph

1000cc Clubman's
1949 (3M) Doug Lashmar, Vincent
  HRD, 76.30mph/
  122.79kph
1950 (4M) A Phillip, Vincent HRD,
  78.85mph/126.90kph
1951–52 Not held
1953 (4M) G P Douglass, Vincent
  HRD, 81.54mph/
  131.23kph

LIGHTWEIGHT 250cc

1951 (4M) Tommy Wood, Guzzi,
  81.39mph/130.98kph
1952 (4M) Fergus Anderson, Guzzi,
  83.82mph/134.90kph
1953 (4M) Fergus Anderson, Guzzi,
  84.73mph/136.36kph
1954 (3M) Werner Haas (FRG), NSU,
  90.88mph/146.26kph
1955 (9C) Bill Lomas, MV Agusta,
  71.37mph/114.86kph
1956 (9C) Carlo Ubbiali (Ita), MV
  Agusta, 67.05mph/
  107.91kph
1957 (10C) Cecil Sandford, Mondial,
  75.80mph/121.99kph
1958 (10C) Tarquinio Provini (Ita), MV
  Agusta, 76.89mph/
  123.74kph
1959 (10C) Tarquinio Provini (Ita), MV
  Agusta, 77.77mph/
  125.16kph
1960 (5M) Gary Hocking (SRho), MV
  Agusta, 93.64mph/
  150.70kph
1961 (5M) Mike Hailwood, Honda,
  98.38mph/158.33kph
1962 (6M) Derek Minter, Honda,
  96.68mph/155.59kph
1963 (6M) Jim Redman (SRho),
  Honda, 94.85mph/
  152.65kph

1964 (6M) Jim Redman (SRho),
  Honda, 97.45mph/
  156.83kph
1965 (6M) Jim Redman (SRho),
  Honda, 97.19mph/
  156.41kph
1966 (6M) Mike Hailwood, Honda,
  101.79mph/163.82kph
1967 (6M) Mike Hailwood, Honda,
  103.08mph/165.89kph
1968 (6M) Bill Ivy, Yamaha,
  99.58mph/160.26kph
1969 (6M) Kel Carruthers (Aus),
  Benelli, 95.95mph/
  154.42kph
1970 (6M) Kel Carruthers (Aus),
  Yamaha, 96.13mph/
  154.71kph
1971 (4M) Phil Read, Yamaha,
  98.02mph/157.75kph
1972 (4M) Phil Read, Yamaha,
  99.68mph/160.42kph
1973 (4M) Charlie Williams, Yamaha,
  100.05mph/161.01kph
1974 (4M) Charlie Williams, Yamaha,
  94.16mph/151.54kph
1975 (4M) Charles Mortimer,
  Yamaha, 101.78mph/
  163.80kph
1976 (4M) Tom Herron, Yamaha,
  103.55mph/166.65kph

LIGHTWEIGHT 125cc

1951 (2M) Cromie McCandless,
  Mondial, 74.85mph/
  120.46kph
1952 (3M) Cecil Sandford, MV
  Agusta, 75.54mph/
  121.57kph
1953 (3M) Leslie Graham, MV
  Agusta, 77.79mph/
  125.19kph
1954 (10C) Rupert Hollaus (Aut),
  NSU, 69.57mph/
  111.96kph
1955 (9C) Carlo Ubbiali (Ita), MV
  Agusta, 69.67mph/
  112.12kph
1956 (9C) Carlo Ubbiali (Ita), MV
  Agusta, 69.13mph/
  111.25kph
1957 (10C) Tarquinio Provini (Ita),
  Mondial, 73.69mph/
  118.59kph
1958 (10C) Carlo Ubbiali (Ita), MV
  Agusta, 72.86mph/
  117.26kph
1959 (10C) Tarquinio Provini (Ita), MV
  Agusta, 74.06mph/
  119.19kph
1960 (3M) Carlo Ubbiali (Ita), MV

Right *Ingeborg Stoll-Laforge of
Germany, seen here as passenger for
the Frenchman Jacques Drion
during the revived sidecar race in
1954. Miss Stoll-Laforge was the
first woman ever to compete in the
TT races. Sadly, both she and Drion
lost their lives in a tragic accident
two years later*

  Agusta, 85.60mph/
  137.76kph
1961 (3M) Mike Hailwood, Honda,
  88.23mph/141.99kph
1962 (3M) Luigi Taveri (Swi), Honda,
  89.88mph/144.65kph
1963 (3M) Hugh Anderson (NZ),
  Suzuki, 89.27mph/
  143.67kph
1964 (3M) Luigi Taveri (Swi), Honda,
  92.14mph/148.28kph
1965 (3M) Phil Read, Yamaha,
  94.28mph/151.73kph
1966 (3M) Bill Ivy, Yamaha,
  97.66mph/157.17kph
1967 (3M) Phil Read, Yamaha,
  97.48mph/156.88kph
1968 (3M) Phil Read, Yamaha,
  99.12mph/159.52kph
1969 (3M) Dave Simmonds,
  Kawasaki, 91.08mph/
  146.58kph
1970 (3M) Dieter Braun (FRG),
  Suzuki, 89.27mph/
  143.67kph
1971 (3M) Charles Mortimer,
  Yamaha, 83.96mph/
  135.12kph
1972 (3M) Charles Mortimer,
  Yamaha, 87.49mph/
  140.80kph
1973 (3M) Tommy Robb, Yamaha,
  88.90mph/143.07kph
1974 (3M) Clive Horton, Yamaha,
  88.44mph/142.33kph

SIDECAR

1923 (3M) Freddie Dixon/Walter Perry, Douglas, 53.15mph/85.54kph

1924 (4M) George Tucker/George Hammond, Norton, 51.31mph/82.58kph

1925 (4M) Len Parker/K J Horstman, Douglas, 55.22mph/88.87kph

1926-53 Not held

1954 (10C) Eric Oliver/Les Nutt, Norton, 68.87mph/110.84kph

1955 (9C) Walter Schneider (FRG)/Hans Strauss (FRG), BMW, 70.01mph/112.67kph

1956 (9C) Fritz Hillebrand (FRG)/Manfred Grünewald (FRG), BMW, 70.03mph/112.70kph

1957 (10C) Fritz Hillebrand (FRG)/Manfred Grünewald (FRG), BMW, 71.89mph/115.70kph

1958 (10C) Walter Schneider (FRG)/Hans Strauss (FRG), BMW, 73.01mph/117.50kph

1959 (10C) Walter Schneider (FRG)/Hans Strauss (FRG), BMW, 72.69mph/116.98kph

1960 (3M) Helmut Fath (FRG)/Alfred Wohlgemuth (FRG), BMW, 84.10mph/135.35kph

1961 (3M) Max Deubel (FRG)/Emil Hörner (FRG), BMW, 87.65mph/141.06kph

1962 (3M) Chris Vincent/Eric Bliss, BSA, 83.57mph/134.49kph

1963 (3M) Florian Camathias (Swi)/Alfred Herzig (Swi), FCS BMW, 88.38mph/142.23kph

1964 (3M) Max Deubel (FRG)/Emil Hörner (FRG), BMW, 89.12mph/143.42kph

1965 (3M) Max Deubel (FRG)/Emil Hörner (FRG), BMW, 90.57mph/145.76kph

1966 (3M) Fritz Scheidegger (Swi)/John Robinson, BMW, 90.76mph/146.06kph

1967 (3M) Siegfried Schauzu (FRG)/Horst Schneider (FRG), BMW, 90.96mph/146.39kph

1968 (3M) *500cc:* Siegfried Schauzu (FRG)/Horst Schneider (FRG), BMW, 91.09mph/146.60kph

1968 (3M) *750cc:* Terry Vinicombe/John Flaxman, BSA, 85.85mph/138.16kph

1969 (3M) *500cc:* Klaus Enders (FRG)/Rolf Engelhardt (FRG), BMW, 92.48mph/148.83kph

1969 (3M) *750cc:* Siegfried Schauzu (FRG)/Horst Schneider (FRG), BMW, 89.83mph/144.57kph

1970 (3M) *500cc:* Klaus Enders (FRG)/Wolfgang Kalauch (FRG), BMW, 92.93mph/149.56kph

1970 (3M) *750cc:* Siegfried Schauzu (FRG)/Horst Schneider (FRG), BMW, 90.20mph/145.16kph

1971 (3M) *500cc:* Siegfried Schauzu (FRG)/Wolfgang Kalauch (FRG), BMW, 86.21mph/138.74kph

1971 (3M) *750cc:* Georg Auerbacher (FRG)/Hermann Hahn (FRG), BMW, 86.86mph/139.79kph

1972 (3M) *500cc:* Siegfried Schauzu (FRG)/Wolfgang Kalauch (FRG), BMW, 91.85mph/147.82kph

1972 (3M) *750cc:* Siegfried Schauzu (FRG)/Wolfgang Kalauch (FRG), BMW, 90.97mph/146.40kph

1973 (3M) *500cc:* Klaus Enders (FRG)/Rolf Engelhardt (FRG), BMW, 94.93mph/152.78kph

1973 (3M) *750cc:* Klaus Enders (FRG)/Rolf Engelhardt (FRG), BMW, 93.01mph/149.69kph

1974 (3M) *500cc:* Heinz Luthringhauser (FRG)/Hermann Hahn (FRG), BMW, 92.27mph/148.49kph

1974 (3M) *750cc:* Siegfried Schauzu (FRG)/Wolfgang Kalauch (FRG), BMW, 96.59mph/155.45kph

1975 (3M) *500cc:* Rolf Steinhausen (FRG)/Joseph Huber (FRG), Busch König, 95.94mph/154.40kph

1975 (3M) *1000cc:* Siegfried Schauzu (FRG)/Wolfgang Kalauch (FRG), BMW, 97.55mph/156.99kph

1976 (3M) *500cc:* Rolf Steinhausen (FRG)/Joseph Huber (FRG), Busch König, 96.42mph/155.17kph

1976 (3M) *1000cc:* Mac Hobson/Mick Burns, Yamaha, 97.77mph/157.34kph

1977 (3M) *1st Leg:* George O'Dell/Kenny Arthur, Yamaha, 100.03mph/160.98kph

(3M) *2nd Leg:* Mac Hobson/Stu Collins, Yamaha, 99.75mph/160.53kph

Overall: Rolf Steinhausen (FRG)/Wolfgang Kalauch (FRG), König

1978 (3M) *1st Leg:* Dick Greasley/Gordon Russell, Yamaha, 101.76mph/163.76kph

(3M) *2nd Leg:* Rolf Steinhausen (FRG)/Wolfgang Kalauch (FRG), Yamaha, 93.67mph/150.75kph

Overall: Jock Taylor/Kenny Arthur, Yamaha

1979 (3M) *1st Leg:* Trevor Ireson/Clive Pollington, Yamaha, 102.14mph/164.38kph

(3M) *2nd Leg:* Trevor Ireson/Clive Pollington, Yamaha, 100.79mph/162.21kph

Overall: Ireson/Pollington

1980 (3M) *1st Leg:* Trevor Ireson/Clive Pollington, Yamaha, 98.13mph/157.92kph

(3M) *2nd Leg:* Jock Taylor/Benga Johansson (Swe), Yamaha, 103.55mph/166.65kph

Overall: Taylor/Johansson

1981 (3M) *1st Leg:* Jock Taylor/Benga, Johansson (Swe), Yamaha, 107.02mph/172.23kph

(3M) *2nd Leg:* Jock Taylor/Benga Johansson (Swe), Yamaha, 104.55mph/168.26kph

Overall: Taylor/Johansson

1982 (3M) *1st Leg:* Trevor Ireson/Donnie Williams, Yamaha, 106.29mph/171.06kph

(3M) *2nd Leg:* Jock Taylor/Benga Johansson (Swe), Yamaha, 106.09mph/170.74kph

Overall: Roy Hanks/Vince Biggs, Yamaha

1983 (3M) *1st Leg:* Dick Greasley/Stu Atkinson, Yamaha, 104.25mph/167.77kph

(3M) *2nd Leg:* Mick Boddice/Chas Birks, Yamaha, 105.11mph/169.16kph

Overall: Nick Edwards/Brian Marris, Yamaha

1984 (3M) *1st Leg:* Mick Boddice/Chas Birks, Yamaha, 103.97mph/167.32kph

(3M) *2nd Leg:* Steve Abbott/Shaun Smith, Yamaha, 105.29mph/169.45kph

Overall: Abbott/Smith

1985 (3M) *Race A:* Dave Hallam/John Gibbard, Yamaha, 104.45mph/168.10kph

(3M) *Race B:* Mick Boddice/Chas Birks, Yamaha, 105.27mph/169.42kph

1986 (3M) *Race A:* Lowry Burton/Pat Cushnahan, Yamaha, 104.53mph/168.22kph

(3M) *Race B:* Nigel Rollason/Donnie Williams, Phoenix, 103.81mph/167.06kph

1987 (3M) *Race A:* Mick Boddice/Donnie Williams, Yamaha, 104.76mph/168.59kph

(3M) *Race B:* Lowry Burton/Pat Cushnahan, Yamaha, 105.53mph/169.83kph

1988 (3M) *Race A:* Mick Boddice/Chas Birks, Yamaha, 106.26mph/171.02kph

(3M) *Race B:* Mick Boddice/Chas Birks, Yamaha, 106.46mph/171.33kph

1989 (3M) *Race A:* Dave Molyneux/Colin Hardman, Yamaha, 104.56mph/168.27kph

(3M) *Race B:* Mick Boddice/Chas Birks, Yamaha, 107.17mph/172.47kph

1990 (3M) *Race A:* Dave Saville/Nick Roche, Yamaha, 100.72mph/162.09kph

(2M) *Race B:* Dave Saville/Nick Roche, Yamaha, 100.17mph/161.21kph

FORMULA ONE

1959 (3M) *500cc:* Bob McIntyre, Norton, 97.77mph/ 157.35kph

(3M) *350cc:* Alastair King, AJS, 94.66mph/152.34kph

FORMULA 750

1971 (3M) Tony Jefferies, Triumph, 102.85mph/165.52kph

1972 (5M) Ray Pickrell, Triumph, 104.23mph/167.74kph

1973 (5M) Peter Williams, Norton, 105.47mph/169.74kph

1974 (6M) Charles Mortimer, Yamaha, 100.52mph/ 161.77kph

50cc

1962 (2M) Ernst Degner (FRG), Suzuki, 75.12mph/ 120.89kph

1963 (3M) Mitsuo Itoh (Jap), Suzuki, 78.81mph/126.83kph

1964 (3M) Hugh Anderson (NZ), Suzuki, 80.64mph/ 129.78kph

1965 (3M) Luigi Taveri (Swi), Honda, 79.66mph/128.20kph

1966 (3M) Ralph Bryans, Honda, 85.66mph/139.47kph

1967 (3M) Stuart Graham, Suzuki, 82.89mph/135.01kph

1968 (3M) Barry Smith (Aus), Derbi, 72.90mph/117.32kph

CLASSIC TT

1975 (6M) John Williams, Yamaha, 105.33mph/169.51kph

1976 (6M) John Williams, Suzuki, 108.18mph/174.10kph

1977 (6M) Mick Grant, Kawasaki, 110.76mph/178.25kph

1978 (6M) Mick Grant, Kawasaki, 112.41mph/180.90kph

1979 (6M) Alex George, Honda, 113.08mph/181.98kph

1980 (6M) Joey Dunlop, Yamaha, 112.72mph/181.41kph

1981 (6M) Graeme Crosby (NZ), Suzuki, 113.58mph/ 182.79kph

1982 (6M) Dennis Ireland (NZ), Suzuki, 109.21mph/ 175.76kph

1983[1] (6M) Rob McElnea, Suzuki, 114.81mph/184.77kph

1984 (6M) Rob McElnea, Suzuki, 116.12mph/186.88kph

[1]*Known as the Senior Classic TT in 1983 because the traditional Senior TT was not run*

PRODUCTION RACES

1300cc
1989 (4M) Dave Leach, Yamaha, 115.61mph/186.06kph

1000cc
1974 (4M) Mick Grant, Triumph, 99.72mph/160.48kph

750cc
1967 (3M) John Hartle, Triumph, 97.10mph/156.27kph
1968 (3M) Ray Pickrell, Dunstall, 98.13mph/157.92kph
1969 (3M) Malcolm Uphill, Triumph, 99.99mph/160.92kph
1970 (5M) Malcolm Uphill, Triumph, 97.71mph/157.25kph
1971 (4M) Ray Pickrell, Triumph, 100.07mph/161.05kph
1972 (4M) Ray Pickrell, Triumph, 100.00mph/160.93kph
1973 (4M) Tony Jefferies, Triumph, 95.62mph/153.89kph
1974-88 Not held
1989 (4M) Carl Fogarty, Honda, 114.68mph/184.56kph

500cc
1967 (3M) Neil Kelly, Velocette, 89.89mph/144.66kpg
1968 (3M) Ray Knight, Triumph, 90.09mph/144.99kph
1969 (3M) Bill Penny, Honda, 88.18mph/141.91kph
1970 (5M) Frank Whiteway, Suzuki, 89.94mph/144.74kph
1971 (4M) John Williams, Honda, 91.04mph/146.51kph
1972 (4M) Stan Woods, Suzuki, 92.20mph/148.38kph
1973 (4M) Bill Smith, Honda, 88.10mph/141.78kph
1974 (4M) Keith Martin, Kawasaki, 93.85mph/151.04kph

250cc
1967 (3M) Bill Smith, Bultaco, 88.63mph/142.64kph
1968 (3M) Trevor Burgess, Ossa, 87.21mph/140.35kph
1969 (3M) Tony Rogers, Ducati, 83.79mph/134.85kph
1970 (5M) Charles Mortimer, Ducati, 84.87mph/136.59kph
1971 (4M) Bill Smith, Honda, 84.14mph/135.41kph
1972 (4M) John Williams, Honda, 85.32mph/137.31kph
1973 (4M) Charlie Williams, Yamaha, 81.76mph/131.58kph
1974 (4M) Martin Sharpe, Yamaha, 86.94mph/139.92kph

Production TT Handicap
1975 (10M) Dave Croxford/Alex George, Triumph, 99.60mph/160.29kph
1976 (10M) Bill Simpson/Charles Mortimer, Yamaha, 87.00mph/140.01kph

Class A
1984-85 for 100-250cc bikes; 1986 and 1988 for 751-1300cc four-stroke bikes
1984 (3M) Phil Mellor, Yamaha, 92.58mph/148.99kph
1985 (3M) Matt Oxley, Honda, 94.84mph/152.63kph
1986 (3M) Trevor Nation, Suzuki, 111.99mph/180.23kph
1987 Not held
1988 (4M) Dave Leach, Yamaha, 114.32mph/183.98kph

Class B
1984-85 for 251-750cc bikes; 1986-88 for 601-750cc four-stroke/401-500cc two-stroke bikes
1984 (3M) Trevor Nation, Honda, 102.24mph/164.54kph
1985 (3M) Mick Grant, Suzuki, 104.36mph/167.95kph
1986 (3M) Phil Mellor, Suzuki, 109.23mph/175.78kph
1987 (3M) Geoff Johnson, Yamaha, 109.98mph/177.00kph
1988 (4M) Steve Hislop, Honda, 112.29mph/180.71kph

Class C
1984-85 for 751/1500cc bikes; 1986 and 1988 for 401-600cc four-stroke/250-400cc two-stroke bikes
1984 (3M) Geoff Johnson, Kawasaki, 105.28mph/169.43kph
1985 (3M) Geoff Johnson, Honda, 113.69mph/182.97kph
1986 (3M) Gary Padgett, Suzuki, 102.98mph/165.73kph
1987 Not held
1988 (4M) Brian Morrison, Honda, 108.42mph/174.49kph

Class D
For 400cc four-stroke/250cc two-stroke bikes
1986 (3M) Barry Woodland, Suzuki, 99.82mph/160.64kph
1987 (3M) Barry Woodland, Yamaha, 102.98mph/165.73kph
1988 (4M) Barry Woodland, Yamaha, 102.21mph/164.49kph

SCHWEPPES JUBILEE TT
1977 (4M) Joey Dunlop, Yamaha, 108.87mph/175.21kph

TT FORMULA ONE
1977 (4M) Phil Read, Honda, 97.02mph/156.14kph
1978 (6M) Mike Hailwood, Ducati, 108.51mph/174.64mph
1979 (6M) Alex George, Honda, 110.27mph/177.46kph
1980 (6M) Mick Grant, Honda, 105.29mph/169.45kph
1981 (6M) Graeme Crosby (NZ), Suzuki, 111.81mph/179.94kph
1982 (6M) Ron Haslam, Honda, 113.33mph/182.39kph
1983 (6M) Joey Dunlop, Honda, 113.71mph/183.00kph
1984 (6M) Joey Dunlop, Honda, 111.68mph/179.73kph
1985 (6M) Joey Dunlop, Honda, 113.95mph/183.38kph
1986 (4M) Joey Dunlop, Honda, 112.96mph/181.79kph
1987 (6M) Joey Dunlop, Honda, 115.03mph/185.12kph
1988 (6M) Joey Dunlop, Honda, 116.25mph/187.09kph
1989 (6M) Steve Hislop, Honda, 119.36mph/192.09kph
1990 (6M) Carl Fogarty, Honda, 118.35mph/190.47kph

TT FORMULA TWO
1977 (4M) Alan Jackson, Honda, 99.36mph/159.90kph
1978 (4M) Alan Jackson, Honda, 99.35mph/159.89kph
1979 (4M) Alan Jackson, Honda, 101.55mph/163.43kph
1980 (4M) Charlie Williams, Yamaha, 96.24mph/154.88kph
1981 (4M) Tony Rutter, Ducati, 101.91mph/164.01kph
1982 (4M) Tony Rutter, Ducati, 108.05mph/173.89kph
1983 (4M) Tony Rutter, Ducati, 108.20mph/174.13kph
1984 (4M) Graeme McGregor (Aus), Yamaha, 108.78mph/175.06kph
1985 (6M) Tony Rutter, Ducati, 107.79mph/173.47kph
1986 (4M) Brian Reid, Yamaha, 109.72mph/176.57kph
1987 (6M) Steve Hislop, Yamaha, 110.40mph/177.67kph

TT FORMULA THREE

1977 (4M) John Kidson, Honda, 93.28mph/150.12kph

1978 (4M) Bill Smith, Honda, 94.48mph/152.04kph

1979 (4M) Barry Smith (Aus), Yamaha, 97.82mph/ 157.43kph

1980 (4M) Barry Smith (Aus), Yamaha, 91.98mph/ 148.03kph

1981 (4M) Barry Smith (Aus), Yamaha, 99.66mph/ 160.39kph

1982 (4M) Gary Padgett, Yamaha, 96.17mph/154.77kph

SENIOR 350cc

1982 (6M) Tony Rutter, Yamaha, 108.53mph/174.66kph

JUNIOR 350cc

1982 (6M) Phil Mellor, Yamaha, 107.44mph/172.91kph

CLASSIC HISTORIC TT

1984 (3M) *500cc:* Dave Roper (USA), Matchless, 96.11mph/ 154.67kph

1984 (3M) *350cc:* Steve Cull, Aermacchi, 94.26mph/ 151.70kph

SUPERSPORT 600

1989 (4M) Steve Hislop, Honda, 112.58mph/181.18kph

1990 (4M) Brian Reid, Yamaha, 111.98mph/180.21kph

SUPERSPORT 400

1989 (4M) Eddie Laycock, Suzuki, 105.27mph/169.42kph

1990 (3M) Dave Leach, Yamaha, 107.73mph/173.37kph

125cc

1989 (2M) Robert Dunlop, Honda, 102.58mph/165.09kph

1990 (3M) Robert Dunlop, Honda, 103.41mph/166.42kph

TT RECORDS

MOST TT WINS (all races)

Riders	Bikes
14 Mike Hailwood 1961–79	82 Yamaha
13 Joey Dunlop 1977–88	59 Honda
10 Stanley Woods 1923–39, Giacomo Agostini (Ita) 1966–75	42 Norton
9 Siegfried Schauzu (FRG) 1967–75	34 MV Agusta
8 Phil Read 1961–77, Charlie Williams 1973–80, Charles Mortimer 1970–78	28 Suzuki
7 Mick Grant 1974–85, Tony Rutter 1973–85, Mick Boddice 1983–89	27 BMW
6 Jimmy Guthrie 1930–37, Geoff Duke 1949–55, Jim Redman (SRho) 1963–65, John Surtees 1956–60	14 Triumph
	13 BSA
	10 Velocette
	11 Guzzi

MOST SENIOR TT WINS

Riders	Bikes
7 Mike Hailwood	19 Norton
5 Giacomo Agostini (Ita)	13 MV Agusta
4 Stanley Woods, John Surtees	9 Suzuki
3 Alec Bennett, Harold Daniell, Geoff Duke, Joey Dunlop	8 Honda
2 Howard Davies, Jimmy Guthrie, Charlie Dodson, Ray Amm (SRho), Tom Herron, Mick Grant, Rob McElnea	4 Sunbeam

MOST JUNIOR TT WINS

Riders	Bikes
5 Stanley Woods, Giacomo Agostini (Ita)	12 Norton
4 Charlie Williams	11 Yamaha
3 Jimmy Guthrie, Freddie Frith, Jim Redman (SRho)	9 MV Agusta
2 Eric Williams, Alec Bennett, Mike Hailwood, Geoff Duke, John Surtees, Joey Dunlop, Tony Rutter, Charles Mortimer, Con Law	8 Velocette
	7 Honda
	5 AJS

MOST SENIOR/JUNIOR TT WINS

Riders	Bikes
10 Giacomo Agostini (5 Sen/5 Jun)	31 Norton
9 Stanley Woods (4/5), Mike Hailwood (7/2)	22 MV Agusta
6 John Surtees (4/2)	15 Honda
5 Alec Bennett (3/2), Jimmy Guthrie (2/3), Geoff Duke (3/2), Joey Dunlop (3/2)	13 Yamaha
4 Freddie Frith (1/3), Charlie Williams (0/4)	9 Suzuki
3 Harold Daniell (3/0), Ray Amm (2/1), Jim Redman (0/3)	

Two of the most successful TT riders, Mike Hailwood (right) and Giacomo Agostini. Between them they have won 24 races, including the Senior TT on 12 occasions

WINNERS OF SENIOR AND JUNIOR TT IN SAME YEAR

1931 Tim Hunt	1953 Ray Amm	1968–70 Giacomo Agostini
1932–33 Stanley Woods	1957 Bob McIntyre	1972 Giacomo Agostini
1934 Jimmy Guthrie	1958–59 John Surtees	1985 Joey Dunlop
1951 Geoff Duke	1967 Mike Hailwood	1988 Joey Dunlop

MOST TOP THREE PLACES IN SENIOR TT

8 Stanley Woods (4 x 1st; 1 x 2nd; 1 x 3rd)	5 Alec Bennett (3 x 1st; 1 x 2nd; 1 x 3rd)	4 Jimmy Simpson (2 x 2nd; 2 x 3rd)
8 Mike Hailwood (7 x 1st; 1 x 3rd)	5 John Surtees (4 x 1st; 1 x 2nd)	4 Freddie Frith (1 x 1st; 3 x 3rd)
6 Jimmy Guthrie (2 x 1st; 4 x 2nd)	4 Harry Langman (2 x 2nd; 2 x 3rd)	4 Geoff Duke (3 x 1st; 1 x 2nd)
6 Giacomo Agostini (5 x 1st; 1 x 2nd)	4 Peter Williams (4 x 2nd)	4 Joey Dunlop (3 x 1st; 1 x 3rd)

THREE RACE WINS IN ONE WEEK

1961 Mike Hailwood; Lightweight 125cc, Lightweight 250cc, Senior TT	1985 Joey Dunlop; TT Formula One, Junior TT, Senior TT	1989 Steve Hislop; Supersport 600, TT Formula One, Senior TT
1967 Mike Hailwood; Lightweight 250cc, Junior TT, Senior TT	1988 Joey Dunlop; TT Formula One, Junior TT, Senior TT	

ISLE OF MAN TT CIRCUITS

ST JOHN'S CIRCUIT

Length: 15.81mile/25.44km
Lap record: 53.15mph/85.54kph,
Harry Bowen, BAT, 1910
1st TT: 1907, won by Charlie
Collier, Matchless

DEVIL'S ELBOW

BARREGARROW

GLEN HELEN

PEEL

LAUREL BANK

BALLIG BRIDGE

BALLACRAINE

ST JOHN'S

CLYPSE COURSE

Length: 10.79mile/17.36km
Lap record: 80.22mph/129.10kph,
Tarquinio Provini (Ita), MV Agusta,
Lightweight 250cc TT, 1959
1st TT: 1954 Ultra-lightweight TT
won by Rupert Hollaus (Aut), NSU

BALLACOAR CORNER

CRONK-NY-GARROO

CREG-NY-BAA

BRANDISH CORNER

MORNEY CORNER
BEGOADE

CRONK-NY
-MONA

HALL CORNER

EDGES CORNER

SIGNPOST
CORNER

ONCHAN
NURSERY BENDS

WILLASTON CORNER

GOVERNOR'S BRIDGE

PARKFIELD CORNER

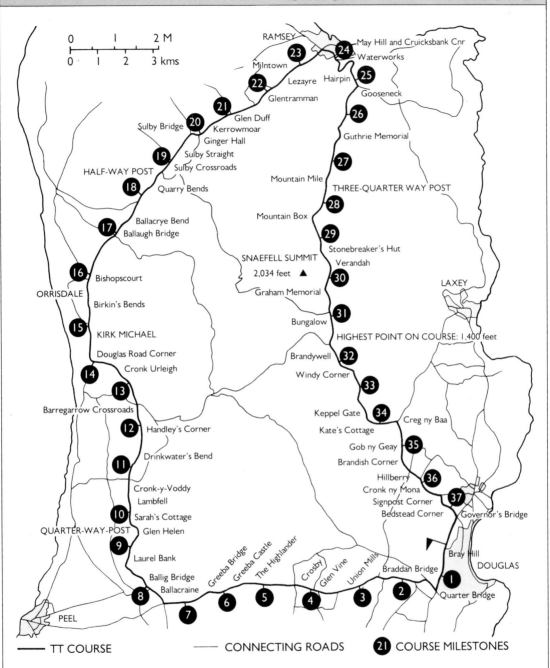

0 1 2 M
0 · 1 2 3 kms

RAMSEY

May Hill and Cruicksbank Cnr
Waterworks

Milntown

Lezayre

Hairpin

Glentramman

Gooseneck

Glen Duff

Kerrowmoar

Guthrie Memorial

Ginger Hall

Sulby Bridge

Sulby Straight

Sulby Crossroads

THREE-QUARTER WAY POST

HALF-WAY POST

Mountain Mile

Quarry Bends

Mountain Box

Ballacrye Bend

Ballaugh Bridge

Stonebreaker's Hut

Verandah

Bishopscourt

SNAEFELL SUMMIT

2,034 feet ▲

LAXEY

ORRISDALE

Graham Memorial

Birkin's Bends

Bungalow

KIRK MICHAEL

Douglas Road Corner

HIGHEST POINT ON COURSE: 1,400 feet

Cronk Urleigh

Brandywell

Windy Corner

Barregarrow Crossroads

Handley's Corner

Keppel Gate

Creg ny Baa

Drinkwater's Bend

Kate's Cottage

Gob ny Geay

Cronk-y-Voddy

Brandish Corner

Lambfell

Hillberry

Sarah's Cottage

Cronk ny Mona

Glen Helen

Signpost Corner

QUARTER-WAY-POST

Bedstead Corner

Governor's Bridge

Laurel Bank

Bray Hill

Ballig Bridge

Greeba Bridge

Greeba Castle

DOUGLAS

Ballacraine

The Highlander

Crosby

Glen Vine

Union Mills

Braddan Bridge

Quarter Bridge

PEEL

—— TT COURSE   —— CONNECTING ROADS   ㉑ COURSE MILESTONES

MOUNTAIN COURSE

Length:	37.73mile/60.71km
Lap record:	122.63mph/197.35kph, Steve Hislop, Honda, 1990
1st TT:	1911 Junior TT, won by Percy Evans, Humber

MILESTONES

First 50mph lap: 1909 Harry Collier, Matchless
First 60mph lap: 1924 Jimmy Simpson, AJS
First 70mph lap: 1926 Jimmy Simpson, AJS
First 80mph lap: 1931 Jimmy Simpson, Norton
First 90mph lap: 1937 Freddie Frith, Norton
First 100mph lap: 1957 Bob McIntyre, Gilera
First 110mph lap: 1976 John Williams, Suzuki
First 120mph lap: 1989 Steve Hislop, Honda
Outright lap record
122.63mph/197.35kph Steve Hislop, Honda, 1990
First 100mph lap on a 250cc machine
1965 Phil Read, Yamaha
First 100mph lap on a 125cc machine
1968 Bill Ivy, Yamaha
First British machine to lap at 100mph
1960 Norton, ridden by Derek Minter. It was also the first
100mph lap on a single cylinder machine
First race winner with an average speed of 100mph
1960 John Surtees, MV Agusta, Senior TT. Runner-up
John Hartle also averaged more than 100mph
First race in which the first three all averaged 100mph
1963 Senior TT; 1st Mike Hailwood, MV Agusta,
104.64mph; 2nd John Hartle, Gilera, 103.67mph; 3rd Phil
Read, Gilera, 100.10mph
First lap under 30 minutes (Mountain Circuit)
1930 Wal Handley, Rudge, 29min 41sec
First lap under 25 minutes (Mountain Circuit)
1938 Harold Daniell, Norton, 24min 52.6sec

First lap under 20 minutes (Mountain Circuit)
1978 Pat Hennen (USA), Suzuki 19min 53.2sec
First foreign machine to win Senior TT
1911 Indian (USA), filled first three places
First disqualification
1911 Charlie Collier, disqualified from 2nd place in the
Senior TT for taking on board fuel illegally
First winner of Senior TT on a 350cc machine
1921 Howard Davies, AJS
First massed start
1924 for the newly instituted Ultra-lightweight TT
First rider to win two races in one week
1925 Wal Handley, Junior TT, Ultra-lightweight TT
First foreign winner of any TT
1937 Omobono Tenni (Ita), Lightweight TT
First non-British winner of the Senior TT
1939 Georg Meier (Ger), BMW
First female competitor
1954 Miss Ingeborg Stoll-Laforge (FRG), passenger to
Jacques Drion (Fra) in sidecar race, they finished 5th
First US winner of a TT
1984 Dave Roper, who won the 500cc class of the
Historic TT on a Matchless
Oldest TT winner
1987 Lowry Burton who won the Sidecar Race B at the
age of 49

*Bob McIntyre on his Gilera during the historic Senior
TT of 1957, when he became the first man to lap the
Mountain Course at over 100mph*

MANX GRAND PRIX

Held every September, the Manx Grand Prix is a training ground for aspirant professional riders who get their first taste of the gruelling Mountain Course at the Isle of Man.

The Manx was spawned from the TT races, which had become increasingly more professional in the post-First World War years; the enthusiastic amateur was left trailing because of his inability to command sponsorship deals from manufacturers. The Isle of Man authorities were also mindful of the fact that their rift with the Auto-Cycle Union in 1922 nearly cost them the TT races. So the Manx Motor Cycle Club, with the approval of the ACU, started the amateur series with a stipulation that only riders who had not previously taken part in an international race, or been the holder of a world motorcycle speed record, could take part.

The first Manx Amateur Road Race took place on 20 September 1923 with 33 riders competing in two categories, 350cc and 500cc, and riding concurrently over five laps of the Mountain Course. Then in 1928, separate races were held for the two classes and became known as the Senior (500cc) and Junior (350cc) Grands Prix.

Because it became difficult to identify the true amateur from the 'shamateur', who received sponsorship from petrol, oil, spark-plug or tyre companies, for example, the races became known as the Manx Grand Prix in 1930.

A Lightweight class (250cc) was introduced in 1933; and in 1957–8, because of the large number of entrants for the Senior and Junior events, additional races, known as Newcomers' races, had to be organised for those riders who did not start the Senior and Junior Grands Prix.

Newcomers' events for the Senior, Junior and Lightweight classes were re-introduced in 1978, and in 1983 the Classic races made their debut.

Riders who have previously competed in a TT or Grand Prix race, or are over the age of 40, are ineligible to compete in the Manx Grand Prix and in the late 1950s a rule was introduced stating that no winner of a Manx Grand Prix could enter again, other than in the Classic races.

WINNERS

All from British Isles unless otherwise stated

MANX AMATEUR ROAD RACE CHAMPIONSHIPS

1923 *500cc:* Len Randles, Sunbeam, 52.77mph/84.93kph
  350cc: Ken Twemlow, New Imperial, 52.46mph/84.43kph
1924 *500cc:* Len Randles, Sunbeam, 56.71mph/91.27kph
  350cc: R C Brown, Sunbeam, 54.20mph/87.23kph
1925 *500cc:* H G Dobbs, Norton, 59.97mph/96.51kph
  350cc: J Morton, New Gerrard, 57.75mph/92.94kph
1926 *500cc:* Rex Adams, AJS, 58.46mph/94.08kph
  350cc: W A Empsall, Velocette, 52.00mph/83.69kph
1927 *500cc:* Tim Hunt, Norton, 57.66mph/92.79kph
  350cc: S Gates, Velocette, 51.87mph/83.48kph

SENIOR GRAND PRIX

1928 Tim Hunt, Norton, 67.94mph/109.34kph
1929 Norman Lea, Norton, 64.02mph/103.03kph
1930 Ralph Merrill, Rudge, 69.49mph/111.83kph
1931 Spug Muir, Norton, 71.79mph/115.53kph
1932 Norman Gledhill, Norton, 67.32mph/108.34kph
1933 Harold Daniell, Norton, 76.98mph/123.89kph
1934 Doug Pirie, Norton, 79.19mph/127.44kph
1935 J K Swanston, Norton, 79.62mph/128.14kph
1936 Austin Munks, Norton, 78.88mph/126.95kph
1937 Maurice Cann, Norton, 81.65mph/131.40kph
1938 Ken Bills, Norton, 84.81mph/136.49kph
1946 Ernie Lyons, Triumph, 76.73mph/123.48kph
1947 Eric Briggs, Norton, 78.34mph/126.08kph
1948 Don Crossley, Triumph, 80.63mph/129.76kph
1949 Geoff Duke, Norton, 86.06mph/138.50kph
1950 Peter Romaine, Norton, 84.12mph/135.38kph
1951 Dave Bennett, Norton, 87.05mph/140.09kph
1952 Derek Farrant, Matchless/AJS, 88.65mph/142.67kph
1953 Denis Parkinson, Norton, 89.68mph/144.33kph
1954 George Costain, Norton, 80.95mph/130.28kph
1955 Geoff Tanner, Norton, 91.38mph/147.06kph
1956 Jimmy Buchan, Norton, 90.83mph/146.18kph
1957 Alan Holmes, Norton, 91.43mph/147.14kph

MANX GRAND PRIX **WINNERS**

1958 Ernie Washer, Norton,
92.94mph/149.57kph
1959 Eddie Crooks, Norton,
94.87mph/152.68kph
1960 Phil Read, Norton,
95.38mph/153.50kph
1961 Ned Minihan, Norton,
93.69mph/150.78kph
1962 Joe Dunphy, Norton,
91.83mph/147.79kph
1963 Griff Jenkins, Norton,
96.10mph/154.66kph
1964 Selwyn Griffiths, Matchless,
96.27mph/154.93kph
1965 Malcolm Uphill, Norton,
89.69mph/144.34kph
1966 Tom Dickie, Matchless,
94.30mph/151.76kph
1967 Jimmy Guthrie, Norton,
94.98mph/152.86kph
1968 Jack Findlay (Aus), Norton,
90.14mph/145.07kph
1969 Gordon Daniels, Matchless,
93.43mph/150.36kph
1970 Roger Sutcliffe, Matchless,
94.41mph/151.94kph

1971 Nigel Rollason, Yamroll,
94.42mph/151.95kph
1972 David Hughes, Matchless,
93.66mph/150.73kph
1973 Paddy Reid, Yamaha,
96.89mph/155.93kph
1974 Boris Murray, Yamaha,
93.28mph/150.12kph
1975 Sammy McClements, Yamaha,
101.04mph/162.61kph
1976 Les Trotter, Suzuki,
98.47mph/158.47kph
1977 Steve Davies, Yamaha,
100.48mph/161.71kph
1978 George Linder, Suzuki,
102.28mph/164.60kph
1979 Clive Watts, Suzuki,
105.27mph/169.42kph
1980 Geoff Johnson, Yamaha,
103.43mph/166.45kph
1981 Dave East, Suzuki,
106.26mph/171.01kph
1982 Gordon Farmer, Yamaha,
100.48mph/161.71kph
1983 Nick Jefferies, Suzuki,
105.16mph/169.24kph

1984 Dave Pither, Honda,
105.59mph/169.93kph
1985 Buddy Yeardsley, Suzuki,
103.81mph/167.07kph
1986 Grant Goddings, Suzuki,
106.58mph/171.52kph
1987 Brian Raynor, Yamaha,
107.20mph/172.52kph
1988 Paul Hunt, Kawasaki,
110.69mph/178.14kph
1989 Nigel Barton, Honda,
111.53mph/179.49kph
1990 Simon Beck, Honda,
110.57mph/177.95kph

JUNIOR GRAND PRIX

1928 Harry Meageen, Rex Acme,
61.58mph/99.10kph
1929 Norman Lea, Velocette,
65.24mph/104.99kph
1930 Doug Pirie, Velocette,
61.63mph/99.18kph
1931 Doug Pirie, Velocette,
69.59mph/111.99kph

Malcolm Uphill won the 1965 Senior Grand Prix, riding a Norton. He completed the 'double' that year by winning the Junior race on an AJS

Many riders have won the hearts of the Isle of Man fans over the years, and few have been more popular than Runcorn's Kevin Riley, who won the 1977 Junior Grand Prix on a Yamaha

1932 J H Carr, New Imperial,
69.27mph/111.48kph
1933 Austin Munks, Velocette,
74.14mph/119.32kph
1934 John White, Norton,
75.59mph/121.65kph
1935 Freddie Frith, Norton,
76.02mph/122.34kph
1936 Austin Munks, Velocette,
73.93mph/118.98kph
1937 Maurice Cann, Norton,
76.23mph/122.68kph
1938 Ken Bills, Norton,
78.76mph/126.75kph
1946 Ken Bills, Norton,
74.18mph/119.38kph
1947 Eric Briggs, Norton,
74.64mph/120.12kph
1948 Denis Parkinson, Norton,
78.20mph/125.85kph
1949 Cromie McCandless, Norton,
81.82mph/131.68kph

1950 Don Crossley, AJS,
82.59mph/132.92kph
1951 Robin Sherry, AJS,
82.61mph/132.95kph
1952 Bob McIntyre, AJS,
85.73mph/137.97kph
1953 Frank Fox, Norton,
84.73mph/136.36kph
1954 Derek Ennett, AJS,
86.33mph/138.93kph
1955 Geoff Tanner, Norton,
88.46mph/142.36kph
1956 Jimmy Buchan, Norton,
88.54mph/142.49kph
1957 Alan Holmes, Norton,
89.13mph/143.44kph
1958 Alan Shepherd, Bancroft/AJS,
89.08mph/143.36kph
1959 Peter Middleton, Norton,
88.73mph/142.80kph
1960 Ellis Boyce, Norton,
90.04mph/144.91kph

1961 Frank Reynolds, AJS,
81.28mph/130.81kph
1962 Robin Dawson, AJS,
89.02mph/143.26kph
1963 Peter Darvill, AJS,
92.48mph/148.83kph
1964 Dave Williams, MW Special,
92.54mph/148.93kph
1965 Malcolm Uphill, AJS,
91.22mph/146.80kph
1966 George Buchan, Norton,
92.86/149.44kph
1967 John Weatherall, Norton,
82.22mph/133.93kph
1968 Jack Findlay (Aus), Norton,
89.85mph/144.60kph
1969 Robin Duffty, Aermacchi,
92.31mph/148.56kph
1970 Clive Brown, Aermacchi,
93.74mph/150.86kph
1971 Steve Moynihan, Aermacchi,
91.17mph/146.72kph

1972 Ken Huggett, Aermacchi,
95.56mph/153.79kph
1973 Phil Haslam, Yamaha,
99.42mph/160.00kph
1974 Boris Murray, Yamaha,
96.10mph/154.66kph
1975 Wayne Dinham, Yamaha,
101.24mph/162.93kph
1976 Joe Lindsay, Yamaha,
101.30mph/163.03kph
1977 Kevin Riley, Yamaha,
102.63mph/165.17kph
1978 Steve Ward, Yamaha,
100.33mph/161.47kph
1979 Clive Watts, Suzuki,
105.58mph/169.59kph
1980 Mike Kneen, Yamaha,
103.94mph/167.28kph
1981 Dave Broadhead, Yamaha,
105.91mph/170.45kph
1982 Andy Cooper, Yamaha,
102.85mph/165.52kph
1983 Chris Fargher, Yamaha,
104.54mph/168.24kph
1984 Ian Newton, Yamaha,
103.64mph/166.79kph
1985 Gary Radcliffe, Yamaha,
103.16mph/166.02kph
1986 Bud Jackson, Yamaha,
103.75mph/166.96kph
1987 Craig Ryding, Kimoco,
104.57mph/168.29kph
1988 Steve Hazlett, Yamaha,
105.13mph/169.19kph
1989 Dave Montgomery, Yamaha,
105.11mph/169.16kph
1990 Stanley Rea, Yamaha,
101.93mph/164.04kph

LIGHTWEIGHT MANX GRAND PRIX

1933 Ron Harris, New Imperial,
66.47mph/106.97kph
1934 W D Mitchell, Cotton,
63.49mph/102.18kph
1935 Ron Harris, New Imperial,
68.56mph/110.34kph
1936 Denis Parkinson, Excelsior,
65.68mph/105.70kph
1937 Denis Parkinson, Excelsior,
69.68mph/112.14kph
1938 Denis Parkinson, Excelsior,
71.05mph/114.34kph
1946 L W Parsons, Rudge,
65.11mph/104.78kph
1947 Austin Munks, Guzzi,
70.63mph/113.67kph
1948 Dickie Dale, Guzzi,
73.37mph/118.08kph
1949–63 *Not held*
1964 Gordon Keith, Greeves,
86.19mph/138.71kph
1965 Dennis Craine, Greeves,
88.37mph/142.22kph
1966 Bob Farmer, Aermacchi,
86.20mph/138.73kph
1967 Brian Ball, BA Special,
81.35mph/130.92kph
1968 Frank Whiteway, Suzuki,
88.52mph/142.46kph
1969 Alex George, Yamaha,
90.63mph/145.85mph
1970 Alan Steele, Yamaha,
90.44mph/145.55kph
1971 Charlie Williams, Yamaha,
93.99mph/151.26kph
1972 Phil Carpenter, Yamaha,
95.06mph/152.98kph

1973 Dave Arnold, Yamaha,
97.23mph/156.48kph
1974 Eddie Roberts, Yamaha,
90.35mph/145.40kph
1975 Alan Jackson, Yamaha,
96.59mph/155.45kph
1976 Danny Shimmin, Yamaha,
99.07mph/159.44kph
1977 Dave Hickman, Yamaha,
99.95mph/160.85kph
1978 Clifford Paterson, Yamaha,
96.25mph/154.92kph
1979 Con Law, Yamaha,
101.78mph/163.80kph
1980 Steve Williams, Yamaha,
99.31mph/159.82kph
1981 Graham Cannell, Rotax,
103.19mph/166.07kph
1982 Robert Haynes, Yamaha,
88.03mph/141.67kph
1983 Chris Fargher, Rotax,
103.25mph/166.16kph
1984 Sean McStay, EMC,
104.35mph/167.94kph
1985 David Johnston, EMC,
101.88mph/163.96kph
1986 Ralph Sutcliffe, Armstrong,
101.77mph/163.78kph
1987 Craig Ryding, Kimoco,
102.45mph/164.88kph
1988 Phil McCallen, Honda,
105.68mph/170.08kph
1989 Nick Turner, Yamaha,
104.96mph/168.92kph
1990 Gavin Lee, Yamaha,
107.88mph/173.62kph

SENIOR CLASSIC

1983 John Goodall, Matchless,
94.68mph/152.37kph
1984 Dave Pither, Matchless,
97.05mph/156.19kph
1985 Neil Tuxworth, Matchless,
96.01mph/154.51kph

1986 Alan Dugdale, Matchless,
98.31mph/158.21kph
1987 Dave Pither, Matchless,
100.22mph/161.29kph
1988 Phil Nicholls, Seeley,
99.28mph/159.78kph

1989 Bill Swallow, Seeley,
100.53mph/161.79kph
1990 Bob Heath, Seeley,
99.68mph/160.42kph

JUNIOR CLASSIC

1983 Paul Barrett, Harley-Davidson,
93.28mph/150.12kph
1984 Lawrence Parris, Aermacchi,
92.69mph/149.17kph
1985 John Stephens, Honda,
93.00mph/149.67kph

1986 Bill Swallow, Honda,
94.50mph/152.08kph
1987 Richard Swallow, Aermacchi,
96.98mph/156.07kph
1988 Richard Swallow, Aermacchi,
100.02mph/160.97kph

1989 Richard Swallow, Aermacchi,
97.76mph/157.33kph
1990 Richard Swallow, Aermacchi,
98.10mph/157.88kph

LIGHTWEIGHT CLASSIC

1983 Richard Fitzsimmons, Suzuki,
83.38mph/134.19kph
1984–87 *Not held*

1988 George Linder, Yamaha,
89.25mph/143.63kph
1989 David Smith, Aermacchi,
87.06mph/140.11kph

1990 Marek Nofer, Suzuki,
91.96mph/148.00kph

NEWCOMERS' – SENIOR RACE

1957 Ned Minihan, Norton,
88.90mph/143.07kph
1958[1] Peter Richardson, Norton,
85.06mph/136.89kph
1959-77 *Not held*
1978 Dave Ashton, Suzuki,
81.25mph/130.76kph
1979 Dave Raybon, Yamaha,
94.84mph/152.63kph
1980 Steve Richardson, Yamaha,
90.20mph/145.16kph

1981 Mike Pellow, Yamaha,
98.16mph/157.97kph
1982 Ian Ogden, Suzuki,
96.28mph/154.95kph
1983 Stephen Carthy, Suzuki,
99.47mph/160.08kph
1984 Ted Byers, Suzuki,
95.72mph/154.05kph
1985 Tom Knight, Ducati,
95.60mph/153.85kph

1986 Jim Hunter, Suzuki,
100.35mph/161.50kph
1987 Colin Gable, Suzuki,
105.23mph/169.35kph
1988 Allan McDonald, Suzuki,
107.11mph/172.38kph
1989 Chris Morris, Honda,
104.01mph/167.39kph
1990 Paul Orritt, Yamaha,
105.96mph/170.53kph
[1] *Known as the Senior Snaefell race*

NEWCOMERS' – JUNIOR RACE

1957 Dennis Pratt, AJS,
82.94mph/133.48kph
1958[1] Gordon Bell, Norton,
84.15mph/135.43kph
1959-77 *Not held*
1978 Robert Brew, Yamaha,
88.11mph/141.80kph
1979 Roger Luckman, Yamaha,
97.17mph/156.38kph
1980 Kenny Shepherd, Yamaha,
98.13mph/157.92kph

1981 Norman Brown, Yamaha,
103.76mph/166.99kph
1982 Gary Hislop, Yamaha,
99.96mph/160.87kph
1983 Robert Dunlop, Yamaha,
102.46mph/164.89kph
1984 Gary Cowan, Yamaha,
101.69mph/163.65kph
1985 Ashley Gardner, Yamaha,
98.45mph/158.44kph

1986 Ian Jones, Yamaha,
96.23mph/154.86kph
1987 Billy Craine, Yamaha,
100.77mph/162.17kph
1988 Charles Morgan, Yamaha,
98.03mph/157.76kph
1989 Dave Hedison, Yamaha,
95.11mph/53.06kph
1990 Lee Pullen, Spondon,
103.28mph/166.21kph
[1] *Known as the Junior Snaefell race*

NEWCOMERS' – LIGHTWEIGHT

1978 Phil Mellor, Yamaha,
85.27mph/137.23kph
1979 Andy McGladdery, Yamaha,
94.49mph/152.07kph
1980 Gary Padgett, Yamaha,
97.55mph/156.99kph
1981 Buddy Yeardsley, Yamaha,
96.81mph/155.80kph
1982 Brian Lund, Yamaha,
97.08mph/156.24kph

1983 Barrie Middleton, Yamaha,
94.56mph/152.18kph
1984 Phil Ames, Yamaha, 95.25mph/
153.29kph
1985 Carl Fogarty, Yamaha,
94.78mph/152.53kph
1986 George Higginson, Decorite,
97.92mph/157.58kph
1987 Ian Morris, Yamaha,
96.81mph/155.80kph

1988 Phil McCallen, Honda,
103.53mph/166.62kph
1989 Pat Sefton, Kawasaki,
96.89mph/155.93kph
1990 Mick Lofthouse, Kawasaki,
100.89mph/162.37kph

RECORDS

WINNERS OF TWO RACES IN ONE YEAR

Norman Lea (Senior GP & Junior GP)
1929
Austin Munks (Senior GP & Junior GP)
1936
Maurice Cann (Senior GP & Junior
GP) 1937
Ken Bills (Senior GP & Junior GP)
1938
Eric Briggs (Senior GP & Junior GP)
1947
Geoff Tanner (Senior GP & Junior GP)
1955

Jimmy Buchan (Senior GP & Junior
GP) 1956
Alan Holmes (Senior GP & Junior GP)
1957
Malcolm Uphill (Senior GP & Junior
GP) 1965
Jack Findlay (Senior GP & Junior GP)
1968
Boris Murray (Senor GP & Junior GP)
1974
Clive Watts (Senior GP & Junior GP)
1979

Chris Fargher (Senior GP & Junior
GP) 1983
Dave Pither (Senior GP & Senior
Classic) 1984
Craig Ryding (Senior GP & Junior GP)
1987
Phil McCallen (Lightweight GP &
Lightweight Newcomers') 1988

Nobody has won more Manx Grand Prix races than Denis Parkinson. He achieved five wins in a 17-year career between 1936 and 1953, the last year bringing him eventual success in the Senior Grand Prix

MOST WINS (all races)

5 Denis Parkinson (3 x Lightweight GP; 1 x Senior GP; 1 x Junior GP)

4 Austin Munks (2 x Junior GP; 1 x Senior GP; 1 x Lightweight GP)

4 Richard Swallow (4 x Junior Classic)

3 Doug Pirie (2 x Junior GP; 1 x Senior GP)

3 Ken Bills (2 x Junior GP; 1 x Senior GP)

3 Dave Pither (2 x Senior Classic; 1 x Senior GP)

FASTEST LAP

114.02mph/183.50kph Phil Hogg, Yamaha, 1988 Senior GP

FIRST 100mph LAP

1974 Phil Haslam, Yamaha, Junior GP

FIRST FEMALE RIDER

1989 Gloria Clark, Senior Newcomers' Race

WINNERS OF BOTH SENIOR MANX GRAND PRIX AND SENIOR TT

Harold Daniell (GP 1933, TT 1938, 1949)
Geoff Duke (GP 1949, TT 1950–51, 1955)

Phil Read (GP 1960, TT 1977)
Jack Findlay (GP 1968, TT 1973)

RACING IN THE USA

Racing in the United States takes place under the auspices of the American Motorcyclist Association (AMA), which was founded in Chicago in 1924 with the aim of providing organised events for the many motorcycle enthusiasts across America. They moved their headquarters to Columbus, Ohio in 1928 and are now situated in the Westerville district of the city.

Early organised events were mostly dirt-track meetings, with occasional road races. Even in the post-Second World War years, when the road racing World Championship was launched, the emphasis in the US was still on dirt-track racing and the fast growing moto-cross branch of the sport.

The AMA and FIM had long since fallen out and it was not until the 1970s that the rift was healed and the AMA became affiliated to the governing body once more. By then, road racing was becoming increasingly popular and the AMA's return to the FIM meant that the top European riders could race in America without fear of losing their FIM licences. It also opened the door for the many talented American riders to make their mark on the European Grand Prix circuit.

The Americans have long been advocates of Formula 750 racing and, coincidentally, shortly after the AMA's re-admission to the FIM, the latter introduced its 750cc series in 1973.

The leading US championship are the AMA Grand National Championships, National Road Race Championships and the Supercross National Championships. The best known of all US road races is the famous Daytona 200, held every March over 57 laps of the 3.56mile/5.73km track at the Daytona International Speedway in Florida.

America had to wait a long time for her first world road racing champion, and that honour eventually fell to Kenny Roberts who won the 500cc crown in 1978. He completed a hat-trick of successes and since then, the United States has been the dominant nation in the 500cc class, winning the title no fewer than seven times in the 1980s thanks to Roberts, Eddie Lawson and Freddie Spencer. They have started the nineties in the same way, with Wayne Rainey becoming the first champion of the new decade.

But it is not just at road racing that America has become dominant in recent years; they have also become one of the strongest moto-cross nations and have won the Moto-Cross des Nations every year since 1981.

AMA
GRAND NATIONAL
CHAMPIONSHIP

This season-long championship was launched in 1954 when Bobby Hill of Columbus, Ohio, won the first ever race at Daytona Beach. Eighteen races made up the inaugural championship and since then, the number of races has varied over the years. In 1990 the championship was a 17-race series. Between 1954–85 the championship combined dirt-track and road races, but since 1986 the AMA has recognised separate road race champions.

WINNERS

All from the United States. Figures in brackets indicate number of race wins during the season.

1954 Joe Leonard, Harley-Davidson (8)
1955 Brad Andres, Harley-Davidson (5)
1956 Joe Leonard, Harley-Davidson (2)
1957 Joe Leonard, Harley-Davidson ·(4)
1958 Carroll Resweber, Harley-Davidson (2)
1959 Carroll Resweber, Harley-Davidson (3)
1960 Carroll Resweber, Harley-Davidson (4)
1961 Carroll Resweber, Harley-Davidson (2)
1962 Bart Markel, Harley-Davidson (6)

1963 Dick Mann, Matchless/BSA (1)
1964 Roger Reiman, Harley-Davidson (2)
1965 Bart Markel, Harley-Davidson (3)
1966 Bart Markel, Harley-Davidson (2)
1967 Gary Nixon, Triumph (5)
1968 Gary Nixon, Triumph (2)
1969 Mert Lawwill, Harley-Davidson (4)
1970 Gene Romero, Triumph (3)
1971 Dick Mann, BSA (4)
1972 Mark Brelsford, Harley-Davidson (3)
1973 Kenny Roberts, Yamaha (3)
1974 Kenny Roberts, Yamaha (6)
1975 Gary Scott, Harley-Davidson (2)
1976 Jay Springsteen, Harley-Davidson (7)
1977 Jay Springsteen, Harley-Davidson (6)
1978 Jay Springsteen, Harley-Davidson (6)
1979 Steve Eklund, Yamaha/Harley-Davidson (3)
1980 Randy Goss, Harley-Davidson (1)
1981 Mike Kidd, Harley-Davidson/Yamaha (2)
1982 Ricky Graham, Harley-Davidson (4)
1983 Randy Goss, Harley-Davidson (2)
1984 Ricky Graham, Honda (6)
1985 Bubba Shobert, Honda (5)
1986 Bubba Shobert, Honda (9)
1987 Bubba Shobert, Honda (7)
1988 Scott Parker, Harley-Davidson (5)
1989 Scott Parker, Harley-Davidson (10)
1990 Scott Parker, Harley-Davidson (7)

MOST TITLES

4 Carroll Resweber
3 Joe Leonard, Bart Markel, Jay Springsteen, Bubba Shobert, Scott Parker
2 Dick Mann, Gary Nixon, Kenny Roberts, Randy Goss, Ricky Graham

MOST RACE WINS

Figures in brackets indicate Dirt Track/Road Race wins
40 (40/0) Jay Springsteen 1975–85
38 (33/5) Bubba Shobert 1982–88
36 (36/0) Scott Parker 1979–90
33 (15/18) Kenny Roberts 1974–84
28 (28/0) Bart Markel 1960–71
27 (19/8) Joe Leonard 1953–61
24 (12/12) Dick Mann 1958–72
24 (24/0) Ricky Graham 1980–86

AMA
NATIONAL SUPERBIKE
ROAD RACE CHAMPIONS

WINNERS

1986[1] Fred Merkel, Honda (2)
1987 Wayne Rainey, Honda (3)
1988 Bubba Shobert, Honda (2)
1989 Jamie James, Suzuki (1)
1990 Doug Chandler, Kawasaki (4)
[1] *Known as the Road Race Series*

MOST RACE WINS

10 Wayne Rainey 1986–87
6 Kevin Schwantz 1987–88
5 Randy Renfrow 1986–90
5 Doug Polen 1988–90
3 Bubba Shobert 1987–88

AMA
SUPERCROSS
NATIONAL CHAMPIONSHIP

The AMA Supercross Championship was born out of the National Moto-Cross Championship which was launched in 1972. Two years later Pierre Karsmakers, on a Yamaha, won the first race in the newly instituted Supercross Championship at Daytona Beach. The inaugural championship, for 250 and 500cc machines, consisted of just five rounds. The 1990 championship was over 17 rounds. Since 1976 the championship has been limited to machines with a maximum capacity of 250cc.

WINNERS

Figures in brackets indicate number of race wins during the season
1974 *250cc:* Pierre Karsmakers, Yamaha (1)
     500cc: Gary Semics, Kawasaki (0)
1975 *250cc:* Jim Ellis, Cam-Am (4)
     500cc: Steve Stackable, Maico (2)
1976 Jim Weinert, Kawasaki (2)
1977 Bob Hannah, Yamaha (6)
1978 Bob Hannah, Yamaha (6)
1979 Bob Hannah, Yamaha (6)
1980 Mike Bell, Yamaha (6)
1981 Mark Barnett, Suzuki (6)
1982 Donnie Hansen, Honda (4)
1983 David Bailey, Honda (3)
1984 Johnny O'Mara, Honda (5)
1985 Jeff Ward, Kawasaki (1)
1986 Rick Johnson, Honda (6)
1987 Jeff Ward, Kawasaki (5)
1988 Rick Johnson, Honda (7)
1989 Jeff Stanton, Honda (5)
1990 Jeff Stanton, Honda (4)

MOST TITLES

3 Bob Hannah
2 Jeff Ward, Rick Johnson, Jeff Stanton

MOST RACE WINS

28 Rick Johnson 1984–89
27 Bob Hannah 1977–85
19 Jeff Ward 1984–90
16 Mark Barnett 1979–85
12 David Bailey 1983–86
10 Broc Glover 1980–88
10 Mike Bell 1978–83

Top *The North Turn at Daytona*

Above *Brad Andres (8) leads Billy Meier at Torrey Pines. Andres is one of four men to have won America's most prestigious race, the Daytona 200, on three occasions*

DAYTONA 200

This 200-mile (321.87km) race, over 57 laps of the 3.56mile (5.73km) road course at the Daytona International Speedway, Daytona Beach, Florida, is the best known annual motorcycle race in the United States. It was first held in 1937 over a beach circuit, and was won by Ed Krentz, out of a total of 98 entrants. The race moved to a different track – though still on the beach – in 1948, and it remained there until 1961 when it moved to a 2-mile (3.22km) road track at the International Speedway. It was extended to 3.81 miles (6.13km) in 1973, to 3.87 miles (6.23km) in 1976 and to its present length in 1985. Despite a modification to the back straight chicane in 1989, it remained the same length.

WINNERS

All from the United States unless otherwise stated

1937 Ed Krentz, Indian, 73.34mph/118.03kph
1938 Ben Campanale, Harley-Davidson, 73.99mph/119.08kph
1939 Ben Campanale, Harley-Davidson, 76.68mph/123.40kph
1940 Babe Tancredi, Harley-Davidson, 75.11mph/120.88kph
1941 Billy Matthews (Can), Norton, 78.08mph/125.66kph
1942–46 *Not held*
1947 John Spiegelhoff, Indian, 77.14mph/124.14kph
1948 Floyd Emde, Indian, 74.01mph/119.11kph
1949 Dick Klamfoth, Norton, 86.42mph/139.08kph
1950 Billy Matthews (Can), Norton, 88.55mph/142.51kph
1951 Dick Klamfoth, Norton, 92.81mph/149.36kph
1952 Dick Klamfoth, Norton, 87.71mph/141.16kph
1953 Paul Goldsmith, Harley-Davidson, 94.25mph/151.68kph
1954 Bobby Hill, BSA, 94.24mph/151.66kph
1955 Brad Andres, Harley-Davidson, 84.57mph/136.10kph
1956 John Gibson, Harley-Davidson, 94.21mph/151.62kph
1957 Joe Leonard, Harley-Davidson,

98.52mph/158.55kph
1958 Joe Leonard, Harley-Davidson, 99.86mph/160.71kph
1959 Brad Andres, Harley-Davidson, 98.70mph/158.84kph
1960 Brad Andres, Harley-Davidson, 98.06mph/157.81kph
1961 Roger Reiman, Harley-Davidson, 69.25mph/111.45kph
1962 Don Burnett, Triumph, 71.98mph/115.84kph
1963 Ralph White, Harley-Davidson, 77.68mph/125.01kph
1964 Roger Reiman, Harley-Davidson, 94.83mph/152.62kph
1965 Roger Reiman, Harley-Davidson, 90.04mph/144.91kph
1966 Buddy Elmore, Triumph, 96.58mph/155.43kph
1967 Gary Nixon, Triumph, 96.23mph/158.08kph
1968 Cal Rayborn, Harley-Davidson, 101.29mph/163.01kph
1969 Cal Rayborn, Harley-Davidson, 100.88mph/162.35kph
1970 Dick Mann, Honda, 102.69mph/165.27kph
1971 Dick Mann, BSA, 104.74mph/168.56kph
1972 Don Emde, Yamaha, 103.36mph/166.34kph
1973 Jarno Saarinen (Fin), Yamaha, 98.18mph/158.00kph
1974 Giacomo Agostini (Ita),

Yamaha, 105.10mph/169.00kph
1975 Gene Romero, Yamaha, 106.45mph/171.32kph
1976 Johnny Cecotto (Ven), Yamaha, 108.77mph/175.05kph
1977 Steve Baker, Yamaha, 108.85mph/175.18kph
1978 Kenny Roberts, Yamaha, 108.37mph/174.41kph
1979 Dale Singleton, Yamaha, 107.69mph/173.31kph
1980 Patrick Pons (Fra), Yamaha, 107.55mph/173.09kph
1981 Dale Singleton, Yamaha, 108.52mph/174.65kph
1982 Graeme Crosby (NZ), Yamaha, 109.10mph/175.58kph
1983 Kenny Roberts, Yamaha, 110.93mph/178.52kph
1984 Kenny Roberts, Yamaha, 113.14mph/182.09kph
1985 Freddie Spencer, Honda, 102.99mph/165.74kph
1986 Eddie Lawson, Yamaha, 106.03mph/170.64kph
1987 Wayne Rainey, Honda, 106.83mph/171.92kph
1988 Kevin Schwantz, Suzuki, 107.80mph/173.49kph
1989 John Ashmead, Honda, 96.32mph/155.02kph
1990 David Sadowski, Yamaha, 98.38mph/155.11kph

MOST WINS

3 Brad Andres, Dick Klamfoth, Roger Reiman, Kenny Roberts
2 Ben Campanale, Joe Leonard, Cal Rayborn, Dale Singleton, Billy Matthews, Dick Mann

FASTEST LAP

111.87mph/180.04kph Thomas Stevens, Yamaha, 1990

OTHER RACES & CHAMPIONSHIPS

INTERNATIONAL CUP

Motorcycle racing as a competitive sport evolved from the International Cup races at the turn of the century. Like the Gordon Bennett Cup, their four-wheeled counterpart, the International Cup races were initially organised by the French – in this case, the Auto-Cycle Club of France.

The first race was in 1904, and came a year after a challenge match between the French and British, which Frenchman Maurice Fournier won at a reported speed of 80mph/128.75kph.

Teams from Britain, Austria, Denmark and Germany, as well as the host country, entered the 1904 International Cup. The British were completely outclassed, although the race was to become famous for its appalling organisation and subsequent accusations of cheating. There was even an instance of nails scattered around but only on one half of the road . . . the French team knew which half they were on! The hosts also had the luxury of being able to pick up spares *en route* thanks to a travelling motorcycle touring the circuit in the opposite direction. The other teams were not allowed such a facility. The result was therefore never officially declared – much to the disgust of the French, of course.

The following year the race was organised by the newly-formed FICM who managed to do what the French ACC could not do: run a well-organised event with no accusations of cheating labelled against them, which did their credibility no harm.

Britain managed a third placing through Harry Collier in 1906; it was the year of the last International, as one year later it was superseded by the Isle of Man TT. But the International Cup, despite its brief and chequered history, should never be forgotten because of the important role it played in the promotion and development of motorcycle racing as a sport.

RESULTS

1904
Dourdan Circuit, Nr. Paris, September 25 (167.77miles/270km)
1 Léon Demester (Fra), Griffon, 44.99mph/72.41kph
2 Franz Jomann (Aut), Lurin-Klément
2 Ingilbert (Fra), Griffon
Race declared void after accusations of cheating

1905
Dourdan Circuit, Nr. Paris, July 1 (167.77miles/270km)
1 Wenzel Wondrick (Aut), Laurin-Klément, 54.50mph/87.71kph
2 Léon Demester (Fra), Griffon*
3 Joseph Giuppone (Fra), Peugeot
* Subsequently disqualified for illegally changing a wheel

1906
Circuit de Putzau, Austria, July 8 (154.60miles/248.80km)
1 Edward Nikodem (Aut), Puch, 47.87mph/77.04kph
2 Louis Obruba (Aut), Puch
3 Harry Collier (UK), Matchless

Weighing in for the first International Cup at Dourdan, near Paris, in 1904

ULSTER GRAND PRIX

Northern Ireland's premier race formed a round of the first World Championship in 1949, and remained part of it until 1971. First held in 1922 over the 16.5mile (256.55km) Clady Circuit in Belfast, for many years it had all classes racing simultaneously after staggered starts. The race moved to its present-day home at Dundrod, near Belfast, in 1953.

Because of the political problems in Northern Ireland, there was no race in 1972; but it returned the following year and has since been one the United Kingdom's top events each year, as racing takes in a 7.5 mile (12.07km) stretch of public roads. The Formula One event is one of the rounds counting towards the TT Formula One World Championship.

In 1990 Steve Hislop lapped the circuit at 123.72mph/199.11kph, the fastest lap ever recorded in a race in Britain.

WINNERS

1922
Over 600cc: Norman Metcalfe, Brough-Superior, 53.38mph/85.91kph
600cc: Hubert Hassall, Norton, 60.57mph/97.48kph
350cc: Freddie Andrews, JAP, 49.65mph/79.90kph
250cc: Wal Handley, OK, 52.39mph/84.31kph
1923
Over 600cc: *No finishers*
600cc: Joe Craig, Norton, 62.99mph/101.37kph
350cc: Jimmy Shaw, Zenith-JAP, 60.02mph/96.59kph
250cc: Wal Handley, Rex Acme, 55.95mph/90.04kph
1924
Over 600cc: Stanley Woods, New Imperial, 57.54mph/92.46kph
600cc: Joe Craig, Norton, 67.86mph/109.21kph
350cc: Freddie Andrews, New Imperial, 59.54mph/95.82kph
250cc: Jack Porter, New-Gerrard, 59.16mph/95.11kph
1925
Over 600cc: Stanley Woods, New Imperial, 65.26mph/105.03kph
600cc: Joe Craig, Norton, 72.04mph/115.94kph
350cc: Jack Burney, Enfield, 65.60mph/105.57kph
250cc: Billy Colgan, Cotton, 57.48mph/92.51kph
1926
Over 500cc: Joe Craig, Norton, 64.31mph/103.50kph
500cc: Graham Walker, Sunbeam, 70.43mph/113.35kph
350cc: Wal Handley, Rex Acme, 68.89mph/110.87kph
250cc: Syd Crabtree, JAP, 60.44mph/97.27kph
1927
Over 500cc: A de Gourley, Norton, 66.12mph/106.41kph
500cc: Jimmy Shaw, Norton, 74.15mph/119.33kph
350cc: Charlie Dodson, Sunbeam, 71.55mph/115.15kph
250cc: Billy Colgan, Cotton, 63.35mph/101.95kph
1928
Over 500cc: George Brockerton, Zenith, 67.17mph/108.10kph
500cc: Graham Walker, Rudge, 80.08mph/128.88kph
350cc: Frank Longman, Velocette, 74.31mph/119.59kph
250cc: F Taylor, OK Supreme, 65.41mph/105.27kph
1929
500cc: Graham Walker, Rudge, 80.63mph/129.76kph
350cc: Leo Davenport, AJS, 76.23mph/122.68kph
250cc: Frank Longman, OK Supreme, 67.21mph/108.16kph

1930
500cc: Stanley Woods, Norton, 80.56mph/129.65kph
350cc: Leo Davenport, AJS, 75.19mph/121.01kph
250cc: Sid Gleave, SGS, 67.63mph/108.84kph
1931
500cc: Stanley Woods, Norton, 86.43mph/139.10kph
350cc: Leo Davenport, Norton, 79.43mph/127.83kph
250cc: E Mitchell, Rudge, 72.63mph/116.89kph
1932
500cc: Stanley Woods, Norton, 85.15mph/137.04kph
350cc: H G Tyrell-Smith, Rudge, 77.89mph/125.35kph
250cc: Ted Mellors, New Imperial, 73.34mph/118.03kph
1933
500cc: Stanley Woods, Norton, 87.43mph/140.70kph
350cc: Wal Handley, Velocette, 83.63mph/134.59kph
250cc: Charlie Dodson, New Imperial, 76.53mph/123.16kph
1934
500cc: Walter Rusk, Velocette, 88.38mph/142.23kph
350cc: Jimmy Simpson, Norton, 84.93mph/136.68kph
250cc: George Knott, Rudge, 77.08mph/124.05kph
1935
500cc: Jimmy Guthrie, Norton, 90.98mph/146.42kph
350cc: Wal Handley, Velocette, 86.65mph/139.45kph
250cc: Arthur Geiss (Ger), DKW, 79.16mph/127.40kph
1936
500cc: Freddie Frith, Norton, 92.00mph/148.06kph
350cc: Ernie Thomas, Velocette, 86.82mph/139.72kph
250cc: Ginger Wood, New Imperial, 78.76mph/126.75kph
1937
500cc: Jock West, BMW, 91.64mph/147.48kph
350cc: Ted Mellors, Velocette, 85.58mph/137.73kph
250cc: Ernie Thomas, DKW, 81.83mph/131.69kph
1938
500cc: Jock West, BMW, 93.98mph/151.25kph
350cc: Ted Mellors, Velocette, 87.85mph/141.38kph
250cc: Ernie Thomas, DKW, 80.48mph/129.52kph
1939
500cc: Dorino Serafini (Ita), Gilera, 97.85mph/157.47kph
350cc: Stanley Woods, Velocette, 91.65mph/147.50kph
250cc: Les Martin, Excelsior, 76.08mph/122.44kph
1940–46 *Not held*
1947
500cc: Artie Bell, Norton, 91.25mph/146.85kph
350cc: Johnny Lockett, Norton, 84.77mph/136.42kph

250cc:	Maurice Cann, Guzzi, 78.78mph/126.78kph	

1948

500cc:	Enrico Lorenzetti (Ita), Guzzi, 85.55mph/137.68kph
350cc:	Freddie Frith, Velocette, 80.16mph/129.01kph
250cc:	Maurice Cann, Guzzi, 72.47mph/116.63kph

1949–71 Results can be found in the **World Road Race Championships** section on pages 15–51 with the exception of the following, which were not classified as World Championship races:

1951 125cc: Cromie McCandless, Mondial, 77.46mph/124.66kph

Not classified because of insufficient entrants

1954 500cc: Ray Amm (SRho), Norton, 83.87mph/134.98kph

Not classified because race distance reduced due to adverse weather

1972 *Not held*

1973

500cc:	John Williams, Yamaha, 104.26mph/167.79kph
350cc:	John Williams, Yamaha, 103.72mph/166.92kph
250cc:	John Williams, Yamaha, 100.39mph/161.56kph
Sidecar:	Dennis Keen, König, 87.77mph/141.25kph

1974

500cc:	Tony Rutter, Yamaha, 104.75mph/168.58kph
350cc:	Tony Rutter, Yamaha, 104.07mph/167.48kph
250cc:	Austin Hockley, Yamaha, 100.57mph/161.85kph
Sidecar:	Dave Edgington, König, 91.58mph/147.38kph

1975

1000cc:	Percy Tait, Yamaha, 106.97mph/172.15kph
500cc:	Melvyn Robinson, Yamsel, 98.18mph/158.01kph
350cc:	Ray McCullough, Yamaha, 106.85mph/171.96kph
250cc:	Tony Rutter, Yamaha, 102.34mph/164.70kph

1976

1000cc:	Geoff Barry, Yamaha, 112.17mph/180.52kph
500cc:	Stan Woods, Suzuki, 109.46mph/176.16kph
350cc:	Ray McCullough, Yamaha, 108.63mph/174.82kph
250cc:	Ray McCullough, Yamaha, 105.19mph/169.29kph

1977

1000cc:	John Williams, Yamaha, 114.97mph/185.03kph
500cc:	John Williams, Suzuki, 113.41mph/182.52kph
350cc:	Tom Herron, Yamaha, 111.16mph/178.89kph
250cc:	Tom Herron, Yamaha, 108.14mph/174.03kph
Sidecar:	Mick Boddice, Yamaha, 102.62mph/165.15kph

1978

1000cc:	Tom Herron, Yamaha, 116.71mph/187.83kph
500cc:	John Williams, Suzuki, 111.95mph/180.17kph
350cc:	Jon Ekerold (SAf), Yamaha, 111.44mph/179.35kph
250cc:	Tom Herron, Yamaha, 107.50mph/173.00kph
TT Formula 1:	Tom Herron, Honda, 110.46mph/177.77kph
Sidecar:	Mick Boddice, Yamaha, 102.52mph/164.99kph

1979

1000cc:	Joey Dunlop, Yamaha, 115.34mph/185.62kph
500cc:	Joey Dunlop, Suzuki, 112.76mph/181.47kph
350cc:	Donny Robinson, Yamaha, 110.73mph/178.20kph

250cc:	Ray McCullough, Yamaha, 107.61mph/173.18kph
TT Formula 1:	Ron Haslam, Honda, 112.90mph/181.69kph
TT Formula 2:	Alan Jackson, Honda, 99.70mph/160.45kph
TT Formula 3:	Barry Smith (Aus), Yamaha, 94.90mph/152.73kph

1980

1000cc:	Joey Dunlop, Suzuki, 116.39mph/187.31kph
500cc:	Donny Robinson, Suzuki, 111.83mph/179.97kph
350cc:	Ray McCullough, Yamaha, 109.58mph/176.35kph
250cc:	Joey Dunlop, Yamaha, 107.71mph/173.34kph
TT Formula 1:	Graeme Crosby (NZ), Suzuki, 114.32mph/183.98kph
TT Formula 2:	Charlie Williams, Yamaha, 100.68mph/162.03kph
TT Formula 3:	Ron Haslam, Honda, 96.70mph/155.62kph

1981

1000cc:	Ron Haslam, Honda, 108.54mph/174.68kph
500cc:	Gary Lingham, Suzuki, 101.50mph/163.35kph
350cc:	Graeme McGregor (Aus), Yamaha, 102.77mph/165.39kph
250cc:	Tony Rutter, Yamaha, 95.90mph/154.34kph
TT Formula 1:	Ron Haslam, Honda, 105.95mph/170.51kph
TT Formula 2:	Phil Mellor, Yamaha, 96.89mph/155.93kph
TT Formula 3:	Barry Smith (Aus), Yamaha, 86.65mph/139.45

1982

1000cc:	Roger Marshall, Suzuki, 118.30mph/190.39kph
500cc:	Paul Cranston, Yamaha, 107.29mph/172.67kph
350cc:	Ray McCullough, Yamaha, 110.30mph/177.51kph
250cc:	Donny Robinson, Yamaha, 104.34mph/167.92kph
TT Formula 1:	Ron Haslam, Honda, 116.72mph/187.84kph
TT Formula 2:	Tony Rutter, Ducati, 100.73mph/162.11kph

1983

500cc:	Roger Marshall, Honda, 110.86mph/178.41kph
350cc:	Brian Reid, Yamaha, 97.76mph/157.33kph
250cc:	Brian Reid, Yamaha, 98.69mph/158.83kph
TT Formula 1:	Joey Dunlop, Honda, 107.38mph/172.81kph
TT Formula 2:	Phil Mellor, Yamaha, 110.16mph/177.29kph

1984

500cc:	Joey Dunlop, Honda, 118.17mph/190.18kph
350cc:	Trevor Steele, Yamaha, 106.37mph/171.19kph
250cc:	Joey Dunlop, Honda, 110.55mph/177.91kph
TT Formula 1:	Joey Dunlop, Honda, 114.28mph/183.92kph
TT Formula 2:	John Weeden, Yamaha, 101.03mph/162.59kph

1985

500cc:	Joey Dunlop, Honda, 116.14mph/186.91kph
350cc:	Steve Cull, Yamaha, 111.43mph/179.33kph
250cc:	Joey Dunlop, Honda, 111.96mph/180.18kph
TT Formula 1:	Joey Dunlop, Honda, 114.45mph/184.19kph
TT Formula 2:	Brian Reid, Yamaha, 111.19mph/178.94kph

1986

1000cc:	Joey Dunlop, Honda, 118.29mph/190.37kph
350cc:	Eddie Laycock, Yamaha, 111.51mph/179.46kph
250cc:	Steve Cull, Honda, 102.60mph/165.12kph
Superstock:	Phil Mellor, Suzuki, 111.60mph/179.60kph
TT Formula 1:	Neil Robinson, Suzuki, 110.42mph/177.70kph
TT Formula 2:	Eddie Laycock, Yamaha, 105.27mph/169.42kph

1987

350cc: Brian Reid, Yamaha, 108.28mph/174.26kph
*Only one race completed. Meeting cancelled following
fatal accident to Klaus Klein (FRG) at end of the first lap
of the Formula 1 race*

1988

1000cc: Eddie Laycock, Honda,
                 120.14mph/193.35kph
350cc (Race A): Brian Reid, Yamaha, 109.09mph/175.56kph
350cc (Race B): Joey Dunlop, Honda, 112.31mph/180.75kph
Superstock: Nick Jefferies, Honda, 101.66mph/163.61kph
TT Formula 1:   Carl Fogarty, Honda, 111.01mph/178.65kph

1989

1000cc: Carl Fogarty, Honda, 120.50mph/193.93kph

Supersport 600: Brian Reid, Yamaha, 112.25mph/180.65kph
Supersport 400: Eddie Laycock, Suzuki,
                108.95mph/175.34kph
350cc: Eddie Laycock, Yamaha,
                106.73mph/171.77kph
TT Formula 1:   Steve Hislop, Honda, 118.02mph/189.93kph
Sidecar: Derek Brindley, Sabre, 98.81mph/159.02kph

1990

1000cc: Steve Hislop, Honda, 121.46mph/195.47kph
Supersport 600: Steve Cull, Yamaha, 113.43mph/182.55kph
350cc: Brian Reid, Yamaha, 116.03mph/186.73kph
125cc: Robert Dunlop, Honda,
                104.78mph/168.63kph
TT Formula 1:   Joey Dunlop, Honda, 120.87mph/194.52kph

*Sidecar racing returned to the Ulster Grand Prix after an absence of 13 years in 1969 and the race was won by
Germany's Klaus Enders and passenger Rolf Engelhard. They repeated their success the following year*

MOST WINS

14 Joey Dunlop
 7 Stanley Woods, Giacomo
    Agostini, Mike Hailwood, Ray
    McCullough, Brian Reid

6 John Williams, John Surtees
5 Wal Handley, Maurice Cann, Tony
   Rutter, Tom Herron, Ron Haslam,
   Eddie Laycock, Carlo Ubbiali

EUROPEAN CHAMPIONSHIPS

The first European Road Racing Championships were introduced by the FICM in 1938. Champions were declared in each of three classes; 500, 350 and 250cc, after a series of eight races, and the rider gaining the most aggregate points from the three classes was the outright champion. The series was held over seven rounds the following year but then the war intervened.

The FICM abandoned the series after the war, although individual Grand Prix racing, in its pre-war form, resumed in 1947, and two years later the FIM launched its World Championships. The European Championships were revived in 1981.

George Meier, the first overseas rider to win the Senior TT, was the inaugural 500cc European Road Race champion

CHAMPIONS

1938
500cc: Georg Meier (Ger), BMW
350cc: Ted Mellors (UK), Velocette
250cc: Ewald Kluge (Ger), DKW
Outright champion: Ewald Kluge (Ger)
1939
500cc: Dorini Serafini (Ita), Gilera
350cc: Hermann Fleischmann (Ger), DKW
250cc: Ewald Kluge (Ger), DKW
Outright champion: Ewald Kluge (Ger)
1939–80 *Not held*
1981
500cc: Leandro Becheroni (Ita), Suzuki
250cc: Herbert Hauf (FRG), Yamaha
125cc: Pier Luigi Aldrovandi (Ita), MBA
 50cc: Giuseppe Ascareggi (Ita), Minarelli
Sidecar: John Barker (UK), Yamaha
1982
500cc: Fabio Biliotti (Ita), Suzuki
250cc: Reinhold Roth (FRG), Yamaha
125cc: Stefano Carracchi (Ita), MBA
 50cc: Zdravko Matulja (Yug), Tomos
Sidecar: Mick Barton (UK), Yamaha

1983
500cc: Peter Skold (Swe), Suzuki
250cc: Carlos Cardus (Spa), Rotax
125cc: Willi Hupperich (FRG), MBA
 80cc: Hubert Abold (FRG), Zündapp
Sidecar: Keith Cousins (UK), Yamaha
1984
500cc: Eero Hyvärinen (Fin), Suzuki
250cc: Gary Noel (UK), Exactweld
125cc: Norbert Peschke (FRG), MBA
 80cc: Richard Bay (FRG), Casal
Sidecar: Hans-Rudolf Christinat (Swi), Yamaha
1985
500cc: Marco Gentile (Swi), Yamaha
250cc: Massimo Matteoni (Ita), Honda
125cc: Pier Francesco Chili (Ita), MBA
 80cc: Gunter Schirnhöfer (FRG), Krauser
Sidecar: Frank Wrathall (UK), Yamaha
1986
500cc: Massimo Messere (Ita), Honda
250cc: Hans Lindner (Aut), Rotax
125cc: Claudio Nacciotti (Ita), MBA
 80cc: Bruno Casanova (Ita), Unimoto
Sidecar: Bernd Scherer (FRG), Yamaha

1987
500cc: Manfred Fischer (FRG), Honda
250cc: Javier Cardelus (Spa), Cobas
125cc: Adi Stadler (FRG), MBA
 80cc: Julian Miralles (Spa), Derbi
Sidecar: Jean-Louis Millet (Fra), Yamaha
1988
500cc: Alberto Rota (Ita), Honda
250cc: Fausto Ricci (Ita), Aprilia
125cc: Emillio Cuppini (Ita), Garelli
 80cc: Bogdan Nikolov (Bul), Krauser
Sidecar: Toni Wyssen (Swi), Yamaha
1989
500cc: Peter Linden (Swe), Honda
250cc: Andrea Borgonova (Ita), Aprilia
125cc: Gabriele Debbia (Ita), Aprilia
 80cc: Jaime Mariano (Spa), Casal
Sidecar: Ralph Bonhorst (FRG), LCR
1990
Supersport 600: Howard Selby (UK), Yamaha
Superbike: Richard Arnaiz (Ita), Honda
250cc: Leon Van der Heyden (Hol), Aprilia
125cc: Javier Debon (Spa), JJ Cobas
Sidecar: Darren Dixon (UK), Yamaha

BRITISH CHAMPIONSHIPS

The first British Road Racing Championships were held in 1959 when the results of one meeting constituted the 'championship'. It did not become a season-long championship until 1966 when it replaced the ACU Road Racing Stars championships, which had been launched in 1958.

The ACU Stars returned in 1973 when the British Championship was for solo and sidecar categories only. It has subsequently reverted to being a multi-class championship under different guises, and with a variety of different sponsors, in the 1980s.

WINNERS

(All from the British Isles unless otherwise stated. Based on result of one meeting only up to 1965.)

1959

500cc:	Mike Hailwood, Norton
350cc:	Alastair King, AJS
250cc:	Mike Hailwood, Mondial
125cc:	Mike Hailwood, Ducati
Sidecar:	Florian Camathias (Swi), BMW

1960

500cc:	Bob McIntyre, Norton
350cc:	Bob McIntyre, AJS
250cc:	Mike Hailwood, Ducati
125cc:	Mike Hailwood, Ducati
Sidecar:	Florian Camathias (Swi), BMW

The start of the Mallory Park leg of the 1973 British Solo Championship. Number 1 is Barry Sheene with his 500cc Suzuki

1961
500cc: Derek Minter, Norton
350cc: John Hartle, Norton
250cc: Mike Hailwood, Honda
125cc: Percy Tait, Ducati
Sidecar: Pip Harris, BMW
1962
500cc: Derek Minter, Norton
350cc: Derek Minter, Norton
250cc: Derek Minter, Honda
125cc: Dan Shorey, Bultaco
50cc: Hugh Anderson (NZ), Suzuki
Sidecar: Colin Seeley, Matchless
1963
500cc: Derek Minter, Gilera
350cc: Phil Read, Norton
250cc: Tommy Robb, Honda
125cc: Hugh Anderson (NZ), Suzuki
50cc: Hugh Anderson (NZ), Suzuki
Sidecar: Colin Seeley, Matchless
1964
500cc: Derek Minter, Norton
350cc: Mike Duff (Can), AJS
250cc: Phil Read, Yamaha
125cc: Frank Perris, Suzuki
50cc: Hugh Anderson (NZ), Suzuki
Sidecar: Chris Vincent, BSA
1965
500cc: Bill Ivy, Matchless
350cc: Dan Shorey, Norton
250cc: Mike Duff (Can), Yamaha
125cc: Dave Simmonds, Tohatsu
50cc: Chris Vincent, Suzuki
Sidecar: Chris Vincent, BMW
1966
500cc: John Cooper, Norton
350cc: John Cooper, Norton
250cc: Peter Inchley, Villiers
125cc: Rod Scivyer, Honda
Sidecar: Owen Greenwood, BSA
1967
500cc: Ron Chandler, Matchless
350cc: Dave Croxford, AJS
250cc: Derek Chatterton, Yamaha
125cc: Martin Carney, Bultaco
Sidecar: Owen Greenwood, BSA
1968
500cc: Dave Croxford, Seeley
350cc: Alan Barnett, AJS
250cc: John Cooper, Yamaha
125cc: Jim Curry, Honda
Sidecar: Peter Brown, BSA
1969
500cc: Dave Croxford, Seeley
350cc: Pat Mahoney, Yamaha
250cc: Dave Browning, Yamaha
125cc: Charles Mortimer, Villa
50cc: Geoff Ashton, Garelli
Sidecar: Chris Vincent, BSA
1970
500cc: Peter Williams, Matchless
350cc: Derek Chatterton, Yamaha
250cc: Steve Machin, Yamaha
125cc: Barry Sheene, Suzuki

50cc: Frank Whiteway, Suzuki
Sidecar: Chris Vincent, BSA
1971
750cc: Percy Tait, Triumph
500cc: Percy May, Norton
350cc: Tony Rutter, Yamaha
250cc: Steve Machin, Yamaha
125cc: Barry Sheene, Suzuki
Sidecar: Chris Vincent, BSA
1972
750cc: Dave Potter, Norton
500cc: Jim Harvey, Yamaha
350cc: Mick Grant, Yamaha
250cc: Steve Machin, Yamaha
125cc: Steve Machin, Yamaha
Sidecar: Norman Hanks, BSA
1973
Solo: Dave Croxford, Norton
Sidecar: Gerry Boret, König
1974
Solo: Stan Woods, Yamaha
Sidecar: Mac Hobson, Yamaha
1975
Solo: Roger Marshall, Yamaha
Sidecar: Mac Hobson, Yamaha
1976
Solo: Steve Parrish, Yamaha
Sidecar: Dick Greasley, Yamaha
1977
Solo: Roger Marshall, Yamaha
Sidecar: Bill Hodgkins, Yamaha
1978
Solo: Steve Manship, Yamaha
Sidecar: Derek Jones, Yamaha
1979
Solo: Keith Huewen, Yamaha
Sidecar: Dick Greasley, Yamaha
1980
Solo: Steve Manship, Suzuki
Sidecar: Jock Taylor, Yamaha
1981
Solo: Bob Smith, Suzuki
Sidecar: Jock Taylor, Yamaha
1982
Solo: Roger Marshall, Suzuki
Sidecar: Bruce Ford-Dunn, Yamaha
1983
500cc: Roger Marshall, Honda
250cc: Neil Robinson, Yamaha
Sidecar: Bruce Ford-Dunn, Yamaha
1984
500cc: Wayne Gardner (Aus), Honda
250cc: Donnie McLeod, Yamaha
125cc: Robin Appleyard, MBA
80cc: Jamie Lodge, Suzuki
TT Formula 1: Wayne Gardner (Aus), Honda
TT Formula 2: Phil Mellor, Yamaha
Sidecar: Steve Abbott, Yamaha
1985
500cc: Roger Marshall, Honda
250cc: Niall Mackenzie,

Armstrong
TT Formula 1: Roger Marshall, Honda
TT Formula 2: Des Barry (NZ), Yamaha
Sidecar: Steve Webster, Yamaha
1986
1300c: Roger Burnett, Honda
TT Formula 1: Mark Phillips, Suzuki
TT Formula 2: Ray Swann, Kawasaki
250cc: Niall Mackenzie, Armstrong
125cc: Dave Lowe, MBA
1987
1300cc: Roger Marshall, Suzuki
250cc: Gary Cowan, Honda
125cc: Robin Milton, MBA
Sidecar: Steve Webster, Krauser
1988
TT Formula 1: Darren Dixon, Suzuki
125cc: Alex Bedford, Honda
Production: Jamie Whitham, Suzuki
Junior Stock: Mike Edwards, Yamaha
Senior Stock: Brian Morrison, Honda
Open Sidecar: Steve Webster, Yamaha
F2 Sidecar: Nick Hamblin, Yamaha
1989
TT Formula 1: Steve Spray, Norton
Supersport 600: Paul Brookes, Yamaha
Supersport 400: Ian McConnachie, Kawasaki
250cc: Ian McConnachie, Yamaha
125cc: Rob Orme, Honda
Production: Dean Ashton, Honda
Open Sidecar: Barry Brindley, Yamaha
F2 Sidecar: Derek Brindley, Yamaha
1990
TT Formula 1: Mark Linscott, Yamaha
Supersport 600: John Reynolds, Kawasaki
Supersport 400: John Yates, Kawasaki
250cc: Rob Orme, Yamaha
125cc: Rob Orme, Yamaha
Production: Dean Ashton, Yamaha
Open Sidecar: Rob Fisher, Suzuki
F2 Sidecar: Dave Saville, Yamaha

MOST TITLES

7 Roger Marshall
6 Mike Hailwood, Derek Minter, Chris Vincent
4 Hugh Anderson (NZ), Dave Croxford, Steve Machin

TRANSATLANTIC CHALLENGE

Inaugurated in 1971 shortly after the American Motorcyclist Association (AMA) returned to full membership of the FIM. The series was designed to formulate a common set of rules for Formula 750 racing on both sides of the Atlantic, and to do this a challenge series between riders from the United States and Great Britain was established.

The series was traditionally held over the Easter weekend at selected British circuits. The last two-nation event was in 1986, the British team being joined by Commonwealth riders the following year. In 1988, the format changed again to a four-team series involving two teams from Great Britain, one from the United States and a European team. The series came to a halt in 1988 – though there was an event of sorts the following year known as the Eurolantic Challenge, when Great Britain beat a multi-national 'Eurolantic' team – but it is being revived in 1991.

RESULTS

(Each nation's top scorer in brackets)

1971
Great Britain   183 (Ray Pickrell 76, Paul Smart 76)
United States 137 (Dick Mann 46)
1972
Great Britain   255 (Ray Pickrell 69)
United States 212 (Cal Rayborn 69)
1973
Great Britain   416 (Peter Williams 84)
United States 398 (Yvon du Hamel 84)
1974
Great Britain   416 (Barry Sheene 88)
United States 401 (Kenny Roberts 93)
1975
Great Britain   243 (Pat Mahoney 45)
United States 278 (Dave Aldana 51)
1976
Great Britain   412 (Barry Sheene 77)
United States 384 (Steve Baker 92)
1977
Great Britain   379 (Barry Sheene 79)
United States 410 (Pat Hennen 83)
1978
Great Britain   435 (Dave Potter 74)
United States 379 (Pat Hennen 92)

1979
Great Britain   352 (Barry Sheene 63)
United States 448 (Mike Baldwin 88)
1980
Great Britain   369 (Keith Heuwen 59)
United States 443 (Kenny Roberts 92)
1981
Great Britain   466 (John Newbold 72)
United States 345 (Dale Singleton 65)
1982
Great Britain   491 (Barry Sheene 95)
·United States 313 (Dave Aldana 56)
1983
Great Britain   245 (Ron Haslam 70)
United States 198 (Randy Mamola 60)
1984
Great Britain   136 (Ron Haslam 44)
United States 259 (Randy Mamola 67)
1985
Great Britain   336 (Wayne Gardner (Aus) 74)
United States 254 (Randy Mamola 78)
1986
Great Britain   314 (Roger Burnett 73)
United States 214 (Kevin Schwantz 84)

1987
Great Britain & Commonwealth 745.5 (Richard Scott (NZ) 123.5)
United States 933.5 (Kevin Schwantz 165)
1988
1. Great Britain I   586 (Roger Burnett 124)
2. United States   570 (Doug Polen 142)
3. Europe   287 (Jari Suhonen (Fin) 78)
4. Great Britain II 281 (Roger Marshall 72)

WINS

12 Great Britain/Commonwealth
 6 United States

FORMULA 750

The FIM Formula 750 Championship was the forerunner of the 750cc World Championship which existed between 1977–79.

Formula 750 became popular in Britain in the early 1970s having been introduced as a separate category in the United States in 1969. Pressure was put on the FIM to increase its upper world championship limit from 500 to 750cc, which eventually came in 1977 with the launch of the Formula 750 World Championship. Formula 750 lost its world championship status in 1979.

FIM FORMULA 750 CHAMPIONSHIP

1973
1 Barry Sheene (UK), Suzuki, 51pts
2 John Dodds (Aus), Yamaha, 47pts
3 Jack Findlay (Aus), Suzuki, 45pts

1974
1 John Dodds (Aus), Yamaha, 27pts
2 Patrick Pons (Fra), Yamaha, 22pts
3 Jack Findlay (Aus), Suzuki, 16pts

1975
1 Jack Findlay (Aus), Yamaha, 46pts
2 Barry Sheene (UK), Suzuki, 45pts
3 Patrick Pons (Fra), Yamaha, 42pts

1976
1 Victor Palomo (Spa), Yamaha, 61pts
2 Garry Nixon (USA), Kawasaki, 59pts
3 John Newbold (UK), Suzuki, 47pts

FORMULA 750 WORLD CHAMPIONSHIP

1977
1 Steve Baker (USA), Yamaha, 131pts
2 Christian Sarron (Fra), Yamaha, 55pts
3 Giacomo Agostini (Ita), Yamaha, 45pts

1978
1 Johnny Cecotto (Ven), Yamaha, 97pts
2 Kenny Roberts (USA), Yamaha, 92pts
3 Christian Sarron (Fra), Yamaha, 55pts

1979
1 Patrick Pons (Fra), Yamaha, 154pts
2 Michel Frutschi (Swi), Yamaha, 132pts
3 Johnny Cecotto (Ven), Yamaha, 126pts

SHELL OILS ACU SUPERCUP SERIES

A televised series launched in 1989, it is held over five rounds at Donington Park, Cadwell Park, Thruxton, Mallory Park and Brands Hatch.

CHAMPIONS

1989
TT Formula 1: Steve Spray, Norton
Superbike: Brian Morrison, Honda
Supersport 600: Rodney Knapp (NZ), Yamaha
250cc: Steve Patrickson, Yamaha
125cc: Steve Patrickson, Honda
Sidecar: Steve Webster, LCR Krauser

1990
TT Formula 1: Terry Rymer, Yamaha
Supersport 600: John Reynolds, Kawasaki
250cc: Steve Hislop, Honda
125cc: Ian McConnachie, Honda
Sidecar: Robert Fisher, Suzuki

MOTO-CROSS

Moto-cross, also known as Scrambling, is a specialised branch of motorcycle sport and commands the very best relationship between rider and machine. The first moto-cross race was organised in 1924 by a group of enthusiasts from Camberley, Surrey, who wanted to stage a southern version of Yorkshire's famous Scott Trial, but without the 'observed' sections of the trial. Because it did not contain these observed sections, the ACU could not grant it trials status; and after one of the 80 starters commented that it would be a 'fair old scramble', the new branch of motorcycle sport was so named. The race took place at Frimley, Surrey, and was won by Arthur Sparkes. More than half of the entrants were forced to retire due to the severity of the course, or machine failure. But this first 'scramble' was nonetheless a great success.

Before the war it was predominantly a British sport, but it became popular in post-war Europe and in 1947 France, Belgium, Holland and England each sent five-man teams to compete for the Moto-Cross des Nations, an international team competition for riders on 500cc machines.

A 250cc event was inaugurated in 1961 and this became known as the Trophée des Nations; again it was for teams. In 1981 a 125cc series, known as the Coupe des Nations, was launched. However, all three merged into one three-class competition in 1985 under the title of Moto-Cross des Nations.

The FIM organised its first individual championship in 1952, the 500cc European Championship, and in 1957 they inaugurated a 250cc class.

That same year the FIM upgraded the 500cc championship to 'world' status, eventually doing the same with the 250cc class in 1962. A 125cc World Championship event was introduced in 1975, two years after being launched as the European Championship. The only other new category to be included in the World Championship programme is for sidecars, making its debut in 1980. Each World Championship meeting is divided into two races and points are awarded in each; the aggregate points gained at the meeting count towards the championship, which normally consists of 12 rounds.

WORLD CHAMPIONSHIPS

500cc

1957 1 Bill Nilsson (Swe), AJS
2 René Baeten (Bel), FN
3 Sten Lundin (Swe), BSA
1958 1 René Baeten (Bel), FN
2 Bill Nilsson (Swe), AJS
3 Sten Lundin (Swe), Monark
1959 1 Sten Lundin (Swe), Monark
2 Bill Nilsson (Swe), Crescent
3 Dave Curtis (UK), Matchless
1960 1 Bill Nilsson (Swe), Husqvarna
2 Sten Lundin (Swe), Monark
3 Don Rickman (UK), Metisse
1961 1 Sten Lundin (Swe), Lito
2 Bill Nilsson (Swe), Husqvarna
3 Gunnar Johansson (Swe), Lito
1962 1 Rolf Tibblin (Swe), Husqvarna
2 Gunnar Johansson (Swe), Lito
3 Sten Lundin (Swe), Lito
1963 1 Rolf Tibblin (Swe), Husqvarna
2 Sten Lundin (Swe), Lito
3 Jeff Smith (UK), BSA
1964 1 Jeff Smith (UK), BSA
2 Rolf Tibblin (Swe), Husqvarna
3 Sten Lundin (Swe), Lito
1965 1 Jeff Smith (UK), BSA
2 Paul Friedrichs (GDR), CZ
3 Rolf Tibblin (Swe), Husqvarna
1966 1 Paul Friedrichs (GDR), CZ
2 Rolf Tibblin (Swe), CZ
3 Jeff Smith (UK), BSA
1967 1 Paul Friedrichs (GDR), CZ
2 Jeff Smith (UK), BSA
3 Dave Bickers (UK), CZ
1968 1 Paul Friedrichs (GDR), CZ
2 John Banks (UK), BSA
3 Ake Jonsson (Swe), Husqvarna

1969 1 Bengt Aberg (Swe), Husqvarna
2 John Banks (UK), BSA
3 Paul Friedrichs (GDR), CZ
1970 1 Bengt Aberg (Swe), Husqvarna
2 Arne King (Swe), Husqvarna
3 Ake Jonsson (Swe), Husqvarna
1971 1 Roger De Coster (Bel), Suzuki
2 Ake Jonsson (Swe), Maico
3 Adolf Weil (FRG), Maico
1972 1 Roger De Coster (Bel), Suzuki
2 Paul Friedrichs (GDR), CZ
3 Heikki Mikkola (Fin), Husqvarna
1973 1 Roger De Coster (Bel), Suzuki
2 Willy Bauer (FRG), Maico
3 Jaak Van Velthoven (Bel), Yamaha
1974 1 Heikki Mikkola (Fin), Husqvarna
2 Roger De Coster (Bel), Suzuki
3 Adolf Weil (FRG), Maico
1975 1 Roger De Coster (Bel), Suzuki
2 Heikki Mikkola (Fin), Husqvarna
3 Gerrit Wolsink (Hol), Suzuki
1976 1 Roger De Coster (Bel), Suzuki
2 Gerrit Wolsink (Hol), Suzuki
3 Adolf Weil (FRG), Maico
1977 1 Heikki Mikkola (Fin), Yamaha
2 Roger De Coster (Bel), Suzuki
3 Gerrit Wolsink (Hol), Suzuki
1978 1 Heikki Mikkola (Fin), Yamaha
2 Brad Lackey (USA), Honda
3 Roger De Coster (Bel), Suzuki
1979 1 Graham Noyce (UK), Honda
2 Gerrit Wolsink (Hol), Suzuki

Brad Lackey, the 1982 world champion, is the only American to have won the 500cc crown

3 André Malherbe (Bel), Honda
1980 1 André Malherbe (Bel), Honda
2 Brad Lackey (USA), Kawasaki
3 Håkan Carlqvist (Swe), Yamaha
1981 1 André Malherbe (Bel), Honda
2 Graham Noyce (UK), Honda
3 Håkan Carlqvist (Swe), Yamaha
1982 1 Brad Lackey (USA), Suzuki
2 André Vromans (Bel), Suzuki
3 Neil Hudson (UK), Yamaha
1983 1 Håkan Carlqvist (Swe), Yamaha
2 André Malherbe (Bel), Honda
3 Graham Noyce (UK), Honda
1984 1 André Malherbe (Bel), Honda
2 Georges Jobé (Bel), Kawasaki
3 Dave Thorpe (UK), Honda
1985 1 Dave Thorpe (UK), Honda
2 André Malherbe (Bel), Honda
3 Eric Geboers (Bel), Honda
1986 1 Dave Thorpe (UK), Honda
2 André Malherbe (Bel), Honda
3 Eric Geboers (Bel), Honda
1987 1 Georges Jobé (Bel), Honda
2 Kurt Nicoll (UK), Kawasaki
3 Kees van der Ven (Hol), KTM
1988 1 Eric Geboers (Bel), Honda
2 Kurt Nicoll (UK), Honda
3 Dave Thorpe (UK), Honda
1989 1 Dave Thorpe (UK), Honda
2 Jeff Leisk (Aus), Honda
3 Eric Geboers (Bel), Honda

1990 1 Eric Geboers (Bel), Honda
2 Kurt Nicoll (UK), KTM
3 Dirk Guekens (Bel), Honda

250cc

1962 1 Torsten Hallman (Swe), Husqvarna
2 Jeff Smith (UK), BSA
3 Arthur Lampkin (UK), BSA
1963 1 Torsten Hallman (Swe), Husqvarna
2 Vlastimil Valek (Cze), CZ
3 Igor Grigoriev (USSR), CZ
1964 1 Joël Robert (Bel), CZ
2 Torsten Hallman (Swe), Husqvarna
3 Victor Arbekov (USSR), CZ
1965 1 Victor Arbekov (USSR), CZ
2 Joël Robert (Bel), CZ
3 Dave Bickers (UK), Greeves
1966 1 Torsten Hallman (Swe), Husqvarna
2 Joël Robert (Bel), CZ
3 Petr Dobry (Cze), CZ
1967 1 Torsten Hallman (Swe), Husqvarna
2 Joël Robert (Bel), CZ
3 Olle Petersson (Swe), Husqvarna
1968 1 Joël Robert (Bel), CZ
2 Torsten Hallman (Swe), Husqvarna
3 Silvain Geboers (Bel), CZ
1969 1 Joël Robert (Bel), CZ
2 Silvain Geboers (Bel), CZ

3 Olle Petersson (Swe), Suzuki
1970 1 Joël Robert (Bel), Suzuki
2 Silvain Geboers (Bel), Suzuki
3 Roger De Coster (Bel), CZ
1971 1 Joël Robert (Bel), Suzuki
2 Håkan Andersson (Swe), Husqvarna
3 Silvain Geboers (Bel), Suzuki
1972 1 Joël Robert (Bel), Suzuki
2 Håkan Andersson (Swe), Yamaha
3 Silvain Geboers (Bel), Suzuki
1973 1 Håkan Andersson (Swe), Yamaha
2 Adolf Weil (FRG), Maico
3 Heikki Mikkola (Fin), Husqvarna
1974 1 Gennady Moisseyev (USSR), KTM
2 Jaroslav Falta (Cze), CZ
3 Harry Everts (Bel), Puch
1975 1 Harry Everts (Bel), Puch
2 Håkan Andersson (Swe), Yamaha
3 Willy Bauer (FRG), Suzuki
1976 1 Heikki Mikkola (Fin), Husqvarna
2 Gennady Moisseyev (USSR), KTM
3 Vladimir Kavinov (USSR), KTM
1977 1 Gennady Moisseyev (USSR), KTM
2 Vladimir Kavinov (USSR), KTM
3 André Malherbe (Bel), KTM
1978 1 Gennady Moisseyev (USSR), KTM
2 Torleif Hansen (Swe), Kawasaki
3 Hans Maisch (FRG), Maico
1979 1 Håkan Carlqvist (Swe), Husqvarna
2 Neil Hudson (UK), Maico
3 Vladimir Kavinov (USSR), KTM
1980 1 George Jobé (Bel), Suzuki
2 Kees van der Ven (Hol), Maico
3 Dimitar Ranguelov (Bul), Husqvarna
1981 1 Neil Hudson (UK), Yamaha
2 Georges Jobé (Bel), Suzuki
3 Kees van der Ven (Hol), KTM
1982 1 Danny la Porte (USA), Yamaha
2 Georges Jobé (Bel), Suzuki
3 Kees van der Ven (Hol), KTM
1983 1 Georges Jobé (Bel), Suzuki
2 Danny la Porte (USA), Yamaha
3 Kees van der Ven (Hol), KTM
1984 1 Heinz Kinigadner (Aut), KTM

2 Jacky Vimond (Fra), Yamaha
3 Jeremy Whatley (UK), Suzuki
1985 1 Heinz Kinigadner (Aut), KTM
2 Jacky Vimond (Fra), Yamaha
3 Gert-Jan van Doorn (Hol), Honda
1986 1 Jacky Vimond (Fra), Yamaha
2 Michèle Rinaldi (Ita), Suzuki
3 Gert-Jan van Doorn (Hol), Honda
1987 1 Eric Geboers (Bel), Honda
2 Pekka Vehkonen (Fin), Cagiva
3 Jürgen Nilsson (Swe), Honda
1988 1 John van den Berk (Hol), Yamaha
2 Pekka Vehkonen (Fin), Cagiva
3 Rodney Smith (USA), Suzuki
1989 1 Jean-Michel Bayle (Fra), Honda
2 Pekka Vehkonen (Fin), Yamaha
3 John van den Berk (Hol), Yamaha
1990 1 Alessandro Puzar (Ita), Suzuki
2 Pekka Vehkonen (Fin), Yamaha
3 John van den Berk (Hol), Suzuki

125cc

1975 1 Gaston Rahier (Bel), Suzuki
2 Gilbert De Roover (Bel), Zündapp
3 Antoin Baborawsky (Cze), CZ
1976 1 Gaston Rahier (Bel), Suzuki
2 Jiri Churavy (Cze), CZ
3 Marty Smith (USA), Honda
1977 1 Gaston Rahier (Bel), Suzuki
2 Gerard Rond (Hol), Yamaha
3 André Massant (Bel), Yamaha
1978 1 Akira Watanabe (Jap), Suzuki
2 Gaston Rahier (Bel), Suzuki
3 Gerard Rond (Hol), Yamaha
1979 1 Harry Everts (Bel), Suzuki
2 Akira Watanabe (Jap), Suzuki
3 Gaston Rahier (Bel), Yamaha
1980 1 Harry Everts (Bel), Suzuki
2 Michèle Rinaldi (Ita), Gilera
3 Eric Geboers (Bel), Suzuki
1981 1 Harry Everts (Bel), Suzuki
2 Eric Geboers (Bel), Suzuki
3 Michèle Rinaldi (Ita), Gilera
1982 1 Eric Geboers (Bel), Suzuki
2 Corrado Maddii (Ita), Gilera
3 Michèle Rinaldi (Ita), Gilera
1983 1 Eric Geboers (Bel), Suzuki
2 Michèle Rinaldi (Ita), Suzuki
3 Jim Gibson (USA), Yamaha
1984 1 Michèle Rinaldi (Ita), Suzuki
2 Corrado Maddii (Ita), Cagiva
3 Kees van der Ven (Hol), KTM

1985 1 Pekka Vehkonen (Fin), Cagiva
2 Dave Strijbos (Hol), Honda
3 Corrado Maddii (Ita), Cagiva
1986 1 Dave Strijbos (Hol), Cagiva
2 John ven den Berk (Hol), Yamaha
3 Massimo Contini (Ita), Cagiva
1987 1 John van den Berk (Hol), Yamaha
2 Dave Strijbos (Hol), Cagiva
3 Jean Michel Bayle (Fra), Honda
1988 1 Jean-Michel Bayle (Fra), Honda
2 Dave Strijbos (Hol), Honda
3 Pedro Tragter (Hol), Honda
1989 1 Trampas Parker (USA), KTM
2 Alessandro Puzar (Ita), Suzuki
3 Mike Healey (Fra), KTM
1990 1 Donny Schmit (USA), Suzuki
2 Bobby Moore (FRG), KTM
3 Stefan Everts (Bel), Suzuki

SIDECAR

1980 1 Reinhardt Böhler (FRG), Yamaha
2 Hans Bächtold (Swi), Yamaha
3 Bruno Schneider (Aut), Hedlund/EML
1981 1 Tom van Heugten (Hol), Yamaha
2 Josef Brockhausen (FRG), Yamaha
3 Jan Bakens (Hol), Yamaha
1982 1 Erik Bollhalder (Swi), Yamaha
2 Josef Brockhausen (FRG), Yamaha

3 Tom van Heugten (Hol), Yamaha
1983 1 Erik Bollhalder (Swi), Yamaha
2 Josef Brockhausen (FRG), Yamaha
3 Reinhardt Böhler (FRG), Yamaha
1984 1 Hans Bächtold (Swi), EML
2 Tom van Heugten (Hol), Folan
3 Reinhardt Böhler (FRG), Wasp
1985 1 Hans Bachtöld (Swi), EML
2 August Müller (Hol), Honda
3 Tom van Heugten (Hol), Folan
1986 1 Hans Bachtöld (Swi), EML
2 August Müller (Hol), Honda
3 Tom van Heugten (Hol), Folan
1987 1 Hans Bachtöld (Swi), EML
2 August Müller (Hol), Honda
3 Rijn van Gastelk (Hol), KTM
1988 1 Christoph Hüssler (Lie), KTM
2 Walter Netterscheid (FRG), Maico
3 Andréas Fuhrer (Swi), Kawasaki
1989 1 Christoph Hüssler (Lie), VMC-KTM
2 Benny Janssen (Hol), EML-Honda
3 Eimbert Timmermans (Hol), Kawasaki
1990 1 Benny Janssen (Hol), EML-Honda
2 Michael Garhammer (FRG), EML-Jumbo
3 Andréas Fuhrer (Swi), VMC-Kawasaki

Joël Robert (nearest to camera) in action during the 1965 Brands Hatch 'Scramble of the Year'

MOST WORLD TITLES

500cc
5 Roger De Coster
3 Paul Friedrichs, Heikki Mikkola,
  André Malherbe, Dave Thorpe
250cc
6 Joël Robert
4 Torsten Hallman
3 Gennady Moisseyev

125cc
3 Harry Everts, Gaston Rahier
2 Eric Geboers
Sidecar
4 Hans Bachtöld
2 Erik Bollhalder, Christoph Hüssler

ALL CLASSES

6 Joël Robert (all 250)
5 Roger De Coster (all 500), Eric
  Geboers (2 x 500, 1 x 250, 2 x 125)
4 Heikki Mikkola (3 x 500, 1 x 250),
  Torsten Hallman (all 250), Harry
  Everts (1 x 250, 3 x 125)

EUROPEAN CHAMPIONSHIPS

500cc
1952 Victor Leloup (Bel) FN
1953 Auguste Mingels (Bel) FN
1954 Auguste Mingels (Bel) FN
1955 John Draper (UK) BSA
1956 Les Archer (UK) Norton
*Became World Championship in
1957*

250cc
1957 Fritz Betzelbacher (FRG) Maico
1958 Jaromir Cizec (Cze) CZ
1959 Rolf Tibblin (Swe) Husqvarna
1960 Dave Bickers (UK) Greeves
1961 Dave Bickers (UK) Greeves
*Became World Championship in
1962*

125cc
1973 André Malherbe (Bel) Zündapp
1974 André Malherbe (Bel) Zündapp
*Became World Championship in
1975*

MOTO-CROSS DES NATIONS

CHAMPIONS

(Names in brackets are the highest finishers, who counted towards the championship. Over the years the number has varied from 2–4)

1947 GREAT BRITAIN (Bill Nicholson, Bob Ray, Fred Rist)
1948 BELGIUM (Marcel Cox, Nic Jansen, André Milhoux)
1949 GREAT BRITAIN (Harold Lines, Bob Manns, Ray Scovell)
1950 GREAT BRITAIN (John Draper, Basil Hall, Harold Lines)
1951 BELGIUM (Nic Jansen, Victor Leloup, Marcel Meunier)
1952 GREAT BRITAIN (Phil Nex, Brian Stonebridge, Geoff Ward)
1953 GREAT BRITAIN (Les Archer, John Draper, Geoff Ward)
1954 GREAT BRITAIN (Dave Curtis, Brian Stonebridge, Geoff Ward)
1955 SWEDEN (Lars Gustafsson, Sten Lundin, Bill Nilsson)
1956 GREAT BRITAIN (John Draper, Jeff Smith, Geoff Ward)
1957 GREAT BRITAIN (Dave Curtis, Brian Martin, Jeff Smith)
1958 SWEDEN (Lars Gustafsson, Ove Lundell, Bill Nilsson)
1959 GREAT BRITAIN (John Draper, Don Rickman, Jeff Smith)
1960 GREAT BRITAIN (Dave Curtis, Don Rickman, Jeff Smith)
1961 SWEDEN (Ove Lundell, Bill Nilsson, Rolf Tibblin)
1962 SWEDEN (Gunnar Johansson, Bill Nilsson, Rolf Tibblin, Ove Lundell)
1963 GREAT BRITAIN (Arthur Lampkin, Derek Rickman, Don Rickman, Jeff Smith)
1964 GREAT BRITAIN (Derek Rickman, Don Rickman, Jeff Smith)
1965 GREAT BRITAIN (Arthur Lampkin, Don Rickman, Jeff Smith)
1966 GREAT BRITAIN (Dave Bickers, Arthur Lampkin, Don Rickman)
1967 GREAT BRITAIN (Dave Bickers, Vic Eastwood, Jeff Smith)
1968 SOVIET UNION (Evgeniy Petushkov, Vladimir Pogrebniak, Leonid Shinkarenko, Arnis Angers)
1969 BELGIUM (Roger De Coster, Silvain Geboers, Joël Robert, Jef Teuwissen)
1970 SWEDEN (Bengt Aberg, Jan Johansson, Christer Hammargren)
1971 SWEDEN (Bengt Aberg, Olle Petersson, Ake Jonsson, Christer Hammargren, Arne Kring)
1972 BELGIUM (Roger De Coster, Joël Robert, Jaak van Velthoven, René van de Vorst)
1973 BELGIUM (Roger De Coster, Silvain Geboers, Jaak van Velthoven)
1974 SWEDEN (Bengt Aberg, Håkan Andersson, Ake Jonsson, Arne Kring)

MOTO-CROSS

1975 CZECHOSLOVAKIA (Antonin Barborovsky, Jiri Churavy, Miroslav Novacek, Zdenek Velky)
1976 BELGIUM (Roger De Coster, Harry Everts, Gaston Rahier, Jaak van Velthoven)
1977 BELGIUM (Roger De Coster, André Malherbe, Jean Paul Mingels, Jaak van Velthoven)
1978 SOVIET UNION (Vladimir Kavinov, Valeriy Khudiakov, Valeriy Korneyev, Gennady Moisseyev)
1979 BELGIUM (Roger De Coster, Harry Everts, André Malherbe, Yvan van der Broeck)
1980 BELGIUM (Georges Jobé, André Malherbe, Yvan van der Broeck, André Vromans)
1981 UNITED STATES (Donnie Hansen, Danny la Porte, Johnny O'Mara, Chuck Sun)
1982 UNITED STATES (David Bailey, Danny Chandler, Jim Gibson, Johnny O'Mara)
1983 UNITED STATES (David Bailey, Mark Barnett, Broc Glover, Jeff Ward)
1984 UNITED STATES (David Bailey, Johnny O'Mara, Rick Johnson, Jeff Ward)
1985 UNITED STATES (David Bailey, Ron Lechien, Jeff Ward)
1986 UNITED STATES (David Bailey, Rick Johnson, Johnny O'Mara)
1987 UNITED STATES (Bob Hannah, Rick Johnson, Jeff Ward)
1988 UNITED STATES (Rick Johnson, Ron Lechien, Jeff Ward)
1989 UNITED STATES (Mike Kiedrowski, Jeff Stanton, Jeff Ward)
1990 UNITED STATES (Damon Bradshaw, Jeff Stanton, Jeff Ward)

TROPHÉE DES NATIONS

1961 GREAT BRITAIN (Dave Bickers, Arthur Lampkin, Jeff Smith)
1962 GREAT BRITAIN (Dave Bickers, Arthur Lampkin, Jeff Smith)
1963 SWEDEN (Lars Forsberg, Torsten Hallman, Cenneth Loof)
1964 SWEDEN (Torsten Hallman, Ake Jonsson, Olle Petersson)
1965 *No result. Due to adverse conditions, meeting cancelled after first leg won by the British quartet of Alan Clough, Dave Bickers, Arthur Lampkin, and Geoff Smith*
1966 SWEDEN (Torsten Hallman, Olle Petersson, Ake Tornblom)
1967 SWEDEN (Steffan Eneqvist, Torsten Hallman, Olle Petersson, Ake Jonsson)
1968 SWEDEN (Bengt Aberg, Bengt-Arne Bonn, Christer Hammargren)
1969 BELGIUM (Roger De Coster, Silvain Geboers, Joël Robert)
1970 BELGIUM (Roger De Coster, Silvain Geboers, Joël Robert)
1971 BELGIUM (Roger De Coster, Silvain Geboers, Jaak van Velthoven)
1972 BELGIUM (Roger De Coster, Silvain Geboers, Jaak van Velthoven)
1973 BELGIUM (Roger De Coster, Silvain Geboers, Jaak van Velthoven)
1974 BELGIUM (Roger De Coster, Gaston Rahier, Harry Everts, Jaak van Velthoven)
1975 BELGIUM (Roger De Coster, Gaston Rahier, Harry Everts, Jaak van Velthoven)
1976 BELGIUM (Roger De Coster, Harry Everts, Gaston Rahier, Jaak van Velthoven)
1977 BELGIUM (Roger De Coster, Harry Everts, André Malherbe, Jaak van Velthoven)
1978 BELGIUM (Roger De Coster, Harry Everts, Gaston Rahier, Jaak van Velthoven)
1979 SOVIET UNION (Vladimir Kavinov, Valeriy Khudiakov, Valeriy Korneyev, Gennady Moisseyev)
1980 BELGIUM ((Harry Everts, Georges Jobé, André Malherbe, André Vromans)
1981 UNITED STATES (Donnie Hansen, Danny la Porte, Johnny O'Mara, Chuck Sun)
1982 UNITED STATES (David Bailey, Danny Chandler, Jim Gibson, Johnny O'Mara)
1983 UNITED STATES (David Bailey, Mark Barnett, Broc Glover, Jeff Ward)
1984 UNITED STATES (Broc Glover, Rick Johnson, Johnny O'Mara, Jeff Ward)
Merged with the Moto-Cross des Nations in 1985

COUPE DES NATIONS

1981 ITALY (Michèle Rinaldi, Corrado Maddii, M Miele, Alberto Barozzi)
1982 ITALY (Michèle Rinaldi, Corrado Maddii, Giuseppe Andreani, M Magarotto)
1983 BELGIUM (Eric Geboers, Marc Velkeneers, Thierry Godfroid, J Blancquert)
1984 HOLLAND (Kees van der Ven, John van den Berk, Jan Postema, John Hensen)
Merged with the Moto-Cross des Nations in 1985

MOST TITLES

Moto-Cross des Nations	Trophée des Nations
15 Great Britain	11 Belgium
10 United States	5 Sweden
9 Belgium	4 United States
7 Sweden	2 Great Britain
2 Soviet Union	1 Soviet Union
1 Czechoslovakia	
	Coupe des Nations
	2 Italy

MOST COMBINED TITLES

21 Belgium
17 Great Britain
14 United States
12 Sweden
3 Soviet Union
2 Italy
1 Czechoslovakia, Holland

TRIALS & ENDURO

Originally held to test the reliability of a machine over demanding terrain, the trial is one of the oldest forms of motor sport. As machines became more reliable, it was the ability of the rider to master his machine under such conditions that came to the fore, and the skill of remaining on the bike without touching the floor became one of the major features of the sport. Severe 'observed points' are set aside and special emphasis is placed on these by the judges. An emphasis on time also became a feature of trials – riders are given a certain amount of time to reach pre-determined check points.

The most famous of all is the Scottish Six Day Trial, which was first held in 1909 and is based around the Fort William area. However, one of the toughest is the Scott Trial, set on the North Yorkshire Moors and originally a closed event for employees of the Scott factory at Saltaire, West Yorkshire. It became an open event in 1920.

Enduro riding is a contest between man, machine, the elements, and time only. Observed points do not form a part of Enduro riding but penalties are incurred for failing to reach pre-determined check-in points within a certain time limit.

One of the leading events in the Enduro calendar is the International Six Days Enduro, until 1984 the International Six Day Trial. A team competition, it was first held in 1913 and based around the Carlisle area of England. It is now staged in a different country each year. Up to 1984, the leading events were the Premier Trophy, for six-man teams, and the Silver Vase, for four-man teams. However, the Premier Trophy became the World Trophy in 1985 (known as the Senior event); and the Vase became the Junior Trophy (known as the Junior event), contested by four-man teams of riders under the age of 23.

The individual World Trials Championship was launched in 1975, with 14 rounds in different countries making up the championship. A team championship, known as the Trial des Nations, was introduced in 1984. Teams originally competed for the FIM Cup, but in 1987 the event was elevated to world championship status.

WORLD TRIALS CHAMPIONSHIP

INDIVIDUAL

1975
1 Martin Lampkin (UK), Bultaco, 101(131)pts
2 Yrjö Vesterinen (Fin), Bultaco, 100(142)pts
3 Malcolm Rathmell (UK), Montesa, 99(134)pts
Constructors' champions: Bultaco
(Best 8 rounds only counted)

1976
1 Yrjö Vesterinen (Fin), Bultaco, 93(124)pts
2 Malcolm Rathmell (UK), Montesa, 87(112)pts
3 Martin Lampkin (UK), Bultaco, 85(110)pts
Constructors' champions: Bultaco
(Best 8 rounds only counted)

1977
1 Yrjö Vesterinen (Fin), Bultaco, 107pts
2 Ulf Karlsson (Swe), Montesa, 101pts
3 Malcolm Rathmell (UK), Montesa, 100pts
Constructors' champions: Bultaco

1978
1 Yrjö Vesterinen (Fin), Bultaco, 128pts
2 Martin Lampkin (UK), Bultaco, 126pts
3 Bernie Schreiber (USA), Bultaco, 125pts

Constructors' champions: Bultaco
1979
1 Bernie Schreiber (USA), Bultaco, 114pts
2 Yrjö Vesterinen (Fin), Bultaco, 105pts
3 Ulf Karlsson (Swe), Montesa, 92pts
Constructors' champions: Bultaco

1980
1 Ulf Karlsson (Swe), Montesa, 121pts
2 Bernie Schreiber (USA), Bultaco, 111pts
3 Yrjö Vesterinen (Fin), Montesa, 94pts
Constructors' champions: Montesa

1981
1 Gilles Burgat (Fra), SWM, 122pts
2 Ulf Karlsson (Swe), Montesa, 87pts
3 Yrjö Vesterinen (Fin), Montesa, 86pts
Constructors' champions: Montesa

1982
1 Eddy Lejeune (Bel), Honda, 162pts
2 Bernie Schreiber (USA), SWM, 129pts
3 Gilles Burgat (Fra), SWM, 126pts
Constructors' champions: Honda

1983
1 Eddy Lejeune (Bel), Honda, 156pts
2 Bernie Schreiber (USA), SWM, 123pts
3 Thierry Michaud (Fra), SWM, 95pts
Constructors' champions: Honda

1984
1 Eddy Lejeune (Bel), Honda, 214pts
2 Thierry Michaud (Fra), Fantic, 212pts
3 Bernie Schreiber (USA), SWM, 152pts
Constructors' champions: Honda
1985
1 Thierry Michaud (Fra), Fantic, 231pts
2 Eddy Lejeune (Bel), Honda, 195pts
3 Steve Saunders (UK), Honda, 185pts
Constructors' champions: No title awarded
1986
1 Thierry Michaud (Fra), Fantic, 197pts
2 Steve Saunders (UK), Honda, 187pts
3 Eddy Lejeune (Bel), Honda, 183pts
Constructors' champions: Honda
1987
1 Jordi Tarres (Spa), Beta, 202pts
2 Diego Bosis (Ita), Aprilia, 170pts
3 Thierry Michaud (Fra), Fantic, 168pts
Constructors' champions: No title awarded
1988
1 Thierry Michaud (Fra), Fantic, 202pts
2 Jordi Tarres (Spa), Beta, 197pts
3 Donato Miglio (Ita), Fantic, 169pts
Constructors' champions: Fantic
1989
1 Jordi Tarres (Spa), Beta, 223pts
2 Thierry Michaud (Fra), Fantic, 193pts
3 Diego Bosis (Ita), Aprilla, 178pts
Constructors' champions: Fantic
1990
1 Jordi Tarres (Spa), Beta, 224pts
2 Diego Bosis (Ita), Aprilia, 195pts
3 Donato Miglio (Ita), Fantic, 180pts
Constructors' champions: No title awarded

MOST TITLES

Riders
3 Yrjö Vesterinen, Eddy Lejeune, Thierry Michaud, Jordi Tarres

Constructors
5 Bultaco
4 Honda
3 Beta
2 Montesa, Fantic

TEAM

(1984–86 FIM Cup; 1987–90 Trial des Nations)
1984 FRANCE (Philippe Berlatier, Gilles Burgat, Thierry Michaud, Fred Michaud)
1985 FRANCE (Philippe Berlatier, Gilles Burgat, Thierry Michaud, Pascal Couturier)
1986 FRANCE (Philippe Berlatier, Gilles Burgat, Thierry Michaud, Pascal Couturier)
1987 ITALY (Diego Bosis, Renato Chiaberto, Donato Miglio, Carlo Franco)
1988 FRANCE (Philippe Berlatier, Thierry Girard, Thierry Michaud, Pascal Couturier)
1989 SPAIN (Jordi Tarres, Amos Bilbao, Andreu Codina)
1990 FRANCE (Thierry Girard, Bruno Camozzi, Philippe Berlatier)

INTERNATIONAL SIX DAY ENDURO

SENIOR EVENT (6-man teams)

(1913–84 Premier Trophy; 1985 World Trophy)
1913 Great Britain
1920 Switzerland
1921 Switzerland
1922 Sweden
1923 Sweden/Great Britain
1924 Great Britain
1925 Great Britain
1926 Great Britain
1927 Great Britain
1928 Great Britain
1929 Great Britain
1930 Italy
1931 Italy
1932 Great Britain
1933 Germany
1934 Germany
1935 Germany
1936 Great Britain
1937 Great Britain
1938 Great Britain
1939 *Results not approved by FICM*
1940–46 *Not held*
1947 Czechoslovakia
1948 Great Britain
1949 Great Britain
1950 Great Britain
1951 Great Britain
1952 Czechoslovakia
1953 Great Britain
1954 Czechoslovakia
1955 West Germany
1956 Czechoslovakia
1957 West Germany
1958 Czechoslovakia
1959 Czechoslovakia
1960 Austria
1961 West Germany
1962 Czechoslovakia
1963 East Germany
1964 East Germany
1965 East Germany
1966 East Germany
1967 East Germany
1968 West Germany
1969 East Germany
1970 Czechoslovakia
1971 Czechoslovakia
1972 Czechoslovakia
1973 Czechoslovakia
1974 Czechoslovakia
1975 West Germany
1976 West Germany
1977 Czechoslovakia
1978 Czechoslovakia
1979 Italy
1980 Italy
1981 Italy
1982 Czechoslovakia
1983 Sweden
1984 Holland
1985 Sweden
1986 Italy
1987 East Germany
1988 France
1989 Italy
1990 Sweden

Top right *One of Britain's best known and most successful trials riders, Arthur Lampkin, seen here in action on his 249cc BSA in 1965*

1952 Czechoslovakia
1953 Czechoslovakia
1954 Holland
1955 Czechoslovakia
1956 Holland
1957 Czechoslovakia
1958 Czechoslovakia
1959 Czechoslovakia
1960 Italy
1961 Czechoslovakia
1962 West Germany
1963 Italy
1964 East Germany
1965 East Germany
1966 West Germany
1967 Czechoslovakia
1968 Italy
1969 West Germany
1970 Czechoslovakia
1971 Czechoslovakia
1972 Czechoslovakia
1973 United States
1974 Czechoslovakia
1975 Italy
1976 Czechoslovakia
1977 Czechoslovakia
1978 Italy
1979 Czechoslovakia
1980 West Germany
1981 Italy
1982 East Germany
1983 Sweden
1984 Holland
Became the Junior Trophy in 1985

JUNIOR TROPHY
(4-man teams, Under-23)

1985 East Germany
1986 Italy
1987 East Germany
1988 Italy
1989 Finland
1990 Sweden

SILVER VASE (4-man teams)

1924 Norway
1925 Great Britain
1926 Great Britain
1927 Great Britain
1928 Great Britain
1929 Great Britain
1930 *Not held*
1931 Holland
1932 Great Britain
1933 Great Britain
1934 Great Britain
1935 Germany
1936 Great Britain
1937 Holland
1938 Germany
1939 *Results not approved by FICM*
1940–46 *Not held*
1947 Czechoslovakia
1948 Great Britain
1949 Czechoslovakia
1950 Great Britain
1951 Holland

SCOTTISH
SIX DAY TRIAL

The Edinburgh Motor Cycle Club was formed in 1908 following the amalgamation of smaller clubs in the area. The new club's first secretary was Campbell McGregor, and in 1909 he proposed plans for a five-day trial to be held over large areas of the Scottish Highlands. Such was the popularity of the first event that it became the now famous Six Day Trial in 1910, although there does remain some doubts as to whether it was held over five or six days in both 1910 and 1911.

Prior to 1932, when for the first time an award was made for the best individual performance, all riders who completed the event within a predetermined number of penalty points received either a gold or silver medal. In the first trial in 1909, R H Salveson and S J K Thomson did not lose any points and each received gold medals.

A magnificent picture capturing the 'trials' and tribulations of the Scottish Six-Day Trial!

1971 Mick Andrews, Ossa
1972 Mick Andrews, Ossa
1973 Malcolm Rathmell, Bultaco
1974 Mick Andrews, Yamaha
1975 Mick Andrews, Yamaha
1976 Martin Lampkin, Bultaco
1977 Martin Lampkin, Bultaco
1978 Martin Lampkin, Bultaco
1979 Malcolm Rathmell, Montesa
1980 Yrjö Vesterinen (Fin), Montesa
1981 Gilles Burgat (Fra), SWM
1982 Bernie Schreiber (USA), SWM
1983 Toni Gorgot (Spa), Montesa
1984 Thierry Michaud (Fra), Fantic
1985 Thierry Michaud (Fra), Fantic
1986 Thierry Michaud (Fra), Fantic
1987 Jordi Tarres (Spa), Beta
1988 Steve Saunders, Fantic
1989 Steve Saunders, Fantic
1990 Steve Saunders, Beta

Sidecar
1932 Harold Flook, Norton
1933 Ted Morris, Baughan
1934 Harold Flook, BSA
1935 Alex Calder, Triumph
1936 Harold Flook, BSA
1937 Harold Flook, Norton
1938 Stuart Waycott, Velocette
1939 Frank Whittle, Panther
1940–46 *Not held*
1947 Harold Taylor, Ariel
1948 Harold Tozer, BSA
1949 *Not held*
1950 Harold Tozer, BSA
1951–57 *Not held*
1958 Jack Oliver, BSA
1959 Peter Roydhouse, Norton
1960 Sam Seston, BSA
Sidecar event discontinued

Jacky Ickx (Bel), six times the winner of the Le Mans 24-Hour motorcar race, competed in the 1963 Scottish Six Day Trial

WINNERS (SINCE 1932)

(All from the United Kingdom unless otherwise stated)
Solo
1932 Bob MacGregor, Rudge
1933 Len Heath, Ariel
1934 Jack Williams, Norton
1935 Bob MacGregor, Rudge
1936 Billy Tiffen (Jnr), Velocette
1937 Jack Williams, Norton
1938 Fred Povey, Ariel
1939 Allan Jefferies, Triumph
1940–46 *Not held*
1947 Hugh Viney, AJS
1948 Hugh Viney, AJS
1949 Hugh Viney, AJS
1950 Artie Ratcliffe, Matchless
1951 John Draper, BSA

1952 John Brittain, Royal Enfield
1953 Hugh Viney, AJS
1954 Artie Ratcliffe, Matchless
1955 Jeff Smith, BSA
1956 Gordon Jackson, AJS
1957 John Brittain, Royal Enfield
1958 Gordon Jackson, AJS
1959 Roy Peplow, Triumph
1960 Gordon Jackson, AJS
1961 Gordon Jackson, AJS
1962 Sammy Miller, Ariel
1963 Arthur Lampkin, BSA
1964 Sammy Miller, Ariel
1965 Sammy Miller, Bultaco
1966 Arthur Lampkin, BSA
1967 Sammy Miller, Bultaco
1968 Sammy Miller, Bultaco
1969 Bill Wilkinson, Greeves
1970 Mick Andrews, Ossa

MOST WINS (SOLO)

5 Sammy Miller, Mick Andrews
4 Hugh Viney, Gordon Jackson
3 Martin Lampkin, Thierry Michaud, Steve Saunders

MOST WINS (SIDECAR)

4 Harold Flook
2 Harold Tozer

GIACOMO AGOSTINI

In terms of achievement, Italy's Giacomo Agostini stands head and shoulders above all other Grand Prix riders. His total of 15 world titles and 122 Grand Prix wins puts him well clear of his rivals and his 10 Isle of Man TT wins is a figure bettered only by Mike Hailwood and Joey Dunlop.

Born in 1943 at Lovere, near Bergamo in northern Italy, Agostini started road racing at the age of 20 on a 175cc Morini after two years hill-climbing. As a Morini works rider he captured his first major title in 1964 when he beat Tarquinio Provini for the Italian 250cc crown, as the Italian fans witnessed the birth of a new idol.

Count Domenico Agusta, head of the MV Agusta empire, was quick to sign the talented youngster for his 1965 Grand

Road racing's most successful rider, Italy's Giacomo Agostini. In an 11-year career from 1965–76, he won a record 122 races and a record 15 world titles

CAREER HIGHLIGHTS

Year	Grand Prix Wins		World Titles	TT Wins
	350cc	500cc		
1965	3	1		
1966	3	3	500cc (MV Agusta)	Jnr (MV Agusta)
1967	1	5	500cc (MV Agusta)	
1968	7	10	350cc & 500cc (both MV Agusta)	Jnr & Snr (both MV Agusta)
1969	8	10	350cc & 500cc (both MV Agusta)	Jnr & Snr (both MV Agusta)
1970	9	10	350cc & 500cc (both MV Agusta)	Jnr & Snr (both MV Agusta)
1971	6	8	350cc & 500cc (both MV Agusta)	Snr (MV Agusta)
1972	6	11	350cc & 500cc (both MV Agusta)	Jnr & Snr (both MV Agusta)
1973	4	3	350cc (MV Agusta)	
1974	5	2	350cc (Yamaha)	
1975	1	4	500cc (Yamaha)	
1976	1	1		

TOTAL GRAND PRIX WINS: 122 (54 x 350cc; 68 x 500cc)

Prix team to complement the already abundant skills of Mike Hailwood. Although Hailwood left the MV team at the end of 1965, Count Agusta, who had seen his machines capture the 500cc world title but never in the hands of an Italian rider, was confident that Agostini would put matters straight and in 1966 his dreams were fulfilled when Agostini captured the title. The Agostini–Hailwood battles in 1966 and 1967 were to become the finest head-to-head confrontations the world of road racing has seen.

That first title was to herald the start of 'Ago's domination of the 500cc class as he went on to win the title seven years in succession, before being beaten by team-mate Phil Read for the title in 1973.

It was not only as the 500cc supremo that Agostini won world titles; at 350cc he won every championship from 1968–73 for the MV team. And in 1970 he equalled Mike Hailwood's record of winning 19 Grand Prix races in one season.

The Isle of Man TT races formed part of the World Championship during Agostini's reign as champion and he soon established himself as a firm favourite with the island's race fans. He made his TT debut in 1965 when he finished third in the Junior race. Between 1966 and 1972 he went on to win five Senior and five Junior TTs, but it was after the death of his great friend Gilberto Parlotti, in the 125cc race in 1972, that he became another of the island's critics, and never competed in the TT again. He lapped the Mountain Course at over 100 miles per hour no fewer than 65 times.

By the end of 1973 he had become unhappy at MV and made the move to Yamaha. He duly retained his 350cc crown the following year, but was un-able to prevent Phil Read and MV retaining the 500cc title. Then in 1975 Agostini was the 500cc champion for a record eighth time.

He returned to MV in 1976 and, appropriately, his record 122nd and last Grand Prix win was for the famous Italian manufacturer in the 1976 West German Grand Prix (500cc); his first ever Grand Prix success had been in the same race, and for the same manufacturer, 11 years earlier.

He had a brief spell at Suzuki before a final season with Yamaha in 1977, after which he retired from riding to become the manager of the Yamaha team.

GEOFF DUKE

Britain's Geoff Duke was unquestionably the finest motorcyclist of the 1950s, winning six world titles and six Isle of Man TTs. But Duke was not only a fine champion; he was also an innovator. He introduced the lightweight one-piece leather outfit and brought to the sport a dashing new style of riding.

Duke was born at St Helens, then in Lancashire but now Merseyside, in 1923 and started riding a BSA at moto-cross and trials events after the Second World War. His skill was soon spotted by one of the leading riders of the day, Artie Bell, and he introduced Duke to the Norton factory, where he was given a job.

He was nearly 26 years old when he made his road racing debut, on a 350cc Norton at the 1948 Manx Grand Prix. He was leading at the half-way stage but was forced to pull out after his machine split its oil tank. But the following year Duke made his mark by capturing the Senior Clubman's TT, and a couple of months later he won the Senior Manx Grand Prix.

His emerging talent was all the more evident in 1950 when he followed up his Manx success by winning the Senior TT, to gain his first world championship victory. But on the revolutionary 'featherbed' Norton he missed out on the championship itself by a mere point when pipped by the Italian Umberto Masetti.

The following year, however, Duke became the first man to win the world 350 and 500cc titles in one year. In addition he won the Junior and Senior TT races, both in record times.

Despite holding on to his 350 crown in 1952 he could only finish 7th in the 500cc class. His Norton was no longer competitive enough for the strong challenge being made by the Italian manufacturers, so at the end of the year Duke moved to Gilera after a brief spell trying his hand at car racing. He celebrated his first season with the Italian team by recapturing his 500cc title, which he duly retained in 1954 and 1955.

Duke then missed most of the 1956 season after the FIM imposed a six-month ban on him, because of his support for an unofficial riders' strike during the 1955 Dutch TT. Injuries sustained during the 1957 Italian Grand Prix curtailed his activities that season too, and in 1958 he left Gilera and returned to Norton. He also had a brief spell with BMW in 1958.

He quit riding in 1960 and retired to the Isle of Man, scene of some of his finest triumphs. He made a brief return in 1963 as boss of the Scuderia Duke racing team which was formed with the help of borrowed 1957 Gileras, but despite such talented riders as Derek Minter,

John Hartle and Phil Read in the team, it was not a successful venture.

Geoff Duke was the first of the modern-day racers, and present-day riders owe him an enormous debt. For his services to the sport he was awarded the OBE in 1951, only the second motorcycle rider after Freddie Frith to be so honoured.

A very young Geoff Duke trying his hand at moto-cross before he became one of road racing's outstanding riders in the 1950s

CAREER HIGHLIGHTS

Year	Grand Prix Wins		World Titles	TT Wins
	350cc	500cc		
1949	–	–		Snr Clubman's (Norton)
1950	1	3		Snr (Norton)
1951	5	4	350cc & 500cc (both Norton)	Snr & Jnr (Norton)
1952	4	–	350cc (Norton)	Jnr (Norton)
1953	–	4	500cc (Gilera)	
1954	–	5	500cc (Gilera)	
1955	–	4	500cc (Gilera)	Snr (Gilera)
1956	–	1		
1957	–	–		
1958	1	1		

TOTAL GRAND PRIX WINS: 33 (11 x 350cc; 22 x 500cc)

JOEY DUNLOP

Every decade has produced a new 'favourite son' amongst Isle of Man racing enthusiasts and in the 1980s Ulsterman Joey Dunlop was their new hero as he became the undisputed 'King of the Mountain'. A colourful character, the quietly-spoken Dunlop has won a staggering 13 TT races since 1977, and only a crash at Brands Hatch in 1989 has prevented him equalling or bettering Mike Hailwood's rec-

ord of 14 wins.

Born at Ballymoney, Northern Ireland in 1952, Dunlop started racing at the age of 18. The first of his Isle of Man successes came in the 1977 Jubilee TT when he powered his Yamaha around the Mountain Course at over 108mph/174kph. But he did not emerge as a winner again until taking the 1980 Classic TT with an outstanding display on the Rae Racing Yamaha; he pushed the absolute lap record up to 115.22mph/185.43kph on the sixth and last lap.

Riding a Honda, Dunlop won the Isle of Man Formula One TT

race in 1983, having finished third and second in the previous two years. The win helped him to retain his TT Formula One world title.

He added a third consecutive Formula One world title in 1984 and in doing so, won his second consecutive Isle of Man Formula One TT. He was already gaining a reputation for being one of the island's top riders, but in 1985 he wrote himself into TT folklore when he emulated the great Mike Hailwood and won three races in one week, winning the TT Formula One and the Junior and Senior TTs. That took his tally of wins

A trio of popular British riders. On the left is Ron Haslam, and Mick Grant is on the right shaking hands with Joey Dunlop after the Ulsterman had won the 1980 Classic TT on a Yamaha. It was the second of Joey's 13 TT wins, just one short of Mike Hailwood's all-time record

on the island to seven, and in winning the junior and senior races in one year he became the first rider to do so since Giacomo Agostini in 1972.

Dunlop was honoured with the MBE in the 1986 New Year's Honours list and he celebrated with his eighth TT success on the Isle of Man, and a fifth successive Formula One world title. He lost his world title, by three points, to the Italian Virginio Ferrari the following year, but managed to retain his Isle of Man Formula One title and

regain the Senior TT. Those two wins took his total Isle of Man successes to 10, level with the great Stanley Woods.

He was still four wins short of Mike Hailwood's record, but he pulled himself to within one of that total in 1988, when he became only the second man after the aforementioned 'Mike the Bike' to win three races in a week on *two* occasions, as he repeated his trio of wins from 1985.

Joey Dunlop certainly established himself as one of the great TT riders of all time, ranking alongside Woods, Hailwood, and Agostini. Sadly, a bad smash at Brands Hatch during the 1989 Eurolantic Challenge, when he was involved in an accident with the Belgian Stéphane Mertens, forced him to miss the 1989 TT races. However, his brother Robert maintained the

family tradition by winning the 125cc TT.

Joey returned to racing in 1990 but could not add to his Isle of Man total. Towards the end of the season, though, he did enjoy his first win since his accident when he captured the final round of the TT Formula One world championship at the Ulster Grand Prix. The way he rode gave every indication that Joey Dunlop was on his way back, ready to challenge Hailwood's all-time TT record.

KLAUS ENDERS

West German Klaus Enders has won more world sidecar titles than any other man. His total of six is two better than that of other well-known riders Rolf Biland, Eric Oliver, and Max Deubel.

Enders was a talented rider who took no chances. He was born at Giessen, near Frankfurt, in 1937 and started racing both solos and three-wheelers in 1960. But it was as the next in a long line of talented German sidecar riders that he was to

CAREER HIGHLIGHTS

Year	World Titles	TT Wins
1977		Jubilee Classic (Yamaha)
1980		Classic TT (Yamaha)
1982	TT Formula One (Honda)	
1983	TT Formula One (Honda)	TT Formula One (Honda)
1984	TT Formula One (Honda)	TT Formula One (Honda)
1985	TT Formula One (Honda)	Snr, Jnr & TT Formula One (all Honda)
1986	TT Formula One (Honda)	TT Formula One (Honda)
1987		Snr & TT Formula One (both Honda)
1988		Snr, Jnr & TT Formula One (all Honda)

make his name in the late sixties and early seventies.

All his world titles were for the German manufacturer BMW, who had been producing world sidecar champions since 1954; Enders was carrying on the tradition of his fellow Germans Wilhelm Noll, Wilhelm Faust, Fritz Hillebrand, Walter Schneider, and Deubel, all of whom had held a monopoly on the world title between 1954 and 1966. Enders himself then captured his first title, in 1967, and though he lost it to Helmut Fath the following year, he was champion again in 1969 and 1970.

Another German, Horst Owesle, took the title in 1971 while Enders enjoyed his 'retirement' from three wheels to race four-wheeled BMWs. But the retirement lasted just twelve months because he was tempted back into sidecar racing and re-captured his world title in 1972, holding on to it for three years before retir-ing again at the end of 1974.

Klaus Enders also made his mark on the Isle of Man TT races. He made his debut in 1966 and the following year fin-ished second. His first success on the island came in 1969 when he won the 500cc sidecar race with a new record speed of 92.48mph/148.83kph. He retained his title the following year, again with a new race rec-ord. In 1973 Enders won both the 750 and 500cc TTs, creating lap records in both races.

Altogether Enders won 27 Grand Prix races; he was part-nered to victory by Rolf Engelhardt on 23 occasions and by Wolfgang Kalauch on the other four. He also enjoyed Isle of Man success with both.

Klaus Enders, winner of a record six world sidecar titles. His 27 race wins in the sidecar class is bettered only by Switzerland's Rolf Biland

CAREER HIGHLIGHTS

Year	Grand Prix Wins Sidecar	World Titles	TT Wins
1967	5	Sidecar (BMW) [1]	
1968	–		
1969	4	Sidecar (BMW) [1]	500cc Sidecar (BMW) [1]
1970	5	Sidecar (BMW) [1/2]	500cc Sidecar (BMW) [2]
1971	–		
1972	4	Sidecar (BMW) [1]	
1973	7	Sidecar (BMW) [1]	500cc & 750cc Sidecar (both BMW) [1]
1974	2	Sidecar (Busch) [1]	

Passengers: [1] *Rolf Engelhardt* [2] *Wolfgang Kalauch*

TOTAL GRAND PRIX WINS: 27 (all Sidecar)

MIKE
HAILWOOD

Britain's most famous racer, Mike Hailwood, doing his best to keep warm!

The son of a wealthy motorcycle dealer, Oxford-born Mike Hailwood became the biggest name in motorcycling and is universally regarded as the finest racer of all time. His record of 14 TTs, 10 world titles and 76 Grands Prix, backs up that claim.

Born in 1940, Mike started racing at the age of 17 and in his first year won the 250cc race at the Cookstown 200 in Ireland. The following year, 1958, saw him win the 125, 250 and 350cc classes in the ACU Star Championships, and he went one better in 1959 by adding the 500cc title to the other three. He repeated the achievement in 1960 to make it two successive clean sweeps.

He had made his TT debut in 1958 and finished third in the Lightweight 250cc, while his first win in a world championship race came in the 125cc class at the 1959 Ulster Grand Prix. In 1960 he became the second man after Derek Minter to lap the Isle of Man's Mountain Course at over 100mph on a single-cylinder machine. Both

men did it that year in the Senior TT, but Minter achieved the feat on the second lap, while Mike did it one lap later. A prize of £100 had been offered for the first rider to reach this milestone – ironically, by Stan Hailwood, Mike's dad!

Mike enjoyed the first of many great seasons in 1961. He became the first man to win three races at the Isle of Man TT in one week, when he won the Senior, Lightweight 125cc, and Lightweight 250cc TTs – he also came close to winning the Junior race but his AJS let him down 15 miles from the finish. He followed up those successes by capturing his first world title when he became the 250cc champion on a Honda. It was to herald the start of a seven-year domination of road racing by one of the sport's favourite sons.

He won the first of four successive 500cc world titles in 1962, each for the Italian MV Agusta team, and in the 1965 season he won eight of the ten rounds in the 500cc championship. The following year, after joining Honda, he won a stag-

CAREER HIGHLIGHTS

Year	Grand Prix Wins				World Titles	TT Wins
	125cc	250cc	350cc	500cc		
1959	1	–	–	–		
1960	–	–	–	–		
1961	1	4	–	2	250cc (Honda)	Snr, Light 250 & Light 125 (all Honda)
1962	–	–	1	5	500cc (MV Agusta)	Jnr (MV Agusta)
1963	–	1	2	7	500cc (MV Agusta)	Snr (MV Agusta)
1964	–	–	–	7	500cc (MV Agusta)	Snr (MV Agusta)
1965	–	1	1	8	500cc (MV Agusta)	Snr (MV Agusta)
1966	–	10	6	3	250cc & 350cc (both Honda)	Snr & Light 250 (both Honda)
1967	–	5	6	5	250cc & 350cc (both Honda)	Snr, Jnr & Light 250 (all Honda)
1978	–	–	–	–		TT Formula One (Ducati)
1979	–	–	–	–		Snr (Suzuki)

TOTAL GRAND PRIX WINS: 76 (2 x 125cc; 21 x 250cc; 16 x 350cc; 37 x 500cc)

In addition Hailwood won the TT Formula One world title in 1978

gering 19 races in all classes, as he won the 250 and 350cc world titles and was narrowly beaten by his former team-mate Giacomo Agostini for the 500cc crown. Two more TT successes that year took his TT tally to nine, just one behind Stanley Wood's all-time record, but 1967 saw him capture the record outright when, for the second time, he won three races in one week. He made it a memorable year by retaining his 250 and 350cc world titles, but he was again runner-up to 'Ago' in the race for the 500cc title.

Mike retired at the end of the 1967 season and shortly afterwards was honoured with the MBE for his services to motorcycling. He then turned his attentions to racing on four wheels, having previously had a flirtation with Formula One car racing in 1963. He won the European Formula Two title in 1972 and in 1973 was awarded the George Medal for bravery after pulling Clay Reggazoni from his blazing Ferrari at Kyalami. The following year he was himself injured after crashing at the Nürburgring and it signalled the end of his four-wheeled career.

He lived in New Zealand for a while, but found the temptation of a motorcycle comeback too great and in 1978, at the age of 38, the great man was seen racing around the Isle of Man again. He duly increased his TT wins total to 13 when he won the Formula One TT on his Ducati, the race also clinching his 10th world title. Remarkably, Mike won TT number 14 the following year when he won his record seventh Senior TT. But it was to be his last success; he retired once again and less than two years later lost his life in a car accident near to his Birmingham home, when going out to buy fish and chips with his two children. Sadly his daughter

Michelle also died in the accident. It was an ironic end to one of motorcycling's finest ambassadors, who had cheated death at over 100 miles per hour for more than 20 years.

EDDIE LAWSON

In 1989 Eddie Lawson silenced those critics who had slammed his previous world title successes when he rode magnificently to take the world 500cc title for the fourth time.

Born in California in 1958, he started racing in 1975. His first major success was in winning the 1981 US Superbike Championship on a Kawasaki, and that same year he made his Grand Prix debut on a 250cc Kawasaki at Hockenheim.

Lawson was one of many talented Americans who started to make an impact on the 500cc scene in the 1980s and he emerged as one of the leading riders of the decade. In his second full Grand Prix season, in 1984, he clinched the crown on the Marlboro Yamaha by 31

points from his fellow American Randy Mamola. But his critics immediately claimed the victory as a 'hollow' one, because the defending champion Freddie Spencer was not fully fit. And there was the same cry when Lawson regained his title in 1986; the 'fit' Spencer had won back his crown by a mere eight points from Lawson the previous season.

Still with Giacomo Agostini's Yamaha team, Eddie finished third in the championship in 1987 and the following year was champion for a third time. But again he had his critics. This time they claimed his Yamaha was superior to runner-up Wayne Gardner's Honda, and that it was machinery rather than man which won the championship.

But when he retained the title in 1989 he won a lot of admirers for the way he rode. Previously labelled as 'Steady Eddie', he pushed himself and rode magnificently to power his Honda to the title and beat off the challenge from those other talented Americans, Wayne Rainey and

Eddie Lawson, the only American to win four world road racing titles

Kevin Schwantz. Eddie has never had a good relationship with the press, but he made them eat their words after a great fourth championship.

He is a dedicated professional who has one aim in Grand Prix racing: to win races, which he has done on 30 occasions. He returned to the Yamaha team in 1990 after just one season at Honda, but could not retain his title, thanks largely to an accident at Laguna Seca in the second race of the championship, which forced him to miss five rounds. He switched teams again in 1991, moving to the Italians, Cagiva.

Californian Lawson started his career as a moto-cross and dirt-track rider and he still enjoys taking part in moto-cross events.

CAREER HIGHLIGHTS

Year	Grand Prix Wins 500cc	World Titles
1984	4	500cc (Yamaha)
1985	3	
1986	7	500cc (Yamaha)
1987	5	
1988	7	500cc (Yamaha)
1989	4	500cc (Honda)
1990	–	

TOTAL GRAND PRIX WINS:
30 (all 500c)

ANGEL NIETO

Spain's first world champion, Angel Nieto, was unquestionably the 'King of the Lightweights'.

He won the 50cc world title six times between 1969 and 1977, and the 125cc title on seven occasions between 1971 and 1984. His total of 13 world titles and 90 Grand Prix wins is second only to Giacomo Agostini's all-time total.

Born at Zamora, not far from the Portuguese border, in 1947, he started work as a 12-year-old with a local motorcycle dealer and at 16 he was racing on a Barcelona-built Derbi. He joined the Derbi works team in 1964 and made his world championship debut in the 50cc event at that year's Spanish Grand Prix. But the talented youngster had to wait until 1969 for his first Grand Prix win, which came at the Sachsenring in the East German Grand Prix. He followed that with a win in the Ulster Grand Prix and those successes, together with consistent riding throughout the season, were enough to give him his first world title.

He retained his title the following year and in 1971 captured his first 125cc world championship, appropriately at Jarama, home of the Spanish Grand Prix. A year later he was a double world champion at 50cc and 125cc, only the second man to achieve such a double.

In 1973 he moved to the Italian Morbidelli team but without success. He stayed only one year before returning to Derbi, but they were no longer competitive and it meant another barren season for Nieto in terms of championship success. However, a move to Kreidler in 1975 saw him regain his 50cc crown with six Grand Prix wins. He moved to Bultaco, another Spanish manufacturer, in 1976 and retained his 50cc crown, which he held on to again the following year.

After that he concentrated on the 125cc class and went on to capture five more world titles for Minarelli and Garelli between 1979 and 1984. He wound up his career riding 80cc Derbis and a 125cc MBA before eventually quitting at the end of 1986. But his career nearly came to a fairytale ending when he led the field in his final race, the 80cc race at Hockenheim, only to be forced out on the final lap.

The senior racing career of Angel Nieto lasted 23 years. He started as a raw and impetuous youngster. But he left the sport as a much respected professional, and an inspiration to the band of Spaniards who have subsequently made their mark in Grand Prix racing.

CAREER HIGHLIGHTS

Year	Grand Prix Wins 50cc	80cc	125cc	World Titles
1969	2	–	–	50cc (Derbi)
1970	5	–	4	50cc (Derbi)
1971	3	–	5	125cc (Derbi)
1972	3	–	5	50cc & 125cc (Derbi)
1973	–	–	–	
1974	–	–	2	
1975	6	–	–	50cc (Kreidler)
1976	5	–	1	50cc (Bultaco)
1977	3	–	3	50cc (Bultaco)
1978	–	–	4	
1979	–	–	8	125cc (Minarelli)
1980	–	–	4	
1981	–	–	8	125cc (Minarelli)
1982	–	–	6	125cc (Garelli)
1983	–	–	6	125cc (Garelli)
1984	–	–	6	125cc (Garelli)
1985	–	1	–	

TOTAL GRAND PRIX WINS: 90 (27 x 50cc; 1 x 80cc; 62 x 125cc)

ERIC OLIVER

Eric Oliver was probably the finest sidecar racer Britain has produced and in 1949 he confirmed himself as the world's best when he became the first world champion in that class.

Born in Sussex in 1911, Oliver started racing both solo and sidecar machines before the war and learned his skills grasstracking. He made his TT debut as a solo rider in 1937. When sidecars returned to the island in 1954, after an absence of 29 years, Oliver was the inevitable winner. With Les Nutt in the chair, the pair triumphed over the Germans Hillebrand and Noll with more than two minutes to spare.

By then Oliver had won himself four world titles. The first was in the championship's inaugural year when, with Denis Jenkinson as his passenger, he won the title on his Norton-Watsonian by five points from the Italian pair Ercole Frigerio and Edoardo Ricotti. Oliver had the distinction of winning the first ever sidecar world championship race, at Bremgarten, Switzerland, in 1949.

With a new passenger, Lorenzo Dobelli of Italy, Oliver retained his crown in 1950 by

winning all three legs of the championship and in 1951, again with Dobelli in the chair, the title was retained.

An accident cost him his chance of a fourth successive title in 1952 and he lost his crown to fellow Britain Cyril Smith, but Eric was champion again in 1953 when, with new partner Stanley Dibben, he won the title by six points from Smith. But that was to be his swansong. He won three more races the following year when he teamed up with Les Nutt, but the powerful German combinations came to the fore of sidecar racing and it was to be 23 years before Britain produced another world three-wheel champion.

Eric Oliver (second right) seen with his Norton back-room team at Montlhery, France, in 1949

It was during the 1954 Belgian Grand Prix that Eric introduced his famous kneeler sidecar unit which formed the basis of all modern-day three-wheeled units.

With the German teams proving too strong Eric quit Grand Prix racing in 1955. He died in 1981 at the age of 70.

PHIL READ

The career of Phil Read, one of the finest natural talents road racing has seen, spanned 27 years, during which time he always had the ability to get the best out of every machine he rode.

Born at Luton in 1939, he served as an apprentice engineer and, unlike most young lads, was encouraged to take up motorcycle racing by his

CAREER HIGHLIGHTS

Year	Grand Prix Wins Sidecar	World Titles	TT Wins
1949	3	Sidecar (Norton) [1]	
1950	3	Sidecar (Norton) [2]	
1951	3	Sidecar (Norton) [2]	
1952	2		
1953	3	Sidecar (Norton) [3]	
1954	3		Sidecar (Norton) [4]

TOTAL GRAND PRIX WINS: 17 (all Sidecar)

Passengers: [1] *Denis Jenkinson,* [2] *Lorenzo Dobelli,* [3] *Stanley Dibben,* [4] *Les Nutt*

mother! His first race was on a 350cc BSA at Mallory Park in 1956, but he first came to prominence in 1960 when he won the Senior Manx Grand Prix on a Norton. The following year he won the Junior TT on his TT debut, the Senior TT that year being won by Mike Hailwood. Seventeen years later they were still rivals on the island and both were still chasing titles.

In 1963 Geoff Duke signed Phil for his new Scuderia Duke team. While the venture was not a successful one, Phil did enough to impress Yamaha and he joined the Japanese team for a five-year spell.

In his first season with his new team, he pipped the Honda of Jim Redman to the 250cc title and repeated his success the following year. After finishing runner-up to Hailwood in 1966 and 1967, he was engaged in a great season-long battle with Yamaha team-mate Bill Ivy in 1968 and managed to regain the title. But how close it was!

The two Yamaha riders dominated the ten-round series, winning five races each. They ended up with identical points and the

Phil Read was awarded the MBE in the 1979 Birthday Honours List. He went to Buckingham Palace to collect his award on a Quasar machine

only way to separate them was to add up the aggregate times of each rider in all the races in which both were classified. That involved adding up the times of

four races and Read managed to capture the title by a margin of just over two minutes.

Read made it a double celebration in 1968 by capturing the

CAREER HIGHLIGHTS

Year	Grand Prix Wins				World Titles	TT Wins
	125cc	250cc	350cc	500cc		
1961	–	–	1	–		Jnr (Norton)
1962	–	–	–	–		
1963	–	–	–	–		
1964	–	5	–	1	250cc (Yamaha)	
1965	1	7	–	–	250cc (Yamaha)	Light 125 (Yamaha)
1966	1	–	1	–		
1967	2	4	–	–		Light 125 (Yamaha)
1968	6	5	–	–	125cc & 250cc (both Yamaha)	Light 125 (Yamaha)
1969	–	1	1	–		
1970	–	–	–	–		
1971	–	3	–	–	250cc (Yamaha)	Light 250 (Yamaha)
1972	–	2	1	-		Light 250 (Yamaha)
1973	–	–	–	4	500cc (MV Agusta)	
1974	–	–	–	4	500cc (MV Agusta)	
1975	–	–	–	2		
1976	–	–	–	–		
1977	–	–	–	–		Snr (Suzuki), & TT Formula One (Honda)

TOTAL GRAND PRIX WINS: 52 (10 x 125cc; 27 x 250cc; 4 x 350cc; 11 x 500cc)

125cc title, again with Ivy in second place. Furthermore, he also won the 125 TT for the third time.

Yamaha withdrew their Grand Prix works team at the end of 1968 but Phil kept riding privately-entered machines and in 1971 he regained the 250cc title. Later that year he teamed up with Agostini in the MV Agusta team as part of their continued attack on the 500cc title, and in 1973 he ended 'Ago's seven-year reign as champion when he won the first of two successive 500cc titles. Agostini beat him into second place in the 1975 championship. Phil then left MV and moved to Suzuki but he announced his retirement at the end of the 1976 season.

However, with six TT wins to his credit and despite his having been one of the island's critics following the death of Gilberto Parlotti in 1972, Phil came out of retirement to take part in the 1977 races. He won the TT Formula One race on a factory Honda and the Senior TT on a works Suzuki. He carried on racing in the TT until 1982 when he was 43 years of age.

Often outspoken, his arguments with fellow riders were much publicised. But Read had a great natural talent that made him one of the most successful 250cc Grand Prix riders. And for his services to the sport he was honoured with the MBE in 1979.

JIM REDMAN

There was nothing spectacular about the riding of Rhodesian Jim Redman. He took no risks and was a firm believer that a bike didn't need to be pushed to its maximum speed to win a race. And his six world titles and 45 Grand Prix wins are testament to that belief.

Although born near Hampstead, London, in 1931, he emigrated to Rhodesia as an 18-year-old and ran a garage in Bulawayo before starting racing in his new country at the age of 24. He returned to England in 1958 and his first race was at Brands Hatch; he finished second to Derek Minter. He returned to Rhodesia in 1959, having become disillusioned with the sport, but the following year he was back again and within two years he was a world champion.

Initially riding Nortons and the occasional Ducati, Jim became a member of the new Honda team in 1960 and got his Grand Prix chance when he replaced Tom Phillis on the 125 in the Dutch TT. He finished fourth, and was also seventh in the 250cc race.

By 1962 Jim was Honda's leading 250 and 350cc rider and that year he won both world titles, a feat he repeated in 1963. He held on to his 350 title for

Jim Redman celebrates after winning the 250 and 350 races at the 1963 Dutch TT. He went on to become world champion in both classes that year, thus repeating the same double of a year earlier

two more years, but had to succumb to the talents of Phil Read in the 250 championship; their clashes in those two years were amongst the most memorable the class has ever seen.

In addition to adding a fourth consecutive 350cc world title in 1965, Jim also completed a hat-trick of Junior and Lightweight 250 TT doubles on Honda factory bikes.

He competed in the 1966 500cc world championship, his first attempt at the title since his Norton days, but despite winning the West German and Dutch races, he could finish only fifth in the championship table and thus failed to fulfil one

CAREER HIGHLIGHTS

Year	Grand Prix Wins				World Titles	TT Wins
	125cc	250cc	350cc	500cc		
1961	–	2	–	–		
1962	1	6	4	–	250cc & 350cc (both Honda)	
1963	1	4	5	–	250cc & 350cc (both Honda)	Jnr & Light 250 (both Honda)
1964	2	3	8	–	350cc (Honda)	Jnr & Light 250 (both Honda)
1965	–	3	4	–	350cc (Honda)	Jnr & Light 250 (both Honda)
1966	–	–	–	2		

TOTAL GRAND PRIX WINS: 45 (4 x 125cc; 18 x 250cc; 21 x 350cc; 2 x 500cc)

of his great ambitions.

After an accident in the 1966 Belgian Grand Prix, Redman announced his retirement and returned to South Africa to look after his business interests. He received an MBE in 1964 for his services to motorcycle sport.

KENNY ROBERTS

Kenny Roberts may have appeared to be a dour rider, but he was a dedicated professional who earned himself a place in road racing history as the first American world champion. Furthermore, by winning the 500cc title three years in succession he emulated the feats of the greats of the sport, Geoff Duke, John Surtees, Mike Hailwood and Giacomo Agostini.

Hailing from Modesto, California, Roberts was born in December 1951 and started racing at the age of 14 on a local dirt track. He turned to road racing when he was 20 and won his first AMA Grand National event on a Yamaha at Houston, Texas, on 29 January 1972. He finished fourth in the cham-

pionship, but the following season he became the youngest ever champion at 22. He retained his title in 1974, was second in 1975 and third the following year.

He had tried the European circuits for the first time in 1974; four years on, after winning the Daytona 200, he returned to make a serious attack on the world 500cc title, which Britain's Barry Sheene had held for the previous two years. It was Pat Hennen who paved the way for American riders, by winning the 1976 Finnish Grand Prix, but it was now up to Roberts to take over as the top American.

He opened his Grand Prix account by winning the 250cc class at the opening race of the 1978 season, in Venezuela. Sheene won the 500cc race but Roberts posted his intentions in the next round at Jarama, and two weeks later the Californian won his first 500cc Grand Prix at Austria's Salzburgring. It was the first of three consecutive wins that put him top of the championship table and, ironically, he clinched his first world title on Sheene's 'home ground' at Silverstone, with one race to spare.

He retained his title with ease the following year, when he also

announced his plans for a breakaway World Series in the hope of getting a better deal for the Grand Prix riders. But it never materialised. Roberts, however, went on to secure his third consecutive world title when he beat off the challenge from compatriot Randy Mamola.

Injury and inferior machines put him out of contention in 1981 and 1982 but the following year he was back to his best and engaged in a terrific battle for the championship with another American, Freddie Spencer. In the end Roberts had to be content with second place, edged out by just two points.

Kenny quit at the end of that season to take charge of the Yamaha team, with whom he had enjoyed every one of his 24 Grand Prix successes.

CAREER HIGHLIGHTS

	Grand Prix		
Year	Wins		World Titles
	250cc	500cc	
1978	2	4	500cc (Yamaha)
1979	–	5	500cc (Yamaha)
1980	–	3	500cc (Yamaha)
1981	–	2	
1982	–	2	
1983	–	6	

TOTAL GRAND PRIX WINS: 24
(2 x 350cc; 22 x 500cc)

Kenny Roberts, chased by Barry Sheene at Silverstone in 1979. Roberts dethroned the Englishman as 500cc world champion in 1978 and made sure he held on to his title for another two years. The battles between these two top riders in that era were amongst the best the sport has seen

BARRY
SHEENE

Barry Sheene probably did more to popularise motorcycling amongst British people than any other man. It was not just his much-publicised, dramatic, high-speed crashes which caught the eye, but also his great personality and riding skills.

Born in London in 1950, he first attracted attention as a 20-year-old when he captured the British 125cc title just two years after making his debut on a Bultaco at Brands Hatch. He made his mark in Europe in 1971 when, riding a 125 Suzuki, he won his first Grand Prix at Spa. He won three races in this, his first championship year, and finished a close second to Angel Nieto. He also won the 50cc race at the Czechoslovakian Grand Prix.

He joined the Yamaha works team in 1972 but a year later teamed up with Suzuki GB, and it was with them that he was to go on and enjoy some of his finest moments in the sport.

He captured the Formula 750 title in 1973 but two years later his career nearly came to an end when he was involved in a crash

Barry Sheene, Britain's 500cc world champion in 1976 and 1977. Britain has not produced such a character since then, nor has she produced another 500cc world champion

CAREER HIGHLIGHTS

Year	Grand Prix Wins			World Titles
	50cc	125cc	500cc	
1971	1	3	–	
1972	–	–	–	
1973	–	–	–	
1974	–	–	–	
1975	–	–	2	
1976	–	–	5	500cc (Suzuki)
1977	–	–	6	500cc (Suzuki)
1978	–	–	2	
1979	–	–	3	
1980	–	–	–	
1981	–	–	1	

TOTAL GRAND PRIX WINS: 23 (1 x 50cc; 3 x 125cc; 19 x 500cc)

at Daytona at over 175mph/281kph. Seven weeks later, though, Sheene was back on his bike and riding at Cadwell Park. Later in the year he went on to win his first 500cc Grand Prix when he beat champion-elect Giacomo Agostini at Assen in the Dutch TT. It was to be the first of nineteen 500cc race wins for Sheene, and in securing his first 'senior' win, he became the first and only man to win world championship races at both 50 and 500cc.

Sheene was hungry for the

500cc crown in 1976 and won the first three races with outstanding rides. At the end of the season he had plenty to spare as he captured his first title from Finland's Teppi Länsivuori and America's Pat Hennen. It was a similar story twelve months later when the ever-popular Briton won the title by 27 points from another American, Steve Baker. A virus didn't help Barry's championship cause in 1978 and, despite a great season-long battle with Kenny Roberts, he lost his title and thus missed out on a hat-trick of wins. And in 1979, his last with Suzuki, he finished third in the championship behind Roberts and Virginio Ferrari.

For the next campaign Barry ran his own team, using production Yamahas, but they were not good enough to prevent Roberts winning his third consecutive title.

Just as he was showing signs of his old form in 1982, and challenging for his third world title, Sheene was hit by a series of misfortunes and had a bad accident whilst practising for the British Grand Prix at Silverstone; he broke both legs after colliding with a fallen bike at over 150mph/241kph. But yet again the gutsy Londoner bounced back and in 1983 he was racing Suzukis again. After riding a far from competitive machine in 1984 he decided to call it a day; but ever-popular, he was never short of work and landed several television appearances. He also tried his hand at truck-racing before eventually emigrating to Australia.

Barry Sheene flirted with danger many times, but after just one appearance in the Isle of Man TT races, in 1971, he vowed never to return to the island because it was too dangerous, and he stuck to his word. However, he became one of the most outstanding small-circuits racers in the 1970s, and had it not been for the arrival of Kenny Roberts his tally of two world championships would almost certainly have been greater.

JOHN SURTEES

John Surtees arrived on the motorcycling scene in the early 1950s as a determined young man. And it was that determination which carried him to seven world titles on two wheels – and one on four wheels – as he became the only man to win the world titles at both of motor sports senior codes.

Surtees was born at Westerham, Kent, in 1934. His father Jack was a South London motorcycle dealer who raced sidecars at grass-track meetings and it was as his father's passenger that young John got his first taste of the sport.

But Surtees wanted a career as a solo rider and at Thruxton in 1951 he first caught the eye when he finished second – on a Vincent which he had tuned himself – to Geoff Duke and his powerful Norton. He made his Grand Prix debut in that year's Ulster Grand Prix, but his glory days were still a few years away.

His TT debut came in 1954, and the following year he became a member of the works Norton team. His first Grand Prix win was on a 250cc NSU in the Ulster Grand Prix of that year, 1955, but his fortunes took a dramatic upturn in 1956 after being signed by the crack Italian team MV Agusta.

He landed the 1956 Senior TT and followed that with Grand Prix wins in Holland and Belgium to win the first of four 500cc world titles. The following season, though, was one of near misses, as he finished third in the World Championship and was runner-up to Bob McIntyre in the Senior TT. But it was back to winning ways with a vengeance in 1958.

He won both the Senior and Junior TT at the Isle of Man, and went on to capture both the 350 and 500cc world titles, the latter after winning six of the seven rounds. He repeated both doubles in 1959 and was even more dominant in the 500cc class, as he won all seven races. In those two seasons he won all 25 Grand Prix races he entered, but it must be said that it was during a period when MV had the Grand Prix scene more or less to themselves and had very little opposition.

Nevertheless, Surtees remarkably made it a hat-trick of 350 and 500cc championships in 1960 when, again, his dominance of the senior class showed, with his winning five of the seven rounds. One of those wins was in the Senior TT as he became the first man to win that race in three successive years.

Barely a month after winning his third successive Senior TT, Surtees competed in his second Formula One car race and finished second to Jack Brabham in the British Grand Prix at Silverstone. He had started his four-wheeled career in a Ken Tyrrell Formula Junior Cooper, but he had now ventured into the world of Formula One.

Surtees quit the two-wheeled branch of the sport and turned his attentions full-time to car racing in 1961. After a season with Cooper and then Lola, he joined the Ferrari team in 1963 and within two seasons he was a world champion again, this time on four wheels. He quit Ferrari midway through the 1966 season and rejoined

Cooper, finishing runner-up to the great Jack Brabham in the world championship.

He had subsequent spells with Honda and BRM before racing his own Surtees-Ford in 1970 and 1971. He retired at the end of the 1971 season but his cars continued in Formula One until 1978. Sadly they never rewarded him with a Grand Prix win.

John Surtees was a very insular sort of person, but he was tremendously skilful and had a great determination to win, as his rivals in the latter part of the 1950s would certainly confirm.

John Surtees and his proud mother Dorothy with the youngster's collection of trophies, as a successful career was unfolding. Surtees was unusually fortunate to have the backing of his mother – many have tried to dissuade their sons from taking up the sport

CAREER HIGHLIGHTS

Year	Grand Prix Wins			World Titles	TT Wins
	250cc	350cc	500cc		
1955	1	–	–		
1956	–	1	3	500cc (MV Agusta)	Snr (MV Agusta)
1957	–	–	1		
1958	–	6	6	350cc & 500cc (MV Agusta)	Snr & Jnr (MV Agusta)
1959	–	6	7	350cc & 500cc (MV Agusta)	Snr & Jnr (MV Agusta)
1960	–	2	5	350cc & 500cc (MV Agusta)	Snr (MV Agusta)

TOTAL GRAND PRIX WINS: 38 (1 x 250cc; 15 x 350cc; 22 x 500cc)

STANLEY WOODS

Until the arrival of Mike Hailwood, Stanley Woods was the undisputed 'King of the TT', and his total of ten wins has been surpassed only by Hailwood and Joey Dunlop.

Ulsterman Woods first learned his riding skills on an Indian sidecar combination at the age of 13. The first bike of his own was a two-stroke 250cc Sun, and that was the beginning of a career that would see him emerge as a master tactician and one of the best road racers of the pre-war days.

He first entered the TT races in 1922 but had to sell many of his possessions to raise the money to get to the Isle of Man. He made his debut on a Cotton and finished fifth in the Junior TT, despite a potentially nasty accident when he set fire to himself and his bike during a refuelling stop.

The following year Woods won the first of his record 10 TTs when he took the Junior race, again on a Cotton. Riding a Norton he won his first Senior TT in 1926 and the following year he enjoyed wins in Belgium, Switzerland and Holland. In 1932 he had the first of two successive Junior and Senior TT doubles, which confirmed him as the most outstanding rider of the decade. He remains one of just three men to win both races in successive years.

He quit Norton at the end of 1933 and rode as a freelance for Husqvarna in 1934 and Moto Guzzi the following year, when he increased his TT tally to eight with wins in the Senior and Lightweight events with new lap records in both races.

Woods also raced for the German DKW team in 1935 but he returned to a British manufacturer in 1936 when he joined the Velocette team and in the two years before the outbreak of the war he won two more Junior TTs taking his overall TT total to 10. His five Junior successes still stands as a record.

Stanley intended racing after the war, but in the immediate years he felt that he wasn't fit enough. Then when he was sufficiently fit to ride, he wisely thought that at 44 years of age he might be too old to take on the Mountain Course, and he retired. But it was not the last the Isle of Man fans saw of Stanley Woods. In 1957 he was seen practising on a Guzzi and lapped the circuit at over 80mph/129kph. But that's all it was, a practice – and a bit of fun for the 53-year-old and for the Isle of Man fans who idolised him for many years.

Stanley Woods won 10 TT races between 1923 and 1939. The record stood for over a quarter of a century until surpassed by Mike Hailwood

CAREER HIGHLIGHTS

Year	TT Wins
1923	Jnr (Cotton)
1926	Snr (Norton)
1932	Snr & Jnr (both Norton)
1933	Snr & Jnr (both Norton)
1935	Snr & Lightweight (both Guzzi)
1938	Jnr (Velocette)
1939	Jnr (Velocette)

LEADING MANUFACTURERS

DERBI

In recent years, Spanish riders have been highly successful in the smaller capacity classes of the World Championships. But the Barcelona Derbi factory have been producing world champions since the 1960s when Angel Nieto, the undisputed 'King' of the small bikes, captured his first title. He went on to win 30 races for them at either 50, 80 or 125cc.

The factory produced pedal cycles to start with, but owner Don Simeon Rabassa decided to start making motorcycles, and like many other Spanish manufacturers he resisted the temptation to build moto-cross machines but concentrated on small capacity road racing bikes. When in 1966 Australian Barry Smith won the Austrian Grand Prix, it heralded the start of a long and successful involvement for Derbi with Grand Prix racing.

However, having won four successive manufactuers' titles at 50cc and 125cc from 1969–72, Derbi then pulled out of competitive racing. But a decade later they had returned and Spaniards Jorge Martinez and 'Champi' Herreros have followed Nieto's footsteps and captued world titles on the famous Derbi *marque*.

WORLD ROAD RACING CHAMPIONS

125cc: Angel Nieto (1971–72), Jorge Martinez (1988)
80cc: Jorge Martinez (1986–88), Manuel Herreros (1989)
50cc: Angel Nieto (1969–70, 1972)

MANUFACTURERS' TITLES

125cc: 1971–72, 1988
80cc: 1986–88
50cc: 1969–70

GILERA

From the start of the World Championship in 1949 until 1957 when they pulled out of road racing, Gilera had won a remarkable 33 races in the 500cc class, captured the manufacturers' title three times and produced six world champions.

In 1936 Giuseppe Gilera acquired the Rondine *equipe* which had been producing a very successful four-cylinder engine, and it was this engine which formed the basis of Gilera's post-war operation, upon which he was to build a successful road racing machine.

The Gilera company was actually founded in 1909 but it was not until after the acquisition of Rondine that it attracted publicity. They started producing powerful machines and in 1937 Piero Taruffi captured the world speed record on a Gilera. Mussolini, just as he did with car racing, used this success as part of his propaganda campaign. Suddenly, the name of Gilera was to be heard across Europe.

Anticipating the banning of superchargers after the war, Gilera started producing a new engine and in 1948 they launched their new machine at the Dutch TT. It weighed 70lb less than the successful British Norton and was a sensational development. It had poor handling, but compensated with devastating speed.

Having won two world titles, with Umberto Masetti in the saddle, Giuseppe Gilera wanted to make sure he kept his grip on the title and in recruiting Britain's Geoff Duke, he was assured of having one of the best riders of the day in his team.

The factory had also started producing 350s, and captured the 350cc crown; while at the Isle of Man in 1957, history was made when Bob McIntyre, on a Gilera, became the first man to lap the Mountain Course at over 100mph. But that was to be the company's last momentous year. Increased costs and a declining motorcycle market forced them to pull out of road racing. Gileras were in fact seen in the 500cc championship in 1963, when the factory agreed to lend Geoff Duke some machines for his newly formed Scuderia Duke team, but the venture did not last long and the name of Gilera eventually disappeared from the road racing scene.

WORLD ROAD RACE CHAMPIONS

500cc: Umberto Masetti (1950, 1952), Geoff Duke (1953–55), Libero Liberati (1957)

MANUFACTURERS' TITLES

500cc: 1953, 1955, 1957
350cc: 1957

SENIOR TT WINNERS

Geoff Duke (1955), Bob McIntyre (1957)

HARLEY-DAVIDSON

Harley-Davidson has been the biggest name in American motorcycle manufacturing for the whole of this century. The company was founded in 1901 when William Harley and Arthur Davidson joined forces to start work on their first machine. Since then, many other US manufacturers have come and gone but Harley-Davidson still remain and are the States' top bike-producer.

In 1904 Harley and Davidson produced a mere eight machines from a small wooden shed in the Davidson family's rear garden. Two years on, they had increased output to 50 machines and it grew from there.

While early Harley-Davidsons were used for racing, they were standard 'stock' models which were privately entered. However, the company started its own racing division in 1914 and the team soon established themselves as the outstanding outfit in the years leading up to the First World War. After the war they continued their dominance of dirt-track racing in the United States, but also developed a machine specifically to concentrate on the world speed record, which they captured in 1923 when Britain's Freddie Dixon achieved a speed of 106.8mph/ 171.88kph. They had to wait until 1970 before recapturing it; Cal Rayborn then twice upped the record. In between they had scooped all major US titles including the first nine AMA Championships (1954–62) and, prior to the arrival of the Japanese machines, were the most successful machine in the Daytona 200.

The company made its first serious challenge on the Grand Prix circuit in the 1970s, and between 1974 and 1978, Franco Uncini (Ita), Gianfranco Bonera (Ita), Michel Rougerie (Fra) and Walter Villa (Ita) partnered the Harley-Davidson 250cc to 24 Grand Prix successes, with Villa winning three consecutive world titles.

WORLD ROAD RACE CHAMPIONS

350cc: Walter Villa (1976)
250cc: Walter Villa (1974–76)

MANUFACTURERS TITLES

250cc: 1975

The 1923 Harley-Davidson sporting, on which Freddie Dixon captured the world speed record

HONDA

Honda's emergence in the world of road racing in the 1960s was one of the most exciting developments in the sport for many years. Originally they concentrated on the small bike categories, but eventually found success at 250 and 350cc levels. Their remarkable run of success paid dividends for the company, who invested a fortune in the sport; sales of road bikes soared worldwide and at the end of the decade they were the world's biggest producer of motorcycles.

The company was founded in 1948 by Soichiro Honda, and within 20 years he had increased his number of employees from 34 to over 16 000. Honda first mooted the idea of entering his machines at the Isle of Man in 1954, but on visiting the island he found the Italian manufacturers were producing far more powerful machines so he went back to the drawing board and it was not until 1959 that his first bike was seen at the TT, when he entered the 125cc race.

Whilst his entrants failed to get in the first three, they did prove themselves to be riding reliable machines for the gruelling Mountain Course. Within two years, Australian Tom Phillis had become the first Honda world champion, and between that time and 1967, when they pulled out of road racing, such notable riders as Luigi Taveri, Jim Redman and Mike Hailwood had all captured world titles on Honda machines, totalling nearly 150 Grand Prix race wins between them.

Hailwood had been recruited to ride their new six-cylinder 500cc machine in 1966 – their first venture into the 500cc championship – and while he was runner-up in the riders' championship, Honda still managed to capture the manufacturers' title.

They announced plans to return to Grand Prix racing in 1979 but their machines were no match for the more competitive Yamaha and Suzuki outfits. However, a serious return in 1982 saw Honda eventually produce their first 500cc world champion the following year when the American Freddie Spencer took the title. Since then Honda has returned to the fore of Grand Prix road racing as well as most other branches of motorcycle sport.

Honda revolutionised the world of Grand Prix racing in the early sixties. Initially they concentrated on the little bikes, but within a couple of years they had taken control of the 250 and 350cc classes. This is the 350 on which Jim Redman won the 1963 world title

WORLD ROAD RACE CHAMPIONS

500cc: Freddie Spencer (1983, 1985), Wayne Gardner (1987), Eddie Lawson (1989)
350cc: Jim Redman (1962–65), Mike Hailwood (1966–67)
250cc: Mike Hailwood (1961, 1966–67), Jim Redman (1962–63), Freddie Spencer (1985), Anton Mang (1987), Sito Pons (1988–89)
125cc: Tom Phillis (1961), Luigi Taveri (1962, 1964, 1966), Loris Capirossi (1990)
50cc: Ralph Bryans (1965)

MANUFACTURERS' TITLES

500cc: 1966, 1983–85, 1989
350cc: 1962–67
250cc: 1961–63, 1966–67, 1985–89
125cc: 1961–62, 1964, 1966, 1989–90
50cc: 1965–66

SENIOR TT WINNERS

Mike Hailwood (1966–67), Joey Dunlop (1985, 1987–88), Roger Burnett (1986), Steve Hislop (1989), Carl Fogarty (1990)

KAWASAKI

Kawasaki are another of the famous Japanese manufacturers who have benefited from road racing success. They are very much fourth behind the 'Big Three' in terms of success, but in the late seventies and early eighties they dominated the 250 and 350cc classes through South African Kork Ballington and West Germany's Anton Mang.

They first made their mark in the 500cc class in 1971 when Britain's Dave Simmonds won the Spanish Grand Prix, but it was in the 250cc class that they were outstanding and won 45 World Championship races between 1977 and 1983; they were manufacturers' champions four times.

Kawasakis were first seen at a Grand Prix at Suzuka in 1965 when four-stroke twin and two-stroke single 125s made their debut. Suzuki and Yamaha were very active in road racing at the time, and it took four years before Kawasaki produced their first world champion when Simmonds rode a four-year-old 125

to the championship. It was also on the 125, in 1969, that he gained Kawasaki's first TT success.

Despite their success with the smaller bikes, they moved into Formula 750, and they have also made machines good enough to compete at the highest level of endurance racing and motocross. They have also produced bikes set to challenge for the world speed record, and in 1978 Don Vesco twice increased his own record on a Kawasaki.

WORLD ROAD RACE CHAMPIONS

350cc: Kork Ballington (1978–79), Anton Mang (1981–82)
250cc: Kork Ballington (1978–79), Anton Mang (1980–81)
125cc: Dave Simmonds (1969)

MANUFACTURERS' TITLES

350cc: 1978–79, 1981–82
250cc: 1978–81
125cc: 1969

SENIOR TT WINNERS

Mick Grant (1975)

MOTO GUZZI

Guzzi started racing in the early 1920s, and by the time war broke out they were one of the outstanding racing teams in Europe. In 1939 they even had the audacity to outrace the German 250s in their own Grand Prix. It was the sort of propaganda that Mussolini revelled in.

The company's headquarters were at Como and they built their famous wind tunnel at Mandello, near Novara. Moto Guzzi first came to prominence in 1935 when Britain's Stanley Woods won both the senior and lightweight TTs on Guzzis. It was to herald the start of a domination across Europe, ended only by the outbreak of war.

After the war their 250 single-cylinder machine continued to dominate, and when the World Championship was launched in 1949, their own Bruno Ruffo

Moto Guzzi's 500cc in 1955. Despite their best efforts, they failed to make an impact in that class after the early fifties

was the first 250cc champion and, of course, Guzzi took the manufacturers' title. Having won three 250cc titles they concentrated on the 350cc class in 1953, with a similar machine but a bigger engine. At the first attempt, they captured the title thanks to Britain's Fergus Anderson. They followed that success with four more titles at that category in the next five years.

The man largely responsible for Guzzi's success was Giulio Carcano, who placed emphasis on designing streamlined machines rather than concentrating solely on improving engine power as many other manufacturers did at the time.

Guzzis attacked the 500cc class but without the same success, and had only three race wins in nine years before their withdrawal from racing in 1957, when they handed over the mantle of top Italian manufacturer to MV Agusta.

However, they were only out of racing for a couple of years, and in the early Sixties they returned to Grand Prix racing;

Right *The names of Giacomo Agostini and MV Agusta are synonomous. They have been the most successful rider/manufacturer combination in Grand Prix history*

in 1962 Britain's Arthur Wheeler finished third for them in the 250cc championship. But by then, the Grand Prix scene was dominated by the Japanese manufacturers and Guzzi could no longer reclaim their place amongst the world's elite. Their challenge for further world championship glories ended in the early seventies.

WORLD ROAD RACE CHAMPIONS

350cc: Fergus Anderson (1953–54), Bill Lomas (1955–56), Keith Campbell (1957)
250cc: Bruno Ruffo (1949, 1951), Enrico Lorenzetti (1952)

MANUFACTURERS' TITLES

350cc: 1953, 1955–56
250cc: 1949, 1951–52

SENIOR TT WINNERS

Stanley Woods (1935)

MV AGUSTA

When Gilera and Guzzi pulled out of racing at the end of 1957, MV Agusta took over as Italy's top manufacturer, and became so dominant in the solo world championships that they won every manufacturers' title in three consecutive years from 1958–60.

Agusta began in 1923 as an aircraft company, and was inherited in 1927 by Count Domenico Agusta, son of the founder. After the war, he founded the Meccanica Verghera Agusta motorcycle factory at Gallarate, near Milan,

and in 1948 they produced their first racing bike, a 125cc two-stroke.

Their first machine won the Italian championship, but the Count wanted to attack the new World Championships and for this purpose he recruited the services of Pietro Remor from Gilera and got him to build a four-cylinder 500cc machine. However, their first 500 was not very successful; it had a good engine but the steering was poor.

To help with their assault on world titles they turned to the leading British riders of the day. Les Graham was recruited to ride the 500 and Cec Sandford to ride their 125. It was Sandford, in 1952, who became MV's first world champion, but

it was a home-grown rider, Carlo Ubbiali, who was to dominate the 125 class in the latter part of the fifties, winning the title five times between 1955 and 1960.

Britain's John Surtees and Mike Hailwood, and Rhodesia's Gary Hocking, had between them lifted the sport's top prize, the 500cc championship, on four occasions for MV, but the Count had one dream to fulfil: winning the 500cc world title with an Italian rider aboard. In 1966 that dream was duly turned into reality when Giacomo Agostini took the title for the first of seven successive years, all for MV. Agostini's last title for MV was in 1972, the year after the 64-year-old Count Agusta died.

Between 1956 and 1973, MV won the 500cc manufacturers' title every year but two, and also enjoyed enviable success in the TT races, where they first competed in 1951. Within 20 years, had become the second most successful manufacturer after Norton, who had been competing on the island since 1907. Again, MV owed a great deal of their success to Agostini.

WORLD ROAD RACE CHAMPIONS

500cc: John Surtees (1956, 1958–60), Gary Hocking (1961), Mike Hailwood (1962–65), Giacomo Agostini (1966–72), Phil Read (1973–74)

350cc: John Surtees (1958–60), Gary Hocking (1961), Giacomo Agostini (1968–73)

250cc: Carlo Ubbiali (1956, 1959–60), Tarquinio Provini (1958)

125cc: Cecil Sandford (1952), Carlo Ubbiali (1955–56, 1958–60)

MANUFACTURERS' TITLES

500cc: 1956, 1958–65, 1967–73
350cc: 1958–61, 1968–72
250cc: 1955–56, 1958–60
125cc: 1952–53, 1955–56, 1958–60

SENIOR TT WINNERS

John Surtees (1956, 1958–60), Gary Hocking (1962), Mike Hailwood (1963–65), Giacomo Agostini (1968–72)

NORTON

Norton is one of the biggest names in motorcycling, and for over a quarter of a century they produced some of the finest machines road racing has seen. In 1988, after more than a decade away from the sport, the name of Norton returned, much to the delight of motorcycling enthusiasts.

Norton's success goes back to the early days of the sport; at the first TT in 1907, Rem Fowler rode a privately-entered Norton (with a Peugeot engine) to victory in the twin cylinder class.

The Norton factory was established in 1902 by James L Norton, but despite Fowler's success at the Isle of Man, it was not until the 1920s that works Nortons made an impression in the TT. In 1924 they achieved their first success, firstly with George Tucker in the sidecar event and then in the Senior TT with Alec Bennett riding. The following year the company's founder died, but the company carried on and greater glories were not too far away.

By 1927 their overhead-valve single-cylinder machine was capable of speeds of 100mph (160.93kph), and that same year they produced their overhead-camshaft engine which was to make them the sport's most dominant manufacturer during the 1930s. However, as the decade started to come to a close they were falling behind the continental manufacturers in power, although the Nortons compensated their lack of speed with magnificent handling.

It was expected that the Nortons would be completely outclassed after the war but they were given a 'reprieve' when the FIM banned the use of superchargers, which their rivals had

One of their most successful Norton eras was the early 1950s. This is one of the works 350s from 1954

been using. Norton stuck to their single-cylinder engine, fitted to a new frame which gave even better holding. This became known as the 'featherbed' and for the early post-war years Norton remained one of the leading racing teams.

Inevitably the European manufacturers copied the revolutionary Norton frame and that, coupled with their powerful four-cylinder engines, meant that Norton was soon left behind. In 1955 they withdrew their factory machines from road racing. But privately-entered production Nortons still appeared, and in 1961 Mike Hailwood won the Senior TT at an average speed of 100.60mph/161.90kph.

Birmingham-based Norton was taken over by Associated Motorcycles Limited, who made the Matchless and AJS, but they eventually folded and Norton was restructured in 1966 as Norton Villiers. They returned to road racing in the increasingly popular Formula 750 and Production races, and in 1972 the John Player Norton team was formed; but, after just three seasons, the tobacco company withdrew its support.

Happily, Norton's name is back on the road racing scene, and judging by the performance of their revolutionary rotary engine in 1990, they could well be returning to some of their former successes.

WORLD ROAD RACE CHAMPIONS

500cc: Geoff Duke (1951)
350cc: Geoff Duke (1951–52)
Sidecar: Eric Oliver (1949–51, 1953), Cyril Smith (1952)

MANUFACTURERS' TITLES

500cc: 1950–52
350cc: 1951–52
Sidecar: 1949–53

SENIOR TT WINNERS

Alec Bennett (1924, 1927), Stanley Woods (1926, 1932–33), Tim Hunt (1931), Jimmy Guthrie (1934, 1936), Freddie Frith (1937), Harold Daniell (1938, 1947, 1949), Artie Bell (1948), Geoff Duke (1950–51), Reg Armstrong (1952), Ray Amm (1953–54), Mike Hailwood (1961)

SUZUKI

Suzuki was the second Japanese manufacturer – after Honda – to win a world title when Ernst Degner (FRG) won the inaugural 50cc world championship in 1962.

Remarkably, the Suzuki factory, at Hamamatsu, near Nagoya, started life as a clothing factory but diversified in the post-war recession into motorcycle manufacture in 1952. Their first machine was a two-stroke in 1954, and within five years of entering Grand Prix racing they were the largest producer of two-stroke machines.

They had been trying their hand, unsuccessfully, in the 125cc class but they came into their own in the newly instituted 50cc class in 1962 through Degner, who had fled East Germany in 1961, and immediately been recruited by the Suzuki racing team.

Their successful 50cc machine was a modified 125, but following their success they produced another version of the 125 which, this time, proved to be more competitive, and in 1963 they duly lifted the 50 and 125cc world titles. However, with spiralling costs and interest in the smaller bikes declining, Suzuki, like Honda, announced they were quitting racing at the end of 1967. Hans-Georg Anscheidt still captured the 1968 50cc title, on a privately-entered Suzuki machine, and in 1970 Dieter Braun's privately-entered 125 also carried him to a world title.

Suzuki aimed for the American market in the early seventies and built 500 and 750cc models which were based on production machines; in 1974 they produced their famous square-four racer. Barry Sheene, who joined

Barry Sheene was Suzuki's first 500cc world champion in 1976, and the following year he made it a notable double for the Japanese manufacturer

the Suzuki GB works team, became the factory's first 500cc world champion in 1976. He retained the title the following year and since then the Italian pair of Marco Luchinelli and Franco Uncini have also won the title.

Suzuki have also produced some very reliable off-road bikes and Belgium's Roger de Coster won all five of his 500cc moto-cross world titles on a Suzuki; the company have also provided machines for other well-known Belgian moto-cross world champions like Joël Robert, Georges Jobé, Gaston Rahier and Harry Everts.

WORLD ROAD RACE CHAMPIONS

500cc: Barry Sheene (1976–77), Marco Lucchinelli (1981), Franco Uncini (1982)
125cc: Hugh Anderson (1963, 1965), Dieter Braun (1970)
50cc: Ernst Degner (1962), Hugh Anderson (1963–64), Hans-Georg Anscheidt (1966–68)

MANUFACTURERS' TITLES

500cc: 1976–82
125cc: 1963, 1965, 1970
50cc: 1962–64, 1967–68

SENIOR TT WINNERS

Jack Findlay (1973), Phil Read (1977), Tom Herron (1978), Mike Hailwood (1979), Graeme Crosby (1980), Mick Grant (1981), Norman Brown (1982), Rob McElnea (1984)

YAMAHA

The Yamaha company was founded in 1888, but for 67 years it was known only for its musical instruments; then, in 1955, they produced their first motorcycle. Six years later they built their first racing machine, and in a relatively short time, they have become one of the leading road racing teams, dominating the 500cc World Championship in recent years.

Although they first raced at the 1961 French Grand Prix, their first full season was not until 1964, when Britain's Phil Read won five rounds of the 250cc class to take the championship by four points from Honda's Jim Redman. It was a great achievement for the team, which was to become the already-established Honda's biggest rival. Read retained his world title the following year and in the Junior TT he became the first man to lap the Mountain Course at over 100mph on a 250cc machine.

The 125 and 250 machines were reliable bikes and the increase in sales from 26 000 in 1958 to nearly 500 000, in little more than 10 years, speaks volumes for their popularity.

After Honda and Suzuki pulled their works teams out, at the end of 1967, Yamaha dominated the 250cc class. But the factory felt little satisfaction in sweeping the board with no effective opposition, and they too officially pulled out of racing, although riders like Phil Read continued racing with their privately entered two-stroke twins.

Yamaha subsequently returned to road racing and like other manufacturers turned their attentions to Formula 750; in particular, to the American market. And indeed, it is through American riders Kenny Roberts, Eddie Lawson and Wayne Rainey that Yamaha has dominated the world 500cc championship in the 1980s.

Their total of 149 250cc wins is more than 50 better than Honda's total; in the 500cc class they have won 84 races, second only to MV Agusta. In terms of world champions, Yamaha have produced 28 solo champions and won 29 manufacterers' titles, records which are almost identical to Honda's. But if, by way of a 'tie-breaker', one includes Yamaha's sidecar world titles, they can clearly claim to be the most successful Japanese Grand Prix team of all time.

WORLD ROAD RACE CHAMPIONS

500cc: Giacomo Agostini (1975), Kenny Roberts (1978–80), Eddie Lawson (1984, 1986, 1988), Wayne Rainey (1990)
350cc: Giacomo Agostini (1974), Johnny Cecotto (1975), Takazumi Katayama (1977), Jon Ekerold (1980)
250cc: Phil Read (1964–65, 1968, 1971), Rod Gould (1970), Jarno Saarinen (1972), Dieter Braun (1973), Jean-Louis Tournadre (1982), Carlos Lavado (1983, 1986), Christian Sarron (1984), John Kocinski (1990)
125cc: Bill Ivy (1967), Phil Read (1968), Kent Anderson (1973–74)
Sidecar: George O'Dell (1977), Rolf Biland (1978–79, 1981, 1983), Jock Taylor (1980), Werner Schwarzël (1982), Egbert Streuer (1984–86), Steve Webster (1987–89)

MANUFACTURERS' TITLES

500cc: 1974–75, 1986–88, 1990
350cc: 1973–77, 1980
250cc: 1964–65, 1968, 1970–74, 1977, 1982–84, 1990
125cc: 1967–68, 1973–74
Sidecar: 1977–87

SENIOR TT WINNERS

Phil Carpenter (1974), Tom Herron (1976)

INDEX

Page numbers in *italics* refer to illustrations